Where the Wind Blows

Cover Design by Matthew Wyne

Photographs and Charts by Author

Additional copies can be obtained from:
www.amazon.com

Where the Wind Blows

Heyward Coleman

Vermillion Press
2013

Where The Wind Blows

Contents

Acknowledgements

Special thanks are due to the many people who encouraged us to take our trip despite the many difficulties involved and to those who faithfully read and gave feedback on the frequent emails and letters I wrote describing our adventures.

I am also grateful to our family, especially my mother, for their enthusiastic support for our adventure and their help along the way in mailing us care packages and tending to our affairs back home. Thanks to Nan Morrison for the skillful use of her red pen (she actually ran out of red ink on this one) and for her kind words of encouragement and efforts in ferreting out and correcting mistakes. And thanks to Matthew Wine for designing the cover of this book.

For Charlotte, Heyward, Alex, and Margot
who made the trip possible.

Chapter 1
The Trip Begins

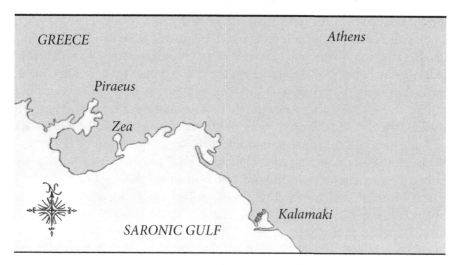

Charlotte had been watching the tanker for some time. It was headed for Cape Knidos, which we had just rounded, and it was becoming clear that we would need to make a turn to stay well clear of its path. But the required turn was also a jibe. Whether it was a false sense of security because the following wind didn't feel strong or whether it was a simple case of overconfidence, I'm still not sure. But the blame was mine. I told Charlotte to bring the rudder over and jibe the boat.

Everything seemed to happen in slow motion. As the boom crashed overhead, the main sheet caught on the steering column. The column snapped like a match stick, and the whole mechanism was thrown across the boat and onto the deck. Charlotte had been flung with it and was up against the lifelines and halfway out of the boat. The now-out-of-control boat was continuing its turn and, if nothing were done, would head for another jibe. Time had frozen. The wheel was lying across the deck. Charlotte was hanging over the lifelines. And the tanker was coming. Our little world had suddenly turned upside down.

***

Almost six months earlier there had been another cataclysmic change in our world—an abrupt end to a fifteen-year business career and the abandonment of all the wild expectations. The successful spin-off of

1

Maritrans—my position as a director, part owner, and senior executive—now all up in smoke. I had been forced to sell my interest and move on.

But what to do next? Uncharacteristically we decided to make it a family decision. Charlotte prepared the favorite family meal, and Alex almost choked over the large spare rib he had half way in his mouth when I broke the news. The children were still recovering from this shock when I dropped the second bomb—I was willing to consider taking a year off before entering the business world again. Secure in the thought that retirement lay far in the future, Charlotte and I had often talked of buying a sailboat and sailing around the world. Knowing that we would probably be too old to do it when the time finally came, we would shut this reality out of our minds and talk in detail of the places we would visit. We avidly devoured books and plans on boat construction and catalogues from numerous yachting supply houses as we mentally built and outfitted our dream craft.

Jokingly Charlotte suggested sailing as a possibility for the businessman's sabbatical that I had just put forth. It wasn't received as a joke. Heyward Junior was ecstatic. He brushed the long blond hair from his eyes and began to lobby in earnest. Was this a possible escape from his upcoming senior year in high school? The proposed trip was pure adventure and unreality at its finest, and he was all for it. Alex, who loves boats, adores sailing, and has a passion for anything mechanical was an easy convert. But Margot required more work.

Margot longed to travel and live somewhere exotic, but was skeptical that life on a yacht would meet her high expectations for adventure. Boldly she put forth her enthusiastic proposal to live in Thailand for a year. But this was rapidly swept aside by her brothers, and she succumbed to the pressure.

With three children jumping up and down and all shouting at the same time, I suddenly realized that Charlotte hadn't been joking at all. Panic set in. They had actually taken me seriously when I had floated my hair-brained idea of a businessman's sabbatical! All eyes were on me—what would I say?

Here is where the MBA and many years of hardened business experience would pay off. Carefully examine the alternatives, list the pros and cons, and then work out a logical choice—maybe even employ a decision tree. As these thoughts raced through my mind I heard myself blurt out:

"Okay, let's do it!"

But there had been some details to work out.

Education? Margot and Alex wanted to continue theirs. Heyward was more ambivalent. We worked out a plan. Margot and Alex would take correspondence courses and pass the sixth and eight grades. But there was one important caveat. They would be responsible for policing themselves. Charlotte and I would only assist in the process. Heyward would also take correspondence courses, but would defer passing his senior year until we returned. It went without saying that he would be responsible for himself. Furthermore he would not need our assistance, thank you very much.

Our home? "Let's sell it and put all of our possessions in storage." Did I really suggest that? Years and years of accumulating and endless hours of loving care for house, garden, and workshop—and I was suggesting that we give it all up—just like that? To my surprise everybody else readily agreed and the decision was made.

Our livelihood? We had the proceeds from the sale of my share of Maritrans which would do for the time being. As for later—why not wait and worry about that later? Was that really Charlotte sitting across the table from me and agreeing to all of this? Or was she only agreeing? It then came to me. She was orchestrating the whole affair!

Come to think of it, she had been acting funny ever since we went back to Harvard Business School for my fifteenth reunion. She had attended the class on managing family relationships while I had attended the one on starting new ventures. I recalled her excited description. The class leader had given an account of his recent experience of leading his entire family on an extended retreat in southern France. He had recounted to the admiring group how this experience not only had strengthened and enriched his family life, but had also opened the path to stunning success in the business world. During that weekend I hadn't learned much about starting new ventures, but Charlotte had obviously learned a lot about managing family relationships.

***

While the concept was simple, implementation was not. Sell our house in Philadelphia, put all of our possessions into storage in our summer home in South Carolina, buy a sailboat, and then plan our trip. One other small matter—it all had to be done rather quickly. It was early June and the day hand of our one-year clock had already started ticking.

June and July were a blur of frantic activity. Packing and the move out of our house in Pennsylvania, the move to South Carolina, and the separate moving truck for my enormous woodworking shop that had occupied three rooms of our basement—and we were determined to do it all ourselves. Part of our objective was to streamline our lives and return to the basics. The astronomically high relocation expense my company had footed in my transfer from Alabama to Pennsylvania ten years earlier had no place in this new life style.

Alex and I were driving the rental truck down Interstate 95 ..s our summer home on Wadmalaw Island where I would store my woodworking tools I wondered if the incredible amount of work was really worth it. In terms of past business income, the savings were relatively small, but in terms of future expenses on the sailboat when I would enjoy no income, they were significant. The same dilemma would present itself time after time over the next year. We had a new yardstick to measure values, but it was hard to put the old one aside.

I had carefully calculated the weight of the lumber from the large cherry tree in our yard. Blighted, it had to come down several months earlier, but unable to watch the tree man hack it to pieces with his chain saw, I had it milled instead. To that weight I had added my best guess of the weight of the table saw, joiner, planer, and other heavy equipment that I had placed on top of the lumber to fill the 24-foot Budget diesel truck to the brim. Although I had checked my calculations several times, I was still nervous about being overloaded.

The first two weighing stations had waved us by, and when Alex saw a U-Haul truck bypass the third we did the same. With only about three more hours to go, Alex and I stopped at a huge and very fancy truck stop. A scale to check truck weight was right in front of the diesel pump. The trip was almost over, but why not? When I went to pay for fuel and got the results, I almost dropped my slurpie—11,128 pounds—we were overweight by over 50 percent.

Cautiously and as slowly as we dared go on the freeway we crept towards Wadmalaw. Visions of a blowout and tools, lumber, and two bodies strewn along the highway filled my mind when Alex broke my chain of thought. "Hey Dad, there's another weighing station ahead." We had asked about the consequences of being overweight back at the Budget office. They had explained that while the fine would probably be pretty stiff, you weren't normally asked to remove excess weight and leave it at the station unless you were really grossly overweight—say by 10 to 20 percent. It looked like the end of the line. With the load I was carrying, I thought they would not only make me unload the entire truck but also would probably throw me into jail. We approached and—what? No trucks? No lights? And then the sign—"closed."

***

We concentrated in earnest on choosing a boat. A close friend in Charleston had taken his family on a year-long sailing trip a few years earlier and provided a wealth of information to help us with our plans—such titles as *After 50,000 Miles, Storm Sailing, How to Repair Your Marine Diesel,*

Twelve Volt Shipboard Systems, and the list went on. I had been reading the three-foot high stack of books Johnnie and Helen had lent me every chance I got. There were thousands of pieces of advice. Each view was definitive and unyielding, and for every one view there were at least a dozen others—equally definitive—that were completely at variance with each other.

FIN KEEL or LONG KEEL? "With its stability in heavy seas, the LONG KEEL is the only logical choice for extended cruising and furthermore..." But in the next book I picked up "Properly designed and built, modern FIN KEEL boats not only handle superbly in heavy seas, but are infinitely preferable to the old LONG KEEL boats in harbors, marinas, and other difficult to maneuver in areas." The books seemed to be about equally divided on this subject until I got to one particularly helpful reference: "probably the best compromise is a LONG FIN KEEL."

Sailor or Motor Sailor? Ketch or Sloop? Fiberglass, wood, steel, aluminum, or cement? Center cockpit or stern cockpit? And all of these questions relate only to the hull. Introduce topics such as anchoring, navigation, sail plans, dinghies and the already exponentially increasing list of alternatives explodes into chaos. Even ropes (called lines on boats) are controversial and can occupy chapters in authoritative books on cruising.

And there was emotional advice. In the last chapter of *After 50,000 Miles*, a particularly authoritative treatise on the cruising life from A to Z, the author preached: "The experience will change your life. But don't wait too long or the game may be up. The frail flesh lasts only so long. Throw up the job and get under way. You only live once." Despite the conflicting advice, there was one point on which there was universal agreement among the experienced seamen whose works I had so carefully scrutinized: "The biggest danger is getting bogged down in the difficulties and never making the trip at all." Somehow I didn't think this was a concern for me and my dedicated crew. After all, I had already "thrown up the job" and there seemed to be a good deal of life left in the "frail flesh" of the Coleman family. It was true, however, that there were still a lot of difficulties that could bog us down. By this time, it was the end of July and I still had not chosen a boat or a destination for our adventure.

By now experts, Charlotte and I carefully outlined the requirements of our craft. An aft cabin for some space to ourselves to preserve our sanity, a ketch rig (two masts) so that the mainsail wouldn't be too big for us to handle, a long keel (we are traditionalists at heart), a relatively shallow draft so that we wouldn't have to worry too much about running aground, and at least three staterooms so that the children could have their own territory. So how did we wind up with a sloop (one mast) with a giant mainsail that took three of us to handle, a fin keel, and a deep draft that would make running aground an ever-constant danger? The answer lies with Minolis.

But part of the blame was Charlotte's. She was responsible for our choice of sailing locations. I have to confess that my heart was with the children. Their arguments for the Caribbean made a lot of sense. Warm water, sunshine, great fishing, and interesting islands—they couldn't understand why we were having such a difficult time with the decision. But Charlotte was adamant. "I'm not going to jerk my children out of school to have them play around in the Caribbean! We should go someplace where there is lots of culture and history and where everyone learns a lot." She then told us for the fiftieth time how much she had enjoyed the trip she had taken in Greece when she was in college. "You just won't believe how pretty it is—you would all just love it." Useless to argue. We would start the trip in the Eastern Mediterranean and then plan from there.

The Sparkman and Stevens-designed Gulf Star 50 appealed to us. A shallow draft ketch with traditional lines, it fit the picture we had been painting from our extensive reading and research. We were delighted when Mike, our broker from Castlemain in Florida, informed us that one was available for purchase in Piraeus, Greece.

Pictures arrived, and I had phone conversations with Paul Weber, the Swiss owner. The *Sun Queen* was beautiful—this was our dream boat. And Mr. Weber, a prominent Swiss businessman, was so nice—he had even offered to show us around Greece if we purchased his boat. But price became an issue. Mr. Weber's expectations exceeded anything approaching reality. Nonetheless, I submitted an offer and Castlemain dispatched an associate in Athens to look at the boat.

Mike was disappointed when he called me. Weber wouldn't come down on the price, and his associate in Athens was not impressed with the condition of *Sun Queen*. But why didn't I call the associate—he had some other ideas for me. It seemed late in the game to be starting over, but that was where I was. The next morning I got up early to try to catch the associate in his office. Gogossis Minolis was the name I had written down.

After two calls to the international operator I finally got the combination of digits that Mike had given me to work. Almost seeing the flow of dollars as time ticked away, I tried to be very organized.

"Hello, Gogossis Minolis please."

"One moment please" from a lady with a strong German accent. Then after an interminable silence as the clock ticked on: "Hello."

"Hello, Gogossis?"

"Yes, Minolis."

"Gogossis, this is Heyward Coleman. I understand from Castlemain that you didn't like the Gulf Star 50?"

"No Heywort, it is not a good boat. Bad shape, lots of osmosis. I took pictures and will send them to you. But listen Heywort, this is not the boat for you. The French boats are much better. I know a 48 foot Jeanneau that I think..."

I interrupted, "Listen Gogossis, could you fax a list of boats to me that are available, then I will call you back.

"Minolis."

"Gogossis?"

"No Minolis. My name is Minolis."

"But Mike told me your name is Gogossis?"

"No, Gogossis is my last name. Please call me Minolis."

"Okay Gogossis, I mean Minolis, I'm sorry, but please fax me the list."

"It's okay Heywort. I'll send you the information. The Jeanneau 48 is the boat for you. I know what I'm talking. There is also a Jeanneau 45 and an Olympia 50 and..."

I didn't care if his name was Gogossis, Minolis, or Aristotle Onassis, the phone conversation was costing me a fortune and I wanted to cut it off until I could get further information.

"Listen, Minolis, please fax the information to me and I will call you back after I have looked it over."

When I received Minolis' fax giving information on the Jeanneau 48 foot Trinidad as well as several other boats, I made the decision. I would fly to Athens to investigate all of these possibilities.

By good fortune another possibility cropped up. A good friend gave us an introduction to Olivier Prouvost who had just purchased the prestigious French sailboat design and construction firm Henri Wauquiez. But that wasn't the end of it. The founder and former owner, Henri Wauquiez had gone on to accept a senior position with Jeanneau—the builder of the very boat Minolis wanted to show to me. These were two people I could rely on to give me very sound advice.

Olivier was easy to track down and was delighted to help me in my quest. He was intrigued with our plans and insisted that he knew just the boat for us. A Henri Wauquiez design—the Amphitrite. He was able to locate two in Southern France that were for sale and suggested that I meet with his representative in Port Grimaud, Monsieur de Kerdrel. I decided to include France in my boat hunting expedition.

***

While I was busy with boats and brokers, Charlotte was busy with home front logistics. We had decided on correspondence courses from the Calvert School out of Baltimore, Maryland for Alex and Margot and had chosen the University of Nebraska's Independent Study for High School Program for Heyward's courses. There was also the matter of lining up schools for the following year when we returned.

Coordinating with the realtors in Philadelphia for the sale of our house and finding someone to rent our summer home while we were gone were also on the list of things to be done. Charlotte's plate was pretty full. In addition, in her spare time, she was to begin organizing the final pack for our trip.

One crisis before I left. Margot had just heard from the Calvert school and they said she had done so poorly on her entrance exam that she probably should repeat the fifth grade. With Margot whimpering in the background, Charlotte and I had a heated discussion that touched on everything from "and this is what we get after paying those outrageous tuitions to Springside School" to "maybe we shouldn't take the trip after all."

But "frail flesh" was not part of Charlotte's character, and after we had finished venting our frustrations she recalled the warning she had received about the Calvert school and their meticulous attention to detail. Margot had taken the test while we were in the middle of our move from Philadelphia and when she was in the process of saying good-by to all of her friends. Obviously her full attention had not been on the Calvert test.

After several more phone conversations a retest arrived. This time Margot was all business, and the result was a stunning success. Yes, the Calvert School would be delighted to welcome Margot into its sixth grade class! Margot was all smiles, and both Charlotte and I silently apologized to Springside for our ugly thoughts.

***

Warm sunshine and the soft Mediterranean air greeted me as I stepped off the plane in Nice. The sense of freedom and excitement I felt were overwhelming. Monsieur de Kerdrel had made it clear that I should plan my arrival in Port Grimaud at 2 P.M. or later so I could meet him after lunch. My two hour delay in sorting out the car rental insurance I didn't want to take in the first place made this easy to accomplish.

Nestled between St. Tropez and St. Maxime, Port Grimaud is an exclusive marina complex with acres of condominiums and yachts. Monsieur de Kerdrel was waiting for me in his small office overlooking the marina.

"*C'étais bièn passé, votre voyage?*"

"*Oui, très bien, merci*" I replied not mentioning the lunch I hadn't had. "*On peut voir les deux Amphitrites?*"

"*Oui, mais il y a une petite problem...*"

In France there is always a little problem. This time it was that one of the boats I was to look at was in Corsica for the week—but never mind, we would look at the one that was still in port. The Amphitrite I saw was beautiful–sleek lines, incredibly sturdy construction, a huge aft cabin. Olivier's advice had been good. This was a formidable vessel. But there were two "*petites problems.*"

The third cabin wasn't actually a cabin at all. It was two small bunks in the passageway between the aft cabin and dinning area. This would be very awkward for the children—we felt strongly that they each needed a measure of privacy, and this arrangement fell short. There was also a matter of equality—the concept from the beginning was that we would all share equally in the work and in the benefits. I knew that our spacious aft cabin compared with the scanty double deck bunks would be the cause of a lot of grumbling.

Price was the other problem. De Kerdrel's quote exceeded the number Olivier had given me by almost 50 percent. The unfavorable exchange rate for the dollar combined with the incredibly high prices in France made it clear to me that it would be unlikely that I would be able to purchase in France.

Even with these problems, however, part of my mission was to evaluate this boat against Minolis' Jeanneau Trinidad. De Kerdrel was offended that I would even talk about the two boats in the same breath, but in response to my question he replied after a long pause: "*L'Amphitrite, C'est une Wauquiez—c'est à dire un bateau très sérieux, tandis que le Trinidad...*" While I thought de Kerdrel's characterization of the Trinidad as a toy was a little extreme, it was obvious to me that he didn't even begin to put the two vessels in the same category.

Back in de Kerdrel's office after our tour of the harbor, I began to develop a very serious case of jet lag. As he called hotel after hotel for me, my head would begin to fall forward and I would almost jerk myself out of the chair as I caught myself before falling asleep. After the sixth "*complet*", it became obvious that I was going to have a very serious problem in finding lodging in this heavily visited portion of Southern France. As the vision of the lightly bearded, medium build Frenchman came into and out focus in my bleary eyes I found myself wondering if there might be a human element there after all. Would he be able to bring himself to the point of generosity of

let me stay on one of the dozen or more boats that were all vacant
er his control, or would he send me on suggesting it would be much
few miles down the road?

After two more refusals, he showed signs of weakening. "*Peut-être
sur un des Bateaux...*" but he didn't finish his thought before the phone on
the other end of the line came to life. "*Oui, oui, oui*" as his head bobbed up
and down "*Attendez un moment s'il vous plaît.*" With his hand cupped over
the receiver he enthusiastically explained that it was only 85 kilometers away
and in a beautiful medieval town in the mountains—and the price was "*pas
chère.*"

The price he quoted didn't sound very "*pas chère*" to me, and I wasn't
at all sure I could stay awake and follow the winding maze of back roads he
had pointed out to me on the map, but it seemed like a better bet than the
chair in his office, so I accepted.

By a stroke of good luck I was able to get Henry Waquiez on the
phone. While the information he gave made me feel good about the next leg
of my trip, the light he gave wasn't solid green. "Yes, Jeanneau makes very
good boats. The Trinidad in particular is well constructed. I think it would
be well suited for your needs."

Coming from the designer who was responsible for the incredibly
successful Wauquiez line of boats, this was a very encouraging endorsement.
But his answer to my question about how he would compare it with the
Amphitrite stayed with me a long time. A long silence and then: "The
Amphitrite is a magnificent boat. I would take it anywhere in the world."

***

Minolis had made a good impression with his get up and go and I
was hopeful that his Trinidad would be the answer. His effusive offer to meet
me at the airport and show me his country stood in sharp contrast with de
Kerdrel's indifference. The flight from Nice to Athens was on time. Minolis
was not. In fact, after an hour of waiting, there was still no Minolis. My after-
hours phone call to his office produced nothing, and I got my first taste of
Minolis' reliability.

Getting up early the next morning to make my phone call to Minolis'
office produced only the same pleasant German accent I had encountered in
my initial call from the states: "I'm sorry Mr. Heyward, Minolis hasn't come
in yet."

"But he was supposed to meet me at the airport last night and
never showed up. I have come the whole way from South Carolina to see

him. When exactly do you expect him in?" I rattled off with ill concealed frustration.

"I'm sorry Mr. Heyward, but Minolis doesn't tell me these things. If you will leave your number I will have him call you back when he comes in. Maybe he will be in this morning."

"MAYBE this morning" I was about to explode, but thinking better of it simply left my number and began my wait.

It didn't take long. "Hallow Heywort —Minolis —Haow are you? Sorry about last night—something very important came up. Listen, I have lots of good boats to show you. Put your hotel clerk on the phone and I will give him instructions for your cab driver."

It was the most expensive cab ride I was to take in Athens. The piece of paper my hotel clerk gave the driver took us down the crowded Singrou Avenue towards Faliro. As we approached one of the world's most polluted bodies of water, unattractive modern architecture interspersed with magnificent statues and ruins gave way to a positively ugly hodgepodge of concrete houses and flat buildings. South of Faliro we followed the shore of the Saronic Gulf to Alimos and Minolis' office.

As I grudgingly paid the driver almost twice the airport fare for a trip of only about two thirds the distance, I marveled at the contrasts. Heavy smog over Piraeus to the northwest, deafening noise over the international airport to the southeast, atrocious concrete structures all about, and yet the sun scintillating over the deep blue water and reflecting off the rocky shoreline made the confused panorama seem beautiful.

Minolis' office was not beautiful, and I was prepared to be angry with him. The pleasant German accent belonged to Christina who welcomed me warmly and led me to an office where a short stocky Greek was either wrestling or dancing with a telephone receiver. Out of the corner of his eye Minolis acknowledged my presence but continued to shout at his correspondent. A lapse into English and a statement hinting that the call was to China—then a look at me to see if I was sufficiently impressed. Finally the shouting match came to an end and Minolis greeted me like a long lost friend and we began to discuss boats.

"Heywort, some bad news. *Argo*, the Trinidad I want to show you is on charter now, but it will be in Volos this weekend and we will drive there to see it. In the meantime I will show you some other boats." Anger turned to disappointment as I realized that I would have to wait five more days before seeing the boat that had led me to Greece, but I remained silent as Minolis led me to his car for a trip to the marina.

Parked a half block up the one way street that led away from Avenue Possidonos, Minolis sped backwards towards the harbor. Nervously peering to the rear I saw a car turn off Possidonos and head towards us. Undaunted, Minolis leaned on his horn and continued in reverse. The intimidated driver swerved to his right into the parking lane. As Minolis sped past, I heard a loud "*Malaka*" from the driver's window and then watched Minolis execute his hard turn in reverse into the parking lane on the busy Possidonos. He then reversed direction and sped into the stream of rapidly moving traffic. Before I had time to recover my senses, he jammed on the brakes and shot into a rapid u-turn and about 50 yards later veered to the right into Kalamaki Marina.

This was the emptiest I was ever to see Kalamaki, but I didn't realize it at the time because all the berths were full. Minolis lamented the fact that so few boats were in but managed to show me two smaller Jeanneaus and an Olympic Adventure. Word spread quickly that there was an American buyer on the scene. As we were leaving the run-down Olympic Adventure, a tall, slightly balding Greek caught up with us and started yelling at Minolis. Minolis yelled back, and I became concerned that a fight was about to break out. The yelling became louder, the movements more animated, and then suddenly they smiled at each other and switched into English. Minolis introduced me to Evianos and explained that he had a Trinidad for sale.

We walked over to Evianos' boat and the Abbot and Costello show began. Minolis' English was much better which gave him a decided advantage. When Evianos showed me the cockpit and told me what nice shape it was in Minolis winked and told me in a low voice how much nicer *Argo* was. As we went through the cabins Minolis pointed out every ding and scratch while Evianos was praising the overall appearance. When we got to the small "extras" Evianos proudly pulled out a large tool box and started to crow about it when Minolis cut him short with "on *Argo* there are two large tool boxes." Not to be out done, Evianos quickly produced two more boxes bringing his total to three.

As we walked away, Minolis was pleased to hear that I liked the layout of the Trinidad, but assured me that the *Argo* was far superior to the boat Evianos had just shown to me. As an afterthought I asked him the name of the boat and owner. "It belongs to Stavos Kiriacoulis of Kiriacoulis Mediterranean Cruises and the name is *Captain Spiros*."

"By the way Minolis, what does *malaca* mean?"

A pause, a pensive stare, and then: "Heywort...Heywort, don't worry...some Greeks, they are not good people...it is a very bad word!"

***

There was plenty to do during the time before going to Volos. I needed to engage a lawyer, find a surveyor, and find out about repair facilities. Although Minolis had offered to take care of all of this for me, I had been in Greece long enough to know better. I did agree, however, to at least meet Minolis' suggestion for a lawyer. After spending more than half an hour looking for King Constantine Ave, I looked at the street sign again. Ave Politehniou—certainly doesn't look like King Constantine. I re-examined my note. Yes, 102 King Constantine Ave was definitely the address Nicolaras had given me in our phone conversation an hour earlier. The owner of the nearby kiosk spoke English and, after scrutinizing my note, pointed to a building a short distance away with 102 clearly marked on the front. To my puzzled look he replied "Oh, they changed the street name five or ten years ago."

Two flights of stairs up, a beautiful young secretary with a miniskirt took my order for cafe frappe. After keeping me waiting long enough to bring home the point that he was a very busy man, Nicolaras glided into the room, gave me a limp handshake, and installed himself behind the huge desk. His personality was as oily as his looks. After some small talk about an aviation deal he and Minolis were working on, he got down to brass tacks. "Getting a certificate of deletion can be difficult in Greece, but I know all the right people. Dracos is a good friend of mine and he can help us."

As he talked I began to realize how vulnerable I was going to be in any transaction I entered into in this strange country. If friends were necessary to conduct business in Greece, who were mine going to be? Getting help from him to protect me against Minolis would be a joke—I couldn't even count on him to give me an accurate street address. I politely listened as Nicolaras droned on about his friends, influence, and power. Fortunately for me, he was a very busy man so it didn't take very long to accomplish my exit. "*Efharisto para poli*" and I was back out in the smoggy air of Piraeus.

I felt lucky when I finally reached Andy at the American Embassy. A close friend who lives in Washington had obtained this high level contact for me from a friend of a friend of theirs who was on the Greek desk in Washington. When I dropped Dan's name, Andy immediately opened up. How was Dan doing? "Fine" I replied as my friend had told me nothing to the contrary and quickly changed the subject. After giving Andy a brief description of my mission I explained that I needed help in three areas. Finding a lawyer, understanding how to get a yacht out from under the Greek flag and under the American flag, and getting advice on purchasing a boat in Greece.

"No problem, Heyward. George is in charge of our legal services and can tell you all about lawyers in Athens and Piraeus. Lilly handles documentation and can help you with flag questions. And Nick, in our economic department, knows a lot about boats and can help you in that area." My conversation with Andy was a breath of fresh air. After a very frustrating morning I was finally getting somewhere. But, as I was to learn many times over, the odyssey I was undertaking was to be a never ending series of ups and downs.

My conversation with George was a definite down. "Yes, Mr. Coleman, I can provide you with a list of lawyers in Piraeus and in Athens. It is a very long list—maybe you want to come in and pick it up."

"George, what I really need is some recommendations for law firms. Is there anyone you have worked with or can recommend as..."

"Mr. Coleman, I'm very sorry, but the Embassy cannot make any recommendations—all we can do is give you a list of firms. You see we can't be in a position of..."

"Yes, George, I understand, but can't you unofficially give me the benefit of your experience and..." It became obvious that this line of questioning was getting me nowhere, but I was finally able to pry out of him that a lady whom he respected very much had recently left the Embassy to go to work for Vgenopoulos and Partners and he gave me their number.

"I'm sorry, Miss Hritakos is no longer with Vgenopoulos, but let me switch you to Miltos Papangelis' office where she worked." There was something appealing about Miltos' honest abruptness and I decided I would chance going to see him. "OK Heyward, you are not far away. My office is 96 Filonos St.—almost at the end—I will expect you." He seemed surprised when I asked him if he were sure they hadn't changed the name of his street lately and then assured me I wouldn't have any trouble finding it.

The narrow elevator at the end of a hall in the unobtrusive building belied the fact that Vgenopoulos was a substantial law firm. This false impression was immediately rectified, however, as I stepped off the elevator. At least half a dozen beautiful miniskirted secretaries bustling about clearly indicated the prestige of the organization. One of them led me into a conference room, and a few minutes later I met Miltos.

Tall, of slight build, and full of nervous energy Milto skipped the small talk and came right to the point. "So, you want to buy a boat in Greece? Who is your broker?"

"Minolis Gogossis. Do you know him? If so do you think he is honest?"

A broad smile and then his quick response. "Nobody in the brokerage business is honest. For that matter nobody in the shipping business is honest. But never mind. Minolis is no worse than most. I will show you how to work with him. But the important thing is to get the certificate of deletion. No matter what Minolis tells you, don't believe him. It takes a long time—maybe thirty days. Don't worry. Dracos is my friend. We will get it quickly.

I was getting a little tired of the "friend" business and who was this Dracos? "How much do you think your legal fees will run?"

"I charge an hourly fee, but don't worry. It shouldn't take much time. Call me when you think you have a deal and we will work on the papers." And before I had a chance to voice my real concerns he was on his feet and heading for the door.

Two more calls to the Embassy put me in touch with Andy's two other contacts. Lilly was a delight and told me she would be happy to help me through the American Flag process. "Yes, getting a certificate of deletion could be a difficult process—don't pay any money until you have it!" She seemed surprised when I asked her if she knew Dracos and replied that she had never heard of him. Nick was helpful and full of advice concerning the economics of buying a yacht in Greece. He agreed to meet with me later and give more guidance.

I was now ready to attack the surveyor problem. Castlemain had suggested that I contact the salvage firm of Loucas Matsos. Here the secretaries were less numerous, older, and only one sported a miniskirt. Mr. Anninos was very pleasant and we immediately hit it off. He would agree to help me find a competent surveyor if I would agree to send him a copy of my log and pictures after our trip so he could write an article for a Greek sailing magazine of which he was an editor.

It was a busy time in his office as one of their ships had just sunk, and the insurance people were coming in to settle the claim. Our conversation had been cut short and I waited patiently as the sole miniskirt prepared a cafe frappe for me. Finally they were done and Mr. Anninos motioned me back into his office.

"Mr. Coleman, I have found just the man to help you—let me introduce you to George Economou."

Tall and thin, slow and methodical—he didn't immediately inspire mistrust. An insurance adjuster and also a surveyor? I was about to inquire about this strange combination when Economou began in a slow very quiet voice: "Mr. Coleman, I am an agent for Lloyds and I also do surveys of yachts. Mr. Anninos has told me that you are about to buy a yacht and you need a survey done?"

A pleasant sparring session and then tentative agreement. If I liked the boat in Volos he could come up on Monday and survey it. I had read a fair amount on the subject and was absolutely set on the idea of having a very thorough inspection before I made a firm commitment on any boat. Mr. Economou had explained that having the critical eye of an insurance agent and the tight wallet of an adjuster made him uniquely qualified to protect me in my purchase. And besides, once he knew the boat, he would be happy to sell me an insurance policy.

On the way out, Mr. Anninos warned me "Don't let anybody put a line on your boat! No matter what trouble you are in, don't accept assistance." A little surprised at this unsolicited advice I asked what I should do if the unfortunate circumstance should present itself. He smiled and presented me with his business card. "Just call Matsos—we will come and get you—and we won't claim salvage rights." Economou nodded in agreement and added "yes, and from an insurance point of view it's very important to get approval before you get any help. Mr. Anninos is a good friend of mine and you can trust him."

Friends and trust. It was becoming a familiar theme. This last exchange left me wondering if Economou was a wise choice for a surveyor, but I was getting to the point where I was going to have to make some rapid choices if I hoped to start the trip before our allotted year was half over.

The next day I arrived at Minolis' office at the time he had suggested. He wasn't there, but Christina was, and she was in an animated conversation with a red-bearded German decked out in dungarees and tee shirt. I could understand enough German to surmise that they were talking about red beard's wife and that their remarks were not very complimentary. As I approached they switched into English and Christina introduced me to Manfred.

"So you are using Miltos" Manfred announced to me. Before I could reply to this astonishing piece of intelligence he continued. "Miltos is the best damn lawyer in Greece! I know. He is representing me against my wife. I bet Minolis won't be happy about this at all. He probably wanted you to use Nicolaras."

Manfred's last statement took me off the defensive and I immediately felt myself warming up to him. Minolis had told me about his wizard German technician but this was not quite what I expected. I was delighted to see some wholesome skepticism and was happy to finally be with someone who was obviously not a member of the "good old Greek" network.

**

16

More boats to see, more administrative matters, a little sight seeing, and then, finally, Saturday came. A call from the desk alerted me that Minolis was waiting in the lobby. As I stepped off the mini elevator with my overnight bag in my hand, Minolis approached me and quickly explained: "A minor girl friend is in the car. I didn't know she was coming until this morning, but I have explained that we have business and I will drop her back at her home in Khalkis on Evia. It's on our way to Volos." In spite of my protests that I didn't mind if she came along, Minolis insisted. "I never mix my social life with business."

Maria vas very pleasant company, and I was sad that we were going to lose her as we approached Evia. At the bridge leading to Khalkis, she and Minolis excitedly explained to me the strange phenomenon that occurs in the river. The water flows rapidly in one direction and then after about six hours stops, reverses direction, and then flows rapidly for another six hours. Legend has it that this phenomenon so mystified Aristotle that he flung himself into the channel because of his inability to explain the cause. It all sounded very romantic, but for the life of me I couldn't see how this differed from the normal tidal flows I was accustomed to seeing on the Atlantic coast.

Leaving me with my thoughts and my camera to photograph this exciting flow, Minolis took Maria to her home. A little over an hour later he reappeared, and I climbed back into his car. "Heywort, what do you think about Maria?" Not knowing exactly what Minolis was driving at I answered noncommittally that I thought she was very pleasant. But he persisted. "Yes, but what about when we stopped for gas, did you notice?"

I had noticed that even though Minolis had been very impatient to get back on the road immediately she had brought us each a small carton of milk-cafe and this had given me the opportunity to also go into the station and buy a couple of pastries.

"Heywort, she didn't even say thank you when you offered her one of your pastries. Maybe she doesn't know English, but still she could at least say 'Efharisto' or something. I am looking for a woman I can be proud of—not one of these crazy secretaries. When she stayed in my apartment, you wouldn't believe. Heywort—she hung all her underclothes on the balcony! What do you think my neighbors they thought?" At this point he swung around and stared at me obviously expecting a response. After a moment or two of my awkward silence he continued. "The neighbors know I am not married. They see the panties and little things. They begin to think I am—how you say?—not a real man. Heywort, it's not funny, I have to worry about what my neighbors they think."

By this time Minolis was getting pretty worked up so I suppressed my laughter and tried to humor him with serious answers. This only served to ignite Minolis's desire to educate me in the mechanics of his love life. Without taking his eyes off the winding road, he reached into his ever present black pouch and fished out a medium sized note book. "Heywort, look at this."

At first I was puzzled. It looked like a financial statement or computer spread sheet. But, upon closer examination, it looked like... no! It couldn't be. But, yes, it was. Neatly penned, in English, there it was. A girlfriend scorecard. Across the top were the desired characteristics and down the left hand side was a long list of names. Opposite each name Minolis had entered a number indicating the rating for each of the characteristics. I tried to act impressed but thought to myself that I hoped that his techniques for purchasing boats was better than his approach towards women.

Finally we reached Volos and *Argo*. Minolis' sales efforts reached a high pitch: "Heywort, this is a fine boat. It's not like the boat Evianos showed you—everything here is in great condition." As we arrived at the quay Minolis interrupted himself in the middle of his sales spiel. "What are these people doing on board? They must be coming in from a charter."

I was new to Greek boat chartering and my opinion didn't count for much, but it seemed strange to me that people returning from a charter would be taking a case of champagne on board. Minolis ignored my remark, shifted into high gear, and marched on board. Deaf ears greeted his Greek tirade so he switched to English. The leader of the "returning charterers" seemed to understand some of what Minolis was saying and replied in French.

"We are going to leave in an hour, but if you would like to see the boat, come aboard." It was a crowd of Parisians and they had almost finished loading their pate, cheese, and wine on board for their two-week charter. The fight was just about to break out when Pandelis Andreolakis arrived at the scene.

Fifteen minutes of shouting in Greek was translated to me as: "Pandelis has decided to charter his boat out one last time, but it will be ready for you to buy when they get back. We can go out now for a ride and you will see how well it handles."

We went through the motions of a sea trial and inspection, but as far as I was concerned it was a non-event. As the French group sailed off, Minolis, Pandelis, and I retired to a cafe and started doing business over a bottle of ouzo. I explained as civilly as possible that unless the boat came off charter immediately I wasn't interested and that further discussions were useless.

It is a credit to Greek entrepreneurship that my objections didn't slow Minolis or Pandelis down in the slightest, and half way through the second bottle we reached an agreement that not only included price, on board spares, and all the accessories that came with *Argo* but also included a plan to get the boat off charter. It was completely dark by the time we arrived at Pandelis' speed boat that was pulled up on a beach not far from a small cafe. We siphoned enough gas from Minolis' car for the trip across the Gulf of Volos, "borrowed" two oars and a life jacket from a neighboring boat, and then set out for the 20 kilometer trip to Vathudi Bay.

It was hard to tell who knew less about what they were doing. Minolis knew a lot about sailboats and seamanship but was totally unfamiliar with the Gulf of Volos. Pandelis knew a little about the geography of the area but practically nothing about boat handling. The fact that the boat itself actually ran was surprising enough, but that after only an hour of running through the pitch black night we actually found Vathudi Bay and the *Argo* was nothing short of a miracle.

We found them seated around a large table in a quaint restaurant on the bay and Minolis made his request. I engaged the ladies in a long conversation about how I planned to sail for a year with my family while Minolis worked on the leader and the other men. While listening to the approving comments from the girls about my plans, I could hear excerpts from Minolis' conversation that suggested that his offer to swap the boat they had chartered for a better boat wasn't being enthusiastically embraced.

In spite of the large platter of souvlaki and two bottles of wine Pandelis had ordered, the situation was degenerating. When Minolis suggested that if his kind offer wasn't accepted, he would personally don scuba gear, remove the propeller from *Argo*, and then have the Port Police arrest the vessel as unseaworthy, all ambiance seemed to disappear from our gathering. While the Parisians were to call Minolis in two days to receive instructions on switching out vessels, it was not at all clear whether or not they would cooperate.

***

During the long trip back to Athens my deep dissatisfaction with Minolis' handling of the entire affair had had time to settle in. When I came into Minolis' office the next morning, he immediately realized he was about to lose a potential customer. I had just finished expressing my disapproval when Minolis made one of his characteristic 180 degree turns.

"Heywort, Heywort, forget about *Argo*. I just talked with Kiriacoulis and he will meet the price Pandelis agreed to." Before I could get a word in edgewise, he continued: "Besides the *Captain Spiros* she has radar, an auto pilot, and a new Genoa sail. You saw what a good boat she was. Heywort, the *Captain Spiros* is the perfect boat for you. You see what I do for you. Ha! Pandelis agrees to a low price for his boat, so we get the low price on the *Captain Spiros*. Not bad, eh? You see, I know what I'm talking—I get the best deal for you."

Against my better judgment, I didn't walk out of Minolis' office immediately. Instead I told him that if he could get the *Captain Spiros* at that price and with auto pilot, radar and a new Genoa I would consider it. The next day we took her out for sea trials. She performed beautifully. Nine knots in light wind. Upon our return Economou pulled up in his sparkling black BMW and we hauled her out for a survey. He and his assistant busily poked around the hull with a knife and took lots of pictures. They certainly looked like they knew what they were doing.

"Eets a very nice boat Meester Coleman. No signs of osmosis. The shaft is a leetle out of line and the rubber in the seems of the teak deck needs to be replaced, but other than that the boat looks very good. My assistant and I will write up a full report and send it to you." That night we put the purchase agreement together. Watching Minolis and Miltos argue as we negotiated the terms was like watching a cobra and a mongoose locked in mortal combat. The negotiations continued well into the night with the cobra taking breaks to call Kiriacoulis to see if he would accept some of the terms I was relaying to my mongoose. Amazingly, we reached agreement, and the next day I was on board a plane with the news for my family. The trip was on.

Chapter 2
The Refit

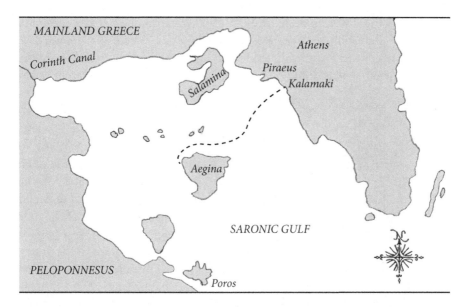

Heyward had agreed to keep his sport coat on in Kennedy Airport to accommodate my desire to look as conservative as possible. But once on the plane, his patience was gone. Off came the coat and out came his tattered shirt. Hair to the shoulders, shirt tails out, and a sash for a belt—he finally felt comfortable. My demands to pull the wrinkled coat back out of the bag that contained his walkman and tapes fell on deaf ears and our argument continued as we stepped off the plane in Athens.

Back on Wadmalaw, packing had not been easy and it had not been casually done. A call to KLM had given me the maximum dimension of baggage and the maximum weight for each piece. We would have no place to store suitcases, so I decided to use cardboard boxes instead. Working backwards, I cut our old moving boxes to the dimensions that yielded the highest possible volume. We were allowed two check on bags each with a maximum weight of 70 pounds per bag. In addition we were allowed one carry on each with a maximum weight of 50 pounds. This gave a grand total of 950 pounds for the five of us plus whatever else we could wear or carry on inconspicuously. With each box on a scale, I had mixed heavy with light until the box weighed exactly the maximum weight and then securely taped and tied them closed. Miraculously the huge pile that had filled our living room had fit almost exactly into the allotted boxes.

It was this hodgepodge of second hand boxes, patched with tape, and wrapped with cords that filled the six baggage carts we pushed before us towards the customs desk. The customs official looked at the carts and boxes and then looked at the five of us. His focus riveted on Heyward. A sneer changed into a smirking smile and out came his pocket knife. Before I realized what he was doing he jabbed his knife into one of the larger boxes and adroitly cut out a square.

The Coleman Family

"Hey, what are you doing? We have clothes in there. Be careful or you are going to slice our things up!" Undaunted he continued his search. As he pulled a pair of underpants and a bag of popcorn out of the hole he had just made, he signaled for me to open the rest of the boxes.

I couldn't believe what was happening. Everything—clothes, books, medicines, fishing equipment—was scattered over the table. He was down to the last box when he finally came upon something that interested him—the Satellite Navigation System I was going to install on the boat. I was trying to explain to him what a Satnav was when suddenly Minolis appeared. A heated argument between Minolis and the official finally led to the official walking off with my Satnav and signaling me to repack my boxes and leave. Minolis explained: "Don't worry Heywort, it's only a formality. Dracos will take care of it. You will get your Satnav back."

I had already come to realize that in Greece nothing is easy, but this was going too far. Under Greek law we had the right to bring electronic equipment into the country as long as it was for our personal use. But as far as the customs official was concerned, Greek law really didn't have very much to do with it. The only thing that gave me any hope that I would ever see my Satnav again was the strong impression the name "Dracos" seemed to have on him.

***

Reality set in hard the next day. With my work list in hand I arrived in Minolis' office at 8:00 A.M. When he finally arrived he explained that Manfred was in Rhodes picking up Mandiki's boat and wouldn't be back for several days.

"But Minolis, you and Manfred promised that he would spend full time on my boat and you would get me ready in a couple of weeks. Look at this list—I can't wait a week before starting and..." Minolis interrupted "Heywort, don't worry, Manfred will get your boat ready like I promised, but it doesn't matter if he starts a few days late. There is a general strike that is stopping practically everything in Greece, so your certificate of deletion will probably get held up also."

Minolis knew he had me locked in and was now putting his efforts on other business. But I was determined that the refit would go smoothly and was ready to focus the full strength of my pent up energy on seeing to it.

Up until this point I was dealing well with the abrupt suspension of my professional career. Aggressively pursuing our sailing adventure had protected me from the frustrations I otherwise would have felt. I was even able to put out of my mind the enormous sense of loss I had felt in leaving a business I had played a major role in developing. Activity was my joy and my salvation.

First it had been the logistics of the move and the excitement of purchasing the boat. I had handled both in the same manner I had handled important business transactions. Now it was the refit. Minolis' office had become my office and I had invaded his telephones, fax, and Xerox machines. This had caused friction, but the yet to be earned commission on *Captain Spiros* was sufficient motivation to bend Minolis into compliance.

There was one leap of faith we needed to make. Although my purchase agreement gave me the right to work on the boat, the vessel was not legally mine until after closing. Any expenses incurred before closing would be at my risk. There could be no closing without the all important certificate of deletion, and that was frozen. Obtaining the certificate was a bureaucratic process and all of the bureaucrats were on strike. Not even so formidable a personality as Dracos could speed things up. Instead of the anticipated two weeks, it looked like the process would take at least a month. We were in a box.

Minolis oozed confidence and urged that we begin work at once. It was a case of the shark hooking the fisherman, and it was a measure of the magnitude of my determination to complete a timely refit that I allowed myself to take the bait. That afternoon we had a family summit and decided to press full steam ahead in spite of the risks. Manfred or no Manfred, we would have engine mechanics, refrigeration people, and sail makers begin immediately. We would do all we could ourselves—cleaning, painting, and light construction.

Minolis arranged help—with healthy commissions on the side— and the *Captain Spiros* became a mass of confusion with parts, people, and equipment everywhere. We worked from early morning until sunset when we would put tools aside, clean up the mess, and wait for Claudine to arrive. Claudine, whose husband was a Greek cardiologist and whom we had met through a friend of Charlotte's, would bring us beer and sit with us to watch the beauty of the sun falling into the Saronic Gulf. She was wonderful. She devoted her evenings to showing us all around Athens and Piraeus and would help me during the day when I needed a translator or local knowledge in my dealings with the boat purchase

The day before *Captain Spiros* was to come out of the water for some of the more extensive repairs, Manfred finally returned. He had left Mandriki's boat in nearby Turkiliminos and was ready to help us—for awhile. Not quite everything we had done was wrong, and he was willing to work hard as long as we kept him well supplied with beer and ouzo. His gruff manner, ready wit, strong work ethic, and incredibly foul language always kept us guessing about what would come next. He was in the throes of a nasty separation with his third wife, but was having a wonderful time with his teenage sweetheart who had left home in Germany to be with him.

The boat was hauled out under Manfred's watchful eye. After placing the chocks and wedges and carefully situating the boat on its cradle, he began to poke around the hull with a chisel. A soft spot. He drove the chisel in and water squirted out. "Its a fucking choke" he shouted as he drove the chisel in several more places with the same results. Several hours later there were two three-foot long cavities in the bottom of the boat—one in front of the keel and the other directly behind it.

We learned all about osmosis that day. A hairline crack is all that is necessary—then water slowly seeps in and travels along the glass fibers. If the crack is left unattended long enough, the water can travel all through the boat and delaminate the fiberglass. The end result can be a severely weakened or even ruined boat. Economou may have looked like he knew what he was doing when he was scraping around with his knife, but the fact that he missed these cracks was, as Manfred delicately put it, "a fucking choke." Fortunately for *Captain Spiros,* the damage was localized forward and aft of the keel. The affected areas were actually void spaces that allowed for a longer keel in a different version of the Trinidad. But somehow Charlotte and I didn't feel very fortunate.

At about this time Minolis drove up. Ignoring the steely looks from all five of us, he immediately began to minimize the importance of the damage. "Heywort, don't worry—the space can be filled in and glassed over—it won't affect the strength of the boat—there was only filler material there in the first place." He then offered some free advice about how to repair the holes and then headed off to another project. Much to Manfred's credit, he did not try to hide the importance of the problem. He agreed, however, that it was not structural and could be repaired without loss in strength of the vessel.

That night was almost the end of our pursuit of the *Captain Spiros*. Although we had expended a lot of money and a great deal of sweat on the boat, we could still walk away. Kiriacoulis and Minolis were dragging their feet on everything they had promised. The radar, the auto pilot, and the new genoa—all important parts of the transaction—had yet to appear. We had also been very disappointed in Manfred's late arrival and the subsequent delay in the refit. The cumulative effect was that we were becoming very tired of the whole affair. The osmosis problem around the keel was the last straw. Charlotte and I debated long into the night about what to do. There were alternatives.

An aggressive Dutch broker had been trying hard to interest us in a 42 foot Tayana ketch that belonged to one of the members of the Pink Floyd. It was a beautiful boat and was loaded with electronics, but had seemed a little "tight" for our space needs. And there was the boat that Nick, another contact from the American Embassy, had suggested. His friend, Mr. Xoutos, was more than willing to sell us his boat. This, along with Tayana ketch, presented very real alternatives to our preset dilemma.

During the day, I had called Economou's office and he was to meet us at the boat the next morning. After talking things over Charlotte and I decided to delay any action until after we had slept on it and talked with Economou. It was a long night!

The next morning we were loaded for bear. Manfred met us at the boat and explained again his proposal for a repair job, but this time he was less critical of the damage. Minolis, fearing the possible loss of a sale, had obviously given him a sound scolding for his earlier comments. Instinctively Minolis knew to avoid Charlotte, but when he arrived that morning he let his guard down. If he had been worried about the loss of a sale before, he was in a near state of panic after the tongue lashing he received from the prospective first mate and mother of the crew of *Captain Spiros*. She had spelled out our alternatives very clearly, and there could be absolutely no doubt about her seriousness.

Normally Minolis would have responded in true Greek fashion with an offensive attempt to shift the blame onto his attacker, but in this instance he had the good sense to realize that his deal hung by a thread. He was all milk and honey—but at the same time still the consummate "used boat salesman". While he was regaling us with his profound knowledge of marine architecture and sound construction, Economou drove up in his black BMW with a driver.

I noted the frightened expression on Manfred's face as Economou, dressed in a conservative business suit, stepped out of his car. "Manfred, I'm counting on you to explain to Economou all of the problems you have uncovered. You might also help me when I ask him how he missed them in his survey." Manfred's cockiness of the day before had entirely evaporated. "Heyward, I have to be careful. I am only a technician. If I get in an argument with a person like that I could find myself at the bottom of Kalamaki harbor!"

The stage was set and the show was about to begin. Two hardened Greeks, each of them determined to show he had not made a mistake, a frightened technician, and a furious wife made for an explosive situation.

First Aid for Captain Spiros

I was less interested in meting out blame than in deciding if the boat could be safely fixed—but I was in the minority. High voices in Greek, German, and English—fingers pointed at faces, at the two holes, and then back at faces. Seeing the commotion, a few other "experts" joined the group and added their unsolicited opinions to the discussion.

Charlotte was convinced that the boat had been badly grounded and everything including the keel had been jarred loose. Minolis thought her theory was ridiculous and tried to rationally explain to her why this could not have happened. Economou was in the difficult position of seeing the irrefutable proof of chronic osmosis that he had failed to detect in his inspection and was trying desperately to find an excuse to justify his omission. Manfred was trying to be as inconspicuous as possible and spoke only when a question was aimed directly at him.

When Economou launched into an explanation that placed the ultimate blame on the crane operator because he had put the boat back in the water so quickly that there wasn't time for an adequate inspection, I had finally had enough. Focusing my attention on Economou I asked: "Does the damage weaken the structure and is it reparable?" He was, after all both the surveyor and the insurer. While I didn't think he was above stretching the truth to cover the carelessness of his inspection, I thought he would have to think long and hard before writing an insurance policy on a vessel that wasn't structurally sound.

He told me what I expected to hear and what I had determined for myself was the case. While the damage necessitated a fairly costly repair, the affected area had only been filler material in the void space that the keel would have occupied in the long keel model. The boat had not been weakened. Minolis was happy, Charlotte was still mad, Manfred was relieved, and Economou quickly disappeared from the scene. The crowd of experts had enjoyed the spectacle and generally concurred with Economou's assessment.

***

We had passed our first crisis of the trip, and we were settling into a routine. But it was a strange routine—so very different from the rigidness of our life in Philadelphia that I would often drift into self-examination. Little things like watching Greek children on their way to school in their neat uniforms would give me guilty pangs. Had I done the right thing in uprooting our lives and pulling our children out of school? Or had the cure been worse than the disease?

The refit had been so consuming that I hadn't had time to dwell on this concern very much. But it was there. Sometimes it would surface when Charlotte and I could break away for a dinner by ourselves and sometimes at night as we discussed the day's activities. At the root were the self-doubts. What was I doing and how had I thrown away such an extraordinary business opportunity? I hadn't minded the six months of eighteen-hour days and seven-day weeks that had led to the Maritrans spin-off. After all, I had emerged as one of the principal owners. It had been every businessman's dream, but as often happens, much bad came with the good. In this case it was bitter conflict among top management over what direction the company should take. I could either follow what I was convinced was a bad course, or stand up for what I believed was right. I had chosen the latter. When the self-doubts set in, Charlotte would soothe, we would rehash the whole affair, and would again conclude it had been the right decision.

***

Manfred became a close friend of the family as the refit progressed. In spite of his gruff manner, we all looked forward to seeing him when he could break himself away from Mandiki to work on our boat. We listened with admiration as he talked about the wooden boat he was about to purchase in Connecticut and of how he was going to fix it up and then run it on charter in the Aegean. He had worked hard all his life and finally his dream seemed within reach.

But I was still a little angry with him for convincing me to buy an incredibly expensive Teflon anti fouling paint. When I had found that the paint was extremely difficult to apply and didn't stick well to the paint that was currently on the bottom, he fiercely defended his position—and his commission—by emphasizing to our children that the alternative paint (that was a fraction of the price and was used on almost every other boat in the Mediterranean) was harmful to the environment and would kill fish. Against my better judgment, but knowing that Manfred was going to apply the paint using his special air brush and would use a special technique, I had given in.

On the day of the painting—exactly one week after we had begun the endless process of sanding, cleaning, sanding, and cleaning to prepare the hull for its gold coat—Minolis drove up and announced that Manfred's wife had left. She had made off with his boat money and was on an airplane headed for her home in Holland. Manfred had turned white and had disappeared in hot pursuit.

Our Professional Painter

This left the five of us, two paint brushes, 10 quarts of liquid gold, and Minolis—who wasn't even about to consider giving a helping hand—to figure out how to get the two coats of paint on the hull in time to meet the firm launch time set for the following day. Minolis quickly evaporated and there we were. While we all felt bad about Manfred's misfortune, we felt worse about the prospect of manually applying the Teflon paint. Experimenting in small patches on the keel I tried thin coats followed by thick coats and thick coats followed by thin coats. I even made a feeble attempt at using Manfred's air gun. But try as I might, the result was consistently a gummy mess. I was about to give up when Charlotte showed us how it was done. With lots of experience on kitchens and children's rooms under her belt, she quickly devised a technique so that the paint went on almost smoothly.

While the painting was in progress, there was a small diversion. A Mercedes rolled up and a young lady stepped out and called for me. Noticing the puzzled look on my face as I approached, she handed me a box and smiled. My Satnav! Dracos had come through. She then handed me a less welcome item. A bill. At first I thought my arithmetic converting Drachmas must be wrong, but she quickly confirmed the correctness of my calculations.

"But this is more than I would have had to pay in taxes even if taxes had really been due. There must be some mistake..."

"No Mr. Coleman, there has been no mistake. You see here on the bill—it took a lot of Mr. Dracos' time -and there was much paper work."

Although I was furious, I made a quick decision. With closing still some time off, and with Dracos the chief player in getting my certificate of deletion, I decided that now was not the time to get into a fight with him. Reluctantly I paid the bill, but, as the young lady drove off, I wondered what was in store next. If this was the type of help I could expect from Minolis' friends, I wasn't sure that I could afford much more of it.

***

Launch date finally arrived. With the overhead crane standing by and Manfred, Heyward, and Alex ready to tend lines, I went to the marina office to inform them the boat was going back into the water and to pay my bill so that the crane could be released to launch. In the true spirit of Greek trust, they didn't want boats launched before money changed hands.

I could see the crane hooking up to my boat as the lady behind the counter explained for the third time that they had a different manager that day, and he had decided to change the system. Paying the bill was not quite good enough. This manager also wanted the owner to authorize the launching in person. And "No, Mr. Coleman, your written authorization isn't sufficient."

Captain Spiros Comes out of the Water

Never mind the fact that I had spent close to a month at the marina and paid rather handsomely for the privilege—the bureaucrat would have it her way. The likelihood of finding Kiriacoulis in his office on Saturday morning was about as likely as finding a Greek you could trust with money—but I tried anyway.

My efforts were rewarded with the appearance of Yannis. Yannis was Kiriacoulis' nephew who claimed to be the owner of *Captain Spiros*. By this time I could see that the boat was clear of the pier and almost in the water. I asked Yannis to come down to the Marina to give us authorization to launch, and without waiting for a response, I left the office to attend to the boat.

The crane operator accepted my payment receipt as sufficient authorization to launch—he hadn't heard about the new system yet—and the *Captain Spiros* was back in her element. Yannis never showed up, and a few hours later a now informed and very angry crane operator came by the boat to give me a piece of his mind. Pretending not to understand what he was saying nor that he was upset, I gave him the traditional Greek greeting—"*yassou*"—and shoved an ouzo in his hand. His hesitation lasted only a moment, and then he joined us in our celebration.

***

The trauma over the hole in the bottom, the enormous amount of work we had completed, the launching, our never-ending difficulties with the Greeks—all of this tended to cement our commitment. There was no longer any thought of turning back. In spite of the fact that the strike was still in progress and closing was not yet in sight, we decided to move onto the boat and treat it like it was ours.

An endless stream of boxes flowed down the two-man elevator in the Hotel Alimos, through the lobby where the entire staff was watching and saying their good-bys, and formed a small mountain on the sidewalk. We knew getting a cab was going to be difficult. The Athens cabs are strictly regulated, and unless they cheat, the prices are very, very low. This doesn't give the drivers much incentive to work, and getting a cab to stop and offer a ride can be tricky.

About the only way the cabbies can make any money is to pick passengers up one at a time until they have their full compliment of four and then charge each of them the meter price from the time they mount to the time they get off. If they can get away with a fairly circuitous route, they are often willing to forego the opportunity to try to double the fare or cheat on giving change.

Under this system, a lone passenger has a fairly good chance of stopping a cab—particularly if he looks mild mannered and pliable. Two passengers and the chances go down significantly. Three passengers and you just as well forget it. With our huge pile of boxes and five passengers, I knew it was going to be a hard sell.

I stationed myself around the corner and out of sight of the hotel and the pile of baggage. Margot took two small boxes and went half way to the corner while I waited for an empty cab to appear. The driver gave me a dirty look when I asked him to turn the corner to pick up my daughter and a couple of boxes, but he grudgingly made the turn and stopped. While Margot was loading the two small boxes, he failed to notice Heyward and Alex just up the street pushing the huge pile towards his cab.

By this time, I had had a chance to exchange "*yassou*'s" with him and tell him about the boat we would live on for the next year. When he caught sight of the others and suddenly realized what was happening, his big frown revealed his inner turmoil. The Greek love for boats, the sea, and families was struggling against his hurt pride in being duped. A heated argument ensued, but I could tell his heart was not really in it. The love of the sea had won out. Three trips to the marina later and, after a generous fare and handsome tip, our new found friend left the *Captain Spiros* and promised to come back to wish us bon voyage.

***

As we maneuvered the newly launched *Captain Spiros* through the Kalamaki Marina it became apparent to me why Minolis had told me back in August the marina was empty when it appeared to me to be full of boats. At that time, there had been only one boat in each slip. Now, for every one boat in a slip, there were two or three other boats clustered about it secured by a combination of mooring lines, anchors, and fenders. The overall effect was a sea of boats randomly clustered about each other and extending two, three, and sometimes even four boats off the main piers. To most seamen, this was an abomination. To the Greeks, it was normal.

Manfred had helped us find a place to nest. Off the second finger pier out from shore we found a place where the boats were only two deep. After setting a stern anchor we nudged our bow in between two boats that in turn had their bows nudged between two other boats—all of them had stern anchors also. Manfred showed us how to tie a special knot on the anchor chain of one of the innermost boats and then helped us with a series of lines from our winches and cleats to winches and cleats on the two adjacent boats. Two bumpers and a life jacket wrapped around our protruding bow anchor demonstrated that we had at least made an effort to prevent the wake of a passing boat from holing our forward starboard neighbor.

Carrying the boxes on board was a bit awkward, but we managed by forming an assembly line and passing the cargo from hand to hand across the boats. Getting ourselves on and off was another matter. Going from our boat to the next was relatively easy. Stand outboard our lifelines, grab the lifelines on the other boat's stern, put a foot on the gunnels, and then—quickly and without looking down—throw your weight forward and step over the lifelines into the cockpit. A similar maneuver gained access to the next boat in—but this is when the tricky part started.

The inboard boat had its bow tied to the pier, but far enough off for protection. For an agile person the jump from bow to pier was easy—but we had not yet developed our sea legs. Coming back on board for the last time that night, we helped each other, but there had to be a last person. Alex was either very tired or very overconfident. His three-foot leap for the three and a half foot gap ended in a loud splash and a lot of cursing. While Heyward and I were fishing him out of the water, Charlotte added to the confusion by continuously yelling: "Alex, keep your mouth shut." We rushed him over to the showers for decontamination when we received our second surprise of the evening. No hot water.

While there was always a certain amount of tension between mother and sons during the trip, it reached a fevered pitch that evening at the door of the showers. Having observed Greek hygiene for the past couple of months we all had a fairly clear idea of what had collected in the incredibly polluted waters of Kalamaki Marina. Charlotte, terrified of hepatitis, cholera, or even the plague, insisted that Alex thoroughly scrub himself and do so as quickly as possible. For his part, Alex, already suffering from chills and shock from his immersion, decided after the first blast of freezing water from the showers that he would rather chance the microbes than lather up in a cold shower.

The shouting match worked its way across the marina and then boat by boat back to our new home. Hot water from the propane stove mixed in buckets with cold water and Alex indulged himself in the first onboard shower/bath of the trip.

***

Two important deliverables were yet to materialize—the auto pilot and the radar.

At the beginning of the refit I had gone over the boat with Kiriacoulis' nephew Yannis. While his forthright and easy going manner was refreshing, the facts he had confronted me with were alarming. "My uncle told you the auto pilot works? He must have been kidding" Yannis explained as he disassembled the actuating arm and spilled out dozens of tiny ball bearings on the table. "Look, the shaft is worn and many of the bearings are missing—it hasn't worked for a long time. The charterers, they don't take care of things."

We had then moved on to the radar, which had yet to make its appearance on board. I was surprised as it was supposed to have been installed prior to my return to Greece. When I questioned Yannis he looked at me with a puzzled expression on his face and then smiled broadly. "I will get Evianos to bring it on board this afternoon" and that was all I could get out of him on the subject.

During my inspection Yannis explained that the boat belonged to him and that he maintained it and often captained it for charter parties. He was very open with me and told me many things about the boat that were to prove to be invaluable later on. As nice as Yannis was, however, I was distressed to hear about the problem with the auto pilot and was not at all optimistic about what I would see when the radar finally arrived.

My pessimism was well founded. Evianos arrived with a huge clunker that took almost half the free space around the navigation table. He also brought the giant dome and a stainless steel mounting bracket for the mast. Yannis' pronouncement that he had never liked the radar because it often ripped the jib was unnecessary—the garden hose and twine wrapped around the stainless steel mounting bracket already had given this hazard away. Whether or not it actually worked was a question I felt was hardly worth asking.

Minolis' response to my outrage had been characteristic. "Heywort, don't listen to Yannis—he doesn't know what he's talking. You know, his uncle bought the boat for him to manage, but every year he loses money. Yannis is not a businessman. That is why his uncle is selling the boat. Don't worry, I will get an electronics expert to look at the auto pilot and the radar—if they are broken, we make Kiriacoulis pay. It's not a problem."

But it was a problem and Minolis' expert made it worse. He repaired the actuator—at considerable expense—but hadn't checked out the part of the system that controlled the actuator. When he came on the boat to look at the controller, I was in the other end of the boat and didn't see him. Hearing the noise from the electric screw driver aroused my curiosity and I came out on deck to see him removing the entire aft end of the cockpit that I had just finished two days work to clean, seal and install.

When I gained sufficient control over myself I asked him in an almost calm voice what he thought he was doing. He took a handkerchief from his immaculately clean coveralls to wipe a small smudge of grease from his hands and sheepishly replied that he hadn't wanted to crawl through the lazaret to connect a wire. Filthy dirty from having crawled through the lazaret myself dozens of times over the past two days to accomplish my repair and furious at the prospect that I would now have to repeat the process to remedy his thoughtless action, I restrained my almost overpowering desire to physically throw him overboard. Clean Jeans then informed me that the controller was faulty, but he had a solution. Simply replace the controller with a new one. But the repairs were going to be more expensive than a new unit.

The expert had also looked at the radar. The unit itself worked, but the cable connecting it had lost its shielding due to corrosion and years of neglect. Running the radar with this cable would cause electronic interference that would prevent any other electronic equipment on the boat from working. Replacing the cable was not possible because it was no longer manufactured, but even if by some miracle he were able to find a cable, installing it in the mast would be extremely expensive. The outlook for my extras was pretty dismal.

**

Riding around with Manfred in his antique VW diesel Rabbit from shop to shop in Piraeus and Turkiliminos was an experience in itself. Costa's stainless steel fabrication shop just behind the Turkiliminos Yacht Club was the hub. After exchanging *Yassous*, studying sketches written out on scraps of paper, and finishing with the mandatory ouzo, we would speed off to the sail maker just across the street from Zea Marina in Piraeus. Costello wasn't comfortable doing business until after we had sampled the special family recipe aqua vita he poured from an old wine bottle. But the new awning and repairs to our old Genoa were coming along nicely as were the stainless steel radar mast for our stern and various other fittings for the boat. Our visits also included the paint shop in Kastela, a machine shop near the commercial harbor, and several specialty chandlers spread throughout Piraeus.

While the sequence of our visits would often change, the last stop was invariable—Manfred's Irish pub near Zea. This was a second home for Manfred, and he knew everyone. Over two or three beers we would discuss the accomplishments of the day, the work scheduled for tomorrow, and the mess into which Manfred's personal life had degenerated. With nothing resolved on any of the topics, Manfred would head back to his small apartment on top of a high hill overlooking Kastela, and I would fight for a taxi ride back to Kalamaki. In a strange way, Manfred and I became very close friends.

**

Closing finally came. Dracos had obtained the certificate of deletion and we were ready to go. At the closing conference in Milto's office, I met

Kiriacoulis for the first time. Older than I imagined and with graying hair, he didn't look like a crook. But, at the same time, he did not exude an honesty that I could count on for fair play. Fortunately our friend, Claudine, had agreed to come to the closing. With her fluent Greek and sharp business mind and with Miltos' legal advice, I felt I had a chance of not being completely fleeced.

The meeting started badly. When I expressed my discomfort at virtually none of the terms of our purchase agreement having been fulfilled both Minolis and Kiriacoulis responded with hostility. Miltos, however, arbitrated and succeeded in hammering out an escrow agreement that held sufficient funds to cover the as-yet-to-be resolved issues of the auto pilot and radar. Miltos was to hold the money and Minolis was to coordinate the repairs. We closed, went through the friendly Greek act, and then Kiriacoulis graciously offered the use of his chauffeured Jaguar to transport Claudine and me back to Kalamaki. The *Captain Spiros* was now mine.

Although the refit was not quite over, we now had a boat and mobility. Manfred rented a house on the nearby island of Aegina and commuted on weekends on a hydrofoil called the *Flying Dolphin*. It did not take him long to talk us into moving our refit to Aegina. The day after closing, Manfred finished repairs to the engine just after sunset, and we were ready to go. The three-hour sail to Aegina in the warm balmy air was pleasant, and we all had a great feeling of freedom. Manfred had brought his guitar, and he and Heyward played as we made the crossing. Harmony reigned until we entered Aegina harbor.

A choice needed to be made of where to anchor. Manfred had proclaimed himself skipper at the outset and I had readily agreed. Not being familiar with the characteristics of the boat, and not knowing the area, I was delighted to have Manfred's help for a familiarization period. Manfred took his job of skipper seriously and had a  definite Prussian view of discipline. When Heyward questioned my choice of mooring locations, Manfred was not pleased. When Heyward persisted in spite of my gentle hints that I wasn't going to change my mind, Mr. Hyde emerged. Manfred's tongue lashing and demeaning description of Heyward's role as a lowly deck hand came as a shattering blow. He had admired the

The Refit Moves to Aegina

bohemian in Manfred and had become quite close to him. This vehement attack was wholly unexpected. Their relationship never fully recovered.

In a way, Heyward was the victim of a fight that was bound to occur, and which in fact had been long overdue. Unlike family life in Philadelphia where decisions could be made in a leisurely fashion and where a certain amount of "family democracy" could be tolerated, we were now in an environment where unquestioning discipline was often a necessity. Manfred and I knew this, but the others did not. Our safety and well being were going to depend on my actions and my judgments and there would be many times when there was no time for debate. Heyward had learned the hard way.

Aegina was now home. The overcrowded stench of Kalamaki marina had been replaced with a charming Greek village. We were moored with our stern facing the pier on the far side of the harbor next to a fishing boat. A gangplank to the shore was pure luxury after the gymnastics in Kalamaki. The village, the beaches, and the entire island were within easy access and we took full advantage of all of them.

There was a woodworking shop, several chandlers, and two excellent hardware stores all within a short walk from our boat. I set up a workshop on a stone ledge on the pier just opposite our boat and continued with the final tasks in preparing the boat for sea. Manfred came to help in the evenings. We were getting close to being ready.

On our third day in Aegina we took a combination outing/sea trials trip to the neighboring island Angistri. Manfred knew a spot where he could bring our stern in so close to shore that we almost touched and secured us with a line to a tree. While the children snorkeled and explored the sea life, Manfred and I worked on the final installation of the stern radar mast that Costa had fabricated for us.

Alex's Octopoli

Alex had speared an "octopoli" the day before and, with spear guns out, both he and Heyward were now trying to top his record. Over the loud protests of both Charlotte and Margot I had cooked Alex's octopoli for dinner. Despite the requisite one hundred beats Alex had given the dead octopoli against a giant rock, it had still tasted a little like shoe leather. I learned afterwards that I should then have boiled it before sautéing it in my gourmet wine sauce.

The next morning Heyward and Alex were trying to provide me with fresh material to redeem my culinary credibility.Lunch time finally came and, to Charlotte's delight, Alex and Heyward had failed to produce another octopoli. Charlotte has never been big on wiggly sea creatures, but this feeling of revulsion took on a special meaning when it came to octopoli. If she never saw another on our trip, it would have been too soon for her. She had had her eye on a small cafe a short distance from where we were moored and our lack of success at fishing gave her the excuse she needed.

Manfred, Heyward, Alex, and I went on ahead. We raced over the slippery stones that jutted out of the water separating the main island from the small island where we were moored and approached the cafe. I was in the middle of a conversation with an Australian family we had met when I noticed that Charlotte and Margot still hadn't arrived. As I walked back to see if I could help them, I saw Charlotte trying to climb over the rocks. It had not occurred to me that they would have trouble, but the rocks were slippery and Charlotte is always very slow and cautious when it comes to climbing of any sort.

At about this time, I saw her foot slip into the shallow water. The rest happened so quickly that I have a hard time remembering exactly but the sequence went something like this. Two or three long brown hose-like objects emerged from the water in the vicinity of Charlotte's foot. Their appearance coincided with a blood-curdling scream of "octopoli." Charlotte then seemed to rise and hop out of the water in a single motion and then leaped from rock to rock along the entire stone trail with a nimbleness that would have been a credit to a mountain goat.

We tried to comfort her by suggesting that it had probably only been an old mooring line, but she would have none of it. When Alex chastised her for not trying to catch it, her steely look signaled us that we had gone too far. Everyone then tried to express their sympathy and their happiness in having gotten her back safe and sound. Heyward and Alex even gave up their impulsive urge to get their spear guns and go after the catch.

On our way back to Aegina we encountered a heavy wind and rain. We tested the auto pilot which did not work at all and other systems on the boat. But we didn't set the sails and try out the reefing system. We should have. There are three items on a sailboat that are absolutely essential: a sound hull, good sails, and a good anchor. We had taken the latter two for granted—a mistake we would pay for later.

***

Manfred was doing a nice job of whipping us into a cruising family. Sailing can accurately be described as hours and hours of relaxed boredom interspersed with moments of sheer panic. Getting under way and mooring are the moments most likely for the sheer panic. Following Manfred's advice we assigned each person a specific duty for both of these evolutions. Alex manned the anchor, Heyward handled lines, Charlotte and Margot placed bumpers to compensate for my errors in judgment, and I took the wheel.

Under Manfred's watchful eye I was in the process of completing my first Mediterranean mooring. In the Mediterranean, mooring space is generally very limited and boats moor with their sterns against the quay and their bows pointed straight out—a stern to mooring. The boats look snug and it may appear to be easy, but it's not. The trick is to drop the anchor at right angles to the chosen spot on the quay and sufficiently far enough from the shore so that it will hold, but not so far as to run out of chain. Once the anchor is placed, the final step is to back in towards the quay as the anchor chain is paid out. With Manfred suggesting the spot, coaxing when to drop the anchor, and gently correcting me in the ticklish job of backing it didn't seem impossibly difficult.

Picturing our clockwise screw rotating counterclockwise while in reverse helped me remember that I would get a strong thrust to the left. Once we started moving, the rudder would begin to have an effect in guiding us and I only had to remember to turn in the opposite direction from the desired path. Keeping in mind that putting the motor in forward to slow our backwards motion would give us thrust to the right because of the then clockwise rotation of the screw and hoping that we wouldn't get any strong gusts of wind that would more or less override any of these control influences, I began my backwards journey to the quay.

Thump, thump, clank, clank—the chain made a horrible noise as it paid out under Alex's watchful eye. I heard him call out that it didn't sound right, but at this point in the maneuver there wasn't much I could do about that. Incredibly, my stern was actually headed for the empty gap between the two sailboats on the quay. Heyward managed to get a line ashore while Margot's bumper placement to port and Charlotte's to starboard kept us from damaging our new neighbors, and we squeezed our way between them on the last few yards of our maneuver. Finally a burst in forward and an order to Alex to hold the anchor chain. We were moored.

Our spot was right in the center of the waterfront opposite the busy cafes. As we settled down to enjoy the view and to compliment ourselves on our successful landing we saw for the first time what we were later to call the green submarine. I had thought the fit between the two boats during our approach had been tight, but the green submarine apparently had different ideas. She was headed, and rather quickly, between us and our neighbor to starboard. We could hear the scream of the anchor chain and to our amazement saw only one person on deck. A petite attractive brunette was everywhere at once, but somehow did not appear to be hurried. The boat looked like a cross between a Sherman tank and a World War I submarine— but as I saw it hurling towards us in reverse and remembered the difficulty of this maneuver, I thought of it more as a torpedo.

Charlotte, ever alert to any impending danger, was quickly up on deck with a bumper and the rest of us weren't far behind. Our precautions weren't necessary. Brigitte had the situation fully under control and *Fratellanza* neatly slipped between the two boats and her ominous steel sides were kept at bay by the bumpers that Brigitte had put in place at the beginning of their maneuver.

We were all still marveling over how one person could do all this when we saw a bearded figure emerge from the pillbox deckhouse. He was followed by two young girls and a young boy. Jean Louis' greeting: "Bon jour *Captain Spiros*" was the beginning of a long friendship.

***

There were a few items that needed to be taken care of before we could relax and visit Aegina. The anchor winch had sounded bad and we needed to take a look. Manfred surveyed the boxy mechanism with its attached motor. He tried releasing the clutch—nothing. The only way to let out chain was to put the motor in reverse—this had been responsible for part of the noise. The whole mechanism was also loose. Manfred shook his head and with characteristic abruptness summed the situation up: "Eets a fucking choke."

Manfred immediately set about to tighten the winch mounting screws, but in doing so snapped off one of the four fittings that secured the winch. The problem had gone from serious to critical. Now the winch would have to come out for repairs. Before doing this, however, we would need to set another anchor. The wind was picking up, and, if our present anchor slipped, we could not reset it without the winch.

Alex and Heyward inflated the flimsy soft bottom dinghy that had come with *Captain Spiros*. Manfred and I carefully lowered the second anchor—a fifty pound Danforth with ten meters of heavy chain—into the boat, attached the chain to the anchor and then attached the end of the chain to a heavy line that we would pay out from the boat. Explicit instructions followed: "Pay the chain out first and when we give you the signal drop the

39

anchor. Keep your feet clear so you don't get tangled and be careful not to let the anchor puncture the dinghy. Now, row hard into the wind and wait for our signal." And then they were off.

In spite of the drag of the line and push of the wind they were successful in positioning the dinghy. Manfred gave the signal and then we both pulled as rapidly as we could on the line to take up slack and prevent the anchor from falling on and becoming entangled in the chain. Pulling became hard and then -yes—it was holding.

Fifteen minutes later Manfred and I struggled to lift the damaged anchor winch out of its compartment and onto the deck. We then slung it onto the back of the folding bike we had purchased in Athens and headed for the sole machine shop on the island. Bad news. The casing was aluminum and there were no facilities to weld aluminum on Aegina. But Manfred always had a solution. On a piece of scratch paper he designed two straps that would give reinforcement and persuaded the machinist to have them ready in two days. It looked pretty crude to me, but I couldn't think of any alternatives so I went along with the plan.

Back at the boat, Charlotte and Brigitte had already become fast friends. Brigitte had pulled out their washing machine and set it up on the pier where she and Charlotte were washing several weeks worth of dirty clothes. The contraption looked like one of the old time agitator washing machines with an open top—except this one was smaller and looked cruder. A long cable to the *Fratellanza's* battery gave it power, and water was provided by a continuous stream of jerry cans that Heyward and Alex shuttled by dinghy from a water tap on the other side of the harbor. Margot was having a great time trying her French out on the three children while the four of them helped with the wash.

Jean-Louis and his family were from Corsica. They had lived on boats in Ajaccio for several years. *Fratellanza*, their most recent vessel, had undergone two conversions under Jean-Louis' special care. This most recent version incorporated many features he had decided he wanted after many years of experience. His addition of a steel cabin over what formerly had been the cockpit—the "pillbox"—gave him a totally enclosed space from which he could pilot his craft while Brigitte took care of the deck. Heavy steel upon heavy steel, the only thing that kept his 42-foot sloop afloat was the huge beam and enormous amount of freeboard. If he grounded, there was more reason to be worried about the rocky bottom than the structural integrity of his craft.

But like many of the French sailors we were to meet, Jean Louis was a real pro and, of course, he kept his *Glennon* at close hand. This book was revered by the French as containing the most authoritative information on sailing and he referred to it regularly. Although he and his family lived on an incredibly tight budget and had practically no discretionary funds, all of the important systems on his boat were of impeccable quality.

Watching Manfred and me remove the anchor winch had worn Jean-Louis out. Things needed to be done slowly and methodically and our frantic activity was a total mystery to him. My troubles, however, did arouse his interest and his sympathy. As we sat around the large rectangular table that occupied most of the stern of *Fratellanza* the conversation turned to the anchor winch. The importance of our problem was beginning to sink in. Our main anchor was a CQR—an all purpose plow anchor that weighed 80 pounds. The 70 meters of 12 millimeter chain added another three hundred pounds. While getting it all up without the use of an anchor winch wasn't completely impossible, it would be so difficult that it would render us almost helpless in an emergency. The only thing that would keep our boat off the rocks in heavy wind was the anchor, and now that system was impaired.

The fact that we had a second anchor deployed made me feel better for the moment, but Jean-Louis was right when he said that the anchor was the heart of a boat. He was very skeptical of Manfred's suggested reinforcement and offered to go to Piraeus with us to get a proper repair.

***

Our days in Aegina were a combination of work and pleasure. With shops of every sort a short walk from our gangway we began to stock the boat in earnest. We also took time to explore and enjoy the wonderful beaches and sights of Aegina. During this time our friendship with Jean-Louis and his family cemented into the strong bonds that can often be formed when people share common goals and face mutual dangers. We took outings together and alternated having dinner on each other's boats. Jean-Louis played the guitar and immediately he and Heyward became close. Joanne was eleven and the oldest. Both Margot and Alex took him under their wings. The middle child, Caroline, had the dark brown hair and penetrating brown eyes of her mother. She loved to be involved in everything that was going on and was always present. The youngest, Chinnouk, had a beautiful voice and long flowing blond hair. Brigitte was the epitome of all that is to be admired in a woman, a mother, and a sailor. Her petiteness belied her enormous energy and skills in every aspect of boat handling.

Our relationship was almost entirely in French. Brigitte was the only one in the family who spoke any English, but Jean-Louis discouraged her use of it. Our dinners would often last until late into the night. Heyward would get into our heated discussions on politics and the quality of life, and we watched with pleasure the process of his French developing as he would search for the proper word and then try to build it into a workable sentence. Alex and Margot were less aggressive in their language efforts, but osmosis was having its effect and their comprehension of French was increasing rapidly.

The highlights of the evenings would come when Jean-Louis and Heyward pulled out their guitars. French ballads alternated with the Grateful Dead as Heyward and Jean-Louis shared their repertoires. Our theme song became Jean Louis' rendition of a song about a French BCBG—a close equivalent to a US Preppie—who trades in his motorcycle boots for a pair of docksiders and devotes his life to the sea.

> *Ce n'est pas l'homme qui prend la mer*
> *C'est la mer qui prend l'homme*
> *Ta Ta Tum*
> *Mais la mer elle m'a pris*
> *Je me souviens un mardi*
> *Ta Ta Tum*

Heyward's Guitar

The evenings would often end with a recital from Chinnouk. Head back, long blond hair flowing down, and blue eyes focused somewhere beyond, her beautiful lilting voice filled the boat drowning out the soft strumming of Jean Loui's guitar in the background.

Jean-Louis had been born again. While he was working on his boat a few years earlier, Christ had appeared to him and told him what he must do to lead a better life. He was firm in his beliefs but not overpowering in sharing them. His family was very religious and they lived their beliefs. The heightened religious awareness brought to us by *Fratellanza* was a welcomed addition to our daily lives. This friendship came at a time when we had a great need for companionship and guidance in our new lives. Jean-Louis may have been right when he declared that our meeting was meant to be.

Jean-Louis had left Ajaccio at the beginning of the summer. The two hours a day he had been putting in on his newspaper distribution job had been too strenuous and he had felt his family needed a break. With their small accumulated savings and a map of St. Paul's travels in the Mediterranean tacked to the bulkhead of their dining room, they had set out for a two-year journey. Naxos and its missionary that was related to their parish back in Ajaccio was their immediate destination. After that they were heading to Turkey where they planned to spend the winter. It developed naturally that we would join them.

***

We were nearing the end of our refit and it was time to begin to settle accounts with Manfred. I had been asking him for a bill for sometime but still had yet to get a response. He had put me off for one reason or another but mainly insisted that he needed to discuss the matter with Minolis before he could bill me. Both Charlotte and I became suspicious. Minolis had comforted Manfred when his wife had run off with all the money with the thought that at least he would have the money from "Heywort" to help him out. Our suspicions were well founded.

One night shortly after the last *Flying Dolphin* arrived from Piraeus, Manfred came on board with an envelope containing his bill. He seemed a little more full of bluster than normal and was slightly nervous. He had finally sat down with Minolis and the envelope contained their joint conniving.

I had been in Greece too long to roll over on this one. I tried to keep the astronomical figure on the last page out of my mind as I studied the components. The number of hours didn't seem to be terribly inflated, but what was this factor of 1.5 applied to most of them? The footnote explained— overtime for weekend and evening work—what was this all about? And the rate. Where had this number come from? It was over twice the figures Manfred, Minolis, and I had discussed.

Manfred did not seem surprised at my angry and puzzled reaction. "What is this overtime all about Manfred? The only time I could get you away from Mandiki was during evenings and weekends. Do you charge Mandiki straight time and hit me with all the overtime? Besides I have never heard of paying an individual contractor overtime, and you and I never discussed the matter. And where does this rate come from? You and Minolis must be out of your minds. This bill is a 'fucking choke.'"

Manfred replied somewhat sheepishly that Minolis had told him I would probably be upset, but that he needed to start with a high number to get a reasonable settlement. Minolis had gone on to warn Manfred that if he didn't bill me soon, I would probably sail away without paying. His instructions to Manfred were to get me to come to his office along with

43

Manfred upon my return to Kalamaki and the three of us would settle on a final amount for the bill.

I was furious. This was the last straw. "Manfred, I refuse to deal with Minolis on this matter under any circumstances. I have kept close track of the hours and I will compare my records with your bill. When you return from Piraeus after your next trip, you and I will come up with a reasonable figure. The matter is strictly between you and me and we don't need any further involvement from Minolis."

When Manfred reported back from his next trip he was nervous. Minolis had pitched a fit when he learned of my refusal to include him in our negotiations. He had complained to Manfred about my use of his office and of how I should compensate him for it—not mentioning, of course, his handsome commission on the sale of *Captain Spiros*. Manfred had felt he was getting in the middle of a situation that was rapidly getting out of control. In the end, however, Minolis had played the martyr and told Manfred to go ahead and negotiate his deal.

Free of Minolis' meddling, Manfred and I quickly worked out a compromise that was fair. We converged on an acceptable number of billable hours and quietly forgot about the demand for overtime. We went back to the hourly rates that Manfred had quoted to me during one of our visits at his Irish pub and consummated our agreement over an ouzo.

Manfred joined us for a farewell dinner that evening. During our time with him we had found him to be an excellent technician, a hard worker, and a good friend. His advice and his mannerisms remained with us throughout our trip and his enrichment of our vocabularies provided an expression that seemed uniquely appropriate for summing up certain situations: "It's a fucking choke."

Before leaving us that night, Manfred reiterated a piece of counseling he had given several times before: "The seas in the Mediterranean are short and steep. Sailing into them is impossible. Don't be in too much of a hurry and sail where the wind blows." As I watched Manfred crossing our gangplank for the last time it occurred to me that this was not just sailing advice he was leaving with us.

***

We needed to return to Kalamaki for two important reasons: an emergency anchor repair and a final resolution to the radar and auto pilot fiasco. The straps for the anchor winch had been so crude that I didn't even bother with reinstallation. By this time I had learned that when Jean-Louis stared at something, shrugged his shoulders, and said nothing, it translated

44

into disapproval. The looks he had given my anchor winch were more in the nature of a horrified rejection rather than mere disapproval, and he had reiterated his offer to accompany us to Kalamaki to have it repaired.

The task at hand was not trivial, and I was glad to have Jean-Louis' assistance. I was now thankful for his practice of avoiding physical activity of any nature when Brigitte was capable of accomplishing the task for him. This reserve of unused energy was going to come in handy. Heyward, Alex and I had already wrestled the Danforth in, but the monster CQR anchor was still out. Charlotte took the wheel and the four of us started horsing in the heavy chain. Getting the best positions and footholds we could, we started pulling. With the motor slowly pushing us forward, our only task was to lift in the chain that was hanging straight down. But the depth was about 15 meters— and 15 meters of chain was very heavy. It didn't take a rocket scientist to figure out what was going to happen when the weight of the anchor was added to the weight of the chain and we all paced ourselves for the real pull. It was worse than I thought it would be, but link by link we finally willed it in. I now fully realized what it meant to be without an anchor winch and was thankful that no emergency had required re-anchoring.

As we began the short trip back to Kalamaki, Jean-Louis' customary lethargy gave way to his passion for sailing, and we put up sails and tested all systems. He silently shrugged his shoulders as we put a first reef in the mainsail. When I pressed him on the matter he would only comment that it's not the way they do it in Glennon. But then he didn't have "La Bible" with him and he agreed to research it as soon as we got back to *Fratellanza*. This was a problem we were going to have to sort out. Unless our auto pilot was designed to make the boat go in circles, it was failing miserably. But the sun was shining, a gentle wind was blowing, and all seemed right with the world. Charlotte fixed us a salad nicoise and our newly installed refrigerator gave us an endless supply of cold beer. The refit was almost over and the trip was about to begin.

We joined the tangle of boats in Kalamaki without mishap. Charlotte pulled out a large canvas bag that would not only support its weight, but would hide the winch's size and bulkiness from the critical eyes of cabdrivers. Traffic was light and Jean-Louis and I had no trouble in hailing a cab and making our way to the machine shop in Piraeus that could weld aluminum.

Necessity has developed a breed of highly ingenious machinists in Greece, and our man was no exception. It had not even occurred to me that we might find parts for the French made Goyot winch, but I had hoped I might find someone who understood how it worked. All four machinists in the shop were as mystified as Jean-Louis and I as to how a clutch had ever worked with the massive square end gears that connected the pulley with the shaft. But they did come up with a solution that could work in an emergency. A strong spring between the two gears would be capable of holding them a fraction of an inch apart so that the pulley could spin freely. If the nut on the end of the shaft could be loosened quickly enough and if the gears didn't catch as they were being disengaged, it was possible that the wildly spinning pulley might not strip the gears in an emergency anchoring. It wasn't an ideal solution (I could see Jean-Louis' shoulders shrugging) but it seemed better than no clutch at all, so I authorized the repair.

Back at Kalamaki, Yannis and Evianos were aboard *Captain Spiros*. Yannis was already half way up the mast and Evianos was about to hand him the radar for installation. I arrived just in time to stop the fiasco. Evianos explained that they were unable to find new cable so they were going to install the radar back in its original position on the mast using the cable that was already in place.

"But Evianos, the shielding is gone and installing it there will prevent my Satnav and other electronic equipment from working. And even if that wasn't the case, the radar is too big to be mounted there and will rip the sails. That's the whole reason I added the stern mast and besides..."

Clearly Evianos wasn't in the least bit interested in my arguments and interrupted: "Mr. Coleman, our job is to install the radar and make it work. If we put it on the mast, it will work. The other electronics... well, that's not our problem. We just want to get the radar working."

By this time Yannis was back on deck and listening quietly to the argument. It seemed clear to me that while he probably didn't wholly subscribe to Evianos' aggressive position, he wasn't going to intercede on my behalf. I had had enough. The auto pilot was hopeless, and now they wanted to jury rig an obsolete radar in a manner that would destroy my other navigation equipment and quite possibly the sails. After saying my final good-bye to Yannis and Evianos, I called Miltos and told him to tell Kiriacoulis that he could keep his radar and auto pilot, and that I was keeping the escrow deposit.

A few minutes later, Miltos called me back and said that Kiriacoulis had agreed, but that there was no need to give him the auto pilot back. He knew money was due on the auto pilot and he didn't want any part of it. Thoroughly sick of the whole affair, I decided to leave the auto pilot in the hands of the negotiating genius who had arranged for its repair in the first place. Minolis wasn't in his office, so I left the semi repaired actuator and the wholly inoperable computer along with its associated cabling on the middle of his desk. He and Kiriacoulis could sort the matter out at their leisure! I then got on the phone and ordered a new auto pilot and new radar from the United States and was assured they would arrive within four days. We then installed the repaired anchor winch, and headed back to Aegina. Brigitte and the children formed our welcoming committee, and we moored next to "Fratellanza."

***

At about midnight I awoke to loud noises and footsteps on the deck right over my head. Everything seemed to be in motion. The wind was howling like a wounded beast. Up on deck, half dressed and half awake, I was struck with all the activity. Half the boats had their engines running and people were everywhere. Jean-Louis was on my bow, and Brigitte was handing him the end of a line. By this time Heyward and Alex had joined me and we took the other end of Brigitte's' line.

A ferocious wind had suddenly come up out of the north-east and was pushing all of our boats away from the *Flying Dolphin* pier and towards the fishing and vegetable boats moored in the north-west corner of the harbor. The wind was blowing at right angles to our anchors and was exerting an enormous amount of force. Jean-Louis' objective was to get a line from *Captain Spiros* to the *Flying Dolphin* pier to keep our anchors from slipping.

Walking from boat to boat and from boats to the pier and then back to boats, we finally succeeded in threading the line to a spot on the pier more or less at right angles to our boat. We then tied it securely. Our boat now acted as an anchor and the other boats attached lines to us to keep themselves in place. The strong wind continued for a couple of hours and then died down. We had just learned our first lesson about how rapidly the weather can change and received our first demonstration of the importance of a stout line to windward.

***

It was now late October and the storm had been a mild precursor of what we could expect when winter finally set in. Jean-Louis was getting anxious about leaving. His many years of experience of sailing in the Mediterranean had taught him to find a place to nest in the winter and avoid putting out to sea again until spring. Our window for a safe passage across the Aegean to Turkey was beginning to close. It was time to leave.

We had spent several nights planning our route across the Cyclades. With travel books, brochures, and pilots spread out we slowly formulated our itinerary for the trip across these fascinating islands. We spent more time reading Fromer than studying Heikell. This was a mistake—but we still had much to learn.

Rod Heikell is the author of an authoritative set of pilot books that cover everything from expected weather patterns and hazards to mariners to advice on shopping and local wines. Almost every boat we encountered on our trip had its volumes of Heikell and in any conversation concerning routing the expression "Heikell says..." was bound to come up. We came to think of Rod Heikell as a close friend and confidant and his pilots were always close at hand.

Our plan was for one last trip to Kalamaki as soon as the radar and auto pilot arrived—and then to set out without delay. I would either install these items en route, or get help installing them when we finally arrived in Turkey.

Although I could not get a confirmation from the shipper that the packages had actually arrived, four days had elapsed since my order and we decided to leave for Kalamaki. This was our first solo on *Captain Spiros* and it felt great. Smooth seas, a beam wind, and the boat performed superbly. What a feeling of independence! Our tasks in Kalamaki appeared to be simple and then we would be off. Everyone was in high spirits. After circling around the marina three times, we finally decided on a spot that seemed a bit less disagreeable than the others. As we were securing lines to the second boat out from the pier, a Greek yachtsman waved to get our attention. Gesturing frantically he shouted in a combination of Greek and English a garbled sentence that we interpreted to mean: "This is my spot, you can't moor here."

This seemed a bit odd to me, particularly as the spot he was claiming as his own was one boat removed from the pier. Besides, we had been in Kalamaki long enough to thoroughly understand the system—which was precisely no system at all. Obviously our new acquaintance had taken us for newcomers to the marina and was going to try to push us around a little. I chose to ignore him and continued with our mooring maneuvers. This pushed him over the edge. Shaking his fists he shouted: "If you don't move immediately, I am going to report you to the port police. If you damage my boat, you are going to have to pay."

As I had already learned, I was either going to have to play the silly game, or acquiesce and move on. I had no intention of doing the latter. "If you want to go to the port police, please, go ahead and do so. This is now my spot, but I don't mind your staying along beside me. But if you damage my boat, you will have to pay dearly." I then turned my back and ignored him. He marched off, furious, and it was the last we saw of him.

When we stepped off the boat, we couldn't believe the sight. Near the spot where our boat had been on shore in its cradle, half a dozen boats were lying on the ground on their sides. The same wind that we had contended with the night before had done its damage in Kalamaki. Visions of the *Captain Spiros* being blown off its cradle made me feel ill. My appreciation for the importance of weather in our new life went up another notch.

***

Miltos was my first order of business. On my way to his office in Piraeus I began to wonder how much over his original estimate my legal bill would be. Had my skepticism been developed to the degree it was to become by the end of our trip I would have been able to make a pretty good guess. The overage was almost exactly equal to the amount he was holding in escrow to cover the radar and auto pilot. Learning that all the trouble and agonizing I had gone through to get the items that were contractually due to me resulted only in lining Miltos' pockets was not a happy thought. But such was the way of Greece.

Miltos agreed to a small reduction in his bill and we parted friends. He assured me that he was only a phone call away if I ever needed more assistance. I wasn't sure I could afford to use his help again, but then I couldn't be sure I wouldn't need it. As I went down his tiny elevator for the last time I said a silent prayer that I would never have to use his firm to fix a hidden problem with the ownership or documentation of my vessel.

We had been warned that getting the autopilot and radar out of customs would not be easy. DHL was the best service available from the states, but I still couldn't get confirmation that my packages had arrived. A call back to the shipper in the US provided me with confirmation that the packages had arrived two days earlier and with a flight number.

They tried to be helpful at Lufthansa, but assured me that customs had no record of my packages. Persistence along with the definitive information on the flight finally paid off. Miss Kraus explained that because of the general strike, customs had accumulated an enormous backlog. Apparently my packages had arrived, but not yet made their way into customs. If I would come to the airport, she would help me locate them.

After waiting in a long line at Lufthansa's airport office, I secured a copy of the shipping papers and went on the back of a messenger's motor bike to an airport freight receiving office. Another line, more bureaucracy, and finally a new set of papers that would get my packages into customs. Off on Stephen's motorbike again to the huge warehouse where the freight arrived and was held for clearance. Our job was to find the packages and use the papers to get them into the customs warehouse. This all seemed so complicated that I was sure that getting them out would have to be easier.

As the motorbike pulled up to the warehouse, I couldn't believe my eyes. Stacks and stacks of boxes of every description were spread over acres of pavement surrounding the warehouse. There were crowds of people pushing, pulling, and poking around. The packages had all been left out in the weather, and the utter disregard that was being given for their care was appalling.

Stephen, flashing papers and speaking rapidly, succeeded in getting us past the guards and into the control area where the mountains of packages were waiting for their entry into Greek Customs. Once in we seemed immune from further scrutiny. Not knowing the size shape, or even number of our boxes the job seemed impossible. We stacked, un stacked, sorted, and tried to look at the various piles from every conceivable angle and direction. Finally I spotted a Raytheon sticker. The box with my radar was located. About two hours later we found the other three boxes containing the auto pilot and other assembly components.

We were now ready to get the items into customs. Stephen wasn't frustrated by the endless chain of people we were bounced between showing now papers now boxes and then papers and boxes. He knew the system. Finally a tall customs official stamped the bill of lading, took the boxes, and handed me a receipt. I thanked Stephen and he zoomed off. Lufthansa's job was done, but my job was just beginning. Now that the boxes had arrived into customs, I had to get them out.

It was getting late, but I still had almost two hours before they closed the offices. Inside there was utter pandemonium as Greek shipping agents and customs brokers battled for front line positions at the various desks. When the papers in my waving hand were finally received by a beefy red faced official, I succeeded in thrusting myself in front of the other bodies crowding the counter. "Ah, Meester Coleman, you are not a custom broker! You are please to go to the passenger terminal and ask for the chief of the airport customs officers. They will take care of you there." And before I could utter a word he had handed me back my papers and redirected his attention to another waving hand of documents. As I was being squeezed and pushed away from my place at the counter I shouted: "But my packages are here, how will they inspect them over at the passenger terminal. I still have more questions! What about..." By this time I had been shoved about three tiers back and was still losing ground, but I did manage to reestablish contact with Redbeef and he assured me that I would get my chance.

It was a hot fifteen minute walk to the passenger terminal, but I force marched it in ten because time was running out. My instincts told me it was going to be a wasted trip, but I felt I had no choice. I began to regret my decision not to engage the services of a custom broker. After my expensive experience with Dracos to retrieve my Satnav, I had decided to do it on my own. The law was clear. If the material was stamped into the *Captain Spiros'* transit log—the equivalent of a passport for a vessel—and if we left Greek waters within 90 days, there was no tax. In principal, all I needed to do was explain the situation to customs.

The chief of airport customs didn't exactly tell me I was crazy, but he made it absolutely clear that there was no possible way for him to handle items that came into the freight terminal. His office took care of passengers and passengers only. He merely shrugged his shoulders when I explained the instructions I had received from Redbeef and told me I should go back and try again.

My briefcase was crammed full of every paper the Greek bureaucrats could possibly demand—passport, ships papers, transit log, and anything else I could find that had even a remote chance of being called for—and it was heavy. The sum was hot, and I was soaked with sweat, but I made it back in less than ten minutes. By this time I was getting really tired. With only fifteen minutes to go before closing bell, I finally made my way back to Redbeef. He didn't seem to recall the exact terms of his earlier instructions to me but pointed out that as there wasn't enough time left in the day to get my packages out of customs, I should come back in the morning—and be sure to bring all my papers.

Over dinner that night, we had a lengthy discussion about what our strategy should be for customs the next morning. The two great loves of the Greeks seemed to be the sea and children. Obviously their love of the sea didn't extend to electronic equipment imported for vessels that would ply it. But Children? Margot volunteered.

Margot and I got an early start. She had on her best dress and I sported a clean shirt and clean trousers. No coat and tie—that would probably make them suspicious. The frantic activity was every bit as great as the day before even though they had been open for less than half an hour. This time I chose a different line. I had had enough of Redbeef.

Margot's presence was a tremendous help. People seemed to push and shove us a great deal less. The fact that she could hold our place in line allowed me to explore around and learn a little more about the situation. In my wanderings, I met Stelios. He described himself as an amateur customs broker and explained how the system worked. On his advice, I switched to the line he was following and finally reached the front.

This time the official concentrated on my papers and seemed willing to deal with me. As he perused the documents he began to frown. "Meester

Coleman, what is the cost of your equipment?" Against all the advice I had been given and in direct contradiction to the instructions I had given to the shipper of my goods, the price, just shy of $5,000 was clearly marked on the documents as well as on the boxes themselves. I had no choice but to confirm the figures that had caused his frown.

"Meester Coleman—electronic equipment and at this high price— I'm afraid the papers you have to fill out are quite long. I suggest you engage a customs broker." Stelios shrugged his shoulders and acknowledged that I had a problem. He had been prepared to help me fill in the "normal paperwork" but I had just been catapulted into a higher category. Stelios suggested a name, and I finally found him. Mr. Opoulos was standing around the table where most of the customs brokers clustered when they had spare time between missions. Mr. Opoulos listened to about half of my story, then interrupted.

"I am very busy now, but maybe next week I can help you. You will, of course, have to pay duty on the equipment. And my fee will be 10 percent of the value of the equipment."

Already angry that I was being forced to use a customs broker, I could hardly believe what he was saying. The Greek system was impossible. I knew that customs brokers flourished because they bribed the customs officials who in turn "encouraged" their use. But this was going too far. My broker was not only going to charge me through the nose, but was also going to force me to pay a tax I didn't legally owe and take his own sweet time in doing it to boot!

Fortunately I had a friend that could help. Two phone calls were all that were necessary to locate Dracos. Yes, he would be glad to help me. His man was no longer at the airport, but if I would come to his office immediately with my papers he would take care of everything. The cab took Margot and me to Dracos' swish office on Singrou Avenue. Neither cold nor warm, Dracos nodded a polite acknowledgment as the petite receptionist ushered me into his office. After quietly studying my papers for a few moments he gave me his verdict.

"You will have to pay the tax of course." Seeing my look of displeasure, he quickly added: "But don't worry, we will simply declare a low value and you won't have to pay much."

I didn't see how we could possibly declare a low value with the price of the material plastered all over the documents and all over the boxes. But I had already learned that Dracos was a formidable character and I was beginning to realize that logic did not play an important part in this delicate process. I remained silent.

"My fee will be $300.00. You will have to also pay the taxes, but they won't be very much. Please leave me your documents and the yacht's transit log. Come back around noon tomorrow and your packages will be ready."

The next morning I took a cab directly to Dracos' office. To my surprise there didn't seem to be any hitches. I gave him the equivalent of $500 in a thick stack of Greek currency and purposefully did not interrogate him about how he had reduced my duty exposure from $1000 to only $200. He gave Niki the keys to his Mercedes and told me to go with him to the airport to pick up my cargo.

Early that afternoon we returned to Aegina—the refit was now complete. The next morning a favorable weather forecast and a confirming reading on Jean-Louis' hand-held anemometer gave us the assurance we needed, and then we were off.

Chapter 3
Crossing the Cyclades and Bodrum

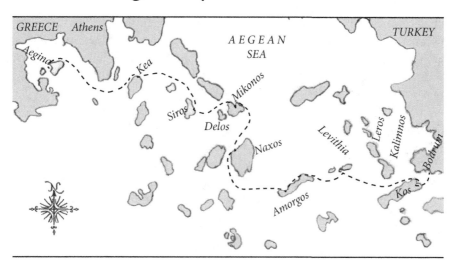

A s we made thie transition from refit to cruising, I found myself again
delving into the past. The trip was absorbing my energies, but the
disappointment was still there.

When Sonat had decided to spin-off Maritrans I was one of three
officers who were to become the principal owners. I also had the job of
coordinating the transaction. There is nothing quite like the sense of power
and fulfillment of structuring a complex company sale, particularly if you
are going to become one of the owners. It was six months of soaring highs
and rock-bottom lows. Time was of the essence, and each day the fate of our
transaction seemed to hang by a thread. Timing was everything and our
"opportunity" had a finite window.

It was Goldman Sachs' idea to use the Master Limited Partnership
structure. Although highly complex and a very time-consuming process, it
yielded the highest dollar value to Sonat and, in the end, that was what it was
all about. It also yielded the highest fees to Goldman and the huge entourage
of tax lawyers, bond lawyers, corporate lawyers, maritime lawyers, and any
other kind of lawyer or investment banker you can think of. I have never
seen so many Gucci shoes and flashy suspenders in one spot as those that
accented our endless series of meetings and drafting sessions.

We followed each competing transaction as they slowly worked
their way to the market place. Macadamia, Motel 6, and Buckeye Pipeline

all became familiar names as we dissected their documents to help us thread our way through our complex venture. We worried a lot about interest rates, tax interpretations, and the general state of the economy. Would the market be right for our deal?

The last month's activities centered on lining up markets and finalizing documents. The race was on, and we had deadlines we couldn't afford to miss. Timing, timing, timing—it was all we talked about. But luck was on our side. Not even the scandal that had resulted in the public arrest of a Goldman Sachs partner slowed us down.

On a warm April afternoon in 1987 champagne corks flew through the rarefied air of the Pepper Hamilton & Scheetz law offices and we congratulated ourselves on our success. We all had a lot to celebrate. Sonat walked away with almost twice as much cash as anyone could have reasonably expected, the investment bankers and lawyers had a pot of over fifteen million dollars to divide among themselves, and we had Maritrans.

What a feeling! Three of us owned the lion's share of a master limited partnership that controlled the largest petroleum shipping company in the country. It seemed too good to be true. And, as it turned out, it was.

***

Fratellanza's smooth departure from Aegina was something we would have to work towards. Our added speed quickly closed their 45 minute lead, however, and we slowed down so we could sail together. Jean-Louis in his blue and white stripped skull cap cut quite an image as he sat on the platform he had constructed across *Fratellanza's* transom. In spite of the distance between our boats and the noises from his motor, we could hear him boom out "*Ce n'est pas l'homme qui prend la mer....*" With Brigitte below at the wheel and *Fratellanza* back at sea on the remainder of its 3000 mile voyage from Corsica to Turkey, Jean-Louis was in his element.

Aboard *Captain Spiros* harmony reigned. The strenuous move from Philadelphia to Charleston, the back breaking refit, the difficulties in purchasing our vessel—they were all behind us now. The trip had finally begun and limitless exciting destinations and adventures lay ahead. Kea was our destination for that night. Our route would take us across the Saronic Gulf, along the southernmost coast of the Greek mainland, and then into the Aegean Sea.

***

The night before I had programmed a number of "way points" into my Satnav to help me follow my planned course. These "way points" are geographical points that I expected to cross during our trip. The Satnav would keep track of them and give me a course and distance upon request. In theory, my little electronic box would continuously keep me posted on exactly where we were and how far we were away from our destination.

Like many things in sailing, there is often a big difference between theory and reality. The reality of the eastern Mediterranean was that in 1989 the little satellites that orbited through the skies and talked to my Satnav were spaced anywhere from one to five hours apart. It was only right after a transit that the Satnav could really be sure of where it was. And even then there was a small imperfection—the formulas it had to solve to determine its position relative to the satellite speeding overhead were so complex that it took about twenty minutes to get a solution. Hence the final position it gave was for twenty minutes earlier and the authoritative latitude and longitude that it would proudly announce with a loud "beep beep beep" was actually only an "estimate" of where we were at that instant based on the very precise knowledge of where we had been twenty

Underway At Last

minutes earlier. Despite these problems, I loved my Satnav. The thought that it was constantly seeking advice from objects speeding through outer space to keep us advised on where we were was both fascinating and comforting.

In reality even my satellite navigation was overkill for much of our sailing in the Mediterranean. Most of the time we were in sight of land and could use piloting to determine our position. This technique relies on sighting familiar landmarks and then carefully measuring the direction they bear from the boat. With a good compass, good charts, and a good eye for identifying the correct object on land that corresponds to the object on the chart, quite accurate results can be obtained using this technique.

But here again, there are pitfalls. The biggest trick is identifying the correct objects on shore. Along the coastline of many of the Greek islands, one hill looks pretty much like another. Even if the compass error is small and the charts are up to date, choosing the wrong objects as originating points for the series of carefully drawn pencil lines on the chart that are all supposed to extend back to the single point that represents your position can result in absolute confusion.

During this first leg of our trip across the Cyclades, I experimented with a combination of all of these methods. The discouragement of becoming hopelessly confused by misidentifying a landmark or making an error in a calculation would become completely eradicated by finally finding an unmistakable landmark or receiving a new Satnav fix.

My mood swung as my confidence in our position changed—it wasn't fun to be lost. But the main trick was to know our precise position when it was time to come into port or when we were to pass close to shoals or reefs. It would take me some time to fully develop my navigation skills.

***

Mt. Ayias Ilias, soaring almost 2,000 feet above Kea, was an unmistakable landmark and I easily made my way into Vourkari Bay. Passing the church on the point as we entered the bay we tried to make sense out of advice Minolis had given prior to our departure. His instructions led us to the beautiful spot just off another small church across the harbor from the docks. Anchored and no lines to shore—this was freedom. We swam, relaxed, and waited for the slower *Fratellanza* to join us.

Jean-Louis circled, eyed the quays on the other shore, and then opted for the most practical alternative. It was fun to watch the quiet precision of their maneuver. Jean-Louis let the anchor go, and Brigitte skillfully backed them to the pier. Timing her short burst of forward perfectly brought them to a stop with the stern platform inches away from the bulkhead.

John Louis

Joanne nimbly jumped to shore and put a line around a bollard to their starboard. Handing the bitter end back to his mother, he took another line and fed it through a ring to port and again passed the end back on board. Securing the end of each line to the winches that are normally used for the jib, Brigitte winched the boat into proper position as Jean-Louis took up slack on the anchor chain. With no tide to contend with, they were able to bring the boat right up to the quay without worrying about changing water levels.

We developed a routine that was to remain with us for most of the trip. Charlotte and I would wake up at 6:00 A.M. to listen to the only English weather forecast that we could receive. The forecast went very quickly and covered the entire Eastern Mediterranean so we would record it and listen more carefully afterwards. We would then consult with *Fratellanza* and make our sail/no sail decision.

The next morning the forecast was good, and from what we could see from our anchorage, the wind and sea looked calm around Kea. After a quick breakfast, Alex and Heyward removed the outboard motor and then lashed the dinghy across our bow. Charlotte and Margot stowed the boat for sea while Heyward, Alex, and I headed us out of the harbor under motor. Once in open waters, Alex and I raised the huge mainsail. This required both of us to go up to the mast. One would pull on the halyard to raise the sail as far as possible by hand while the other stood by with a winch handle for the last part of the evolution. A couple of turns around one of the heavy duty winches mounted on the mast, some hard cranking, and—*voila*—we had a new source of propulsion.

Roller reefing made raising the jib a simpler process. With this system, the jib is mounted on the forward stay and left there. It is retracted by pulling a line that turns a drum attached to the bow stay making it rotate. As it rotates, the jib neatly wraps itself around the stay until finally nothing is left except a neat roll of sail. To let the sail out all that needs to be done is to slowly release the line so that the sail can unroll.

With both sails up, we turned off the motor and enjoyed the silence and beauty of sailing through the Greek Isles. Our route took us along the southern coast of Yiaros, an uninhabited island with a barren and rocky coast. Heikell warned about strong gusts of winds funneling down its mountains when the Meltemi blows, but we were well past the season for the Meltemi and the wind was light so we relaxed.

A little after noon the wind became so light that our speed dropped to two knots. Siros was close and even at our reduced speed we would arrive at Ermoupolis well before dark, but I felt we should minimize our time between ports so I started the motor. While Charlotte was the most vocal on the subject, my entire crew felt that the noise and fumes of the diesel significantly detracted from the pristine surroundings. My argument that keeping our speed up minimized the chances of us encountering a stiff blow fell on deaf ears, and I turned the engine off. After a brief period of calm, the wind picked back up, and we had a brisk sail into Ermoupolis. It was only later that we learned from our slower sailing companions that the wind did become quite strong and only our speed had kept us from having our first sailing crisis of the trip.

Ermoupolis is the capital of the Cyclades, and its large harbor provided many excellent choices for mooring. We opted for a stern to mooring off the town quay where we had an excellent view of the town square. Like many of the cities of the Greek islands, Ermoupolis is laid out with winding streets that lure the visitor to keep wandering and to peer around just one more corner. Ironically the purpose of the layout in ancient times had been just the opposite. It was thought that the complicated maze of the streets would discourage pirates and raiders from entering into the heart of the city and would make pillage and a quick escape more difficult.

***

Soon after moving aboard *Captain Spiros* we had instituted a meal rotation system. It was part of our new democratic life style in which we all shared the benefits and the work. Going from youngest to oldest each person was given an allowance and was responsible for planning, buying provisions, and then cooking the evening meal. To minimize family friction, we decided that the cook should also clean. In this way the chef could profit from the economy of pots and pans and small number of dirtied utensils employed in his well planned dinner.

There had been notable smash hits—Alex's three hamburger patty each banquet topped with home fries, Heyward's famous Greek salad in which the onions he used were so strong he wore a snorkel and mask to protect his sensitive nose and eyes during preparation, and Margot's fresh-baked cookies that topped off her chosen creation of the day.

There had also been some—well, quite frankly—flops. When a meal was particularly unpalatable, references would be made comparing it to my *"octopoli a la shoe leather."* If the meal was worse than just plain bad, it could evoke comparisons with Charlotte's vinegar rice. The mere mention of this evening when Charlotte accidentally made her rice with the vinegar intended for her salad dressing instead of water was enough to set our teeth vibrating and our noses running.

But for meals that were truly awful—those that we even feared to throw overboard because of potential harm to sea life—the only fair comparison could be Heyward's sausage Aegina. Not being able to speak, read, write, or understand Greek tended to be a disadvantage when trying to buy ingredients for meals. Heyward's mistake had been in accepting the neatly packaged, long round object that had been thrust into his hands by the Greek butcher after his sign language and phonetic attempts to make his desire for sausage understood.

Sautéed bell peppers, browned onions (after the mask and snorkel treatment) and finally it was time to add the sausage. The white gooey paste that oozed out of the neat red plastic wrapper didn't look much like sausage. I had not been paying attention to Heyward's labors, so when he asked me to taste it, I was caught off guard.

Two chews into the large spoonful he had handed me and it hit the nerve endings in the roof of my mouth like an electric charge. Not wanting to hurt Heyward's feelings, I managed to wait until I got into the head before spitting out the offending concoction and brushing my teeth. During subsequent trips to the Aegina butcher, we would eye the red packages and wonder what Greek delicacy this white ooze could possibly produce.

But now we were in Ermoupolis and it was time for a splurge. The argument began as we scouted around the town square looking for a suitable establishment. When I would find a particularly appealing taverna and explore the kitchen with the cook, admiring each pot as the chef proudly explained his creation, my enthusiasm would immediately be doused by the children. "Oh, Daddy, gross! Another pot roast place! " And then they would immediately dash off to another of the overpriced tourist traps whose open sign indicated that they hadn't yet realized that the tourist season was over.

The Greeks have done for pizza pie what Mc Donald's has done for the hamburger and on that particular day I wasn't going to compromise. The thousands of Big Macs and Whoppers I had forced down since the birth of our oldest child in the name of family harmony flashed through my mind. No more souvlaki, no more Greek pizza. I wanted a real meal. The argument reached its climax when I signaled Charlotte and the children to join me as I took a seat in a particularly enticing taverna just off the town square. I didn't think emotions could get this high over a single meal, but they did.

Alex saw a few dishes that appealed to him, so he wasn't too excited. But Heyward was in a near frenzy. While I found the depth of his vocabulary and the scope of his imagination in describing the "Pot Roast" dishes quite impressive, Charlotte seemed to feel that his profanity was uncalled for and was becoming quite unhappy about the scene he was causing. Her immediate and unyielding attack on him added fuel to the fire and by this time it looked to me like we were finally out Greeking the Greeks.

Margot came up with the solution. Why not give each person their share of the money and they could choose where they wanted to eat. Charlotte was disappointed to not have our meal a family affair, but recognized the sound logic in Margot's idea. After all, we were certainly getting a full dose of family togetherness on each day of our travels. The children made a bee line to the nearest pizza trap, Charlotte and I settled down to a couple of Amstels and our pot roast meal, and a new tradition was born.

***

The first two legs had been easy, and we were beginning to develop a false sense of security. This changed abruptly on our trip to Mikonos. The seas were relatively calm until we reached open water. A brisk breeze picked up, and we had our first chance to test our reefing system in earnest. Our crudely executed maneuver was a clear demonstration to all of us that we had a lot to learn.

Our first mistake was waiting until we needed the reef before putting it in. The second was to bring the boat directly into the wind and waves to carry out the maneuver. With the boat wildly pitching up and down, Alex and I went up to the mast to lower the mainsail and tend the mass of lines. Although we had practiced in still water, holding on with one hand and sorting through the tangled lines with the other with the boat pitching about wildly was an entirely different matter. Half way through, I heard a loud crashing noise off the port bow. Holding tightly to lifelines and cleats, I pulled my way to the bow and found that our Danforth anchor had broken loose and was now crashing into the side of the boat. It had already punched

Crossing the Aegean

one hole in the boat about two feet above the water line. With Alex's help, I got the anchor back on the bow, lashed it down, and then finished taking the reef.

The wind seemed to come about directly out of Mikonos—proving the description we had heard that in the Mediterranean the wind is always either too strong or too weak—but whatever the strength it's always on your nose. Foul weather gear came out as the wind came up and we learned what a force 6 sea was like in the Aegean. Margot was feeling rather green, Heyward had his ears on—The Grateful Dead at full blast—and was having a great time, and Alex was pestering me to put up our cutter storm sail. I tried, unsuccessfully, to calm Charlotte's mounting concern by assuring her that the winds were well within *Captain Spiros*' capabilities and that we would soon be safely ensconced in Mikonos. In fact, this thought also gave me a great deal of confidence.

When we finally entered Mikonos harbor, I realized, for the first time, how different the conditions in the Aegean are from those I had been accustomed to on the east coast of the United States. The wind was howling down the mountains and right through the center of the harbor with more force than on the open seas. To make matters worse, the large ferry boats had put out additional security lines that effectively blocked entry to all of the good mooring spaces along the quay. The only choice was to anchor which was very difficult because of the deepness and relatively small size of the harbor. After motoring in place against the wind and trying to anchor for about two hours we finally succeeded in getting the anchor to hold. A few minutes later the port police motored over in a small fishing boat and, shouting above the wind and frantically signaling to us, finally succeeded in making us understand that another ferry was coming in and that we needed to move.

Night was beginning to set in, we were all bone tired, and I was really beginning to become concerned. At about this time, *Fratellanza* succeeded in mooring alongside a small excursion boat that was moored outboard a small ferry. With Jean-Louis' help we were able to moor outboard of *Fratellanza*. No sooner were our lines fast than along came the small fishing boat with the port police yelling at us that the innermost ferry would probably be getting underway in a few hours. By this time we had learned our lesson and ignored the port police's advice. If and when the ferry decided to move, we would deal with the matter and not one second before. Jean-Louis had explained to us before and we had just seen first hand that in Greek waters security of one's vessel is sacred. No one, and that includes port police, can make you leave a safe berth if it puts your vessel in danger.

Once the lines were fast, we experienced one of those incredibly rapid changes of moods that were so typical of our new life. We went from tired, waterlogged, and if not frightened then at least very nervous water rats to eager and expectant tourists about to explore one of the most exciting of the Greek Islands—and all in the space of only a few minutes. Not even the bad back that Charlotte had been developing over the past few days could dampen her enthusiasm for a visit of Mikonos. There was, however, one small obstacle that tended to discourage her exuberance—the little matter of getting across *Fratellanza*, the excursion boat, and the ferry boat.

After being well anesthetized with a couple of Amstels, she concentrated on keeping her back straight as I pushed and Jean-Louis pulled to get her up the eight feet from *Fratellanza's* deck to the railing on the stern of the excursion boat. An equal drop from the deck of the of the excursion boat to the deck of the ferry, a small slippery climb from the ferry to the stone wharf, and it was done. We were ready to explore Mikonos.

Windmills, a huge pink pelican that strutted along the waterfront of the harbor like he owned it, and the wonderfully winding streets captured our imaginations and lifted our spirits. It felt great to be on dry land and off

Fratellanza

the rolling deck of the *Captain Spiros.* But most of all, it felt great to be out of the howling wind. When we finally felt we could linger over dinner no longer, we worked our way back to the boat. As we approached the pier and the warmth of Mikonos melted behind us, we became aware again of the immense force of the wind. Our lives had become divided between two worlds—the world of the quiet protected streets and restaurants that we had just left and the precarious world of the howling wind we were about to reenter.

The wind had picked up considerably since we had left—or was it just a distortion of our perceptions after being out of it for several hours? After doubling the lines we went below to get some sleep. Charlotte's and my cabin was directly under the mast and no matter how tightly I pulled the halyards and tied lines to keep them away from the mast, the wind would finally succeed in finding a way of making them flap. The noise of the wind screeching through the rigging and the halyards beating against the mast invaded the warm protection of our cabin and served as a nagging reminder of the elements we were constantly pitted against. "Are the lines holding? Could someone else's boat be slipping? What is that new noise?" were questions that constantly filtered through our minds regardless of whether we were asleep or awake. There was no escape from the relentless wind and no true rest when it blew.

At about three o'clock in the morning I woke up to a squealing whining fury. The fiendish noise was like the wind noises of earlier that evening but much louder. On deck, sleepy, and half dressed I saw that it was blowing even harder. But that was not the source of the cacophonous sounds that had interrupted my sleep. The wind generator on *Fratellanza* was spinning so hard it looked like the whole boat was about to take off. The squealing sound was the sound of bearings going completely wild. I woke Jean-Louis and warned him of the impending disaster, and we got his machine under control—but not without cost. Another blade had been damaged. He was now down from the original four to only two.

The next morning our first winter storm set in and getting underway was completely out of the question. Heikell's description of the narrow channel fringed by reefs and prone to strong wind was all it took for us to scrap our plan to visit Delos.

After three days the storm abated and we decided to leave. We weren't wild about getting underway when the forecast called for a force 4 to 5 but the distance to Naxos was short, and we wanted to be in Turkey before the winter weather had a chance to firmly establish itself. Actually, our big concern was the next leg—the trip from Naxos to Amorgos. Jean-Louis had told us about his friend that had received the *coup de vent* on the southern tip of Naxos, and all of us had read the warning in Heikell with care. Mt. Zeus, a high peak on the southern tip, not only provided a point where wind could funnel down from the mountain top, but also gave a focal point where the winds that were flowing down both the eastern and western coasts could join forces and hurl their power across the sea.

Getting underway was complicated by the fact that *Fratellanza's* reverse didn't always work. With *Fratellanza's* lines still attached to our boat, we used *Captain Spiros'* powerful engine to back away from the excursion boat. My by now proficient line handlers then freed us from our neighbor, we reversed direction, and then swung smartly to port—all without crashing into any other vessels. We were beginning to get our sea legs. This time we raised the sail on the first reef. But as it turned out our precaution was unnecessary. A moderate, steady wind on our beam gave us a most pleasant sail to Naxos. Against our better judgment, but trusting in Jean-Louis' superior seamanship, we allowed ourselves to be convinced to moor to the mole instead of anchoring. *Fratellanza,* with her shallow draft, led the way and found a spot for us where our deep keel wouldn't touch bottom. After much maneuvering we anchored stern to off a small finger quay that jutted from the south side of the mole.

Shortly after mooring the wind began to pick up and by evening it was blowing quite hard. As I began to wish that I was anchored and well away from the mole, a giant ferry entered the harbor. Her stern to mooring was precision itself, and I would have thoroughly enjoyed watching the maneuver if it hadn't been for the spot she had chosen. She now lay squarely on top of both *Captain Spiros'* and *Fratellanza's* anchors with her stern made up to the main mole. With horror, I realized that we were locked in place and our fate was no longer under our control. If our anchor slipped, there was absolutely nothing we could do. It was a long night.

The next morning, the wind showed no sign of letting up, and the weather forecast for the next twenty-four hours called for more of the same. Our boats were holding nicely so we decided to accompany Jean-Louis on his visit to his corresponding evangelical church. Loaded with a heavy picnic lunch, we boarded the morning Trans-Naxos bus bound for Lamanis. The pastor was delighted to receive us and gave us a cook's tour complete with a pre-recorded church service. Our picnic lunch in the middle of a huge pistachio orchard gave us a great view of Mt. Zeus and the origin of the strong winds we would have to contend with on our departure.

Heyward had stayed behind to watch the boats. What he would do if something had happened we didn't know, but it made us all feel better to have someone left in charge. Besides, he was not in the least bit interested in seeing Jean-Louis' church and this had proved to be a graceful out.

It was interesting to watch the progress Heyward was achieving in making the transition into our new life. As a rising senior with a large entourage of friends Heyward had become so absorbed in the crushing demands of social activities with his peers that he was losing sight of the mundane aspects of life that included such things as responsibilities and obligations. It was perhaps an inward recognition of this developing imbalance that had made him such a strong advocate of the trip from the beginning. At any rate, it is not an easy thing for a seventeen-year-old boy to leave his friends and social life behind to live cooped up in a boat with his parents and younger siblings. There was no escape from family togetherness and no tolerance for foisting some portion of one's duties onto others. The load each person needed to carry was significant and was clear for all to see.

While this was a maturing reality for all of us, it was particularly hard hitting for Heyward. But he managed to cope and became quite adept in the various ship's routines. His already well-developed people skills flourished. We never went anywhere that he didn't immediately make friends, and in many ways he led our social activities. His experience with Manfred had been tough, but, he had learned an important lesson from it. I was constantly impressed with his ability to hold his own in practically any conversation on practically any topic, with practically any age.

We could see the boats below in the harbor as we came over the last hill on our return from our outing at Laminas. The wind was still up and we still had a ferry anchored across our bows. The outing had been great, but it was now time to rejoin our problems. We thanked Heyward for his stewardship and settled back into the routine.

The next day the winds were still too high to sail. The children decided to take advantage of our delay to indulge themselves. We had all seen the sign in front of the Apollo Hotel. Hot showers—500 drachmas. The temptation had finally become too much for Heyward, Alex, and Margot. Even though $3.50 represented a substantial portion of their weekly allowances, the craving became unbearable and, loaded with soap and clean towels, they took the windy walk down the mole in quest of the warmth and luxury of unlimited hot water.

They became a little suspicious when the lady explained that it would take an hour to warm the water, but hoping for the best they used the time to have a coke at the hotel bar. After awhile the lady reappeared and at last their treat was at hand. The fact that the water was, as Alex put it, "lukecold" was bad enough—but salt water—that was the killer. Three chilly, disappointed, and very angry children left the Apollo Hotel, $3.50 poorer each, to return to the *Captain Spiros*.

Although the original ferry had left after our second day in Naxos, we found that the normal spot for ferries was off our bows. During several of our nights Charlotte and I awoke to the terrible cacophony of chains being paid out and motors whining as successor ferries defied the force of the strong winds to accomplish the difficult anchoring maneuver. The thought of the wind pushing against the whole length of the ship in an effort to bring it crashing on top of *Captain Spiros* and *Fratellanza* led to sleepless nights— even when the noise was finally over and the maneuver had been safely completed.

The winds blew increasingly harder until on our fifth day when we experienced our first Mediterranean gale. That afternoon Jean-Louis and I rigged stout lines from our bows to a large bollard on the mole. The situation had become similar to the big blow we had experienced in Aegina, but this time we had been able see it developing. The lines would prevent the force of the wind that was beginning to clock around to our starboard beams from exerting undue force on the anchors.

That evening, as the gale was reaching its peak, a port police officer came down the mole and shouted to us to move our lines because a big ferry was coming and would have to use the bollard. Before we could explain our situation, he left. After much discussion, we decided we would rather risk the wrath of the port police than give up our line to windward. When the officer reappeared an hour later, and this time with a friend, we pretended not to understand his request. Over the howling wind they made themselves perfectly clear. A pretty fierce discussion ensued and we learned just how far we could push the port police. We were not at all happy about moving our line to the next bollard up the mole to make room for the ferry, but even this oblique angle gave us additional holding power against the wind.

It was a long night but our anchors held and we awoke to relative calm and a decent weather forecast. The ferry left, freeing our pinned anchors, and we departed for Amargos.

***

Although we had taken the precaution of getting underway on the second reef, the weather remained very calm and the only thing we experienced on passing the feared cape was the thrill of a strong following wind.

Off the beaten path and almost completely void of tourism, Amorgos represented a truer picture of Greek life than anything we had experienced so far. Like most of the Greek islands, it had its own vital ferry link to Piraeus, but supplies and facilities were definitely limited. Two supermarkets, a taverna, and a post office were the primary components of the commercial district of town. Our expectations had already adjusted to the Greek version of a supermarket. Although we never were able to obtain a definitive definition of the term, apparently any establishment that could boast of the combination of canned goods, fresh vegetables and a selection of meats, no matter how small, was considered a bona fide supermarket. While we had experienced some real surprises on other islands, the two supermarkets in Katapola took the cake. Jean-Louis had beaten us to the first store and made off with the five tomatoes and three potatoes that had lined their shelves. Fortunately for us he didn't like beer and the half case of Amstel was still available for sale.

Back at the boats, Jean-Louis had found what he was looking for. The black faucet symbol in the middle of the harbor map of Katapola in Heikell indicated the availability of water. Usually there was a charge but only if someone was there to collect. Jean-Louis had been careful not to look for the tap until well after dark and was in the process of carrying his fifth jerry can back to *Fratellanza* when he saw me watching. "This will be our last chance for water for several days—you should take some on board also."

We were getting a bit low, so I decided to get Charlotte and the children to help. The faucet was about 100 yards from our boat—too far for our hose to reach—the only way was with jerry cans. That night the entire Coleman family became firm believers in the conservation of water. I was reminded of old grammar school math problems:

"Problem: The five man crew of the *Captain Spiros* must fill their 250 gallon water tank using two twenty liter jerry cans. The water supply is 100 yards away. Questions: Can jerry cans rated in liters be used for tanks that hold gallons? Is it fair for Margot, who weighs about half as much as Heyward, to make as many trips as Alex, who is midway between the two in weight and who is still in trouble from slugging his sister the day before? If Charlotte loses her temper and knocks out the captain with a half full jerry can of water, who will navigate?"

While none of us were able to answer the math questions, we did learn one important fact. No matter how many trips each of us made or how many jerry cans we carried, the tanks would never become full. We also found that we became much less compatible with each other while engaged in this operation. After two hours, frustrated and tired, we decided to wait until we could find water within hose distance of our boat to complete the job. In the meantime, we would simply use less water.

***

The next day we headed for our first isolated anchorage—Levithia—an almost totally uninhabited island at the far eastern end of the Cyclades and very close to Turkey. Heyward and Alex wanted to explore and took off in the dinghy while Charlotte, Margot and I relaxed and watched our slower moving companion enter the bay and choose an anchorage. We had noticed all of the small fish around our boat and mentioned it to Jean-Louis. Joanne and Caroline came out on deck with fishing lines and special dough balls that Brigette had prepared for them. Although we had pulled a trolling line behind our boat during every stage of our trip, we had never had so much as a nibble. We were amazed to see the children pull in one after another of the tiny fish. Pretty soon they had almost half a bucketful.

Zodiac Dinghy

The fish soup Brigitte had prepared for us had been delicious, but we were getting worried. It was getting dark and the boys still hadn't returned. Although I wasn't sure, I didn't think they had taken a light. I began to regret not having given them more specific instructions and limitations. Years of boating and mistakes have taught me how utterly confusing darkness can make the water. I was also acutely aware of how little I could do to help them if they got into trouble. There was nothing to do, however, but wait and hope they hadn't taken themselves so far away that they would not be able to find our masthead light and the way back.

Before we had time to become too concerned, we heard the faint sound of the Yamaha and watched a lightless boat slowly emerge from the pitch black dark. That night we had a very frank discussion about prudent boating practices that left little room for doubt about how Charlotte and I felt about after dark exploration.

***

Six o'clock came early and the forecast called for strong winds. But they were coming from the right direction and we were all getting anxious to get to Turkey. As usual, *Fratellanza* beat us out of port. Some fishermen who had put a net out were consolidating their catch as *Fratellanza* glided out of sight around the entrance of the small bay. Our enjoyment of the scene of the father-son team pulling in their nets from their gaily painted boat was cut short by the crackling of the radio

"*Merde! Le moteur est foutu! Brigitte, viens vite!*" and then silence.

We had learned not to interrupt when a crisis was erupting, so we waited patiently for Jean-Louis to regain his composure and deliver his message to us. As prearranged, we were tuned to channel 11. As we waited a mental picture of their situation went through my mind. Their transmission had come three or four minutes after they rounded the eastern point of our bay—this meant that they had probably made open water before their motor failure. Although I couldn't be sure, the ripples that were visible from the point indicated that there was probably a fairly stiff westerly breeze. Since they had put their sails up as they rounded the point, this probably meant that they had the necessary propulsion to keep them off the rocky southern coast of Levithia. But losing a motor near land was always a serious problem and we all stared at the radio receiver with concern written across our faces.

"*Captain Spiros,* this is *Fratellanza*"

Brigitte's calm voice and a return to correct radio procedures indicated that some measure of control must have returned, and I replied with some relief: "*Fratellanza, Captain Spiros,* how can we help you?"

"The motor, he become very hot and we turn it off. We run over a plastic bag we think and it block the cooling water. The wind is very strong but we are OK. We sail for Leros and meet you there, yes? The motor, we don't know yet how much damage she get."

The accident I had dreaded had happened to *Fratellanza*. While I knew that Jean-Louis, with his years of experience, could maneuver and anchor his boat under sail in the tight confines of an Aegean harbor, the prospect of doing it sent chills down my spine. What if he encountered the same conditions we had faced in Mikonos? Under sail he would only get one shot at it and it had to be right. I had thought it out many times.

As we cleared the bay I was glad to feel the strong wind on our stern pushing us towards Leros. We could now see *Fratellanza* with sails full and making good speed. As we passed them, we shouted good luck and promised to scout out the harbor in Leros and give them a report. If conditions were good they could enter under sail. If they were bad, well, the unpleasant solution would be to ride it out even if it meant sailing through the night.

The circumstances brought out the irony of our situation. While it seemed comforting to always be close to land it was in fact very dangerous. When the weather gets really bad, land is the mariner's worst enemy, and trying to enter one of the small, confined, and poorly protected harbors that characterized most of the area could result in disaster. This was especially true at night and was compounded many times over if the motor wasn't working.

When we left the security of a harbor, we always did so with our destination clearly in mind and a large margin for error built in so that we would arrive well before dark. But the weather in the Mediterranean in the winter is absolutely unpredictable, and a full gale can come out of nowhere without any warning. Once at sea, there is no choice but to ride the bad weather out and suddenly all the quaint islands with their inviting coves and anchorages become deadly lee shores ready to devour any prey that is blown down upon them.

By the time *Captain Spiros* was nearing Leros, the wind had shifted to the north and it became clear *Fratellanza* would not be able to make it. By now far behind us, she changed course for Kalymnos, the island just south of Leros. As we approached Leros, we lost sight and then radio contact. We were sorry we were not there to help her, but in reality there was very little we could do. She was a sailboat and built to sail. While we could have put a line on her and towed, it not only would have put our vessel in danger but would have been more dangerous for *Fratellanza*. As long as she had steerage and sails her best alternative was to go it alone. We had made such good time to Leros that we decided to push on to Kos. From there it would be easier to regain contact with *Fratellanza* plus it put us closer to Turkey.

Guidebook in hand Charlotte began: "Ancient Kos had many famous citizens but above them all stands Hippocrates, the great...Gosh, that ship is getting awfully close, Heyward, please be careful... physician of antiquity and the father of modern medicine. We know little of the old healing methods..." The children hated for Charlotte to read them history of any kind and always

71

made a point of showing her that they weren't interested—but this time even Charlotte didn't seem to be paying attention—and she kept pausing to stare at the menacing ship. Not wanting to get into a tanker argument with her, I gently pointed out that the cruise ship she had been riveted on was moored and not a problem. But another problem was about to present itself as we entered the busiest harbor we had seen since leaving Piraeus—how to find a place to moor.

We were now all business. Alex had the anchor ready for letting go, Heyward was ready with two coiled lines at the stern, and Margot had brought all the bumpers on deck and was in the process of positioning them. The harbor was full, but I saw a space on the south end between a sailing yacht and a ferryboat. Was it reserved for ferries? Seeing no sign I gave myself the benefit of the doubt. Completing my second circling of the harbor I turned sharply to the left as I passed the chosen slot. Neutral then reverse. The two points that I had chosen off my port beam remained in line. Our speed was off. I shouted to Alex to drop the anchor. Clank, clank, clank, careful placement of bumpers by Margot and Charlotte, an expert toss by Heyward to a helpful hand on the quay, and we were done.

As we were getting ready for our foray into the bustle of Kos, we heard a voice off our bow: "Michele, there aren't any more places, what are we going to do?" The voice belonged to an attractive blond lady stationed on the bow of a trimaran that was in the process of scouting out the harbor. Although there was some space between the ferry to our starboard and its neighbor, the ferry had a line from its bow across the space and tied to the neighbor.

"But Michele, we don't have the right to take off his line."

Charlotte had established sympathetic eye contact and was therefore a prime candidate for the request the man maneuvering the trimaran was about make. "Stay out of it" I warned Charlotte. "You don't know what trouble is until you start messing with a Greek ferry boat's lines."

Charlotte was already on shore walking past the ferry when the request came:

"Excuse Madame, but could you…" Before Michele could finish his sentence Charlotte pointed further down the quay at a large open space and signaled the trimaran to follow her there. Although a large plaque made it clear that the space was strictly reserved for commercial vessels, mooring there was better than circling around—and certainly better than incurring the wrath of a ferry boat captain. Besides, while possession is nine tenths of the law in other countries, it's often better than the law in Greece. Watching the perfect control Michele had of *Papyrius* as he backed with her twin screws made me regret again not having considered the multihull alternative more seriously when I had been choosing our boat.

Dominique and Michele invited us on board and pointed out all of the advantages of a trimaran. Space, stability, and a shallow draft were the main features. The three hulls allowed such things as full sized cabins and a spacious lounge. Instead of what Charlotte had come to call the "front end loader" their stateroom had a large double bed that actually could be entered from the side. Compared to the acrobatic maneuvers we had to perform to comfortably install ourselves in our bed, this was an incredible luxury. The galley with its four-burner stove and overhead oven was from a different world.

As Michele opened a 1984 St. Emillion that he had added to his fully stocked wine cellar back home in France, we tried not to be too green with envy. He explained that with her enormous width and the two outer hulls *Papyrius* was infinitely more stable than her mono-hull counterparts. During rough, rainy, or cold weather, he would simply shift his steering station to the main salon and drive from the elevated stool on the starboard side while Dominique brought him his *cafe au lait*.

By a glance at Charlotte and a slight nod back from her in acknowledgment we agreed not to air our multi-hull argument in front of Michele and Dominique. Charlotte's aesthetic arguments had won over my practical considerations and we had ruled multi-hulls out early in the game. While I wouldn't have minded rehashing our arguments a little, I was afraid Charlotte would bring up the key point that had polarized her against multi-hulls.

In high winds, multi-hulls could capsize, and once over there was no way to bring them back. While multi-hull supporters acknowledge that this tends to be a disadvantage, they argue that because they do not have a keel with its enormous weight, a hole in a multi-hull will not cause it to sink. The argument then degenerates to who is better off, the multi-hull sailor with his boat upside down and ruined, but still afloat, or the mono-hull sailor with a hole and no boat at all.

Somehow I didn't think it would be polite to bring up this design flaw while Michele and Dominique were proudly showing us around and Charlotte, with her silent nod, had signaled her agreement. They were headed for Bodrum also but only after a week-long visit in Kos. We left saying we looked forward to seeing them again in Turkey.

***

The next morning was very busy. The Greek owner of a supermarket—this one was actually large enough to fit the delicatessen category in US terms—had advised us that good food and many other supplies would be very difficult to find in Turkey. "The Turk people, you know, they are not clean. The meat is very bad. They don't care. You will see. It is more better here in Greece."

Pascal was glad to help us compensate for this fundamental deficiency in Turkish goods by selling us items from his well stocked shelves and freezers. Although his description of what we could expect to find in Turkey was at variance with everything we had read and heard from other cruisers, we were impressed with the variety and quality of his store so we bought, and bought and bought. He even talked us into Greek honey bearing his family name. "You won't get honey like this anywhere in Turkey," he boasted, and we would up with three large jars.

Had it not been for Alex's accidental discovery, Charlotte would have made us all visit the Ascelepion whether or not we were interested in Hippocrates. At first no one believed him when he said that he had seen a real laundromat—"Yea, one that takes coins. And it has lots of machines!" As we had never been able to find anything of the sort in Athens, Piraeus, or any of the islands we had visited, we were all justifiably suspicious. But a reconnaissance trip by Margot and Heyward confirmed Alex's find and we immediately planned our entire morning around this windfall. We finished the laundry just before noon and decided we would leave that day for Bodrum. We were quite concerned about *Fratellanza* and were anxious to join them in Bodrum. We had tried to contact them on the VHF radio the evening before and that morning, but with no luck.

After waiting in line at customs for about fifteen minutes, I was told by the officer that I needed to go to immigration first. While Immigration confirmed that this was true, they pointed out that I would still have to go to the port police before them. Finally getting to the first place third, I reversed the order and succeeded in completing the intricate trail of paperwork that gave me the right to depart from Greek waters. Frustrated, but happy to finally be on my way, I ignored the smirk from the official at the entrance of the building who had initially pointed me in the wrong direction.

***

My crew had everything ready when I returned and we were on our way out of the harbor entrance before one o'clock. With a beautiful day and a brisk breeze from the east, the ten mile trip to Bodrum was going to be quick. Scanning the horizon with my binoculars the small sailboat off our starboard bow looked familiar. Could it be? Over channel 11 on the VHF I inquired: "*Fratellanza, Fratellanza?* Ici *Captain Spiros.*"

Immediately the radio cracked back in reply, "*Ce n'est pas l'homme qui prend la mer,...*" The race for Bodrum was on! It was a classic hare versus tortus affair. *Fratellanza* was well ahead and well upwind, but we had the speed. Nine knots. As we closed, the coastline of Turkey began to unfold. First, the Island off Bitez and then Bodrum itself came into view. The castle of St. Peter, dominating the skyline of the ancient city, began to take shape. What looked like a giant wall of rocks at first started to resemble the breakwater and jetty that were laid out so clearly in the volume of Heikell I was examining.

Excitement reached a fevered pitch. Alex talked me into putting up the cutter sail, but it was so small and poorly cut that it seemed to have no effect on our speed. But even without a boost from the cutter sail, our superior speed had quickly narrowed the gap between our two vessels. *Fratellanza* came within shouting distance, but we decided to let them keep the lead. They had earned it.

"*Hey, Jean-Louis, Ça vas? Hier soir a Kalymnos, cétais bien passé?*"

A big smile, a shrug of his shoulders, and a shout over his shoulder as he went forward to lower the sails: "*de gâteau.*" Apparently the motor overheating had not been a serious problem as we now saw smoke coming from *Fratellanza's* exhaust. We lowered our sails and followed her into the harbor.

Bodrum, or Halicarnassus as it was called in antiquity, was the home of the ancient historian Herodotus and at one time had the most powerful fleet in the Aegean. This wasn't just a new port; it was a new world—east replacing west, mosques and minarets replacing steeples and crosses, and best of all a wonderfully protected harbor that provided ample anchor space in spite of the very large number of boats. But our first priority wasn't to relive history. We needed to find a berth in the marina where we could finish the work that was unfinished when we had left Piraeus. *Fratellanza* had decided to join us there for one night.

The attendant was waiting as we entered the modern marina at the west end of the harbor. He was signaling us to come between the pier and the dock that paralleled it two boat lengths to the east. I had tried to figure out how to take on a mooring, but this was new. To avoid a tangle of anchors, many marinas had moorings, heavy weights with lines attached, and boats would use these to secure one end while the other end was attached to the quay. The result was a Mediterranean mooring without the complication of correct anchor placement. While the concept was great, I wasn't quite sure how we would get the mooring line on board or how it would affect the delicate process of maneuvering. I was about to find out.

Holding a radio with one hand and signaling us with the other, the attendant made it clear that he wanted us to nudge our bow to the bow of the boat where he was perched. It also seemed clear that our assigned resting place was between that bow and the bow of the boat about four meters to its starboard. My mind raced as the distance narrowed. Ten meters, five meters, three meters, and then the attendant was handing Alex a heavy line. "So, that was how we get the mooring line on board," I thought, as I then began to figure out how, in reverse, to turn *Captain Spiros* around almost 180 degrees in the confined space between the two piers to get her stern into the slot. Alex was also undergoing a learning experience. The mooring line, slimy with eelgrass, was hard to grip. Its other end was attached to a heavy chain, which made it even more difficult to handle.

More by will than by skill I accomplished the turn—but the maneuver left the boat at an oblique angle to the slot as we began to back in. Now it was Margot and Charlotte's turn to have a learning experience as they frantically placed bumpers to fend us off our two neighbors. Heyward had just missed his first throw to a person standing on the pier when I shouted to Alex to hold tight on the mooring line. Everything then seemed to happen at once. From the bow: "I can't hold the damn line, it's too slippery and..." From the starboard side: "Margot, come help me with this bumper and bring another—quick we are going to hit... " From just behind me on the stern: "Dad, you are about the hit the dock—do something—quick!"

Of the three problems, Heyward's was the one that needed my most immediate attention. A short burst of forward and we were still. Charlotte and Margot had succeeded in placing their last bumper and avoiding disaster. Alex finally succeeded in getting the slippery line to a bow cleat and Heyward was winching us in on the stern line from his second throw.

All was now still and quiet. We had completed our trans-Aegean voyage and were safely at our destination. While our minds had mainly been on safely docking our vessel, the beauty of Bodrum had not escaped our notice as we had crossed the harbor—St. Peter's castle, the white houses and buildings with flowers everywhere, and behind these, lush green mountains that came down to the city and the sea.

A greeting committee had been forming on the pier during our arrival. Atilla, the caretaker for the Turkish gulet moored to our port, had taken the lines Heyward had tossed. Chris, skipper of the British schooner moored to our starboard, had been watching Charlotte and Margot's bumper placements with great interest as he was applying a coat of varnish to his vessel's immaculate mahogany trim. Rick had used our arrival as an excuse to quit working on his sloop moored about four boats to our port to come over and chat. The marina attendant and his assistant were also there to tell us how to register.

Everybody talked at once and we felt welcome. Heyward brought out cold beer that was immediately accepted by everyone except the two marina personnel. Advice on reefing, shopping, sight seeing and then a little gossip about who was who in the marina community flowed freely. One or two beers later and we had become members of the community.

Of all the advice, one piece was urgent. It was Thursday and the Thursday market was in progress—we should not miss this event. With our giant blue plastic bag in hand, the five of us left the marina and skirted along the waterfront towards the east side of the harbor. The main street that followed the waterfront was picturesque and bustling. About half way to the end where all the market activity was taking place, my head count came to only four. Less than an hour in a new country—actually a new continent—and we had lost Alex.

But Alex had come to be a very independent traveler and we were getting used to his wandering. We weren't too worried when we finally saw him reappear—and we weren't too surprised to see his face merged into something that looked like a cross between a giant Italian hoagie and a Greek Gyro sandwich. Alex had discovered the donner. When he came up for air, he let us each have a bite. Not bad! We then retraced our steps to the greasy stand where Alex had made his purchase. Our gastronomic exploration of Turkey had begun.

The advice about the market had been right. The sidewalks and quays were covered with mountains of ripe vegetables, fresh fruit, and herbs of every description. We had never seen anything like it. Haymarket Square in Boston, the Italian Market in Philadelphia, and even the huge vegetable market in Piraeus were child's play compared to this display of produce. There were so many different varieties of peppers, eggplant, tomatoes, and onions that I couldn't make my mind up which ones to buy. We solved the problem by buying a little of everything. And then there were all the spices. Black peppercorns, green peppercorns, huge piles of saffron, hills of ground cumin and turmeric. Then piles of cilantro, curly and flat leafed parsley, leeks, lettuce of every kind and shape, spinach, and the market went on and on.

Amazingly there was no bargaining. The prices were marked and scrupulously observed. You could look for a bargain—some marked prices were lower than others—and if you looked closely enough, you could usually see the reason for these price differences—but you always paid the posted

77

price. And the prices were incredible. No matter how much we bought, we didn't seem to have to pay real money. The exchange rate was $1,500 Turkish lira per US dollar—and the cost of the vegetables ranged between 50 to 300 lira per kilo. A couple of dollars worth of lira was all it took to have our huge blue bag so heavy that it took two of us to carry it.

We were trying hard to get used to Turkish money. The 1,000 lira note was the same size and looked almost exactly like the 10,000 lira note. We had heard about the honesty of the Turkish people, but our first demonstration came when Charlotte mistakenly paid for five kilos of tomatoes with a 10,000 lira note and started to walk away after she had received about 200 lira in change. The frustrated and actually somewhat angry vendor chased her down the street waving nine 1,000 lira bills.

The marina itself provided many services. A grocery store, a well-stocked chandler, a wine shop, and even showers were housed in white stucco buildings with tile floors that were surrounded by bougainvillea and a rainbow of other flowers. This was luxury. Margot announced that Turkey was the nicest country she had ever seen. We were all a little skeptical about the showers, but the efficient marina attendant who had checked us in had assured me that hot water would be available at 10 A.M. every morning. We would just have to wait and see. Despite the high price of $20.00 US per day we decided to stay while we completed refitting *Captain Spiros*.

At five A.M. came the sun and the call to prayer. Booming over loud speakers a lilting voice in a strange language rattled out its instructions to believers. Although we couldn't understand the words, we knew what the message conveyed and we found it to be a relaxing and reassuring way to begin the day. We were beginning to become fond of Turkey.

***

The marina had told us it would be easy. Take the form they had given us and present it to the officials in the offices at the other end of the harbor—at the end of the quay just past the Knights of St. John's Castle. Then we would have our transit log and entry into the country would be complete. Jean-Louis and I were in great spirits as we headed along the harbor road towards the Castle. Neither one of us believed that the forms the marina had given us would be sufficient and we were each loaded with all of our ship's papers and passports, but with our early start and the advice and help from the marina, we were confident that it could be done quickly.

The officials turned out to be not in one office but in four: passport police, customs, health, and harbor-master. Starting with customs had been a mistake. After making us wait thirty minutes the officer explained that we needed to go to health first. We backtracked to the middle of the harbor, completed the requisite paper work there and then set off to find the harbormaster. We didn't mind getting lost because every wrong turn led to an interesting view or shop—but mild frustration was beginning to set in.

The passport police were the next and were the easiest. After filling out forms for each member of our boats the officers took our passports. Stamp, stamp, stamp... we were almost done. "Go next door to customs, get them to sign here, and then come back to this office" the friendly mustached officer told us as he handed us the form that would become our transit log. I struggled to get out a "*tesekkur ederim*"—saying thank you was almost as difficult as getting the help—and then we headed next door.

The office was empty. But we had talked with the official there at the beginning of our quest two hours earlier. 10:00 A.M. seemed early for lunch so we went back to our friend at passport police. "Keep checking. Someone is always in the office. Lunch doesn't start until 1:00." The "always manned office" continued to be empty so we impatiently waited on a bench outside. Finally the same grouchy official we had met that morning returned. "*Merhaba*" I struggled and forced a friendly smile. Either my pronunciation was so distorted that he couldn't decipher my attempt at "hello" or he simply didn't believe in returning greetings.

When his silent glare became uncomfortable I tried again. "We would like to get transit logs for our sailboats. The passport police gave us these forms and said to..." He cut me off with a shrug of his shoulders, pointed to his watch, and then pointed to his mouth. Apparently his lunch started at 11:45 and he was subtly telling me I should come back in the afternoon. I knew better, but I did it anyway. Jean-Louis cringed as I explained to the official that we had been working all morning to get our transit logs and his signature was the last step. Would he please take just a minute before his lunch to complete our forms? I had just crossed swords with a Turkish official.

Silence, a long scowl, and then: "Bring boat here in afternoon." He then thrust a long form into my hand and growled: "Write everything on boat here. We check boat when he come here." And then he ushered us out of the office and locked the door.

Jean-Louis had already located headquarters for the French sailing community in Bodrum. Hammed's cafe was just up the pier under the shadows of the castle. There was general agreement that we were in trouble. The wind was blowing hard and the difficult maneuvering that would have been necessary to squeeze into the one vacant spot near customs would have been very difficult if not downright dangerous. But that wasn't the worst of it.

Everyone agreed that we were headed for a strip search of our boats. At best this meant days of work to restore the boats to order and at worst it meant damage or confiscation of goods.

Jean-Louis used Corsican logic to solve the problem. Groucho had been in so much of a hurry to feed his face that he hadn't even bothered to look at our paperwork. He hadn't seen our names or the names of our boats. That afternoon two very polite and unhurried ladies took their paperwork through the various offices and obtained transit logs for the *Captain Spiros* and *Fratellanza*. They were so pleasant that even Charlotte's gaffe in thanking Groucho in Greek didn't spoil the process.

***

When we got back to the marina, social hour was well in progress. Heyward and Alex had just returned from fishing with Atilla. He was about two years older than Heyward, was Turkish, spoke fluent English and German, and seemed to be more than just a little crazy. I wasn't paying much attention when he asked to use my radio. I should have been suspicious when he promised not to use my call number, but I was busy and told him to go ahead without giving it any thought. About five minutes later Charlotte came up to me on deck: "I think he has called a girl friend in Germany using our radio and..." Before she had finished I put down my drink and hurried below. When he saw the look on my face he immediately signed off and sheepishly told me not to worry. He had used the call number of another boat—of course it was all right—and I would not receive any charges.

I didn't bother to explain to Atilla that the process of getting a call number from the US Coast Guard for a boat I had purchased while in Greece was a process so complicated that I had decided to bypass this formality. But I did explain that if he so much as touched my radio again I would use ancient Turkish penal codes in dealing with the offending hand.

Ian arrived shortly afterwards. An Australian ex-patriot, Ian was the self-proclaimed social director of the English-speaking community in Bodrum. He was an authority on all topics, and had come to hold court on our boat. We had lots of questions, and, of course, he had all the answers. It wasn't just jealousy that was bothering Atilla as he was eased out of the limelight and the children directed all their admiration to Ian. Ian had caught Atilla with his hand in the cookie jar many times and there was a definite air of animosity between the two of them. Later Ian told me that he had warned Atilla before about his illegal use of radios and would talk with him again.

Rick joined us as the tempo picked up. Between Rick and Ian we obtained the names of all the people we needed to contact to finish our refit.

Knock, knock, knock on our starboard side, and then a shout to Ian from Chris to come with him for happy hour at the marina bar. Ian picked up the longing look in Heyward's eyes and immediately included him in the party. Off they went and thus began Heyward's nocturnal adventures in Turkey.

Early the next morning I succeeded in making contact with Gary, a British ex-patriot and he agreed to install my radar and auto pilot. I was less successful in contacting Yenner, the local sail maker, but at least I was able to find his office and left a note. Things were beginning to come together.

While Charlotte and I worked on the boat, the children occupied themselves with their school work. Up until this point, the work had not been going as well as we had expected. During the refit in Piraeus and Aegina, it had been very difficult for the children to find the time. On our trip across the Cyclades it improved, but there were still rough spots. Both Charlotte and I were determined not to police the school routine. It had been our agreement from the beginning that they were to discipline themselves and we wanted them to learn self-reliance almost as much as we wanted them to pass their courses. The concept was sound, but implementation was not easy. When were we interfering instead of simply providing a quiet place to study?

After much trial and error, we were finally evolving into a system in which we required that they be up and in their study positions at a reasonable hour and that they put in a reasonable amount of work on days when logistics would permit. We tried to stay out of the fights over who sat on which side of the table and who had moved whose books, but we stepped in when discipline was necessary to prevent bodily harm to one of the students.

In Bodrum we began to settle into a routine. School work in the morning for the children, refit work for me, and general boat keeping for Charlotte. We would slack off in the afternoon and by evening were ready to participate in the ritual of social hour and then dinner. Heyward would leave to join Ian, Chris, and their buddies at the local watering holes and the rest of us would enjoy the company of others in the Bodrum sailing community either on our boat or visiting another boat.

***

One day I heard shrieks of laughter and lots of commotion on the gulet to our port. Margot rushed over to our boat and, out of breath, exclaimed: "You won't believe it Dad. Atilla is trying to pull a tooth out and, and... Alex had told him about tying it to a door (a lapse into helpless laughter) and he... and he (more laughter) he tied it to his spear gun and is going to shoot it ." With that she rushed back over to Atilla's boat.

Ever since we had smiled when we learned how much Alex had overpaid Atilla for his large diving knife, Alex seemed to act differently towards him. How much of this tooth business was due to Atilla's normal crazy behavior and how much had been orchestrated by Alex, I wasn't sure, but I decided that I should go over and find out what was going on. Atilla had always looked a little incongruous in the plush surroundings of the luxury gulet he was baby-sitting. But that afternoon the contrast was stark. Stripped down to his bathing suit, his long black hair sticking out everywhere and a long cord protruding from the wild smile on his lips to the shaft of the spear gun he was pointing over the side and into the water, he looked more like someone who had just boarded the vessel to take it over rather than someone paid to be its caretaker.

Sensing that Atilla was about to become a victim of his own boisterous daring, I tried to give him an out. "Is the tooth very loose?"

"No, but it has been hurting me and I think I would like it out." Then, softening a bit he added "Do you think it will work?."

Looking at the stout cord from his mouth to the cocked spear gun, there was no doubt in my mind of whether or not the end result would be an extracted tooth—but my own jaw started aching at the prospect of what he was poised to do, and I gave him the out I thought he had been hoping for all along. "Why not wait until it is very loose—then it will come out easily—and maybe it won't even cause you to miss the fish." Atilla, appearing to be relieved, agreed with my suggestion, and that was the end of it. I was about to add that I would appreciate his not selling the spear gun to Alex, but then thought that this would be interfering and left the young to their mischief without further comment.

***

Remembering the powerful winds and unprotected anchorages we had encountered during our crossing, I found a chandler from whom I purchased a 70-pound fisherman's anchor, 20 meters of 12 mm chain, and 100 meters of large diameter polypropylene line. My unsuccessful search for this material in Naxos when the gale was howling was still fresh in my mind. My security blanket now consisted of three anchors—our 70-pound CQR, our 50-pound Danforth, and our new Fisherman's anchor. In addition we had more than half a mile of heavy lines. Even by Jean-Louis' stringent standards my boat now had a heart.

The refit work was hot and hard. The auto pilot, the radar, water pumps, and bilge pumps, and then back to the auto pilot. I was sick of crawling around in confined areas and figuring out how to tighten a screw where there wasn't enough room to put a screwdriver. Then a visiting expert would point to something else broken or would comment that while my repair job was pretty good, I really hadn't used the proper materials and electrolysis or dry rot would probable get it before the year was out.

Finally we declared an end to the refit, moved out of the marina, and anchored next to *Fratellanza*. After testing the anchor and taking a line ashore to hold us parallel to *Fratellanza*, I realized my mistake—too shallow and too close to shore—but for some reason I turned a blind eye. We missed the early morning *ekmek* (bread baked daily and hot from the ovens) and the hot showers, but the freedom and beauty of being anchored in the harbor more than made up for it and we began to think about what we would do next.

We had the freedom to sail anywhere and the options were endless. North through the Dardanelles, into the Sea of Marmara, then to Istanbul and afterwards the Black sea. Even Russia was in reach. Or we could head south and explore the Turkish coast the whole way down to Antalya. Or Cyprus, then Crete, and then maybe Egypt and North Africa. The situation in Iraq didn't look good—it had been over three months since Saddam Hussein had marched into Kuwait, and there was no sign of him backing down—but we still hoped the situation would be resolved without a war and we weren't overly concerned. Our original plan to winter in the Red Sea had, however, been discarded in the name of prudence.

Every night during our visits with other cruising families the conversation would inevitable turn to future routes. Charts and pilots would cover the limited table space and we would all share plans and stories about far away places. We were still undecided, but our tentative plans called for chasing the sun south and enjoying the exotic and historic coast of Turkey to the Gulf of Fethiye, then to Finike and Kemer, and finally to Antalya. Sipping Pina Collatas in Antalya was the goal—afterwards—who knows?

We were finding that the people we met were becoming the most important part of our experience. We had discovered that there was an entire community whose existence was devoted to cruising. Our purchase of *Captain Spiros,* our hard work in fitting it out, and our accumulated mistakes and adventures had qualified us for full membership into this community— and we loved it. We had gained sufficient experience to determine instantly a great deal about a boat and its crew simply by looking at it.

Cruising boats, with their propensity for practicality and reliability, were easily distinguishable from the flash and pomp of yachts owned and maintained for two weeks of use during the fair weather season. The owner of the latter was inevitably an important Paris businessman, an English lawyer, a German doctor, or some other successful member of the European community. These absentee landlords were referred to as "Yachties" and their greatest pleasure in life was loading their luxury craft with expensive and complex equipment that allowed them to live just as if they hadn't taken the two weeks off from Paris. It didn't matter that the equipment was constantly breaking down—their caretakers had the other fifty weeks of the year to fix the problems.

There was some friction between Cruisers and Yachties. The former were constantly looking at the latter with mixed feelings of jealousy for their money and scorn for the way in which they spent it. It was sheer delight to see some new piece of Yachtie equipment fail miserably or to watch a pale skinned Yachtie fresh off the plane clumsily try his aborted maneuver for the fifth time.

For their part, the Yachties looked down their patrician noses at the homely practices of their Cruising neighbors. How could anyone clutter his deck with bicycles strapped to the lifelines or have anchors attached to make shift brackets on the deck or stern? These yokels were destroying the aesthetic beauty of the lines of their boats. But worst of all was their practice of hanging laundry out where everyone could see it. Why couldn't these nautical nomads have the decency to install essentials such as washing machines and clothes dryers in their boats?

It was fun to watch a Yachtie size up his Cruising neighbor. The smirk at noting the absence of roller furling for the jib, the scowl at seeing the presence of ugly ladder steps built onto the mast, and finally the look of pure disgust and quivering nose as the stare locked onto the inevitable bras, panties, and socks pinned to the lifelines.

But in spite of these differences, the Cruisers tended to get along with the Yachties. It was the third class of sailors that merited the scorn of everyone and were to be avoided at all costs. Charterers. These were the true weekend warriors. Their knowledge of seamanship and boat handling could range anywhere from simply substandard to totally non-existent. The principal qualification was to have at least one member of the crew able to produce a well-written sailing resume. The rest was taken care of by the owners' insurance and a non-refundable damage deposit.

Since all of our travels had been off-season and mostly in remote locations, our contacts had been primarily with cruising boats. Meeting another cruising boat was instant friendship and shared experiences. Invitations for coffee, lunch, or cocktails were automatic and the ensuing discussions were fascinating. Topics bounced from the mechanics of sailing to routes and experiences to home and cultures to politics to religions and to history. Most of the cruisers we met were well educated, well traveled, and very interesting people.

Early in the trip, the children pointed out something important that was happening during these boat visits. Everyone was included. Age did not matter. Heyward was entitled to have his own opinion of what Bush should do about Saddam Hussein, and when Alex went into a long explanation of how a particular mechanical problem could be solved, everyone listened. Margot could address her comments to the German father or could engage in a conversation with his nine year old son who spoke no English. We would all sit around the salon table and spend hours sharing thoughts, experiences, and companionship.

***

Being in a port, anchored, and not pressed to depart for the next destination was relaxing, but we were still not immune from the effects of the weather. During the morning of the third day the wind began to pick up, and we realized the error of our choice in locations—we were too close to shore. The anchor had slipped once and we had had to pay out more anchor chain to make it hold. This put our rudder and keel dangerously close to the rocky shore line. Another slip and we would be in serious trouble. We had to move.

But we had made the classical error of waiting until action was necessary before taking it. Now the wind was up and weighing anchor would be difficult and dangerous. The wind was hard on our beam which put enormous tension on the anchor line. To bring in the anchor we needed to slacken the line from our stern to the shore, let the boat swing into the wind, and then motor up against the wind to the anchor while we winched in the chain. But loosening the stern line would have had the immediate result of crashing our stern into *Fratellanza's* bow. We were stuck.

Although I would often reject Alex's exotic solutions out of hand, this one seemed to make sense and I agreed to try it. With Heyward in the dinghy pushing on our stern with all the strength our Yamaha could muster and Alex stationed at the anchor winch, Charlotte slowly slacked our line to shore. The powerful forward thrust of *Captain Spiros* combined with the valiant efforts of Heyward and the Yamaha moved us slowly towards the anchor and made further action by Margot and Brigitte, who were both standing ready with giant fenders, unnecessary.

We carefully chose a spot in the middle of the harbor. This time I surprised Charlotte by immediately agreeing to her inevitable request for a second anchor. Heyward and Alex moaned and groaned—by now they knew exactly what setting the 60 pound Danforth along with its heavy chain and lines entailed. But they also knew that we were going to stay put for awhile and that putting the anchor out now would be better than waiting for a midnight storm.

Having the boat securely anchored in the middle of the harbor made me feel better about leaving for an overnight exploratory trip to Marmaris to determine if this would be a good base of operations. With two anchors out, separated by about 45 degrees, I felt that no matter how hard the wind blew, the boat would be fine. Charlotte and the children knew how to use two points on shore to tell if the anchor had slipped and had gained more than sufficient experience to execute the various maneuvers to avert disaster in the unlikely event it should become necessary. Anchor watches and motoring in place to ease the tension on the anchor were nothing new to any of us, and I felt comfortable leaving them alone.

***

About a week after arriving in Bodrum, we had been happy to welcome the French trimaran we had met in Kos. Michele and Dominique were only able to stay a short time, however, as they planned to leave their boat in Marmaris and then spend the winter in Paris. Before leaving for Marmaris Michele explained that he had an arrangement with K Technical Services and that I should meet his friend Doan to learn about their capabilities. Michele was going to leave his boat under Doan's care for the winter and return to it in the spring. We had talked about leaving our boat for an extended inland trip during Christmas and we always had a need for specialized repair capabilities, so I thought it would be worthwhile to take Michele up on his offer to make introductions and show me around Marmaris before he and Dominique went into hibernation in Paris.

I boarded a large Pamukkale bus to Mugla and then connected to Marmaris on a little dolmus for the drive through steep mountains covered with a green canopy of pine trees and dotted with thousands of beehives. On a long quay just before the footbridge leading to the marina there was a group of support services shops of all kinds. K Technical was sandwiched between a travel agency and a chandler. The outfit was run by a group of Germans, and I was impressed with the scope of their services. They flew into Germany almost weekly, so hard-to-get parts was their specialty. How they got these parts past the very stringent Turkish customs is something they didn't go into with me, but they assured me that they could find anything I needed.

The associates I met—most of whom were German—had strong technical qualifications. Doan was a special case. The only Turkish associate in the group, he appeared to compensate for his lower level of technical knowledge with a natural aptitude for wheeling and dealing. Although he wasn't with me, I could almost see Jean-Louis' shoulders twitching and thought of his warning: "Never trust a Mediterranean man—especially when he is smiling and friendly." The smile never left Doan's face and he was one of the friendliest people I had ever met. "Ah yes, Heyward, Michele has told me all about you. He is still over at the boatyard getting *Papyrius* ready to come out of water. We will meet and all have dinner together tonight."

I liked Doan immediately and began to ask him about obtaining items for my boat that had been impossible to find. As I listed the items one by one—the German-made anemometer that had never worked, a special part for my stove, a shortwave radio... and the list went on—Doan simply smiled and shrugged his shoulders indicating that obtaining these items would be no problem at all for his prestigious firm. When I mentioned 100 meters of 20-millimeter diameter nylon rope he stopped me: "We have a spool of that in stock. We ordered a roll for an Englishman, but he didn't use it all. Come look."

I couldn't believe my luck and followed him into the crowded store room as he rummaged around and finally produced the coil of line. "Heyward, it is 20-millimeter line and there are only 60 meters, but if you can use it, I will give you a special price." He then quoted me a lump sum that came out to be a very reasonable price for the English made and very high-quality line. When I mentioned, as low key and politely as possible, that it didn't look like 60 meters, he assured me that it had been measured carefully.

While I was looking at the line, trying to make a decision, he was suddenly called away for a quick errand. His absence gave me an opportunity to exercise a little due diligence without offending his friendliness. Eric helped me roll the line out and we measured—41 meters. Suddenly Doan's price didn't look very good.

***

With a couple of hours to kill before dinner, I wandered down the quay and over the footbridge to the marina. A brand new complex, parts of which were still under construction, it was very impressive. The office was well equipped and friendly. A lounge area where people could read their mail and socialize, two multilingual and very helpful receptionists, and a "leave one take one" paperback library—all contributed to a warm ambiance. Amazingly, the price was quite reasonable—in fact only about half that of Bodrum.

It was getting close to time to join Michele, Dominique, and Doan for dinner when the storm began to hit. High wind then huge drops of horizontal rain began to pelt my face as I made my way back over the footbridge to K Technical. The others were waiting and we jumped into Doan's car to avoid the weather. The darkness and curtain of rain made it hard to see anything, and I didn't understand the reason for Doan's sudden frantic veer to our right. He couldn't see anything either, but his memory of seeing a hole that morning measuring about one square meter worked just in time for him to avoid tragedy. The car behind us wasn't as fortunate and I learned a lesson in how the Turks mark their road construction.

Doan ushered us into his favorite lokanta. Only just recognizable as a restaurant from the outside, the inside continued the informality—Plain tables, white unadorned walls, and bottles of water on the tables. No beer or wine here. We followed the owner to the kitchen and chose among the fragrant bins of vegetables, soups, and kebabs. The food was excellent and the prices unexpectedly low—no wonder they tried to keep the lokantas hidden from the tourists.

When we left, water in the streets had become high enough to flow over the top of my shoes and fill them with squishy liquid. I wondered how they were faring in Bodrum and was happy again that we had put out the second anchor. Breakfast, a short walk to the bus station, and then good-bye to Michele and Dominique. I promised to check on their boat when we arrived in Marmaris and told them I hoped we would see them again when they returned from Paris in April. Their tentative plans were to leave early enough in the spring to sail north to the Sea of Marmara and Istanbul before the Meltemi with its powerful northerlies set in.

***

The storm was still pounding Bodrum when I returned. As I walked past the mosque I noted the absence of *Fratellanza* and began to feel uneasy. The weather was fierce, and I could see a lot of activity in the port. *Captain Spiros* was where I had left her and seemed to be riding well. I continued to the marina where I would try to catch a ride out to the anchorage.

At the marina there was a crowd at the end of the outermost dock. As I approached I saw the French couple from Marseilles, Thierry and Jo, handling lines on the end of the dock, Alex in our dinghy, and *Fratellanza* bobbing around on the end of a long line. Alex filled me in. The wind had pushed *Fratellanza* up on the rocks and in her attempt to extricate herself, the motor had failed. Alex and the dinghy had come to the rescue, and disaster had been averted. They were now in the process of trying to secure the vessel to the marina dock.

I couldn't understand all of the heated dialogue that was bouncing from Jean-Louis to Thierry and then back—but the gist centered around how Jean-Louis could secure his vessel safely against the storm but at the same time have it appear he wasn't exactly moored at the marina. He was still smarting over the $20.00 he had paid for his first night in Bodrum. As Alex and I motored away I could still pick up isolated phrases "obligation to provide a safe berth.... we won't go ashore or use the showers... leave early in the morning... *merde*."

The force of the wind was incredible. We were having a hard time holding the dinghy down—how Alex had kept it from capsizing when he had been alone was a mystery. We inched our way into pin pricks of heavy rain and tried not to think of the discomfort. As outlines tuned into shapes we passed one familiar boat after another until finally the transom of *Captain Spiros* was in sight. Some help from Heyward and Margot and we had the motor safely on board and the dinghy lashed to the stern.

Down in the cabin with the hatches shut everybody was talking at the same time. But Alex edged the others out of the conversation as he gave his account of the gulet. "Remember the fancy gulet that was on the pier near the castle? When the storm began, she left the harbor..."

"You have never seen anything like it, they are still picking up boards" Charlotte interrupted.

Alex's glare signaled that it was his story and he didn't need help. "The gulet that had been next to us at the Mosque towed it out of the harbor—I don't think its motor was working."

"Yes, and they went out in this storm—can you believe it?" Charlotte felt compelled to add.

Authoritatively from Alex: "I saw the whole thing—I was standing on the breakwater and..."

Margot interrupted: "Oh goody for you, know it all—I saw it too. You aren't the only one you know!"

"Shut up bitch—I'm telling the story."

"Alex, one more word like that and you are in your cabin for the rest of the day—now apologize to Margot." Charlotte then went back to the popcorn she was fixing.

"OK Mom. Sorry Margot. The two boats went out of the breakwater—the wind was so strong I don't see how they kept from hitting the jetties. Then the rope broke."

"Or someone cut it—I bet it had something to do with the insurance."

"Mom, I'm telling the story. Just fix the popcorn. When the line was gone the gulet went straight up on the rocks. Up and down. I could hear the sound of the wood splitting. The man on the gulet jumped into the water and the other gulet picked him up. The gulet just started to come apart. One mast fell and then the other. Then the boat broke in half. It was awesome!"

We all dove into the popcorn and then I got each person's account of the storm and the sinking of the gulet. I was horrified that I had left them alone in such trying circumstances, but they had handled themselves very well. They had watched the anchors carefully, run the motor for the daily battery charge, and taken very good care of things. But the tragedy of the gulet had presented an image of what could happen, and it stayed with all of us for the rest of the trip.

***

The invitation to dinner with Thierry and Jo on their boat was very special. Fixing a meal in cramped quarters was difficult enough, but inviting two other families turned it into a major undertaking. Thierry and Jo had become close friends with Jean-Louis and Brigitte, and that night we were included in the circle.

When we boarded, Jean-Louis and Thierry were in one of their endless discussions. This time it was on anchoring. "The best way to anchor with two anchors is to tie one on to the other with a long line and then have them both out in one long straight line."

Thierry disagreed strongly. "*Mais Jean-Louis, tu est fou.* When you go to pull them up, you are lifting two anchors at one time. It is not possible!"

"Thierry, you don't listen. I said you use a long line for the second anchor. Of course the line has to be longer than the depth of the water. That way you have the first anchor in before you start lifting the second anchor. Read Glennon!"

"Glennon, Glennon!" Thierry was insulted. "Of course I read Glennon. Do you think Glennon would suggest such a crazy method?" He then pulled himself up, slid across Jo and Brigitte, and started searching through a cabinet over his navigation station.

"*Voila la Bible*" he exclaimed brandishing a thick cloth bound book. "Anchoring. Let's see. Yes here. Ha ha. See, it says 'you must never use two anchors on one line.'" He then thrust the book under Jean-Louis' nose.

Jean-Louis turned red and in a rare display of energy got up from the table, descended into his dinghy, and rowed off. A few minutes later he was back and now with a thick book in his hand.

"*Regarde mon ami*! The preferred method of anchoring with two anchors is to secure the first with a long line and..."

Thierry was dumb struck. Glennon. The Bible. And it said two different things? He grabbed Jean-Louis' book and quickly thumbed through the first few pages. "Ah ha, you see" he said thrusting the book back to Jean-Louis "An earlier edition. You have an old book. Glennon has finally realized their mistake and corrected it in my book."

Thierry and Jo had two young daughters and were just resuming their sailing life. They still owned a restaurant in Marseilles but had left it with a manager. Their boat was exactly the kind of boat I would have chosen if I had had the experience: a forty foot steel ketch with a center cockpit. An aft cabin for Thierry and Jo and two smaller cabins forward for the children. The dining area was open and comfortable, but all space had been utilized. Thierry had made cabinets everywhere but had done it in such a way that it did not detract from the spaciousness of the cabin. Unlike *Captain Spiros* where I had to use inaccessible storage under bunks or behind toilets Thierry's lay-out gave easy access to the endless items that are necessary to support a cruising life.

The ketch rig was ideal for them because the two masts allowed ample sail and good balance for virtually all weather conditions, but precluded the necessity of the very large and hard to handle mainsail that would be necessary on a sloop rig (single mast) of that size. If we had not had three children to help, the giant sail on *Captain Spiros* would have been impossible for just Charlotte and me.

But more than anything I was impressed with their library. Thierry had a complete set of US Pilot Charts on board. Finally I was able to solve the riddle of finishing our trip in the Caribbean. The children, Alex and Heyward in particular, were getting worried about the increasing coldness. They were beginning to lobby hard for sailing to the Caribbean and finishing our trip there. I had argued that it was almost impossible because of the weather, but I didn't have the facts necessary to conclusively prove it.

The pilot charts for December, January, and February made my point. They also were scary. The little circles with the number of gales expected in the center told the story. The whole Mediterranean looked like a disaster area. Our original plan to go to the Red Sea for winter still looked good from a weather point of view—but the worsening situation in Iraq had long since closed that option. But crossing the Mediterranean was out of the question.

Alex had argued that even if we couldn't cross the Mediterranean in the winter, we could hotfoot it across in March and April and then be ready to cross the Atlantic in May. After all the hurricane season really didn't start until July. But the pilot charts said otherwise. March and April still looked like tough months and any crossings would involve waiting out gales in protected ports and making it in any reasonable amount of time would be very difficult. And even if we could make it across by May, we would be beginning our transatlantic voyage at the beginning of the season when tropical storms began to form off the African coast.

***

The social event of the month, Abdul's birthday party, solved the riddle of the sailboat with no mast. The event had been sponsored by the French community and was held in a clubhouse down the quay from Hammed's Cafe. Abdul's French girlfriend told us the sad story of their brief charter business. The charter party had been unhappy when after only one day Abdul had limped back into Bodrum towing his mast, but as a consolation they had one very good story to tell back home about how powerful the Meltemi can really get.

Everyone enjoyed watching Josette dance, and I had an interesting conversation with her husband Bernard about scuba diving. He always brought a full tank with him when he sailed and explained to me how much this helped when anchors became fouled and other similar emergencies occurred.

Alex enjoyed the party the most and surprised us all with a new found interest. She was a true French beauty and both Charlotte and I commended his taste. Unfortunately, she had other plans. But what a great way to try to learn a language!

As usual, the conversations gradually converged on travel plans. Most of the French planned to remain in Bodrum for the winter and had all found spots on the quay close to the water tap just outside of Hammed's cafe. As enjoyable as our life in Bodrum was becoming the purpose of our trip was to explore, and we were becoming restless.

There was one memorable event just before we left Bodrum. Jo had been washing laundry and hanging it over the side of their boat when suddenly her wedding ring dropped off and fell overboard. The tragedy had an enormous effect on the French community, and they were galvanized into action. Bernard donned his scuba gear and headed the effort. He brought up bucket after bucket of mud from six meters below while husbands and wives alike sifted through the muck in a hopeless task to find the tiny ring.

The fact that the project was impossible only spurred their strong French individualism and pride, and they kept trying and trying. Finally, just before dark, after almost eight hours of work they found the ring. Singing, dancing, shouts of *chapeau* and *"viva la France"* filled the night air and was one of our lasting memories of Bodrum, *Fratellanza*, and Hammed's cafe.

***

We said our good-byes and made plans to get underway. Our next objective would be to explore the Gulf of Gokova. The trip to the fuel dock helped us get our sea legs back and after an hour or so of searching about we finally succeeded in finding someone to operate the pumps. The fuel wasn't too expensive, but our good-bye to *Fratellanza* was.

While fuel was being pumped aboard I went over to see Jean-Louis for a last visit. He had unlashed his wind surfer from the lifelines and was in the process of cleaning it when we arrived. Previously Heyward had sailed on Fratellanza's wind surfer and Jean-Louis knew we had an interest. The offer sounded far too high, but I wasn't very comfortable in bargaining with a friend and was about to say that I wasn't interested when I saw the anxious look on Heyward's face. Against my better judgment I offered him half of what he had offered. Fifteen minutes later we returned to our mooring at the center of the harbor with a Mistral board lashed to *Captain Spiros'* lifelines and all the necessary paraphernalia for wind surfing crammed in the bow compartment below.

Jean-Louis understood the weather in the Mediterranean far better than I, and the inactive wind surfer, always underfoot and in the way, served as a constant reminder to me of my Corsican friend's advice to never trust a Mediterranean man who was friendly. But Brigitte, Jean-Louis, and the children had become fast friends and we knew we were going to miss them.

93

Chapter 4
Exploring the Gulf of Gokova and Marmaris

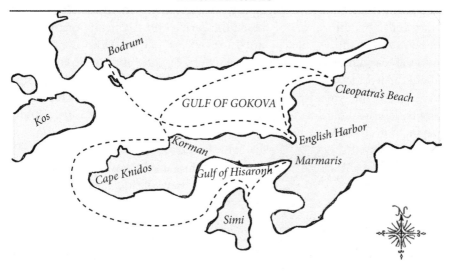

It was time to move on—but we needed good weather. The incident of the gulet was still fresh on our minds and we had no desire to tangle with a gale. We had a full load of fuel, a change of oil for our 80 horse power Perkins, and a full stock of provisions, but gale warnings early the morning of December 7 changed our plans, and we spent a quiet day planning our trip to Degirmen Buku and English Harbor. Our route would take us past the small island of Kara Adasi with its hot springs and then across the Gulf of Gokova and near to its easternmost end. The next morning the weather forecast was good but what I saw outside was not—drizzling rain and an overcast sky. I motored out of the harbor entrance in the dinghy to see what it was like there and saw a small sloop. Curious to see if the small Danish boat knew something I didn't, I motored over to them. "Hello. Where are you headed?"

"Ve are going to Englishman's Cove."

"What do you think about the weather?"

"Oh, Ve get a little vet, but I don't think the wind she vill blow too hard."

I made a quick decision. "We are going there also. Our boat is the *Captain Spiros* and my name is Heyward. Let's keep in touch by radio."

"OK. Ve are *Dina*. Ken and Lisa. Ve monitor channel 7. See you in Englishman's Cove."

I headed back to *Captain Spiros* and filled everyone in on our plans. Ten minutes later we were underway with the dinghy in tow. Atilla had told Alex and Heyward all about the sulfur springs on the neighboring island of Kara Adasi and we had planned to stop for a swim. Hot water flowing into the sea sounded great to everyone. But Charlotte and I were concerned about the weather and we had a long way to go. The argument was beginning to get pretty hot when we heard the loud whirring noise from the stern. Alex almost fell overboard in his mad dash to the bent rod with its line rapidly paying out. There were fish in the Mediterranean after all. By this time we had almost caught up with *Dina*. A quick call on channel 7 assured them that we weren't in distress, and they continued on—wondering why our boat had just done a 180 turn and almost jibbed.

Our First Fish

Charlotte had not let go of the helm. She had simply forgotten she was driving. After all, we had had a line overboard on every leg of our trip and this was the first strike of any kind. Alex's shouts to slow the boat down so he could get the fish in served as a reminder to Charlotte of her role and she whirled around to see where she was going. More important than the direction was the upward motion of the boom. "Holy s---, we are going to jibe" she exclaimed as she turned the wheel as hard as she could. All eyes turned to the boom. Up, up,... then back down... and then Charlotte's maneuver took effect. She had avoided the jibe.

We wanted to land the fish Alex had succeeded in reeling up to the boat, but we didn't want to lose anyone overboard. No time for the elaborate gaff Alex had wanted to construct. Over objections from everyone I reached over the side, grabbed the leader, and flung the fish into the cockpit. Alex and Heyward's loud protests that I was going to lose the fish were drowned out by Charlotte's scream as the fish actually came over the side.

"Don't get it in the cockpit" she shouted jumping out of the way "and don't get it near me."

I reached for the flapping fish and grabbed it by the gills. Blood starting coming out its mouth and all over the teak trim.

"Its a bonito! Who wants a bonito... and it's making a mess all over the boat—throw it overboard right now. This minute! I'm not kidding" as she moved further out of harm's way.

But Alex and Heyward would have none of this—it was our first fish and they wanted to keep it. Margot was indifferent, but, like Charlotte, stayed well out of the way. Heyward went below for a knife, and two minutes later the head and intestines were over the side. I wrapped the five pounder in two plastic bags and put it into our refrigerator—over Charlotte's loud objections. "It's a trash fish and it's going to smell up everything in the refrigerator." But being unwilling to touch the creature and having only one vote put her at a disadvantage, and our catch began its wait for dinner.

***

We had decided to bypass the anchorages along the northern shore of the Gulf of Gokova in favor of the more interesting and more protected anchorages along the eastern shore. English Harbor, which had sheltered English torpedo boats during the war, had a top rating from Heikell for shelter and was reported to be one of the most beautiful spots in the Gulf.

It was drizzling rain when we entered Degirmen Buku and headed for English Harbor. Lush pine forests covered the mountains and came down to the sea. As we rounded the outer point, we watched as an incredibly well protected cove revealed itself. The restaurant and its rickety dock that were marked on our chart were clearly visible, and we saw four other boats snugly at anchor. We could understand why the family aboard *Petit Cheveaux,* whom we had met in Bodrum, had chosen to spend the last two winters in this spot.

We dropped anchor between the forward two boats in about the middle of the cove and then began to scan the harbor and our new neighbors with binoculars. The boat alongside the rickety dock had looked familiar, but the binoculars solved the riddle. *Petit Cheveaux* had apparently decided to make it a third winter in English Harbor.

After radioing *Dina* to let them know we had arrived safely and to give them a few tips on locating the anchorage, I decided to explore the cove. Alex and Heyward had just returned in the dinghy after securing a long stern line to a tree on the far shore so I took the dinghy over to visit *Petit Cheveaux.*

Gerard, his wife, and their two small children were neatly ensconced in their little home tied up to the restaurant's pier. The restaurant was closed for the winter, but the owner still lived there and would give Gerard and other boat owners a ride to Marmaris each Friday when he went to the market. Occasionally *Petit Cheveaux* or one of the other boats would make the trip to Bodrum where they could pick up other supplies. Their cove was secure from winds in any direction and their surroundings were idyllic. It was a perfect place to while away a winter.

Gerard was very interested in our catch and strongly disagreed with Charlotte's characterization of bonito as a trash fish. He dug through a pile of papers in one of his bookshelves and finally found his favorite recipe. *Sauté de ton au paprika.* Other than the fresh cream, we had most of the ingredients on board so I decided to try it on my crew that night. Gerard declined my invitation, but wished us all "*bon apetit.*"

Charlotte was not enthusiastic. "You know what *ton* means, don't you?"

"Yes, but I think it's going to be very good. Especially with the paprika and..."

"*Ton* is tuna fish. And that's no tuna. It's already smelling up the whole boat..."

"Well, bonito is some kind of cousin to a tuna and really looks a lot like tuna." As Charlotte had never seen a tuna fish except in a can or as a fried fillet in a restaurant and as I had actually caught one many years ago in Cape Cod, she reluctantly went along with the program, and I began to prepare my gourmet meal.

While I didn't think the concoction smelled great, I thought Charlotte's comments about the effect it was having on the atmosphere were entirely uncalled for. But once the ball started rolling, everybody else jumped in. Margot wasn't going to eat any fish no matter what it smelled like, so she more or less exempted herself from the conversation. But Alex's snide comments really hurt—after all, I had helped him land the fish—and his allusion to parts of the female anatomy were entirely inappropriate for a child his age no matter what the setting.

But I knew that a generous dousing of paprika and a positive attitude could compensate for a lot, and continued with my creation. Everybody acknowledged that the rice and salad were great, and, although nobody else would believe me, the bonito was pretty good also. My enthusiastic announcement that the next time I would try curry powder instead of paprika met with loud groans.

***

After a quiet day exploring the beauty of Englishman's Cove we decided to depart for Sehir Adalari and the famous Cleopatra's Beach.

Cleopatra had lived on the island and the legend was that she had many barge loads of pink sand brought in from the African coast for her and her lover Mark Anthony. We anchored in the small cove just across from the island—a beautiful spot, but a tricky and potentially treacherous anchorage. There was no protection except in the cove, and our boat took up almost all of the space. We were OK as long we didn't move, but one slip and it would be *Captain Spiros* on the rocks.

The boys bore the brunt of my paranoia, and were thoroughly exasperated when I made them dinghy the lines to new spots on shore for the fifth time. Finally, with an anchor holding the bow at the entrance of the cove and two lines attaching the stern to trees on either side of the head of the cove, I felt comfortable. With no tide, we were able to tension the lines so that the boat wasn't able to move at all.

Right when I was about to declare us safely anchored, a Turkish couple boarded a small fishing boat at the head of the little cove. Before I could even think about moving our lines to let them pass, they motored up. While she was at the wheel, he put an oar under our starboard shore line and ran their boat underneath. As they glided past, the wife broke into a broad smile and threw us two small tangerines. The couple were attractive and friendly and their looks and gestures made us feel at home. We were becoming very attached to Turkey.

As we walked across the island towards the beach we crossed the foundations of an old Roman town and then walked through an ancient amphitheater. There were no fences, signs, or boundaries of any sort—just us, the ruins, and an old man picking up olives from a beautiful old olive grove that covered the whole island. We had noted the slack supervision in the museum at Bodrum's Knights of St. John's Castle, but here there was no supervision at all.

Cleopatra's beach was all we had heard and more. The coastlines of both Greece and Turkey had almost always been a mixture of cliffs, large rocks, and stones. Sandy beaches were rare. Amazingly the pink was still there, and enough of the summer warmth remained for us to enjoy a vigorous swim. On the way back we picnicked under the olive trees, and Margot and Alex treated us to a performance in the amphitheater. We then retired to the solitude of our little cove.

Although the weather had been good during the day, the 6:00 A.M. forecast that morning had called for high winds. With the precarious nature of our anchorage, I hoped that the usual inaccuracy of the forecast held for the night. But it wasn't only the weather that attracted our concern that night.

The *Captain Spiros* schoolroom afloat was looking like it might sink. It didn't take regression analysis or high math to figure out that at the rate Alex and Margot were completing their Calvert lessons there wasn't even a remote chance that they would finish. As I sat at my navigation station fretting about the weather, I picked up a pad of paper, a ruler, and a pen and designed a graph.

The number of boxes next to each name corresponded to the number of weeks left before the end of June. I defined the end of June as D-day and then asked Margot how many lessons she had left. Without thinking much about what I was doing she gave me an answer. The same question to Alex yielded the same results but a considerably larger number. Their curiosity aroused, they gathered around the chart table to see what I was doing. Margot queried: "What's D-day?"

"That's DEAD DAY," I replied. "Anyone not finished their Calvert lessons by then is going to be Dead."

"Ha Ha Ha. Very funny! What are the numbers in the stupid boxes?"

"That, Margot, is the number of lessons each of you are going to complete each week until June. And I'm serious."

After the initial screams and protests, we had a serious family discussion and agreed to adopt the chart. I posted it on the bulkhead behind the navigation station and ordered both Alex and Margot to keep it up to date. The concept had been simple, but the effect was profound. The chart forced both of them to realize how far behind they were but showed them how they could bail themselves out. It also gave them a means to administer the self-discipline they needed to keep themselves on track. Both Charlotte and I had stuck with our resolution to leave the responsibility for their progress with them and we weren't about to change now.

***

The 6:00 A.M. forecast was a little better than the day before, and we got an early start with a steady wind behind us. With the main full out to starboard and the jib out to port (wing and wing) we glided past Degirmen Buku headed for the mouth of the Gulf of Gokova. We had decided to stop at Kormen which was the last protected harbor before the very formidable Cape Knidos at the western tip of the Dorian Peninsula.

Wing on wing was pretty and the ride was usually smooth, but it caused a lot of tension—particularly when Charlotte was steering. In principle it was simple. If the mainsail begins to flap and the boom starts to lift, the boat is close to jibbing and should be veered slightly to windward. If the jib starts to flap, the veer should be to leeward—but only ever so gently.

Overcompensating for a flapping jib or waiting too late to compensate for a lifting boom can result in a jibe.

On *Captain Spiros* a jibe was serious business. As the stern passes across the wind the huge mainsail and its massive boom shifts from being all the way out on one side to all the way out on the other side. If the maneuver is carefully controlled and the boom is drawn up close to the center of the boat just before the turn and then rapidly let out on the other side, all is fine. But if the maneuver is executed inadvertently or too quickly, the boom and sail come crashing across the stern with terrible force and woe be to anything or anyone who is in its path. On a small boat wing and wing can be exhilarating and fun with the only consequence of a miscalculation being a capsized boat and a dip in the

Wing on Wing

water. On a large boat the consequences can range anywhere from mild embarrassment to a crushed skull or a demasted vessel.

Charlotte was giving it all of her attention and actually doing a pretty good job. But as the wind picked up, her habit of verbalizing concerns was resulting in a ceaseless string of questions, warnings, and expletives.

"Oh the jib is flapping, should I come to the right a little? The rudder isn't working, we aren't turning... oh s---!" And a quick turn of the wheel in the other direction. And then "The waves are really getting big. Don't you think we should take a reef in the main?" Muffled groans from our reefers Heyward and Alex. And then "Explain again which way you turn when the main is flapping."

Knowing that Charlotte didn't really expect and certainly didn't need answers to the machine gun fire of questions, we mostly remained silent and enjoyed the ride. One thing was certain. With the attention she was giving it and the extent of her concern, we were not in any danger of jibbing. I laughed to myself when I thought about the advice a close sailing friend, had given to us years ago—"Steer the boat so that the wind feels the same on the back of both ears." It wouldn't be long before I learned that Charlotte's worrying wasn't so far fetched, and that the humorous anecdote about down wind sailing missed the point. Wind tickling the back of an earlobe was an entirely different matter than the awesome force released by the uncontrolled swing of a jibbing boom.

Early that afternoon we spotted the entrance of Kormen. It was a man-made harbor and looked secure. There was only one other boat, a gulet, apparently moored for the winter, so there was plenty of room for us to moor along the quay. To our delight, there was a little restaurant just up the quay from our spot. The town itself consisted of one combination house, general store, and mule shed, but they had coke, beer, and olives so we were able to do a little restocking before treating ourselves to dinner at the restaurant.

The next morning we were greeted with very strong winds from the southeast. Jean-Louis had repeatedly warned us about the wicked winds from the south. "Winds from the north can be strong, but they don't change. They are honest winds. But winds from the south—beware. You never know what they will do." It was no time to deal with Cape Knidos. Instead we decided to remain in Kormen for a day and explore.

Our second day in Kormen began with drizzling rain and weather that clearly said don't leave today. As nothing was pressing to be done, I stuffed a pad of paper in my pocket and began a combination jog and walk along the path that led up into the mountains. The fertility of the land at the base of the mountains and the care with which it was cultivated were impressive. Not a square foot was wasted. It was mid December and tomatoes were still on the vine.

As I left the flat farmlands and started up the mountain, a magnificent view of the coast started to unfold. I chose a comfortable rock from which I could see the jetties of the harbor, the town, and the expanse of azure blue water beyond. It was a good spot to simply sit and think.

Sometimes the mental adjustment to our new life was difficult. This was especially true for me. As a businessman time had always been scarce, and my list of responsibilities had seemed endless. Delegation of duties and responsibilities was something I had learned well, and in my position at Maritrans I had a well oiled machine that I had been completely absorbed in running.

Now this was gone and in its place was the management of our boat, our trip, our family, and myself. The first three were straightforward and absorbed much of the restless energy I was no longer expending on my business. This had been especially true during the refit when even 12 and 14 hour days couldn't seem to get the job done. But managing myself was something I had not yet completely resolved. Charlotte and I talked about it a great deal. It really came down to what the trip was all about. We still weren't sure. Out came the pad. For the tenth or twentieth time I started to write about our experiences. But, as in all of my attempts before, I couldn't focus my thoughts and decide what to write about. Too many thoughts were crowding my mind.

On several occasions I had tried to write about my experience at Maritrans and my abrupt departure, but there was still too much bitterness for me to tackle it. And again there was the lack of focus on what I would write about it. What was I trying to describe? The disappointment over seeing something I had given ten years of my life to help build being systematically dismantled? The hurt pride and resentment over the way I had been treated? Or was it simply disappointment that my investment aspirations had been dashed?

Charlotte had seen it clearly. The effect Steve had been having on me was destructive, and that, combined with the disapproval I felt for how he was handling our company, were beginning to erode my health. She had been right. It had been time to leave. The press release said that I had left to pursue other interests, and it was true as far as it went. But the question kept lurking in my mind. Had I done the right thing or should I have gutted it out and hoped for the best in the end? My wounded ego had told me to stay and try to turn the situation around. My heart had urged me to leave.

And then in my train of thought, Manfred's parting advice for our trip came to mind. "In the Mediterranean, the seas are short and steep and the winds can be high—you can't sail into them. Don't be in too much of a hurry—watch the weather carefully—and then go where the wind blows."

Maybe that was what had happened at Maritrans. With Charlotte's encouragement and after a great deal of soul searching I had done it. I had gone where the wind was blowing me, and that was how I happened to find myself sitting with my back to a large rock in a remote corner of Turkey. I stuffed the pad back into my pocket and began the jog back. Writing would still have to wait.

***

Excitement back on *Captain Spiros. Dina* had arrived, and we now had company. Heyward and Alex had helped them get their boat moored along the quay just forward of ours. The invitation for coffee that night was special, and we had accepted. As we climbed aboard and descended into the main cabin, we were impressed with the neatness and meticulous care in arrangements. Ken was at *Dina's* navigation station and signaled for us to be quiet. With one hand he held a portable radio against his ear and with the other he was rapidly writing on a small pad of paper.

Lisa led us to the table which was just big enough for all of us to squeeze around and put out the pastries that she had baked earlier that day. A moment later Ken joined us with his pad of paper still in hand. "Strong vind tomorrow. Maybe gales. " I was more interested in how he obtained his forecast than the actual results and jotted down channel number and time. An evening forecast—what a luxury. But the channel was shortwave and this capability would have to wait. While we were still in Bodrum I had asked my mother to send to us a shortwave radio, but our prize was still lagging somewhere behind us in the mail.

As the evening progressed, we began a friendship that was to last for an important part of our trip. We were intrigued with Ken's answer to the inevitable question of how he had embarked on his life of sailing. At the height of a successful business career in sales, he and Lisa had decided that there was more to life. They created a long range plan that entailed sailing school, buying a boat, liquidating assets, and investing in such a manner that they could achieve self-sufficiency. How long did it take? Five years. A deeper appreciation had already begun to set in on why we had encountered so many difficulties in trying to do it all in only a few months.

But even with five years of preparation, screw-ups are possible. With great animation they told us about the maiden voyage. After a huge celebration and bon voyage party with all of their friends they sailed out of Denmark early the next morning. "Ve didn't even check the vether. The North Sea and ve didn't even check the vether." They both laughed. "It vas a really bad storm. Ve almost lost the mast. Our friends really laughed ven ve had to come back. Ve don't make the same mistake anymore," he said tapping the piece of paper with his recently scribbled forecast on it.

The 6:00 A.M. Greek forecast agreed with the one Ken had received that night. Strong winds from the south and gale warnings. The wind blew hard and I was thankful for the excellent protection given by the stone jetties that sheltered us from the seas in every direction. The weather remained near gale force for several days, and Cape Knidos began to take on an ominous aspect. But Ken and I were getting anxious to get underway and when we finally received a decent forecast on the evening report, we made preparations to depart the following morning.

Charlotte and I were up early to listen to the weather forecast. It was good. But it didn't look good outside. We walked with Ken and Lisa to the end of the pier to take a look. Not too bad past the jetties. Reluctantly Charlotte went along with the decision, and we made preparations to get underway.

Dina's underway was perfection. The combination foul weather jackets, life vests, and safety harnesses were in keeping with the impeccable quality of everything they had on board. Alex and I stood by to cast off their lines, but what were they doing? Taking a reef while still tied up. Not a bad idea. We handed the lines on board, but they didn't leave the port. Raising the sails while still inside the breakwater? Seemed a little risky as there was so little room to maneuver, but with the seamanship Ken was displaying, this obviously wasn't a problem for *Dina*. By the time they passed the entrance of the harbor under both motor and sail, they were ready for anything. It had been a good lesson for us.

Our plan was to stop at Cape Knidos for lunch and to visit the ruins if the weather was good. The harbor was small, unprotected, and had poor holding. No place to be in a bad blow. But the ruins of the ancient city and the beautiful surroundings would be well worth the stop if conditions permitted.

The wind was from the west and was increasing. Our initial tack put us on a course towards Kos, right about in the middle of the entrance of the Gulf of Gokova. The boat was pounding heavily against the choppy waves and a light rain added to the dismalness of the situation. We were experiencing a

Tension Mounts

little of Manfred's short steep seas. Charlotte's suggestions that we turn back became more frequent as the wind continued to mount.

Alex had secured the dinghy across the bow, but the spider web of lines he had used was beginning to work loose. Suddenly I realized that he had left the middle seat in the dinghy and it was beginning to come out. I climbed forward and, holding tight with one hand, secured the loose lines with the other. I then asked Margot to open the hatch to her room which was just aft of where the dinghy was tied so I could remove the dinghy seat and throw it down. It was a bad call. Almost simultaneously with the opening of the hatch, a huge wave broke over the bow and white water went over me and down the hatch. Margot, her bed, and her whole room were drenched. I threw the seat down and she slammed the hatch shut.

Back in the cockpit a heated argument was developing between Heyward and Charlotte about whether the sea was rough enough to cause any real danger. To Heyward it was pure pleasure and he couldn't see why anyone could have cause for concern. This irritated Charlotte sufficiently for her to launch into her sermon about respect for the sea and its perils. When she began to mix culture with warnings and started to describe what mariners must have felt when they passed the temple of Poseidon at Sounion in their tiny wooden boats, Heyward interrupted:"Poseidon is a pussy!"

His comment had the desired effect and Charlotte almost had an epileptic fit. "Heyward, don't talk like that. It isn't funny at all. I think we should turn back. I don't like this weather at all."

Normally I'm not superstitious, but I was about half way through reading the *Odyssey* and it sure seemed like the little tiff Odysseus was having with Poseidon wasn't paying off for him. But we were getting pretty close to the Cape and I couldn't see much advantage in turning back at that point. I told Heyward to keep his comments to himself and then explained that after we rounded Cape Knidos, we would have the wind on our stern and it would be an easy ride.

By this time all thought of stopping at Knidos was gone. The cape was in sight and looked every bit as ominous as we had heard. In this weather it was a good place to give a wide berth. I wanted plenty of sea room between us and the rocky coast line along the end of the peninsula and kept going a couple of miles extra before making our turn to round the cape.

It always comes a little as a surprise how different it is when the beating is over and the seas and winds are following. Suddenly the howling of the wind and sting of salt spray were replaced by a gentle rolling motion and an almost tranquil quiet. We broke out beer and began to relax. But our celebration was premature.

Charlotte was at the helm and we were wing and wing—with all the accompanying questions and nervousness. The small speck on the horizon had turned into a tanker and its constant bearing off our port bow meant trouble. I had hoped that it would develop some drift as it came closer, but it didn't. We were going to have turn to avoid it, but unfortunately the turn required a jibe.

Focusing my attention on staying clear of the tanker and lulled by the relative calm of a following wind I told Charlotte to turn slowly to starboard to jib the boat. It started with an almost imperceptible motion of the mainsail and boom. A small luffing noise, a slight rise of the boom, and then the boom began its 180 degree swing.

Everything seemed to happen in slow motion. As the boom rocketed overhead with enormous force, the main sheet caught on the steering column and wrenched it out of the deck. Charlotte had been flung with it and was up against the lifelines and half way out of the boat. The boat was now out of control and headed for another jibe. Time had frozen. The wheel was lying across the deck. Charlotte was hanging over the lifelines. And the tanker was approaching. Our little world had suddenly turned upside down.

The slow motion stopped and the action began. Margot helped pull Charlotte back into the cockpit. Somehow my numbed mind remembered that the auto pilot was connected directly to the rudder. I went aft to switch on the pilot and to start the motor. Simultaneously Alex went forward to lower the mainsail and Heyward cranked in the jib. We were back in control.

A Little Help from Margot

It all happened in the space of a few moments, but it felt like forever. Stunned and still shaking, we looked at each other and then watched the tanker pass closely on our port side. For a few minutes we just sat there thinking of all of the awful things that could have happened. A person overboard and a crippled boat for the recovery. The tanker crunching through our boat. Or our out of control boat being pushed up on the rocky lee shore of Cape Knidos. I was thankful for the wide berth we had given the hostile coast.

It was Alex who first broke the silence: "Heyward, do you still think Poseidon is a pussy?" This feeble attempt at humor revived our spirits, and we began to put things back together. Margot held up the steering column while I made a splint with boards, duct tape, and ropes that kept it in place. Amazingly the steering cables had not come loose and we regained manual control of the steering.

We began our postmortem. "I just don't see how it could have broken the steering column" I commented. "Did anyone see exactly how it happened?" "Yes. I saw it" said Heyward "The sheet rope caught on the support poles that surround the steering column. But I don't see how that broke it." A lively discussion followed and we each put forth our theories of what had happened.

The nearest well protected port was Pethi on the Greek island of Simi. We conferred with Dina by radio and agreed to meet them there. As we settled down for the ride to Simi, depression began to set in. Our plans to explore the Gulf of Hisaronu and its myriad of fascinating coves had to be scrapped. After Simi we would have to pray for good weather and limp on to Marmaris. And, worst of all, I would be back in the boat repair business again—less than a month after completing our overhaul.

But beer, popcorn, and the incredibly beautiful countryside of the Dorian Promontory began to cure our moods. After everyone had finished giving their version of what had happened for the tenth time, we all began to realize what we had been through. More importantly, we began to understand what had happened within ourselves. The big challenge had come and we had measured up. When the accident had occurred, we were on our own. Even the thought of calling Turkish or Greek authorities for assistance was, as Manfred would have said, "a fucking choke." Everyone had done the right thing at precisely the right time. Our initiation was complete. We were now a tried and tested cruising family. And despite its eccentricity in shedding its steering column at a most inopportune moment, *Captain Spiros* had proven itself. We had all gained a new sense of confidence in ourselves and in our boat.

***

As we neared the coast of Simi we hauled down our Turkish courtesy flag and replaced it with a Greek flag—no point in irritating the Greeks unnecessarily. The entrance to Pethi was well marked and we made it in without any problems. There was a small tanker unloading at the town pier so we decided to anchor.

After the third attempt we realized that the CQR simply wasn't going to hold. The grass on the bottom was too thick for it to take a bite. While we could have deployed the fisherman's anchor, we were all tired, and I think I would have had a mutiny on my hands if I had suggested digging it out of the bowels of the boat. So, instead, we headed for the opposite side of the pier from the tanker. A potentially perfect docking was marred by too little speed at the beginning of the maneuver and too much at the end. A six-inch-long scar along the starboard side would serve as a reminder to me not to make the same mistake again.

I heard a scream when Margot had finished placing bumpers and had gone down to her room. "There's water everywhere and my bed is soaking wet." Almost scared to look, I removed the soggy mattress from the bottom bunk bed and lifted the cover boards. Six inches of water covered almost half of the tools that I had on board. I opened the door to the forward cabin and discovered worse—water up to the combing at the bottom of the door. The only thing I could see clearly on the floor was the top half of the portable generator I had bought in Piraeus to help me with refit work. Opening the hatch had been a major mistake.

Again we had to mobilize forces. Heyward helped me carry the generator up to the pier while Margot and Charlotte emptied the tool bin and began the tedious job of washing each tool in fresh water. Alex and I then rinsed the generator first with fresh water and then with kerosene. It was a little tricky deciding just how to proceed. Pouring water in the crank case seemed a little unnatural, but we had to assume that salt water had penetrated everywhere. When we were done, the generator actually started. But it sounded sick. Real sick. We put it away and hoped for the best and then went to take care of the other tools. The coat of oil helped, but they never were the same again.

Dina arrived when we were about half way done with our tool cleaning. At precisely the right angle and exactly the right speed, they glided in front of us and handed their lines to Heyward and Alex as their boat came to a complete stop at exactly the right spot. Ken and Lisa had had a nice brisk sail and a pleasant day. But much to their credit they didn't rub it in and were very sympathetic about the problems we had experienced.

That night coffee was on board *Captain Spiros,* and Ken and Lisa helped us sort through the events of the day. Ken approved of our jury rig repairs and was as mystified as we were about the column breaking. He agreed that the stainless steel bar that went from the deck on one side of the column and then up and over it to the deck on the other side should have protected it. For that matter, the column itself should have been able to withstand the strain. In any event, the sheet should never have caught on the column in the first place. The placement of the pulleys was much too far aft on the boom and too close to the column.

He bent to look at the break. "It's not clean, Heyward. Look at the corrosion! It has been broken before." He then poked around and showed the remnants of the very poor repair job. Charlotte's interest was thoroughly aroused. "I noticed when I was painting that the paint was a different color around the base. I asked Minolis about it and he said it was nothing."

Another lesson in Greek ethics. Kiriacoulis and probably Minolis had been fully aware of the previous accident and had withheld the information. Worse than that, Kiriacoulis had deliberately concealed an inadequate repair job on a critical piece of ship's equipment. A decent survey should have been able to detect this piece of deception, but, as we had learned in Kalamaki, Economou couldn't even recognize acute osmosis when it was right under his nose. We hoped there weren't any more surprises in store for us.

Our night in Simi was uneventful. Good weather greeted us in the morning and there was still no visit from the Greek Port Police so we decided to dispense with the formalities and left without either checking in or out of the country. As we rounded Karaburun light on the end of a finger of Turkey that forms the southern boundary of the Gulf of Hisaronu, we hoisted our Turkish courtesy flag again.

The Gulf of Hisaronu—literally the Gulf of Fortresses—had been appropriately named. As we glided down the coast we spotted one ancient fort after another. It was a shame that we couldn't stop, but we felt prudence dictated that we get to Marmaris as quickly as possible to get our steering repaired.

We were relaxing and enjoying the ride when suddenly Margot started yelling. "Quick, come look. A dolphin. Quick. It's jumping out of

The Navigation Center

the water." We went up on the bow where Margot was hanging over the bow pulpit pointing. Flashing through the crystal clear water, a gray dolphin was crisscrossing our path and staying almost perfectly even with the tip of our bow. The white belly and gray back alternated into view as he rolled into his turns. And then, splash, he would shoot up out of the water and then back. Our spirits were beginning to revive.

***

Just after coming through the narrow pass between Keci and Nimara islands that led into Marmaris bay I radioed K Technical. Doan was happy to hear of my arrival and invited me to come to the office after I got settled in the marina.

The Marmaris Marina was the best organized establishment we had seen since leaving the states. Just before arriving, I had radioed the office and they dispatched a harbor-master in a dinghy to lead us to our berth. This time we understood the drill, but the maneuver was more difficult because of the tight fit. I decided to go past the slot and then to back in. The rotation of my screw was such that it would help the turn, and there was practically no wind. It worked perfectly and as we glided into the slot. Alex took the mooring line that was handed to him by the marina attendant. Heyward's line toss was perfect and in a few moments we were moored.

Bob, the owner of *Kalona* that was moored on the other side of the floating pier from us, was our welcoming committee. Originally from California, he and his wife had been living on their 45 foot ketch for many years. She was currently back in California because of an illness in the family. Bob gave us an orientation to the marina and to life in Marmaris.

Shortly after the lines were secured, everyone went off to explore our new surroundings. The marina had a fax machine and a telephone where we could receive as well as make calls. We had returned from the wilderness! I sent two faxes. One to Economou in Piraeus with an accident report, and one to my mother letting her know how to reach us. I had let her know before leaving Bodrum that our next reachable location would be Marmaris and had given her the address of the marina so she could forward mail.

We returned to the boat excited with our new surroundings. I had brought back a stack of mail from the office that had been waiting for us when Alex returned with the astonishing news that there was not one but two large bath houses and each had over 20 showers. And best of all there was hot water.

The first night in Marmaris Bob came aboard for cocktails, and we discussed the repair of the steering column. He cautioned me about using K Technical. While he considered them honest, he was not high on their competence and was downright critical of the prices they charged. On the other hand, he concurred with the recommendation that Ken had given me that I look up Allan on the little Danish sloop *Lykke*.

I had located *Lykke* the night before. As I passed the boat on my way back from the showers I saw Allan on deck and stopped to chat. He, his wife Gitte, and their small daughter had been cruising for sometime. Marmaris was home for the winter, but they were planning to fly back to Denmark for Christmas. Allan worked on repairing boats in the winter which gave him the financial freedom to cruise in the summer. He kept a good stock of tools on board, but also rented a shed on shore where he had a lot of equipment.

His timing did not exactly fit my needs. He was going to leave for Denmark in two days and wasn't going to be back for almost a month. But his assistant, Suleman, would be around and perhaps he would be interested. Allan agreed that he and Suleman would come look at my boat late that afternoon.

Shortly after my conversation with Allan, I walked over to K Technical. Doan greeted me with a big smile and treated me like a long lost friend. I explained our mishap off Cape Knidos and asked if he could come take a look and tell me what was involved to repair the damage. "Heyward, I will be very happy to see what you need. Of course we can fix it. We get parts from Germany every day and we fix your boat very good. But I bring Eric with me. He understand boats very well and he know what to do. Maybe later I take you fishing."

Thirty minutes later I was introducing Doan and Eric to my family. Charlotte's antennas went up immediately—particularly when Doan started talking about taking us all fishing. Eric was German, efficient, and all business. He was also very expensive. While they could get a new column from Germany, Eric recommended removing the column and having the two parts welded back together. The column was aluminum, which made repair very specialized, but Marmaris had very good machine shops and aluminum welding was no problem. He took a quick look at the break and then gave me a number.

After they left, we had a conference. The children immediately proclaimed Doan another Minolis and said I would be crazy to deal with him. I thought they were being a little hard on him, but did agree that the number Eric had given me was unrealistic. We would wait to see what Allan and Suleman had to say.

At about noon a marina attendant called us from the pier and said that there was a fax for *Captain Spiros* at the office. Charlotte and I walked over to pick it up. It was from Economou. Impressed that I had received a reply so quickly, I opened it up and read:

REF: S/Y CAPTAIN SPIROS - 6/12/90 - DAMAGE TO STEERING COLUMN
TKS YOUR FACSIMILE MESSAGE OF YESTERDAY CONTENTS OF WHICH NOTED. YOU ARE KINDLY REQUESTED TO PROCEED TO RHODES ISLAND AND ADVISE US, SO WE CAN ARRANGE FOR IMMEDIATE SURVEY OF DAMAGES SUSTAINED.
KIND REGARDS,
GEORGE ECONOMOU

I handed it to Charlotte and watched her facial expressions carefully as she read. The veins in her neck began to pop out and her face turned red. "Proceed to Rhodes" she gasped. "The steering is broken and he wants us to leave the safety of Marmaris and sail to Rhodes? And he is your insurance agent?" Charlotte then went into some very descriptive language of what she thought of Economou and of all the other Greek "helpers" we had engaged in our travels to date.

I had to agree with her. It was hard to see what the value of an insurance policy was if I had to bring my boat to a Greek island of the insurer's choice before I could make any claim. Suppose I had sunk in Marmaris? Was I supposed to refloat the vessel and then take it to Rhodes to see if my insurance would cover the accident?

As with everything else concerning *Captain Spiros* we now found ourselves very much on our own. I had followed US procedures in covering all risks associated with my vessel—a pre-purchase survey, a lawyer for closing, and a comprehensive insurance policy. But in Greece these rules somehow didn't apply. I had been lulled into a false sense of security because my policy was with Lloyds. But the fact was that my agent was Greek and I was now getting Greek service. We had been Greeked again!

Later Allan and Suleman arrived and made a very thorough inspection of the damage. Allan immediately pointed out that the column had previously been broken and that the repair job had been wholly inadequate. He explained that in welding aluminum, full strength can never be regained and that it had been the wrong thing to do in the first place. But worse than that, the weld job had been poorly executed, and apparently only designed to cosmetically hide the original damage.

Their solution was simple and made a lot of sense: fabricate an aluminum sleeve that would fit over both sections of the column with several inches of overlap on each end and then weld that in place. It would not be as sleek as a new column, but it should be at least as strong as and perhaps even stronger than the original. Like the Greeks, the Turks were ingenious at fixing machinery by manufacturing parts. Making a sleeve and installing it would be no problem. The only catch was to find a section of aluminum tubing of the right diameter—the rest would be straightforward. Suleman felt sure he could find the material.

Allan and Suleman consulted with each other and then gave me a price. It wasn't just the fact that it was less than a third of K Technical's price that persuaded me to use them. Their solution sounded like it would actually work. I gave the go ahead and Suleman started work. An hour later he deposited the steering wheel and binnacle in the cabin and walked off our boat carrying two pieces of mangled aluminum tubing.

It was a strange feeling. *Captain Spiros* with no steering wheel. We were putting a lot of trust in Allan and Suleman. But there was something about both of them that struck me as very straight and honest. Besides, I liked the idea of having someone from the sailing community doing the work. Allan knew what it was like to have broken equipment at sea.

Although Allan was leaving for Denmark in a few days, Suleman would finish the work. They promised me that the job would be done by Christmas. But what if a storm came up in the meantime? I felt very vulnerable. But there was nothing else I could do and the Marmaris marina was by far the securest place we had been since we had started out trip. I decided to relax and leave the work and worrying to Suleman.

While I had been concentrating my energies on getting repairs underway, Charlotte had dealt with another pressing matter. Laundry. The last real cleaning had been in Kos at the Laundromat and our clothes were becoming rather sticky. That afternoon Charlotte had returned to the boat very excited.

"You won't believe the laundry I found today. Alli is great. He will be open tonight and Alex thinks we can get there in the dinghy."

Alli was delighted to meet the rest of us and immediately took drink orders. The laundry Charlotte had brought during the afternoon was still drying, but he urged us to sit down and watch TV while it was finishing. We knew that the situation was deteriorating in Iraq, but we were out of touch and had no idea how bad things had really gotten. That night at Alli's, we were mesmerized by the reports on CNN, and for the first time began to feel we had some cause for concern for our safety. From that point on, we kept close track.

***

Late one afternoon I received a message that a package had arrived at the post office. As it was almost closing time, I hurried to the post office to claim what I was sure was the long awaited shortwave radio. One line led to another and then I finally got the bad news. My package had to go through customs, but there were no customs officers in Marmaris. The notice was simply to summon me to the Marmaris post office to inform me that I needed to proceed to Bodrum where I could claim the package. It sounded like Greece all over again.

Margot decided to come with me and we caught an early morning bus. The trip over the mountains through giant pines jutting up and clear blue water lapping below, and bee hives everywhere reminded me again just how spectacular this portion of the Turkish coast could be. We arrived in Bodrum about mid-day and Margot went to visit with *Fratellanza* while I went directly to the post office.

It started off badly. My notice didn't seem to produce any results, and I was wondering if the package was really there. Finally a lady took interest and went off to look. About 45 minutes later she returned with the customs official. "Meester Coleman, we have your recorder. Eet is an electronics equipment and there of course is due customs duty." He then thumbed through a thick book until he got to the proper page. "Let me see. Ah yes. The duty for a recorder is 700 Deutsche marks." He then stared at me with a silly grin on his face.

"700 Deutsche marks! That's almost 500 dollars. That can't be right. That's more than the radio costs."

"Ah, Meester Coleman, I'm so sorry. But that is what the book says. You see..." and he shoved the book under my face and pointed to some Turkish writing: "Here, you see what it say, it is a recorder."

"Look, this is just a little portable radio, not a recorder. It's not expensive and I'm surprised there is any duty on it at all. Are you sure you have the right page?"

"Yes, Meester Coleman, it is a electronics equipment, a recorder, and this is the page for electronics equipment. I am sorry. I would like to not take money, but I must fill out the form and I have to go by this book."

The lady who had helped me in the first place nodded her agreement. It was beginning to look like I was in a real bind. I needed the shortwave radio very much, but certainly didn't want to pay four or five hundred dollars to claim a one hundred dollar radio.

I pointed to another item on the page that had 15 Deutsche marks written next to it: "What's that?" I inquired.

"That is a, how do you say, a music that goes in the recorder."

"You mean a cassette?"

"Yes, that is it, it is a cassette."

An idea suddenly occurred. "Why don't we say that my electronics equipment is a cassette and then I will pay the 15 Deutsche marks?"

The fact that he didn't get huffy and immediately tell me I was wrong indicated that perhaps there was some softness. "But Meester Coleman, it really isn't a cassette."

"No, I guess not, I replied, but it's not a recorder either. It's really only a little portable radio." I then added hopefully: "but it's probably a lot nearer to being a cassette than a recorder."

The logic of my last statement was not lost on the official, but he suddenly changed tacks. "I would like to help you, Meester Coleman, but you see, eet ees written on your papers that eet is a recorder and I would be in trouble if I tried to change..."

"Are you sure that the papers say it is a recorder?"

"Yes Meester Coleman, I am sure. You see..." and he started to point at part of the papers—but suddenly slowed down and frowned. "It should be here, but there is nothing... eet seems someone has forgotten to..." Silence and then some help from the nice lady. "Well, if nothing is written there, maybe we could fill it in with something else."

I promised not to tell anyone what happened, paid the fifteen Deutsche marks, and left with my "cassette" as quickly as possible before they changed their minds. Back on the boat everybody was excited about the new shortwave. It changed our lives. Suddenly we could get the BBC news forecast every hour and we were back in the civilized world. The timing of receiving this capability had been good—events in the Persian Gulf were degenerating at such a rate that we could hardly turn the radio off.

***

Christmas was getting close, and I spent some time researching vacation alternatives. Charlotte and the children had been lobbying hard for Egypt. Despite the continuing deterioration of the situation in Iraq, we had not completely given up on Egypt, so I went to the travel agency on the quay to see what they could suggest. The price was reasonable and there was availability—even at this late date. We could take a flight the day after Christmas and return a week later. We would have to take a bus to Izmir which was about a five hour ride, but that shouldn't be too bad. And one last item. There was a small insurance surcharge that had just been put into effect the previous week.

"Insurance surcharge? What is it for?"

"It's really nothing Mister Coleman. It only comes to about ten American dollars for each passenger. It's still a very good price."

"Yes, I understand it's a good price, but why did the airlines add an insurance surcharge?"

"Well, Mister Coleman, it's for something they call a War Risk Policy, but it's so small and really nothing to worry about."

If plans for a trip to Egypt weren't already dead, the War Risk Policy surcharge did the trick. Even Charlotte's wild enthusiasm to visit Egypt died a sudden death when I relayed this bit of information.

Helmut and Brigitte, whom we had met upon our arrival in Marmaris, had just returned from a week trip to Istanbul and were fascinated with it. They told us all about the Golden Horn, Topkapi, St. Sophia, the Blue Mosque and then about the colors, the marvelous restaurants, and the excitement. As a businessman before his cruising days, Helmut had traveled to Istanbul many times. His love for the city was infectious, and it didn't take long before we were all convinced. The decision was made.

Helmut gave some good practical advice. Use the Pamukkale Bus Lines. From my trips between Marmaris and Bodrum, I was already familiar with the cut throat competitiveness of the bus lines. It would be helpful to have a preference prior to being subjected to the pulls and offers of the hawkers at the terminal. He also pointed out to us how efficient the buses were in Turkey. There were at least five direct buses from Marmaris to Istanbul each day. He suggested a bus that leaves at around 8:00 A.M. and arrives in Istanbul at about 9:00 P.M.

As Christmas neared, Charlotte and I went for a hike and picnic in a picturesque wooded area that overlooked the harbor. We sat on the bank of a small mountain stream and finished the bottle of red Turkish wine as we contemplated our surroundings. The pine trees were far too big for the *Captain Spiros,* and besides we might get in trouble for cutting one down. But another idea occurred. A branch would do just fine. It was the smallest Christmas tree we have ever had, but it brightened up the cabin of *Captain Spiros* and put us all in a holiday mood.

Lately I had noticed that Margot's mood seemed to be perpetually festive. Could it have anything to do with Claus, the youngest member of the crew of the *Et Au Alt*? No, not possible. After all, she was only eleven. But Charlotte and I decided to keep a sharp eye out anyway. Early in our stay in Marmaris we met the Hjorth family who were cruising in their small sloop *Et Au Alt.* Claus was between Margot and Alex in age and Karina was nearer Heyward's age. Bianne and Deeda were normal people who, like us, had decided to take a year off to see the world, and we immediately became good friends. They had sailed the whole way from Denmark and planned to return to Denmark that summer via the French canals.

***

One night Charlotte and I were in the marina office trying to make a phone call when a whirlwind of energy swept in the door. There were five of them and they were all talking at the same time. They made a beeline to the mailboxes and zeroed in on the one marked H. The youngest boy grabbed the stack of letters from the box and began to thumb through them.

"This one is for me. Yea. Here's one for you, Mom. And two for Mary, and..." This was our first glimpse of the Hoffmans. They had just returned from a trip to Istanbul, Bursa, and the coast of the Sea of Marmara. Hans and Mandy and their three children were Australian and lived aboard a Beneteau named *Mary Lou*. We had just found our second set of close friends in Marmaris.

Brunch on board *Mary Lou* Christmas morning was a memorable event. Hans intrigued us with his stories about rug buying near Bursa. He had become an expert, and the piles of rugs strewn around everywhere in *Mary Lou* proved it. Knowing that space was always at a premium on a cruising boat, I asked him where he was going to put them. He showed me the starboard aft cabin that was Jonathan's room. The mattress looked unusually high—then realization. A stack of rugs at least eight high was sandwiched between the frame and mattress of Jonathan's bed. Hans planned to do the same in each of the other three cabins.

The rugs were spectacular and the stories that Hans had for each one made me want to learn more about the art of Turkish rugs. The other stories Hans told were equally interesting, and we found ourselves deeply engaged in animated discussions on a wide variety of topics.

As Heyward began to take issue with Hans on his views towards the Persian Gulf Crisis, I thought about the enormous changes that had taken place in all of us. Here were the ten of us—different ages, different backgrounds, different nationalities, and, until two days earlier, strangers to each other—but now deeply engrossed in matters ranging from how to cook an egg to whether or not to fight a war. And everyone's opinion was important.

Although Heyward seemed to be too aggressive in stating his views, he was holding his own with Hans and I restrained myself from admonishing him. As the conversation switched to World War II and Hans' description of the role his father had played on the Eastern Front as an SS officer, I held my breath that Heyward would not overstep himself. I needn't have. His comments were well meaning, sensitive, and engaging. In the beginning Heyward had been against military intervention on the part of the US. But the realities of Saddam Hussein's cruel actions had slowly eroded his aversion to the use of force. The whole question had taken on a much more personal note when a close friend from Charleston had volunteered and was now in Saudi Arabia.

Hans' views were also very strong. His father had never returned from the Eastern Front and he grew up hating war and all it stood for. He had moved away from Germany and now lived in Australia. He could see no reason for armed intervention regardless of the circumstances and was very critical of the direction President Bush was taking.

For the Hoffman family, cooking an egg could be equally as controversial as the use of arms. Soft boiled eggs were Hans' specialty and the cooking of them could not be entrusted to anyone else. Room temperature eggs, one cup of water per egg at a brisk boil, immersion for exactly two minutes, and then the immediate removal and placement before the expectant diner. Mandy and the children maintained a careful silence as he went through his ritual, but I could see the only partially concealed smiles as Hans, who was about twice as large as the very limited cooking space on *Mary Lou*, flourished the huge slotted spoon and then stabbed it into the pot just as the second hand was passing 12 on the ship's clock.

We had all dutifully followed Hans' instructions and were ready with salt, pepper, toast, olives, and other condiments spread in little piles around our places on the table. Hans had been impressed with the way Bursa-ites had used their tabletops as combination plates and serving dishes and was importing this culture to *Mary Lou*. I was ready with spoon in hand when my egg was delivered from the swooping slotted spoon and dug in immediately. Hans was right—temperature, consistency, and taste—all were perfect.

***

Christmas was turning out to be a very social day. Charlotte had prepared the traditional *Captain Spiros* Christmas lunch of lamb chops and rice and had invited Bob to join us. Bob was the first cruising American we had met since leaving Piraeus and we enjoyed comparing stories with him. He and his wife had left from California with *Kalona* many years ago and had been everywhere. Although *Kalona* had seen years of wear, Bob kept the varnish fresh and the brass bright. Her lines were traditional and the deck and trim were mostly wood, it was a high maintenance boat, but Bob loved keeping it up.

In a way, having Bob on board for Christmas lunch was a little like being back home. He missed his wife very much and was looking forward to her return in about a month. We missed family and friends at home, and the children were disappointed that Christmas packages had not yet arrived. Charlotte's Christmas decorations and the huge knitted Turkish socks she had bought and stuffed full for all of us helped, but we were all a little lonely anyway.

While we were fascinated with Bob's stories about his adventures since leaving California, I was particularly interested to learn about the use of his ham radio. Several years ago he had obtained his ham license, and it had opened a new world for him. The principal advantage of the ham radio was that it has an extremely long-range. When conditions were right at night, Bob could reach the east coast of the United States. From there a fellow ham radio operator could patch him into a phone line so he could phone his family in California. He had talked to his wife just the night before and would call her again that night. We had found phoning the US from Turkey was not only difficult, but prohibitively expensive—thirty to forty dollars for a three minute call. But calls back home were not the only advantage of the ham radio. Bob had contacts throughout the Mediterranean and made a network call each morning at 9:00 A.M. Although Bob used this mainly for gossip, it served as an invaluable source of information for any boat on the move.

Inevitably our lunch conversation turned to the Gulf Crisis. We were all affected and all becoming more concerned. Judging from the letters and faxes we were getting from home, our family was more concerned than we were. Although the Persian Gulf was almost fifteen hundred miles away, we still felt exposed. Turkey shares a border with Iraq and it wasn't at all clear how involved they might become in any action that might occur. And there was the fact that Turkey was an Islamic country. Although the sympathy of every Turk we met seemed to be clearly with the US, this could change in the event of hostilities.

Bob was not in the least concerned with his safety in Marmaris. His feeling of security was reinforced by his ham network. Two boats that were wintering in Tunisia were part of his morning conference, and they had no plans to move. His friend Jim on *Searcher* was currently wintering in Rhodes and he also felt very secure. But our conversation mainly centered on what was happening and where it would lead rather than how it affected us. While the news seemed very bleak, we all still hoped that Saddam Hussein would eventually back down and leave Kuwait and that the crisis would be defused.

We had planned to leave for Istanbul the following morning, but Suleman had not quite completed the repairs. He seemed to be doing a good job, but I was a little nervous about leaving the finishing touches unsupervised. Everyone had almost finished packing when I began to voice my uneasiness about leaving before Suleman was completely done. When the big argument started, Charlotte supported me and we went to bed planning to postpone the trip a few days.

The following morning Charlotte and I were wide awake when the call to prayer started to boom out. We looked at each other and knew immediately that each of us had the same thought. We got the children up, threw our last articles of clothing in our suitcases, and then went through the check list to secure the boat. Bob was an early riser and immediately agreed to my request to supervise the final repairs and give Suleman the envelope with a check.

Shut all hull valves, store the outboard below decks, empty the refrigerator—some extra groceries for Bob—shut all hatches, stow all extra lines and articles below deck, double check the mooring lines, put the dinghy on the bow, shut off the propane, pump all bilges dry, turn all battery switches to off, remove all trash from the boat, and then we were done. With everyone helping it took less than an hour. By 7:30 A.M. we were on our way to the bus station—and to Istanbul.

∗

Riding in the big Pamukkale bus was pure luxury. It was comfortable and clean, but best of all it was not our responsibility. We pulled out our maps and books and began to plan our adventure. The scenery was varied and interesting. It was Charlotte's first time to see the incredible beauty of the sea and pines from the top of the mountains surrounding Marmaris. The winding road also gave us another look at the eastern end of the Gulf of Gokova and we tried hard to identify landmarks we had sailed past.

Mugla was the first in a series of stops that were to occur every three hours. There was enough time to stretch our legs and ply through the many refreshment stands. There were huge piles of oranges and tangerines everywhere, and fresh orange juice was only five cents a glass. Alex bypassed the orange juice and made a beeline for the nearest donner stand. He had become quite a connoisseur of the delicacy and was particularly looking forward to Bursa where the most famous donner of them all, the Bursa Kebab, had been developed.

Between Mugla and Izmir, the lush green began to turn to brown and deep gorges replaced the sloping mountains to the coast. The children had made friends with their neighbors on the bus and were doing a pretty good job of communicating with them. Charlotte and I were searching our travel books trying to decide on a hotel and restaurants for Istanbul. As each mile clicked away, we felt ourselves relaxing more and more. We were also getting very excited about seeing Istanbul and the north of Turkey.

On the third stop, Alex found a new kind of donner after he had purchased his usual. He didn't really need two, but this was an opportunity he might not find later. Back on the bus I noticed the second greasy package and chided: "Alex, how many of those things are you going to eat?"

"But Dad, this is a new kind of donner. They call it an *iskembe* donner. I just wanted to try it."

"You are going to make yourself sick. I have never seen anybody eat so much junk. But you sure are becoming an expert on greasy meat sandwiches. Maybe you should write a book. Let's see, maybe call it *Turkey on Five Donners a Day*."

Alex didn't think my joke was very funny. But a little while later I heard Margot and Heyward laughing loudly and pointing to Alex. He looked a little green. "Hey Dad, you can have the rest of my donner" he said as he offered me the greasy package that had been diminished by only one bite.

"Don't take it, Dad" Margot managed to get out in spite of her almost hysterical laughter. "Smell it first."

I smelled and then began to join the laughter. "What did you say it was, Alex? *Iskembe*?"

Alex nodded sickly.

I looked in my little pocket dictionary. "I-s-k-a-m-b-e, here it is, yes, *Iskembe*. Tripe! Alex you just bit into a tripe sandwich. How was it? I couldn't possibly take it from you. If you are not hungry now, why don't you just save it for later?"

Just for fun I looked in the dictionary again. ."Look Alex, it says here that donner means to turn or revolve. Maybe an *iskembe donner* is something that turns your stomach. Be sure to include that in your book."

The bus stopped at a crowded terminal in Yalova, a city on the shore of the Sea of Marmara. What now? As the bus entered the long queue to board the awaiting ferryboat we had our answer—we would approach Istanbul by sea. Our last stop on the bus and in Asia was Uskudar. Across

The Bosporous from Topkapi

the Bosporus the lights seemed to go on forever—Istanbul in all its splendor lay before us.

Our six days in Istanbul were packed with excitement. The city was vibrant with activity, a strange and wonderful mixture of people and cultures. Across the street from the Grand Bazaar with its miles of shopping alleys was a shiny new Pizza Hut. Europeans, Asians, Turks, and Arabs, people from every walk of life, filled the crowded sidewalks and weaved through the stand still traffic that jammed the streets. How could they get so many people and so many vehicles all in one place?

The children's tolerance for sightseeing and for supervision was definitely limited. The initial onslaught to Topkapi had been acceptable, but after that we had to revert to our old practice of splitting up for part of the day so that the children could pursue their interests while we pursued ours. By the third day they were ready to try the busses on their own. With trepidation we finally agreed to let them head to the Taksim area on their own. The only stipulation was that they stay together and that they each keep a copy of the hotel address and phone number in their pockets. Late that night they recounted their trip to us. The bus had been a piece of cake, but watching the Karate Kid dubbed in Greek with Turkish subtitles had been less than satisfactory.

The highlight was our trip up the Bosporus. While we were in line to purchase our ferry tickets, a tall, rather skinny man came up to Heyward and asked how much we were paying. He then quoted a price substantially below the number Heyward had given him and said he would charter his boat to us for that amount. He pointed to a small, but pleasant, little ferryboat moored beside the quay. "You get off when we stop and see many things. My boat, she is a nice boat. You have fun with me and I tell you all about sights. "He then gave us a big smile and doffed his cap. "You come this way with Stephon—we will have very nice trip."

He seemed congenial enough and his craft looked like it would do nicely, so we

On Our Way to the Black Sea

followed him over to a forty-foot boat with a small wheel house forward and an awning covering two rows of seats in the stern. The gay colors covered most of the rust and it had only a slight list to starboard. In the wheel house an older man with a skull cap gave us a one tooth smile and waved us aboard. We had just put ourselves in the hands of Stephon and his helmsman Monk for our twenty-mile trip up the Bosporus.

Just as we were about to get underway, Stephon spotted an Austrian couple and their small child and persuaded them to come aboard. When I asked Stephon if they were going to join us, he thought I was complaining, and before I could explain otherwise lowered our price by twenty percent.

A few minutes later we worked our way out of the crowded Golden Horn and turned to the North towards the Black Sea. Our first stop was

Rumeli Hisar. In 1452 Mehmed the Conqueror had constructed this massive fort in only three months and then used it to achieve his conquest of Constantinople. We had just completed the long climb up to the top of the walls when the rain started. But even with the rain coming down and the weather getting colder, we continued our exploration of this remarkable achievement. Standing on one of the turrets we stared at the barely visible shore of Asia on the other side of the Bosporus and could visualize the frenetic armies of Mehmed throwing up this massive structure in order to overcome the last bastion of Christianity in Turkey.

Stephon was keeping his promise and continuously spouted out anecdotes and history as we wove our way up the Bosporus alternating stops between the European and Asiatic shores. His stories became better as the level of his large bottle of Raki became lower. It was getting colder and we were soaking wet, but Stephon produced a stack of shag blankets and we wrapped ourselves up and watched history glide by.

Our last stop was on the Asian side at Anadolufeneri, just at the entrance to the Black Sea. Stephon led us to a quaint seafood restaurant where we enjoyed fresh fish that we picked from a tank and had grilled on the porch. He joined us for a beer and then we began the trip back.

There were more stories that Stephon wanted to recount, but his

Castle of Kilitbahir

speech became difficult as the bottom of the Raki bottle came into sight. The sea became choppy and Stephon began to turn green. The loud gasping noises made it hard for us to carry on conversations among ourselves, and I became concerned that we might lose our guide overboard, but Monk gave us a knowing look and assured us there was nothing to worry about.

We filled in the history for ourselves as we worked our way down the Asian coast back towards Istanbul. Monk was great company, and we took turns warming up in the tiny wheelhouse and talking with him. Alex was impressed with the small propane heater and urged me to get one when we returned to Marmaris. Back at the pier in Istanbul, we tried to wake Stephon up to thank him and say good-by, but finally had to settle with letting Monk relay our message.

Canakkale was another strategic point oozing with history. The Hellespont or Dardanelles is the choke point where the Sea of Marmara funnels down to the Mediterranean. After getting situated in a modest hotel, Charlotte and I took the ferry across the strait and explored the castle of Kilitbahir—another of the fortresses that Mehmed the Conqueror had built during his campaign to conquer Constantinople. It was an exhilarating feeling to look down on the Hellespont from the ramparts of Kilitbahir and think of the armies of Greeks, Romans, Ottomans, and then in modern times Allies and Germans who had fought over this same turf.

Our visit to Gallipoli was a special experience. In a small cafe near the Kilitbahir fortress, we met an elderly man who said his son was a taxi driver and the best guide in town. Two Turkish teas and a five-minute drive later we arrived at his son's house. Ahmet, emerging a few minutes later, straightened his wrap around sun glasses, finished pulling on his driving gloves, and then set out with us to explore the past. As he drove us through the battle grounds he made them come alive.

He took us to the wide beach where the Australians were supposed to have landed. From there we walked along the coast to the steep cliffs and rocky coast where the buoy the British had anchored off the beach the night before had dragged during the day. Using the buoy as the landmark for their embarkation had resulted in disaster. The war museum, the graves, and the harsh terrain all told the story.

A high point of our stay in Canakkale was a good seafood dinner. We had honed the art of finding a good restaurant and negotiating a reasonable price to a high degree by this stage in our travels in Turkey. The rules were simple. Once a price had been set, no need to check the bill—it would be scrupulously correct. But setting the prices—this was the trick. The smiling waiter that greeted visitors and showed them the magnificent display of produce, meats, and fish was careful to avoid the subject of price. And, of course, there were no menus. The visitor is put at ease and broaching price seems like a breach of etiquette. But we had learned that the unpleasant topic will certainly arise after the dinner is over and surprises often lead to indigestion.

We had developed an interesting technique. No matter how mouth watering the display, none of us would give the slightest indication of interest. I would choose an item that I was certain none of us wanted and politely ask how much. The host, fearing the loss of a sale but still wishing to sell a profitable meal, would quote a medium high price. We would all then feign shock at the high price and act as if about to leave. The host, panicking that he was about to lose five potential clients, would implore us to ask about the other items. My next inquiries would then be directed at the dishes I knew my hungry crowd had been dreaming about eating for the last week. Quotations for these choices were invariably about half the price of my first request. That night, our technique worked famously and we left for Troy the next day with full stomachs.

The cheesy wooden horse that greeted us at the park entrance was in sharp contrast with the informality and lack of infrastructure at historical sites that we had enjoyed in the south, and we wondered if admission would be worth the price. But seeing the ruins themselves drew us in. Was it nine layers or thirteen layers? We couldn't tell, but it gave us a real feeling for the past to wander around the partially completed excavations and try to imagine what it had been like.

The coastline had receded out of sight in the intervening centuries, so it was a little hard to picture the arrival of the Greek fleet, but seeing actual

Ephesus

stones and foundations brought a new sense of reality to Homer. From this point on, Odysseus's trials and tribulations would assume a much greater reality as I continued to slog my way through the *Odyssey*.

Ephesus was our next stop. It was a beautiful clear morning when we quit our bed and breakfast in nearby Selcuk and began our walk down the tree lined avenue. We were wholly unprepared for the site that greeted us as we veered off the main road and finally made it over the last hill. At Ephesus an entire city stretched out before us. Roads, buildings, houses, and a large amphitheater. We walked down the Arcadian Way to the site of the ancient harbor, now dried up, and then worked our way back to the Library of Celsius where we sat on the floor and enjoyed a feast of tangerines. Unlike Troy where we could only try to imagine what it had been like when Helen had walked its streets, we could almost see the bustle of togaed Romans engaged in their engineering and commerce in this vital metropolitan center.

✳✳✳

We returned to Marmaris refreshed and ready to face the elements. Suleman had finished the steering column repairs and *Captain Spiros* looked as if she were ready for sea. While we were all happy to be back and see our friends again, Margot was particularly animated. We had heard enough about Claus during our two week trip to confirm our suspicions and were not at all surprised to see Margot make a beeline to *Et Au Alt* as soon as we arrived at the marina.

Before leaving for our Christmas trip, I had received a distressing letter from our friend WAM about Carl. Carl had been a close friend in college and someone whom I had kept up with ever since. His escapades included living on a sailboat for several years and sailing it in both the Mediterranean and the Caribbean. After that, he had been in the film business. His latest venture had been in barging petroleum and that had culminated in some sort of deal in Venezuela. Carl was vibrant and fun. I had always been fascinated by his free spirit and willingness to try almost anything.

WAM's letter read:

Dear Colemans,

I assume the trip must be more or less successful to date or someone would have reported the contrary by now. At least you must be too busy to write.

I fondly recall once putting my ex and the three girls on the 30-foot *Whisper* and going for three weeks. You met us at Crooked Island. When I returned I told people that it was the best way I knew to make three weeks seem like a year. This was universally misinterpreted as a witty reference to a disaster. It wasn't. Rather a reference for the only way a working Dad could cram in more time with his family. In any event I am interested to know if it holds true for three months.

Distressing news from here, ironically connected to sailing.

Carl has inoperable brain cancer. The prognosis is that he does not have much past this year left. I drove down to Montgomery yesterday to visit with him. He is in good spirits with only minor physical problems at present. He rides to the hounds and is keeping that up and reports that at least no one bitches about him smoking anymore.

Carl and I reminisced about a lot of trips and people and he asked about you and wanted me to let you know of his situation. I think he would really appreciate a letter with a full account of your adventures.

I guess Carl is an excellent example of why one should 'go cruising' or its moral equivalent at the first opportunity or make that opportunity if it does not occur naturally. I certainly envy your adventure.

Smooth sailing, Merry Christmas, Happy New Year!
WAM

Charlotte and I had talked about Carl, WAM, and our trip well into that night. While we had been traveling, I had managed to put it out of my mind. But when we settled back into the routine of *Captain Spiros* there it was—too big to ignore. I took the letter from WAM out of the chart bin at my navigation station and read it for the twentieth time. It was a rainy day and I had nothing pressing to do. I fished the laptop computer out of the chart bin and began:

"Dear Carl" and suddenly the words started pouring out. I began to explain to Carl—or was it to myself—the complex chain of events that had led the five of us to a small sailboat at the eastern edge of the Mediterranean. But, strangely, for the first time it started to make sense. Manfred's advice came back and I could almost see him there with his big smile and glass of ouzo telling me again. "Sail where the wind blows." And more than anyone else I knew, Carl had followed this advice. I spent almost the entire day huddled over the computer and managed to get down the story of our adventure through the trip north. Carl had given me the key. I finally began to understand *what it was all about*. And, for the first time, I could write about it.

***

During our trip north, we had become a little out of touch with current events, but made up for it by listening to the BBC hourly news reports several times a day on our new shortwave radio. The situation in the Gulf had become more serious and it was becoming an increasingly important factor in our plans. President Bush had given Saddam Hussein a January 15 deadline to withdraw from Kuwait and it was beginning to look like a war might actually start. We were not quite sure what we would do if war broke out, but we were considering leaving Turkey if it did.

January 8 was a beautiful day, the forecast was for continued good weather, we had taken on 200 liters of fuel the day before, and there really wasn't any excuse not to leave. But a phenomenon had set in that we were to experience time and again during our trip. Marmaris was comfortable and we had made friends. Inertia had set in, and it was hard to make ourselves move. Leaving the known for the unknown was difficult. We were nervous about the Iraq situation—staying in a marina seemed to be more secure—and we were still nervous about our Cape Knidos experience.

I made a quick trip across the marina to consult with Hans and Mandy about the weather—or had I gone to say good-bye? I still wasn't sure when they welcomed me aboard, but they knew. Veteran cruisers, they had gone through this tug of war themselves many times. Quietly they gave me the assurances I had been seeking and told me again about the places I should visit in the Gulf of Fethiye.

Margot had also known and had made use of the time left to say good-bye to Claus. Bob of *Kalona* and the crew of *Et Au Alt* handled lines for us as we got underway and we waved good-bye to the assembled crew of *Mary Lou* as we motored past on our way to the marina entrance. Our trip to Fethiye had begun.

Chapter 5

Fleeing the War

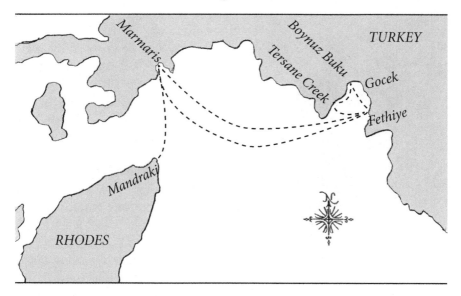

We had thought a lot about where we would go after Marmaris. The weather was beginning to get cold, and we had planned our entire trip around warmth. The Red Sea in winter had been the original goal, but Saddam Hussein had changed all that. Now our thought was to continue south along the Turkish coast.

The Gulf of Fethiye would be first—then Kekova, Finike, and finally a long stretch to Antalya. We had read a lot about Antalya. In addition to the beautiful beaches there were also the fascinating ruins that spanned from the early era of cave dwellers to survivors from Troy to the conquests of Alexander the Great. But it was mainly warmth that we were seeking, and Antalya had taken on a special meaning to us.

There was great excitement when we arrived in the Bay of Fethiye. It had almost become a legend to us. Everyone we had met since we had arrived in Turkey had asked us if we had been in Fethiye yet and then proceeded to give us enticing descriptions of its wonders. "It's a huge bay 10 miles wide and 10 miles deep that is completely protected. No matter how hard the wind blows, there are no waves" or "There are snow-peaked mountains all around and beautiful little anchorages everywhere. Our favorite was Kapi Creek but we also loved Boynuz Buku and there was..." The pages on Fethiye in my

Warm Weather at Last

Heikell were so full of penciled notes about fantastic anchorages that I could hardly read the charts.

As we rounded Kurdoglu Point on the western tip of the bay we could see why people had been so enthusiastic about Fethiye. Snow peaked mountains topped the lush green surroundings and inviting cove after inviting cove opened to our view as we skirted the western shore of the bay. Bloody Marys and our favorite lunch of salad nicoise were part of our celebration. We had finally caught up with warm weather and our spirits soared. The only damper on complete enthusiasm for our new surroundings was Margot's one hundredth request that we go back to Marmaris. While we were all getting a little tired of Margot's obsession with Marmaris, I was happy to note that she was still referring to the port and not directly to Claus. Maybe it would start to recede soon.

We sailed through the narrow passage between the island of Skopea and the eastward curving promontory of Kapu Dag on our way to Bianne and Deeda's favorite spot—Kapi Creek. There we shared the tiny cove with a closed restaurant and a fishing boat that was moored waiting for the next season. The long climb up the hill that protected us from the open water rewarded us with a spectacular view. Warm sun, olive trees everywhere, and wandering goats all contributed to the quiet charm of our little cove.

The next day we experienced the joy of a brisk wind with flat seas as *Captain Spiros* shot across the bay. Hidden behind a large peninsula jutting out from the eastern shore, the town of Fethiye lay waiting. The harbor was very large, peanut shaped, and confusing. We circled twice trying to decide. The fact that no boats were moored in the obvious vacant berths along the quay was troublesome, but none of us wanted to voice our concerns. Our carefully worded questions to the couple on the French sloop were fielded with an equally careful response. We wanted to know if they had chosen to anchor 100 meters offshore because of security concerns, but all we learned was that there was a great vegetable market in progress all day. They seemed pleased, however, when we decided to anchor next to them.

When we dinghied to the main part of town, there was a welcoming party of one. While we were generally very fond of the Turks and found that hospitality when offered was sincere, there was something about the character that helped us with our lines that immediately made us suspicious.

"Hello, you are American?"

His eyes must be very good to have been able to see the American flag we flew on the aft stay of *Captain Spiros*. By this time we had gone to the smallest version on board and didn't bother to unfurl it when it became wrapped around the stay. We tried to avoid him, but it was no use.

"Would you like to come to my restaurant and have tea?"

"No thank you", I replied. "We want to go into town and shop for provisions and we are very busy."

"You need Coca Cola, beer? I get you best price. Okay?"

We temporarily shook him off by entering a shop, but he just waited outside. Carrying groceries was always a source of argument and the children saw the possibility of not having to lug heavy bags of coke and beer to the dinghy. They begged that I give him a chance. When I left the shop and he started his barrage again, I asked him how much he would charge for a case of beer and six liters of coke. His price was reasonable, so I agreed provided he could bring them to our dinghy within an hour.

It was amazing that after seeing so many wonderful open air markets we could still be impressed by another. Instead of piles of produce along the waterfront or along a street, Fethiye had a huge labyrinth of covered stalls that spread through half the city—beautiful tomatoes, peppers, and spices were everywhere. It didn't take long to have our bags full with all we could carry.

Lugging our purchases back to the dinghy we saw three large boxes of coke, a case of beer, and our pesky friend waiting for us. He was all smiles and quoted a figure. I did some quick arithmetic and asked him how he got his total. "I got very good price on the beer, but the coke was expensive—still it is very good buy for you." And with that he started to load the bottles into the dinghy.

"Wait just a minute. The price of the coke is twice what you told me and I said six liters not eighteen."

Not paying any attention to my comments he continued towards the dinghy and only stopped when I blocked his path. "Listen, we appreciate your help, but I don't think we want the coke. Here is your money for the beer. Thank you very much for your help." Charlotte and the children had been quietly loading our stores into the dinghy while this exchange was going on and before he could protest, we left. While he didn't shake his fists, his dark glare left no room for misinterpretation.

On the way back to *Captain Spiros* we stopped by the French boat to chat. When we told them of our bizarre encounter Gerard quickly exclaimed: "So, you met Khadafy!" Francine grimaced and they then both began to tell us all about the strange gypsy who continuously lurks around the waterfront pestering visiting yachtsmen. "We almost warned you but didn't think of it until after you had left. He is a very strange man. I don't know his real name, but everyone calls him Khadafy. We stay away from him."

That night we had a long discussion about the situation in the Persian Gulf and how it affected us. The children listened for the tenth time to the theory Charlotte and I had been putting forth and for the tenth time disagreed. I began: "America is leading the Allies against Iraq and we are one of only a very few American families around. Turkey is an Islamic country and while the people don't seem to side with Saddam Hussein, there could be things going on that we don't understand."

"Yes, and all it takes is one terrorist. Just one terrorist! And who do you think he is going to attack?" Charlotte added. "We are the only Americans around. It's why we keep telling you that you have to be so careful. And Heyward, that's the reason we didn't want you to stay out late with Ahmet in Marmaris. It's just too dangerous!"

This led to the same argument we had had so many times before and that had been an important factor in our decision to leave Marmaris. The children simply refused to recognize that they could possibly be in any danger and refused to heed our warnings about keeping a low profile and staying close to the boat and the marina. Both Charlotte and I knew we would have much better control in places where they didn't have a group of friends and where there would not be any temptation to roam around town at night.

Captain Spiros at Anchor

After provisioning and a little sight seeing, we were ready to continue our exploration of the area. Faithful to the many descriptions we had been given, the bay was flat in spite of brisk winds and our trip across to Tersane Adasi was sheer joy. The French boat that had been next to us in Fethiye was already ensconced at the head of the creek, and it gave us a good feeling to have company. Sheep wandered through old Byzantine ruins that dotted the shore line and we could hear the tinkling of their bells from the cockpit of *Captain Spiros*. Heyward and Alex snorkeled in wet suits while Charlotte and I climbed the peak and watched the sunset.

***

Although we tried to put the Gulf Crisis out of our minds, it was still very much there. The January fifteenth deadline for withdrawal from Kuwait was getting closer and the BBC news could talk of nothing else. But we still hoped against hope that Saddam Hussein would finally give in and that war would be averted. Charlotte and I had discussed contingency plans if war were to break out, but it still seemed so unreal that we hadn't worked out anything definite. About as far as we had gotten was that if war did come, we would probably leave Turkey. But even this wasn't definite and we continued to center our planning on the extended trip along the Turkish coast towards the south. Sipping Piña Coladas in Antalya was the goal.

While we had not yet faced the full reality of the political situation in which we found ourselves, we did begin to take steps to better prepare ourselves for the physical reality of our situation. Our boat was our passport to safety no matter what happened on the political front. But it wasn't going to be a free ride. Knidos had taught us a hard lesson. *Captain Spiros'* hull, sails, and systems were sound and offered protection from the elements. But we were the weak link. No matter how good our equipment, it was always subject to breakdown, and it would be our actions that would make the final difference. While we had told ourselves that if war broke out, we could simply sail to a safer destination, we had finally realized that it was much more complicated. We had seen enough big storms to know that it would take a pretty drastic situation to induce us to leave port in one.

But one thing was certain. We needed to be ready no matter what. The overriding concern and the event that had to be avoided at all costs was "man overboard." At night, falling overboard would almost certainly result in a lost crew member. And even in daylight the odds of recovery weren't very good—particularly in stormy conditions. We had talked the situation through many times and had had some drills, but we were still green. I continued to have nightmares about Knidos and was haunted by the picture of Charlotte hanging on to the lifelines and half out of the boat. What would have happened if she had gone overboard? Would we have been able to recover her?

I insisted that we have more formal training while we were in the protected waters of the bay. Although there was some grumbling, the crew went along with my drills with enthusiasm. "Man overboard, starboard side!" I shouted as I flung Oscar off the starboard bow. Some of Alex's bluster evaporated when he realized how hard it was to bring *Captain Spiros* into the wind, get the sails down, and then retrace the path to Oscar. Margot did not react favorably to my harsh rebuke to her. "Keep your hand pointed at Oscar and don't take your eyes off of him—NO MATTER WHAT. And please be quiet about Marmaris. I'm sick of hearing about it. Particularly now. This is a man overboard drill and it's serious!" Heyward stood on the bow with a boat hook to retrieve the large plastic bag full of empty coke bottles that made up the principal part of Oscar. "Alex, I would give you a three out of ten on your recovery—and just be glad you weren't Oscar. Margot, you are next."

Alex Shows us How

Everybody had their turn and it was good practice. It gave us a little more confidence, but it also served to reemphasize the most important rule on the boat. Don't fall overboard. It's not allowed. Take whatever measures are necessary, but don't go overboard. While I often had trouble getting some concepts across to my highly independently-minded crew, this was one point that was fully understood and accepted.

***

Boynuz Buku was another anchorage that had been highly recommended. We were just dinghying ashore when the boat load of Turkish businessmen arrived to set up their barbecue. Murat invited us to join their party. He was a banker in Gocek, the principal town at the head of the Bay. His friend Chelick was playing an instrument that looked like a cross between a guitar and a lute so Heyward went back to the boat to get his guitar and we joined into the festivities. They offered us grilled fish and grilled chicken which we ate with our fingers and washed down with raki. There were about fifteen of them and they were having a great time. The music and singing got louder and louder and bottles of raki kept coming.

As things seemed to be reaching a climax, a little hairy boar appeared from the woods and began to run about sniffing everything and everyone in sight. The Turks took great delight in chasing the boar about and would roll it over when they could get near enough to touch it. The squealing, the cacophony of the music, and the excited conversations blended into wonderful confusion and we were sad when our friends re-boarded their large fishing boat to return to Gocek.

After a brief visit to Gocek, we headed back to Fethiye. It was January 14—one day before the deadline—and we were getting increasingly nervous. We used the trip across the bay to practice reefing and made fueling our first priority in Fethiye. We had been told by the French boat we had met earlier that getting fuel would be simple, but it was not. I temporarily moored our boat at the town pier we had avoided on our prior visit and phoned the number our French friends had given us to have a truck bring fuel. They said they would be there in an hour so I went back to the boat to wait. In the meantime, Charlotte went to the Fethiye branch of the Turkish Guaranty Bank to get funds. While we were in Bodrum, we had opened up a US Dollar account and used this as our source of money. Given the uncertainty of our situation, we had decided to close the account and keep our cash on board.

Heyward was the first to see him coming down the dock. Khadafy had found us again. "I bet you are waiting for fuel. But they won't come. Everybody is trying to get fuel today." Although I had already arrived at the same conclusion, I didn't like hearing it from him.

"Heyward, you, Alex, and Margot stay with the boat while I go to the filling station to see what I can do."

"Hello my friend. I go with you. I am big help. You will see. We get diesel for your boat!" Khadafy spit out as he stared at me with his beady eyes. Although my initial reaction was to tell him to get lost, I didn't want to leave the boat with him around so I shrugged my shoulders and headed for a cab. He climbed in and we headed for a Mobile filling station on the other side of town. I had to exaggerate a little about how much fuel I needed, but in the end was successful in convincing the owner to dispatch his truck to the yacht pier. Khadafy and I then hopped in the truck.

We topped off both of the 250 litter tanks on *Captain Spiros* and put an additional 70 liters in two jerry cans Alex had purchased earlier. I paid the owner and was about to go back on board when Khadafy approached me with his hand outstretched. "You pay me now. 50,000 Turkish lira please."

I had already decided how I was going to handle this one. "You are my friend. Friends don't charge each other money. I paid for the cab. It was nice of you to come. Thank you." I said and then held out my hand to shake. Khadafy wasn't a happy camper, but I hadn't offered a smaller amount that he could negotiate and he didn't quite know how to react. Before he could say anything I added. "But you are my friend and I want to give you a small gift." I then handed him 5,000 Turkish lira and climbed back on the boat. He gave me a greasy smile and wandered away.

Charlotte had returned during the refueling operation, but we didn't get a chance to talk until after Khadafy had left. "The bank wouldn't give me any money. They absolutely refused to give me any money!"

"What do you mean they wouldn't give you any money?" I asked.

"They said they didn't have any American dollars, but to come back tomorrow and maybe they would have some." Charlotte replied, clearly very upset.

"How about English pounds or German marks?" I asked.

"No western currency at all. The only thing they would give me was Turkish lira."

This was serious. If we returned to Greece, Turkish lira would be useless to us. If we could find anyone who would exchange with us we would be lucky—and even then it would probably be less than fifty cents on the dollar. I went back to the bank with her, but it was useless. We got them to call the Marmaris and Bodrum branches, but the reply was the same. There was no western currency. By this time, it was getting late and there wasn't anything else we could do. We motored back to our old anchorage and mulled over the situation.

We had about a thousand US dollars on board and another thousand dollars in Turkish lira. The boat was fully stocked and fueled. Our water tanks were full. What should we do? Margot's continuous suggestion that we go back to Marmaris was getting tiresome, but it had some merit. We felt very vulnerable in the middle of Fethiye, and knowing Khadafy was at large didn't make us feel any better. While he was probably harmless himself, we didn't like the idea of him blabbing around town that there was an American family living on the big white sailboat in the harbor.

In Marmaris, on the other hand, we would be in the middle of a large marina with very tight security. As we talked things through, we decided that if there were no withdrawal from Kuwait the next day, we would head back to Marmaris and decide what to do from there. In the meantime, we would try the bank again in the morning.

Our French friends were back in Fethiye and said they planned to stay even if war did break out. They acknowledged, however, that they would feel more exposed if they were American. They were sympathetic with our plight at the bank and suggested that we might get our way if we made a big stink and caused a scene. I was sure that the bank had some western currency in spite of their claims to the contrary and decided to follow their advice.

We were at the Guaranty Bank when it opened. "I'm very sorry, but we do not have any American dollars" the teller told me very politely.

"Please take me to the manager; I would like to talk with him." I said in a loud voice.

"I'm sorry, sir, but he is busy and..."

"I don't care if he is busy or not, I am going to see him" I said and headed to the office where a clean-cut man in a conservative business suit was talking on the phone. "Excuse me, but your teller is telling me that your bank doesn't have any money" I said in a very loud voice. By this time we were attracting a good deal of attention and the manager realized he wasn't going to be able to ignore us. He quickly terminated his phone conversation and invited us into his office.

At first I thought he was going to help, but then it became obvious he just wanted to get rid of us. "What do you mean you don't have any money? My account guarantees US dollars. I gave your bank US dollars to open it. Now I want them back. Is your bank now going to cheat me out of my money?" While most of the crowd that had gathered around probably couldn't understand the words, they could certainly follow the drift.

"I am very sorry Mr. Coleman, but we don't have any American dollars left in this branch. The situation in Kuwait is causing many problems."

"How about German marks, or British pounds, or Italian lira, or even Spanish pesetas?"

"No Mr. Coleman, only Turkish Lira."

"How about other branches. Can I get ANY western currency at ANY Guaranty Bank?"

The conversation was useless and I knew it. The only thing I was accomplishing was creating a scene and drawing further attention to the only American family in Fethiye. I did get the banker to call Istanbul and Marmaris and extracted a promise from him that funds in US dollars would be available to us in Marmaris on the next day. But both Charlotte and I realized that the promise was nothing more than a ploy to get us out of his office. We would just have to make do with what we had.

The bank experience along with the fact that Saddam Hussein had not yet withdrawn from Kuwait decided it. By noon we were leaving Fethiye Harbor on our way back to Marmaris.

***

This trip was different from any we had made before. A noon departure meant arrival into Marmaris well after dark. It was drizzling rain and we had not received a morning forecast. We were breaking two of our most important rules. But there was excitement in action and everyone was in high spirits—particularly Margot. Heyward and Alex were also pleased to be heading back to their old friends. We joked about being war refugees but it wasn't very funny. Charlotte and I tried to impress on the children the seriousness of the situation and that they could no longer freely roam about Marmaris, but they were still reluctant to acknowledge any real danger.

The weather deteriorated and changed from drizzles to a constant downpour. I had charts out and studied the approach into Marmaris for the tenth time. We would lose daylight well before approaching the two islands that spread across the entrance of the bay and I would have to use lights and radar to thread my way through the narrow channel. Up until this point the radar I had spent so much time and money on acquiring had seemed like a luxury. Now it was indispensable.

If I had not been through the channel twice before in daylight, I don't think I would have tried it. But when we had left Marmaris a little over a week earlier, I had taken careful mental notes thinking that maybe I might have to return at night. Now I was wrestling with two concerns. The Turkish navigation lights were spotty at best. I had noticed many times that lights that were marked on charts were simply not there or were not working. The flashing red light on the southern tip of Keci Adasi and the flashing white light on the northwestern tip of Nimara Adasi should define the channel, but would they be working? If they were working would we be able to see them? The rain was varying from a steady stream to short bursts of heavy downpours. Suppose we had a downpour as we approached the channel and couldn't see the lights?

Before, the radar had been a toy. Now it was critical. I finally learned the importance of the "rain" button. Pushing this several times got rid of the false readings caused by rain, but also reduced the clarity of true objects. I learned empirically that during the heavy downpours the only way I could clear the screen of the rain was by setting the "rain" so high that the screen became blank and we couldn't see anything. Later I would learn how to make this delicate adjustment and retain some ability to detect other objects, but for the time being I had to face the harsh reality—during the worst downpours we were blind.

As we approached it became completely dark, but I could clearly follow the contour of the coast on radar. A white light ahead marked the spot where we would need to turn north to head towards Marmaris bay. Once we made that turn, we would need to find the flashing red light on the southern end of Keci Adasi. While I was glued to the radar, everyone else was out on deck bundled in foul weather gear with eyes straining. We had all seen the rocky shore around both islands and knew the consequences of missing the channel. The rain was only a drizzle and I could see the islands ahead on radar. But the image on the radar screen was not clear enough to pick out the channel between the two islands—they appeared as one large mass. "We are getting close. It should be just off the port bow. Look hard." I rattled off as I continued to try to adjust the radar.

Silence and then from Alex: "I see it. Red. Yes, it's flashing."

"Good. Call out to me when it comes on" I said looking at my watch. Alex complied while I timed.

"Good, two seconds between flashes. That's Keci Adasi. Yes, I can see the channel now on radar."

Then from Heyward "I see the white light. It's just off the starboard bow." The rest was easy. We glided across the open harbor and into the well lit marina. Claus was waiting at the dock when we moored.

***

We met long into the night with Bob, Bianne and Deeda, and Hans and Mandy. They were concerned, but were going to stay in Turkey. Bob's morning ham radio conference with Rhodes had produced distressing news. *Searcher* had reported that Greek officials had visited each of the boats in Mandraki Harbor to see how many beds they had on board in case they were needed for wounded from the war. Bob was convinced that Marmaris was a safer place to be than Rhodes. Helmut had left for Mandraki that morning to make his monthly pork run, but had planned to stay in Rhodes only long enough to stock up. Bob hoped he would be back the next morning with news of the situation in Mandraki.

The discussion turned onto what exactly was the deadline. Jan. 15 was the last day for withdrawal. Did that mean action would take place on Jan. 16? And, if so, when did Jan. 16 start? Washington time or Kuwait time? It was 10:00 P.M. on Jan. 15 in Marmaris and the only thing that was completely clear was that Saddam Hussein had not withdrawn. What now?

When we awoke the next morning Charlotte and I were still undecided. Leaving Turkey meant making the short sail over to Rhodes, but we didn't like the sound of what Bob had been hearing from *Searcher*. If there was really panic in Rhodes, perhaps we were better off in the security of the Marmaris Marina. But the fact remained that Turkey was an Islamic country and our country was about to go to war with an Islamic country.

We decided to give the bank at Marmaris a try. Maybe the promise was going to be fulfilled. If so, it would give us much greater financial security and would also give us more confidence in Turkey. The bank had no western currency and had no idea when they would have some again. And no, they had not received any special instructions from Fethiye concerning my account. On the way out of the bank Charlotte looked at me and said: "This is crazy. Let's get out of Turkey. Now!"

"I agree. Let's get back to the boat and start the paperwork." Checking out was easier than checking in and it only took two hours to turn in our transit log and clear customs. The officials couldn't have been nicer and each of them urged us to change our minds and stay. But they understood why we wanted to leave and helped us with our checkout. As we started stowing the boat for sea, I watched Claus and Margot staring at each other and talking. They had both been so animated when we had arrived last night. I felt so sorry for them that I didn't ask Margot to help with our final preparations.

Bob came over and gave us the results of his morning ham conference. *Searcher* was going to stay in Rhodes. His correspondents in Monastir, Tunisia were also going to say put. Helmut was going to return to Marmaris so Bob asked him to buy five extra kilos of bacon for him—it might be a long spell without pork. Bianne and Deeda and Hans and Mandy were also going to stay. Ken and Lisa were thinking about leaving, but their boat was out of water undergoing repairs from a recent grounding. It looked like we were the only ones leaving, but we had thought it through and were determined to go.

By 1:30 P.M. we were ready to depart. There was no rain, but the weather looked uncertain. Unless the wind fully cooperated, we chanced a night entrance into Mandraki. It would have been more prudent to wait until morning, but we had made up our minds. At 2:00 P.M. we sailed out of Marmaris bay for the last time. We continued to listen to the hourly BBC news reports, but no one seemed to know what was happening. The only thing that was certain was that the world was in turmoil.

Chapter 6
Our Home in Rhodes

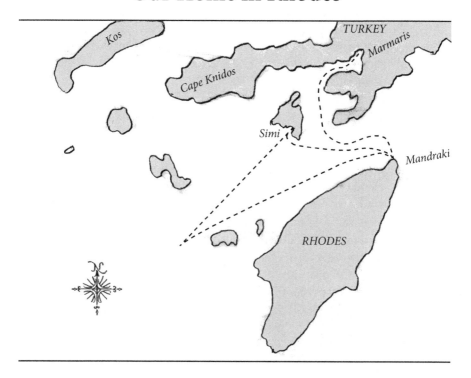

The weather cooperated sufficiently to get us in sight of the headlands of Rhodes before dark. This was helpful because it gave me a chance to start trying to read the coastline while there was still a little light left. But our final approach was going to have to be in darkness. It was a clear night and I could see the contour of the coast very well—but I needed to pick out the entrance of Mandraki harbor. I could see lights and a mammoth structure that I was pretty sure were the castle and walled city. Mandraki should be to the right. But to be absolutely sure I needed to sight the flashing green light that marked the right or northern end of the harbor entrance. A partially submerged jetty extended out and to the north of this point so it was critical to not go beyond the light.

Everybody was straining their eyes, but still no light. Charlotte was getting nervous and interjected: "I just don't understand why they put green lights on the right. Haven't they ever heard about *red right returning*?" It was confusing—like driving on the wrong side of the road in England. In the Mediterranean and for that matter throughout Europe, navigation lights are the opposite as in the US and red right returning becomes green right returning.

But my main concern was in finding the green light. I saw a flashing white light that probably indicated the southern end of the harbor, but still no green! The shore was getting very close and I was just about to turn away when Margot shouted:

"There's a light, but it's red. See. Just next to the white light."

A red light? Disorientation set in and I turned *Captain Spiros* to parallel the coast. Then Charlotte announced a tower in exactly the direction I had expected to see the green light.

A quick look at the chart and suddenly the puzzle unraveled. The tower was where the green light was supposed to be. It was simply burned out. And the red light marked the left side of the entrance to the inner harbor. And, yes, there was a green light just next to it coming into view. The left and right hand sides of the inner harbor opening became clear. I cursed the slovenliness of the Greeks—it wasn't the first time I had found a navigation light that was out or not in place—but it was the first time it had put the safety of my boat and my family in danger.

Mandraki Harbor Entrance

We dropped our sails, headed into the outer harbor, and then turned south towards the inner harbor. The Colossus of Rhodes had been destroyed by an earthquake many centuries before, but we tried to imagine what it had looked like as we sailed between the two jetties across which it had stood back in 300 BC.

***

The horseshoe shaped harbor was packed full of boats and at first we didn't see any free spots. But after circling twice we saw one empty slot along the jetty on the eastern side of the entrance. We approached cautiously and shouted for advice. A figure that we couldn't quite make out replied that it was a good spot, but that we should not drop our anchor too far out as there was a large heavy chain across the harbor—I took his advice and started backing towards the spot. The figure waiting to help us was Helmut. Both he and Brigitte were full of news. No, they weren't nervous about Rhodes and the war. But they planned to return to Marmaris in the morning. They had a very good rate at the Marmaris marina and preferred the protection it afforded their boat to that of Mandraki.

At about this time, two guards with machine guns came up and asked to see our papers. "You will please to check in with the Port Police and Customs in the morning. You can stay here tonight." They then left. Very kind of them, I thought. If they had wanted us to leave at night they would have had to use their guns to convince me.

"The security is very tight" Helmut explained. "The entire harbor is cordoned off and they are checking passports in and out. Don't worry. You shouldn't have any trouble getting a transit log tomorrow." There was still no news from the Gulf. We were all very tired and turned in soon after we had finished securing the boat. It had been quite a day.

We woke up to the 6:OO A.M. BBC news. The war was on. Over 400 sorties had been launched on Iraq during the night. We learned what surgical bombing was all about. By the time the 6:00 A.M. news was over, it was time for the 7:00 A.M. news to begin, and we heard continuous news on the war throughout the morning.

Daylight had yielded another surprise—and this one was pleasant. Rhodes was beautiful. We were moored just to the left of an ancient fort that occupied a circular promontory on the northeast corner of the harbor and on top of which was the white light that had been so important to us the previous evening. To the south and along the eastern sea wall of the harbor were three old and very pretty stone windmills. But the spectacular view was to the south-west. The ancient castle that had been the home of the Knights of St. John for over 200 years was in the center of a walled city.

Our first priority was to check into the country. As soon as we thought there would be a reasonable chance of finding anyone, we made the trip to the south end of the harbor where we were presented with the daunting sight of a World War I tank and soldiers with guns everywhere. But the soldiers were friendly and we were glad for the security. We then walked through the old city and entered the commercial harbor where we found the port police office and began the process of obtaining our transit log.

Customs, the final step in the process, took us back across the commercial harbor, back through the old city, and to the end of the quay that formed the west side of Mandraki harbor. Afterwards we headed to the large open market just off the quay for souvlaki and beer. In spite of the bureaucracy and in spite of the Greeks, it was nice to be back. The souvlaki tasted great.

Our immediate thought was to continue west. But since we had left Fethiye the weather had become steadily worse. When we had crossed from Marmaris, the wind had been quite strong and now was blowing near gale force. From what we could piece together from the morning weather forecasts, the whole Eastern Mediterranean was full of storms. For the time being we had little choice but to sit tight.

We spent a great deal of time devouring the collection of magazines and newspapers we had collected from the town square just across the harbor. The "Herald", the "London Times", "USA Today", the "British Telegraph", the "Wall Street Journal"—we couldn't get enough. Alex was even spending his allowance to get the latest copy of "Time" or "US News and World Reports" to study the detailed articles on missions, aircraft, and weapons.

As we settled in, our concerns about our safety while in Rhodes began to diminish, but our family at home had other thoughts. We were convinced that the weather posed a much more real threat to us than any effects from the Gulf War, but it was hard to convey this to concerned relatives halfway around the world.

The morning of January 20, we had long discussions with neighboring boats about our situation. On our starboard side, a Dutchman, Hans, and his American wife Marge were very nervous about the war and wanted to head west as soon as possible. Their steel boat was made in Holland and was perfection. Alex spent hours admiring the boat and milking information from Hans about every detail. *Alk* was a good example of what the combination of sound construction, a practical layout, and hard work on the part of the owner could yield.

To port there was a delightful French family with whom we immediately became friends. Armand, Genevieve and their young son Benjamin nursed their spacious ketch during the winter and then took charter parties for week long cruises along the Turkish coast in the spring and summer. They were not at all nervous about Turkey, but chose to stay in Rhodes because the mooring fees were very low, and they wanted to be close to Rhodes' Camper Nicholson Office that they used as their central point to coordinate charters

While the rumors about poison gas, nuclear bombs, and terrorism were running rampant, we felt fairly safe where we were. Although the Greeks were extraordinarily concerned about terrorism and had beefed up security everywhere, their main concern was Athens because it had the highest PLO population outside the Middle East. The security measures they were taking around Mandraki and around the commercial harbor seemed to be adequate for the situation in Rhodes.

But the dangers were real. Israel had been bombed three times and no one knew if they would retaliate or not. And then what would be the response from Baghdad if they did retaliate? No matter how much we discussed the situation, it was impossible to arrive at any clear conclusions. All of us would have loved to return to Turkey. We had had a wonderful time during our stay there and wanted to see more. But Charlotte and I were against doing anything that put us closer to the war and we were also very concerned about the children's failure to understand the seriousness of the situation and their unwillingness to take proper precautions. Staying in Rhodes was a possibility and if it hadn't been for the concern of our families we might have chosen this alternative. Putting it all together we decided to move on—but only if we could do so safely.

Charts came out and we benefited from the collective experience of both Armand and Hans. Back to Athens through the Cyclades, a route beset with a myriad of lee shores and poorly protected harbors, was out of the question. Staying in Rhodes would be safer. We would need to head for the open seas of the central Mediterranean and the obvious destination was Malta.

But how would we get there? Island to island with stops in between or a straight shot? With our level of experience, I was not about to undertake a 1,000 mile trip in the middle of winter all in one leg. It would require at least a week and maybe more. And during the trip we would be virtually guaranteed of encountering at least one gale.

Island by island and waiting out bad weather between stops was the other possibility. But the charts presented nothing but bad alternatives. Skirting the southern coast of Crete was a bad choice because of the very poor protection afforded by its ports along that coast. The northern coast was better, but not great. The islands between Rhodes and Crete were also poorly protected. Khalki, Saros, Karpathos, and Kasos all held the lowest rank Heikell awards for shelter. I had already seen how powerful the winds become in winter and had no desire to ride out a gale in a poorly protected anchorage wondering when the anchor was going to drag and allow our boat to be smashed up against a rocky shoreline.

Even if we could safely make it past Crete, there was still the 600 mile stretch between the western end of Crete and Malta. A strong gale from the north during that leg would not only bring discomfort and danger, but also could push us onto the coast of Libya where at a minimum our boat would be confiscated. Winter was the problem. In the summer, a direct sail or island hopping would have been easy and probably a lot of fun. But winter in the Mediterranean is not fun. In ancient times, mariners seldom ventured out during the winter months and in Greece there were actually laws against sailing between November and March.

How about getting a seasoned skipper to help us with a direct sail to Malta? Our neighbors agreed it was feasible, but none of them thought it prudent. I decided to call Minolis the following day to see what he thought about the idea and to see if Manfred would be available. In spite of other shortcomings, Minolis was a very accomplished sailor and I valued his opinion. And all of us had developed a great deal of confidence in Manfred. If Manfred was available and willing to undertake the trip, we thought it was worth a try.

The post office was just across the harbor from us and close to the center square where we bought our newspapers and munched on gyros. It had phone booths and was a good place to make a call. By some fluke Minolis answered the first time I called: "Hallow Heywort. Did you visit the places I tell you? How is *Captain Spiros* ? You are lucky to have such a fine boat!"

I resisted the temptation to complain about the faulty steering column and instead turned the conversation to the effect the war was having in Athens and more specifically what he thought about crossing the Mediterranean at this time of year.

"Everybody here is panic. The airport, you wouldn't believe. Everybody crazy. Soldiers with guns, police stop all the people. But the war is no here. Crazy, crazy, everybody crazy. So, you want to cross the Mediterranean? I tell you *Captain Spiros* she's a good boat. It's not a problem; you just have to be careful."

"Minolis, we think that if we make the trip to Malta, we would like to have an experienced skipper with us. We were thinking about asking Manfred. Do you know how we can reach...?"

Minolis stopped me in mid sentence and replied in rapid fire: "Manfred is very busy. He is working on a boat for the Chinese and then he goes to the United States to see about his boat." And then, a little mellower: "Besides Manfred is not good for skipper to you. I have a very good friend who sailed with me in the race across the Atlantic. You remember, I told you all about my race?"

I remembered all too well the endless series of tales Minolis had told me about his trip. He had chosen a northern route to pick up heavier winds and had a near disaster about half way across. A knock down wind had heeled his boat over so far that his drinking water and fuel had been contaminated by salt water leaking in through the vents. He had only managed to avert aborting his trip by talking a Greek tanker into putting fresh water and diesel fuel in jerry cans and floating them over to him in a life raft.

"My friend Demetri is a very good sailor. He was with me on the trip. I give you his phone number." I then told Minolis about the steering column, but he didn't express much interest and we ended the conversation amicably.

It took a couple more trips to the post office, but later that day I was finally successful in reaching Demetri. Yes, he would be interested in making the trip, but there was a small problem. He had to be in Athens in two weeks for a wedding, but he thought we could complete the trip by then. I agreed to call him the next day to confirm the details.

While the debate was over and we had decided to chance a crossing, there were some pretty varied feelings on the subject. Heyward and Alex, the macho side of the crew, were both in favor of making the trip—Heyward purely for the danger and excitement, Alex because he still wanted to cross the Atlantic and knew that if we didn't get across the Mediterranean soon we would miss the season. Margot was at the other end of the spectrum. She had not acquired the sailing bug and absolutely abhorred the idea of spending a week or more bouncing around on rough seas. And, of course, there was Marmaris—which we still heard about from her at least five times a day. Charlotte wanted to leave Rhodes, wanted to be in Malta, but was not at all enthusiastic about the interim. She wanted to be told that the trip wouldn't be bad, but all the empirical data she had amassed since leaving Aegina three months earlier suggested otherwise.

A phone call to Demetri the next morning completed the arrangements. He would arrive by plane the following morning and we would depart immediately, weather permitting. I told him that since war had broken out we had been unable to get any forecasts at all. He promised to get one just before leaving Athens. The trip was on!

Charlotte and the children spent the day topping off our supplies—particularly lots of salty crackers and snacks. I went over to the largest chandlery on the island, Camper Nichols, and bought the sextant I had been examining for the last three days. While my Satnav should be adequate for the trip, I wanted a back up, and our long trip gave me the excuse I had been looking for to make the purchase. There was lots of excitement that night, and we went to bed early hoping for a third consecutive day of sunshine.

Even before going up on deck I could hear it from our cabin. Wind howling in the rigging. It was from the northwest—just where we would be heading—and strong. Demetri arrived at 7:00 A.M. Tall, young, and confident, Demetri exuded competence. His neatly monogrammed blue duffel bag contained the best foul weather gear we had seen. When he arrived, the wind was between a force 5 and 6. He had forgotten to get the weather forecast before leaving Athens, but didn't seem overly concerned about the situation. He checked our systems, helped stow some items, and waited to see what happened to the weather.

It got worse, not better and by 11:00 was up to a force 7 and still on our nose. By some incredible logic that he claimed was based on a hunch that the wind would shift once we left Rhodes, but was probably based more on his Athens wedding commitment, he suggested we check out of Greece and get underway. By an equally incredible decision making process, we agreed with him and said goodbye to our friends while he walked our passports and transit log through the proper authorities. I was amazed that he could accomplish this so quickly, and shortly after noon we headed *Captain Spiros* back out between the two jetties that had greeted our arrival almost a week earlier.

It started off bad and got worse. After we rounded the northern tip of the island and settled onto our course we found that our wind direction measurements had been correct. Right on our nose. But Demetri, racing sailor that he was, trimmed, tugged, and fiddled with every line on the boat until he had flat full sails and the boat perfectly balanced. He showed us lines we didn't even know existed and taught us how to get the last bit of speed possible from our craft. But talented as he was, Demetri couldn't alter the physics of the situation, and the fact was that our desired course and the direction from which the wind was howling were one and the same.

Modern sailboats are designed to sail close hauled on courses that can take them on tight tacks that are close to the wind direction. And *Captain Spiros* was such a modern sailboat. Demetri had us trimmed and was able to achieve a course only 40 degrees off the wind.

But Mother Nature, the Mediterranean, and Neptune have tricks of their own, and sailing hard into a force 7 wind we received a good demonstration. "Bam, Bam, Bam" as our hull pounded the short steep seas.

Setting out for Malta

We felt the hull shudder and watched the knot meter drop to almost zero as the head on collision with each wall of water sent foaming spray over the decks to drench us.

My little calculator didn't have trigonometric functions and besides I didn't feel well enough to go below decks to calculate the speed made good over our plotted course. But a pretty good guess would have been something less than two knots. And using our motor was out of the question for such a long trip. Experience had taught us that the magnitude and direction of the wind could last one, two days, or even a week.

Margot tried hard not to spill the yellow pail she held between her knees and we tried not to catch her with our harnesses as we stepped over her prone body. Charlotte was white as a sheet but through some kind of miraculous self-control did not vocalize the worries that were written across her face. Alex, who normally would have been dogging Demetri's every move and showering him with a thousand questions was strangely quiet. He was trying hard not to watch Margot and the yellow bucket. Even macho Heyward didn't seem to be having a very good time.

Four hours after leaving Mandraki Demetri and I went below for a conference. "Heywort, I think your crew is no very experience. Maybe going to Malta is not a good idea."

"Demetri, I think my crew is fine, but maybe leaving with a gale on our nose wasn't a very good idea."

Demetri realized it wasn't going to be quite as easy as he had hoped.

"I tell you what Heywort. If we go back now you no have to pay me for anything—just my plane ticket for coming."

Demetri was being more of a statesman than I had expected. He was actually accepting some fault for what had obviously been a very poor decision. I began to wonder if he was all Greek. Softening a little, I offered: "Listen, I think it's too long a trip to try to return to Mandraki and make it in before dark. Simi is a lot closer and it's a nice downwind sail. Why not stop there for the night and we can make a leisurely trip back tomorrow with the wind behind us the whole way? Maybe you could teach us some techniques on reefing and trimming our sails. If we do this, I will pay you for the day and you could get a plane back tomorrow night."

Demetri liked the idea and it was met with enthusiastic acceptance by the entire crew. Within five minutes we had turned around and were headed towards Panormittis on the southwestern tip of Simi. The change was instant. It was like the wind had suddenly stopped blowing and the waves had receded to half their size. We even noted, to our amazement, that the sun was shining and it wasn't very cold. Alex began to rattle off a long list of the things he wanted to try on our trip the next day, Charlotte started talking about what she would fix us for supper, and even Margot started to perk up and look around. It had been the right decision.

It was almost dark when we passed Seskli Island and began to approach Panormittis, but Demetri claimed to know the small bay very well and said that even in pitch black dark he would be comfortable entering. This assurance along with a clear view of the light that marked the eastern side of the bay entrance allayed my concerns and Demetri skillfully guided us into the bay.

After circling the bay, Demetri chose a spot and then went forward to help Alex with the anchor while I took the wheel. I was busy lining up a tree with the monastery on shore to check that I had taken all speed off the boat when I heard a loud shout from Alex:

"No Demetri, don't...there is a problem with the anchor winch..."

The rest of his sentence was drowned out by a deafening noise that sounded like someone had thrown a shovel full of gravel into a washing machine and then put it on spin cycle. "Clak........clak.....clak...clak...clak... clak claaaaaaaaaaaaaaaaaaaaaaaaaaaaaaaaaaaaaaaaaaaaaaak." And then I could hear Alex again.

"Dad, put it in forward, go forward! We are going to lose the anchor!"

I eased it into forward, turned the wheel over to Charlotte, and went up to the bow to see what was happening. I looked in the anchor box with horror. All the chain had run out past the anchor winch and the only thing keeping it attached to the boat was a light piece of nylon line that was tied to the last link. The sole purpose of this line was to provide a means of cutting the anchor loose in an emergency. Any strain on the line would result in the loss of our anchor and 80 meters of heavy chain—and then we really would have an emergency on our hands.

Alex didn't need to tell me what had happened. I could easily surmise. Demetri had become frustrated with Alex's slow release of the anchor by winding it out with the electric winch and, despite Alex's warning that the winch was faulty, had released the clutch. The noise we had heard was a loud argument between the square end teeth on the winch end of the clutch and the square end teeth on the release end as they ground against each other during the uncontrolled spinning of the then freed windlass. The chain had continued out past the windlass and was only saved by the emergency nylon line.

Alex wisely remained silent and Demetri preserved his dignity by horsing in the anchor line and re-engaging it in the winch. He then reasserted his credibility by showing us a technique to keep us from swinging on our anchor.

The wind was strong so we needed a lot of chain to hold us firmly in place. But the bay was narrow and if the wind were to shift during the night, we could become dangerously close to shallow water. Demetri's technique was interesting. He rigged a large galvanized shackle on our spare anchor and then attached this to the anchor chain forward of the winch. He then tied a heavy nylon line to the shackle and used it to let the spare anchor slide down the anchor chain. Once on the bottom the spare anchor would prevent any movement of the chain to the right or left and would thereby prevent any significant shift in our position. The nylon line could then be used to retrieve the Danforth when we were ready to pull up the main anchor. I was impressed. It was a Greek modification of the Glennon technique that Jean-Louis had so proudly shown to us in his old version of *La Bible*.

Charlotte outdid herself for dinner and we sat down to half of the supplies we had stocked up for the long voyage. Maybe this was her insurance policy that we wouldn't change our minds in the morning. Everybody was completely revived and we talked long into the night. Alex asked question after question ranging from his pet project of lazy jacks to how to rig our spinnaker pole. Demetri regaled us with stories of his Atlantic crossing with Minolis and confirmed much of what Minolis had told us previously—except the person assuming the role of superman seemed to take a subtle change in his version. Heyward played his guitar and Margot quietly filched wine when she thought none of us were looking.

Charlotte and I brought out our tape recorder and played back the Greek version of some of our earlier weather forecasts. Demetri translated and we took copious notes. After about an hour of this we had learned enough to be able to understand the major points of the forecast in Greek. Later, this would prove to be of great value.

When it was time to go to bed, Charlotte and I climbed into our front end loader and were instantly asleep. But not for long. I was pulled out of a deep sleep by a loud, low-pitched grinding sound that made the entire hull resonate. It went on for two or three seconds, stopped for about an equal amount of time, and then repeated. By the end of the first grind, Charlotte was also awake and we stared at each other poised to leap out of bed to face the emergency. Before we had a chance to draw ourselves out of our shelf it suddenly occurred to me what was happening.

"It's Demetri's rig! The wind has shifted and the shackle is running up and down the chain." I then looked out our porthole and confirmed my theory. I could gauge our swing by the shifting of the lights on shore and the swings coincided with the periods of grinding. "If it gets too bad, Demetri can get up and fix it" I complained and we both went back to sleep. So much for Greek innovation.

Returning from Aborted Malta Trip

The next day the conditions were about the same, but we had the wind on our stern and the sailing was great. We practiced going between second and third reefs and did it without coming into the wind. Demetri showed us how to rig the spinnaker pole and we reached speeds up to 15 knots. We experimented with various methods of hoving to—a maneuver that entails lashing the wheel and rigging the sails in such a manner that the boat moves very slowly forward in a controlled manner despite very high winds.

But most important, we got Demetri to help us rig an effective preventer that would keep us from having an uncontrolled jibe in down wind sailing. We told Demetri all about our mishap off Cape Knidos and practiced controlled jibe after controlled jibe so that we could avoid its ever happening again. By noon we were getting near to Mandraki so we called an end to our drills and settled down to enjoy the remainder of our exhilarating sail.

Demetri was at the wheel as the force 7 wind propelled us closer and closer to Mandraki. Even though he was skipper, I normally would have been watching closer, but for some reason I wasn't. Instead I was leaning back in my seat, relaxing, and enjoying leaving the worries to Demetri. But as the outline of the harbor and surrounding buildings began to take shape, I suddenly snapped out of my lethargy.

"Demetri, shouldn't we be getting the sails down?" I asked as I went aft and started the motor.

Our normal procedure was to start the motor and get sails down and furled well before entering harbors or restricted maneuvering areas. But Demetri looked unconcerned and didn't seem in any hurry to carry out the maneuver. Whether he was going to try to show us how macho racing sailors bring their boats into harbor in the middle of a gale or whether he was just asleep at the switch, I wasn't sure. But the coast was getting close and we had a very powerful wind behind us pushing. I was just about to insist that he get our sails down when he issued a low key order to Heyward to furl in the jib.

Heyward inserted the handle into the winch and started to crank. He cranked and he cranked, but a strange thing seemed to be happening. The jib wasn't coming in. "Its really getting hard to turn. Alex, come help." Precious seconds slipped by while Alex tried to help Heyward

Suddenly I realized what I should have figured out in the beginning. "The reefing line is jammed" I shouted as I ran to the bow to see if I could free it. But the enormous strain exerted by the winch had jammed the line so tightly between the reel and its housing that I couldn't free it even after Heyward had released the tension.

Things started to happen very fast. Demetri now fully realized the magnitude of his misjudgment, but it was too late. We were wing and wing with the wind square on our stern and hurling us towards the stone jetties along the shore at 12 knots. By this time the rocks were only about a hundred yards away.

Demetri had no choice. He jibed the boat. As the massive boom went wildly crashing overhead, Demetri gallantly tried to prevent the main sheet from wrapping around the steering column. He almost lost his hand in the process. But, unfortunately, the inevitable happened.

Charlotte emerged from the cabin to see the steering wheel flopping around on the deck, Demetri on the bow straining to pull the jib down from its roller reefing track, and Alex in the process of lowering the mainsail— all of this with no steering and our boat heading straight for the rocks. Fortunately, after our experience at Cape Knidos, all of us knew what to do— in a way Charlotte wasn't even surprised.

I regained control of the vessel temporarily with the auto pilot, and then Heyward and Margot helped me put the broken steering column in place so that we regained manual control. Somehow Demetri and Alex got the sails down in very short order and with only about 50 feet between us and the spray-soaked jetty we turned the boat around and entered port.

We limped back to our old slot between Hans and Armand and sat there shaking. I could hardly talk. Cape Knidos seemed like child's play in comparison. We had come within an inch of smashing our boat to pieces. Visions of the hapless gulet in Bodrum came to mind. Both Hans and Armand had seen the whole thing and kindly allowed us time to collect our thoughts before helping us sort out the pieces.

One thing was certain. We were in Rhodes for the war. It would have taken a scud missile attack before we would have even considered leaving again. It was also pretty clear what our next project would be. None of us were in a very good mood.

I was still in a state of shock when Hans came aboard with his tools and began to disassemble the mess that had been our steering column. Demetri looked very contrite and tried to help Hans. Ever alert to try to shift the blame Demetri examined the mangled base of the column. His face lit up. "This has been broken before!"

The Broken Steering Column

I had wondered how my reinforced sleeve could have broken so easily and looked at the piece Demetri held in his hand. The sleeve hadn't broken. The break was below the new sleeve. I took the tube from Demetri and examined it. "You are right, it has been broken before. Damn Kiriacoulis and damn Minolis. The column had been broken not just once but twice. And they covered it up and never told me a damn thing."

Now with more confidence Demetri started to pick up steam. "The column never should have broken, we should have been okay It was the fault of the...

Something inside me snapped and I interrupted Demetri in mid sentence: "Demetri, I warned you about the problem of a jibe and told you what had happened to us at Cape Knidos. You had no business..." But I stopped. Chewing Demetri out wasn't going to fix my steering column, and I was so depressed I simply didn't have the energy.

Hans finished removing the binnacle from the column and removed the base from the deck. All three of us stood looking at the pieces. After a long silence I said to Demetri: "I told you I would pay you for one day and I will. But I expect your help in getting a new steering column. I want you to take the measurements back to Athens with you on the plane tonight and get Costa to make me a new column out of stainless steel. We will use the base to make a template and we will measure the height and diameter before you leave."

To Demetri's credit he immediately agreed to my requests. In spite of his bluster and his Greek instinct to save his pride, he was a seaman at heart and fully understood the position he had put us in. I knew I could trust him to help fix the damage he had caused. We made the template, took the measurements, and an hour later Demetri was gone.

This was the absolute low point of the trip for me. We had almost lost our boat—she would have been dashed to pieces in minutes on the jetty just like the gulet in Bodrum. We were completely immobile so it was impossible to leave Rhodes no matter how bad the war became. But, worst of all, I knew from past experience how difficult it was and how long it was going to take me to repair the steering column.

Hans and Armand tried to cheer us up but without much success. It was with heavy hearts and badly shaken nerves that we all finally climbed into bed. I lay there listening to the wind howling through the rigging until I finally fell into a deep sleep.

***

The next morning I tried to sort things out. Several things seemed clear. One, we were in Rhodes to stay and we should just as well make the best of it. When people had told us they were wintering in such and such a place, we had never understood why they wanted to quit exploring. Now we knew. Two, I was going to have to fix the steering column myself. The last time it had broken I had relied on Suleman to fix it. While I had saved myself some time and effort I had wound up with a second-rate job. In fact it was that way with most things on the boat. No one was going to give the same level of attention to my boat that I could give it. In the end the problem was going to come back to me anyway so I just well struggle with it in the beginning.

This was a very important lesson and one that I was to face throughout the trip. I had to be able to depend on myself and my crew for the final solution for any problem that arose. Hiring Demetri had been a mistake. We had been completely competent to take the boat anywhere it could safely go. The fact of the matter was that our trip was not prudent under the circumstances, and hiring a professional skipper had lulled me into making a decision that I had known was wrong.

The fact that I needed to fix the problem upset me more than anything else to do with the accident. After our extensive refit in Kalamaki and the additional work in Bodrum I was thoroughly sick of working on the boat. The thought of ripping out the stern and crawling into inaccessible spaces to first remove and then reinstall the appropriate mechanisms made me feel ill. When was the work going to end?

I explored around the harbor and obtained advice from German, Italian, Danish, and Norwegian boats—and most of it was pretty good.

The owner of a Danish boat had a small machine shop on board and could fabricate small components. A German on another boat, Alli, had a pretty good welding shop. Gerry on *Sundance* knew about all the major repair facilities in the city and was a wealth of information on tips on how to prevent corrosion and electrolysis.

As I got further into the problem and how to solve it I began to feel better. But it was my long talk with Martino that finally pulled me out of my slump. Although he was over 60 and looked like he would have had trouble fixing a flat tire on a bicycle, Martino had just removed and completely overhauled the diesel engine on his boat. He was proud of himself because, in spite of not knowing much about engines, he had done all of the work himself.

If he could do it, why couldn't I? And why should I resent it? Why not look at it as a challenge and then take pleasure in the final accomplishment? In the end, that is what cruising is all about. No matter what goes wrong, you need to be able to fix it. And if you are going to enjoy cruising you better enjoy fixing things. By the end of the day, I had my plans pretty much in place and was resigned to making the repairs myself.

During the repairs, I talked with our neighbors about various routes for crossing the Mediterranean and the best times of year to do it. One of the boats had come to Greece from Gibraltar that fall and gave us some good advice about what we could expect when we finally made our way west. That night we heard for the first time about the relatively shallow depths between Sicily and Sardinia and the profound effect that this can have on the seas when strong winds blow down from the north. We also concluded that there was no way that we could possibly make it out of the Mediterranean in time to cross the Atlantic before the hurricane season. From that point on, our plans began to focus on getting to the Balearic Islands by summer and terminating our trip there.

***

Margot was all smiles. We had decided that Charlotte would take the Monday morning ferry to Marmaris to withdraw the money we had left with the Turkish Guaranty Bank. Margot would go with her and they would stay for three nights and then return on the afternoon ferry.

Just after taking Margot and Charlotte to the ferry, I saw Alex returning from a foray to the square. But instead of riding the bike, he looked like he was carrying it. As he came closer, it looked like he was carrying not one, but two bikes. "Dad, the bike broke in half. I was going pretty fast and it came apart. I almost killed myself." He looked more rattled than hurt, but the bike looked awful. The combination of salt water and having transported my anchor and heavy line back in Bodrum had done in our sole means of land transportation.

I was about to declare it a total loss when I had a sudden thought. Why not try the welding shop I had seen on the German boat. Alli pulled his welding machine out of the lazaret and hefted it across the gangplank and ashore. It looked like it was in worse shape than the bicycle, but after he ran the long cord to the octopus connection that was serving him and six other boats, he was ready to tackle the job. Barefooted, cut off jeans, no shirt, and scraggly hair that came down six inches past his shoulders, he didn't give the appearance of a seasoned welder. I couldn't decide whether I was worried more about his setting his hair on fire or burning his chest and feet with hot slag. But Alli didn't share my concerns and at the end of ten minutes he had magically rejoined the two halves of the bicycle and we were back in business.

The next day began with very strong winds from the northeast and it set up quite a surge in the harbor. I was glad I had followed Hans' example and rigged snubbers on our two stern lines to the pier. It had been a good use of the two tires I had acquired earlier to use as sea anchors. By tying lines from the tires to the quay and then from the tires to the boat, the tires served as giant rubber bands and greatly diminished the stress on the lines as the surge kept pitching the boat up and down.

While Mandraki Harbor afforded relatively good protection, it was nothing like a well designed marina, and I could now see why people had told me that it would not be a good place to leave a boat unattended. Unlike Marmaris, we would need to be with the boat at all times and this meant we could not use Rhodes as a base for exploration. But that was okay. Rhodes was a beautiful place and we were enjoying making it our home.

The giant ferry from Athens arrived exactly on time. Technically, unaccompanied items were not supposed to be transported for individuals, but Demetri had made special arrangements. I was a little worried, but followed his instructions exactly. The chief load master's memory was immediately refreshed when I handed him a 1,000 drachmas note and a few minutes later I left the ferry with a long bundle tied to my bicycle.

Before returning to the boat, I wanted to locate the machine shop that Gerry had told me about. Four holes needed to be drilled at the top of the column to attach the binnacle, and it was important that they be located exactly. A misinterpretation of Gerry's intricate directions put me in the middle of a large boatyard with sail and motor boats of all descriptions jacked up on blocks and in varying states of disrepair. One boat in particular stood out as being beyond repair. The hull was wooden and the seams were open wide. Four or five different flaking colors merged at various locations along the sides and bottom. At spots where there was no paint at all, the bare wood looked rotten. The deck house was in shambles and the masts and rigging, if there were any, were nowhere around to be seen.

But this did not discourage the three youths that were busy hammering, scraping, and painting as their mother supervised from below. I immediately felt a kinship and introduced myself to the mother: "Hello. My name is Heyward Coleman. Do you know where Yannis' machine shop is?" She introduced herself and told me where I had made a wrong turn. We then got into a long conversation and told each other how we happened to be where we were.

Wendy and her three children were very English. Her accent was like Audry Hepburn's before *Enry Iggins,* and her vocabulary came straight from Barnacle Bill the Sailor. But her honesty and enthusiasm were spellbinding, and I found myself probing deeper and deeper into their saga. Here, finally, was a family and a boat even more ill prepared for their adventure than *Captain Spiros.*

It had all started about a year earlier when she, her three boys, and daughter got a special deal on *Salvator.* It was their dream and they had been full of hope as they sailed it out of the small Spanish shipyard. One motor and countless mishaps later they found themselves sailing in Turkey. For reasons I didn't completely understand, but that had something to do with the Turkish authorities, they had been asked to leave the country. Their arrival in Rhodes had coincided with the loss of their rudder, and they were using the emergency shipyard repair as an opportunity to fix some of *Salvator's* problems.

Wendy introduced me to Peter, Johnnie, and Millie and I noted that they were about Heyward's age. Wendy explained that Edward was in Cyprus picking up a special part for the boat and Peter added: "Yea, and he's a pain in the arse. I hope the bloody towel 'eds get him with a bloody scud miss-isle!" The long silence after Peter's pronouncement seemed to indicate general agreement with his assessment of his missing crew mate, and I quickly changed the subject. "When you get *Salvator* back in the water, please come see us," and I left to find Yannis' shop.

Yannis and his son did an excellent job of locating and drilling the holes, and back on *Captain Spiros* I was delighted to see that the new column fit perfectly. I was also very pleased with the quality of Costa's work. The column was a heavy duty stainless steel pipe welded to a heavy duty flange. If the accident repeated itself, next time it would either be the deck or the sheet rope itself that would go—there was no way that Costa's column could be broken.

I removed the skirt from the stern for the third time and then scraped off all the silicon. By now it was becoming routine and only took three hours. Alex helped and, after a couple of hours of bending ourselves around in impossibly tight places, we finally succeeded in reinstalling the column and reconnecting the steering mechanism. I then applied a fresh coat of silicon and reinstalled the skirt. *Captain Spiros* was again ready for sea.

Heyward fixed a steak dinner for the three of us that night and we had a long talk about the remainder of our trip. With our repairs completed and with life in Rhodes beginning to click, we were in high spirits. Heyward and Alex surprised me by making a strong pitch that we extend the trip for one more year so that we could see more places and finish by crossing the Atlantic. During difficult times I had often wondered if they regretted leaving their home and friends for our adventure. But they were now suggesting that we stay longer. In the magic of that evening I found myself almost agreeing with their wild plan.

At about 8:30 the next morning I was surprised to hear Jim calling me from the quay. Jim was one of the first people we had met when we had arrived in Rhodes. After hearing about all of *Searcher's* broadcasts from Bob in Marmaris we had felt like we already knew him. He had just finished his morning session with Marmaris and had news for me: "Heyward, I just talked with Bob and he wanted me to relay a message to you from Charlotte. Instead of catching the afternoon ferry, she is getting a ride on *Mary Lou.*" I thanked Jim for the information and invited him on board for coffee.

Charlotte and I had been intrigued with his story which was the most similar to mine I had yet encountered. He had been a senior executive with American Express but several years ago decided he wanted to chuck it all and travel the world. His choice of vehicles, however, had been a trawler instead of a sail boat and he had decided to leave home permanently instead of just taking a year off as we were doing. He and his wife Caren were into their fifth year and were thoroughly enjoying themselves.

It was cold and windy and *Mary Lou* had had a rough trip. Poor Margot. But both Charlotte and Margot were beaming when we helped Hans moor his boat across the harbor from us. Hans and Mandy had decided to make a pork run and when they had learned that Charlotte and Margot needed a ride had decided to push their trip up a few days. Heyward, Alex, and I were invited aboard and we heard all about their visit. Charlotte started with an account of her trip to the bank.

161

After telling us that they had been most cooperative and that the teller had even remembered her name, she began her account of how her verbose friend slowly counted out her American dollars.

"Ah ha Mrs. Coleman, what do you think about George Bush? Do you like him? Let's see, that's two thousand dollars. I don't have any more hundreds. Do you want the rest in fifties?"

"Yes, that would be fine" Charlotte had nervously replied in a low voice feeling that all the eyes in the bank were on her.

"But you didn't answer my question. Do you like George Bush. He is really giving it to Saddam Hussein, yes?"

The stack of bills in front of the teller had become over an inch high as she cited the total of four thousand, five hundred and fifty in a voice that was loud enough for everybody in the line to hear. Her fixed stare at Charlotte demanded an answer, so Charlotte replied in whisper that she thought George Bush was a good president and then tried to change the subject. Charlotte had then stuffed the wad of money in her already bulging pocketbook and, hoping nobody would follow, returned to the marina.

Margot had enjoyed seeing Claus, but from what she said or didn't say, it seemed to all of us that some of the flame had died out. At any rate, after her return, the incessant suggestions that we return to Marmaris abruptly halted.

***

Our social life in Rhodes had already been established before our adventure with Demetri. But after returning it really began to take off. This was particularly true for the children. Two Danish boats full of students around Heyward and Alex's ages had arrived shortly after us into Mandraki. The school was sponsored by the Danish government and was for children who had been in trouble. Basically, prospective students had a choice between going to a correctional school or cruising on a boat for a year—what a choice! The students couldn't have been nicer—apparently the concept works—and the instructors were quite competent. Our children were becoming close friends with the students, and while they all had school work in the mornings—formal lessons for the Danes and correspondence courses for our children—the afternoons and evenings were free and they became inseparable.

Like us, the Danish boats were distancing themselves from the war. But in their case orders had come from Denmark. They had been ordered to leave Turkish waters immediately and forbidden to return while the war was in progress. It made us feel more justified about our decision to leave.

Charlotte and I were also settling nicely into life in Rhodes. More than any place in our travels it was becoming a home. Not only did we have our set of friends, but we also began to become familiar with the streets, the shops, the vendors and all the other aspects of the city that were so essential for daily living. It was nice to recognize and be recognized by the butcher or to have our vegetable lady tell us when she expected more fresh artichokes.

Sandy was the organizational center of the marina and of our daily routines. An English lady who spoke fluent Greek, she was the receptionist for Camper Nicholson. All the boats had learned to coordinate through her. We all gave Camper Nicholson's address and fax number as our own, and when correspondence arrived, Sandy would notify us by radio. If she couldn't contact the boat in question, she would give the message to a neighboring boat who would walk the message over.

The Camper Nicholson Office was the social center for Mandraki. I found myself going there almost daily. Coffee was always served and the staff was friendly and helpful. Husbands would go for equipment and advice, and wives would go to send faxes, to make phone calls, or to chat with Sandy. Mandikos, the manager, was very nice, and I would become involved in discussions with him and his people about various problems ranging from how to rig a permanent preventer to how to sell my boat at the end of our trip. While the inventory at Camper Nicholson was meager compared to a well stocked US chandlery, by Eastern Mediterranean standards it was fantastic. Instead of being able to get almost anything you wanted, you could almost always get something not completely dissimilar from what you needed.

The Hamam also became an important part of our lives. Armand had introduced Heyward, Alex, and me to the Turkish Baths during one of our first evenings in Rhodes. The night trip through the old city with quiet evening replacing noisy bustle gave us a better chance to appreciate its charm. At the end of a narrow winding road we entered the Hamam.

An old lady sitting next to a charcoal fire took our 50 drachmas and directed us to the left doorway which was for men. We deposited our clothes in wooden lockers and took only soap and our keys with us. There were two tiled rooms with huge domed ceilings. All around the walls there were stone basins about one foot above the floor. Each of the basins was fed by a spigot just above it. There were no drains in the basins and the water just overflowed the sides and ran down on the floor.

The procedure was simple. You sat next to a basin and dipped the water out with a wooden bowl. You then poured the water onto your head or body. It didn't look like much, but it was. The sensation of the hot water flowing all over our bodies and the warmth of the room was absolutely delicious—especially after the constant cold of our boat. And it felt so good to be clean. The hard part about the Hamam was leaving, but even that was made pleasant by the transition of lingering by the charcoal fire before re-entering the cold night air.

***

Claudine, our friend in Athens, had given us the Stavrianakis' phone number in a fax to Rhodes and I had called them just before Charlotte and Margot had left for Marmaris. John had been very friendly and insisted we join them for their family lunch on Sunday. It was the big event of the week for us and we were very excited when he picked us up in his car. It was a beautiful ride through the country to their home in the town of Koskinou, about 10 miles from the city. John's brother, Michael, had been a patient of Claudine's husband Dennis and they had all become close friends. Katerina, John's wife; their two children Maria and Vicky; Michael and his wife Marits; and Vicky's husband John and their two children were all there to greet us when we arrived. The warm hospitality and genuine interest they showed us gave us a glimpse into an aspect of Greek life we hadn't known existed.

The long table had so much food there was hardly room for our plates. The ladies produced course after course of exotic dishes, and even bottomless pit Alex seemed to get enough to eat. We told the family about our trip and they told us about their lives—the years John, Katerina, Maria, and Vicky had lived in Australia; how Dennis had diagnosed Michael's heart problem and saved his life; the butcher shop John and Vicky owned and wanted us to visit. Before the day was out we felt we had become part of the family. We invited everyone to come to Mandraki the following Sunday to visit us on *Captain Spiros*. And then, all too soon, it was time to leave.

On the trip back, John told us about a friend of his who had a yacht he kept at Mandraki. About five years earlier the friend had been visiting them for the weekend and a violent storm had suddenly broken out. Being concerned about his boat, the friend had driven in the night to Mandraki, left his car at the end of the quay, and went to tend his boat. As the night progressed, the storm became much worse. At its peak, the wind became so strong that it picked up rocks from the breakwater and hurled them into the harbor. That night their friend lost both his boat and his car and very nearly his life. Over half the boats in Mandraki had been either sunk or very badly damaged during that storm. John told us this story not to alarm us, but simply to explain how precarious the weather in Rhodes can be. He added that subsequent modifications to the east quay should prevent the same catastrophe from reoccurring, but still we should be cautious.

***

Gerry on *Sundance* not only gave good advice on technical repairs, he also gave the best exchange rate on the island for drachmas as he converted his repair earnings into US dollars. One day he invited us on board for a beer and gave advice we hadn't expected. "You should go to the boat yard and ask Yannis about the *Captain Spiros*. Ever since you arrived here I thought the boat was familiar. Now I remember. Last year she was here and had a big hole in her. I remember that they had to pump all night. I don't know how bad the damage was. But Yannis would know. He did the work."

Charlotte immediately jumped to the conclusion that this had been the cause of the osmosis and that the boat had sunk and the damage had been terrible. This then led to the usual tirade against Kiriacoulis and Minolis. Whether the story was true or not, and how bad the accident had been if there had been an accident, we never learned. Yannis had already heard that an American family had purchased *Captain Spiros* and immediately clammed up when we went to his shop and started asking questions.

After all the work we had done on the hull in Kalamaki I was certain that if there had been hull damage, it had been adequately repaired and we had a sound bottom. Charlotte was less convinced, but after getting Gerry to take a close look at our boat and rigging and then hearing his pronouncement that everything was in top shape, she let it drop.

Our children and the Danish students were becoming inseparable. After lessons the group would drift from our boat to one of the Danish boats and then to the other Danish boat. Heyward and Catherine were becoming more than good friends, and the second romance of our cruise was in full swing. Charlotte and I worried a little about the whole matter. After all, they were all juvenile delinquents and would have been in reform school if they were back in Denmark. But, on the other hand, we liked each of them as individuals, and they seemed to be well into the process of mending their ways. We decided that it was good for our children to have the exposure and we were also happy for them to have the opportunity for companionship of others their own age.

Armand decided it was time for *L'Ancettra* to return to Turkey. We were sorry to see them go and invited the three of them to dinner the night before their departure. With the war in full swing their prospects for a successful season of chartering looked bleak and we were concerned for them. The life they had chosen had lots of freedom but there was a price. We wished them well as they sailed off the next morning.

By this time, I had fixed nearly everything that needed fixing on the boat. One of the winches on the mast, a loose starboard stanchion, a new preventer system that could be easily rigged for when we were before the wind, a traveler for the stationary block of the main sheet—all of these had finally been crossed off my "to do list." But another interest had crept in to occupy much of my attention.

The new sextant I had bought just before Demetrius' arrival presented a new challenge. I had wanted it as a back up in case the Satnav quit working on our crossing to Malta. Demetri had promised to teach me to use it during our trip, but it had sat unused in its elegant wooden box ever since our aborted trip. As a student at Naval Officer Candidate School I had learned to take a sun line in the school parking lot. But this was different. I wanted to be able to use the sun, the North Star, and the moon to help us know where we were.

Before leaving the US I had bought Chapman's book and the giant two-volume authoritative work by Bowditch. But these works did not contain the information I needed to use the sextant. I still needed sight reduction tables and a nautical almanac, but how could I get them? Sight reduction tables didn't exist in any of the stores in Rhodes and the only nautical almanac I could obtain was an abbreviated version carried in *Reed's Mediterranean Navigator*—but the volume available was for the previous year.

I didn't have any choice. I couldn't simply use tables and standard methods of interpolation. I was going to have to actually learn how the geometry worked and solve a large part of the problem mathematically. Ironically, this difficulty turned an otherwise rote and somewhat boring process into something fascinating. Hans shared a program with me he had written for a hand held calculator, and I began to see how I could do without sight reduction tables. I bought a programmable calculator from the largest department store in Rhodes and after a few days was in business. Hans then taught me how to calculate the correction values for my sextant and before long I was successfully taking sun lines. Hans also taught me how I could get a sun line at sunset even without the sextant. Before long I was getting the feel for it. Other people had different tricks and different methods and I immersed myself in learning the art.

***

I didn't see the boat arrive. In fact I had forgotten all about them. But Heyward had been drawn in like a magnet. When he arrived back at *Captain Spiros* just before dinner he was full of stories. "Dad, this neat boat just came in and I met Peter. He plays the guitar and is really cool." *Salvator* had arrived in Mandraki.

Over the next few days, social hour switched from *Captain Spiros* to *Salvator* and instead of having the mass of teenagers in our cockpit and cabin, the group was enjoying the easy casualness of the English family on *Salvator*. In the water, *Salvator* didn't look quite as bad as she had on shore, but her suffering was still obvious. Through Heyward we learned about Peter's never-ending source of red wine. He had discovered how to purchase in bulk from one the local Rhodes wineries and explained to Heyward that at only twenty cents a pint he couldn't afford not to drink all he could possibly consume.

But the story that was told time after time was the account of the Saturday night outing to a Rhodes discotheque that included our three children, the young from *Salvator* and the entire crews of both of the Danish student boats. Peter and Johnnie had already been pretty well oiled before arriving, but that had been only the beginning.

Johnnie had started the fun by launching into one of his favorite topics: "Where are the fucking yachties tonight? Usually they are here in their fucking space suits." Peter took the cue and pretending to have on a suit of fancy foul weather gear began: "Well mate, I don't care what you say, MY spinnaker pole is bigger than YOUR spinnaker pole and we can make 12 bloody knots event without a spinnaker pole." Johnnie then rejoined with: "Bugger me, but everybody knows that your boat doesn't even have a weather fax or a mobile telephone. If you so much as set a Sperry Topsider on my polished teak deck I'll punch a hole in your Zodiac and wrap your dick up in my roller reefing."

This went on for the better part of the evening with their whole table laughing so hard they were almost crying. From then on we referred to foul weather gear as space suits and we never saw a yachtie again without conjuring up the image of *Salvator* and her raunchy crew.

At the end of the first week of February, *Et Au Alt* arrived in Mandrake. They had begun their long trip back to France where they would enter the French canals and then work their way back to Denmark. It was great to see Bianne and Deeda again and they came aboard for dinner that night. Bianne helped me fill out a list of safe anchorages across the Aegean and gave me a rough idea of his itinerary. He planned to cross over to Simi and then sail up to Kos and from there across the Cyclades and then enter the Saronic Gulf. From there he would go through the Corinth Canal and then on to Corfu.

It was almost exactly the route that I was leaning towards, and we made plans to try to meet somewhere along the way. We agreed to monitor channel 68 on the VHF radio and hoped we would catch up with them in

Galaxidhi, a port just after the Corinth Canal. They had loved Galaxidhi during their trip out and planned to stay there awhile and use it as a base to visit and explore Delphi.

The next day we took them to Vicki and John's butcher shop and they finished stocking for their trip. The selection was so good and John and Vicki were so nice to us that we also decided to purchase hefty supplies. Although we hadn't yet set a date, we knew it wouldn't be too much longer before we would be leaving also.

We were sad to see *Et Au Alt* go, but hoped we would catch up with them later. Going over Bianne's plans had been a big help, and we began to firm up our own plans. We hoped to be ready to leave within the next few weeks.

Sunday was a big day. The Stavrianakis were coming to visit. Charlotte had been getting ready for two days, and Alex had the dinghy all ready to take the grandchildren around the harbor. Things started off badly when Marits almost fell off the gangplank coming aboard. Fortunately I was able to catch her from the shore and Heyward gave her a steadying hand from the boat. The grandchildren found coming onto the large sailboat scary and weren't up to the excitement of cruising around Mandraki harbor in Alex's Zodiac. Margot's boat baked chocolate chip cookies broke the ice and after a short time we found ourselves explaining all the odd aspects of our nautical existence. John and Michele wanted to learn everything about the boat and we thoroughly enjoyed showing it to them. After inviting us all to the wedding of a good friend of their family for that night in Koskinou, Michael again passed out gifts for everyone and they left.

The following week we began to get ready for our departure in earnest. I had repaired almost everything I could find that was broken and we began to top off our provisions. Several more trips to Vicky's, a cab ride to the supermarket by Heyward and Charlotte, and a trip by me to Peter's bulk wine depot and *Captain Spiros* was full to overflowing. We just needed good weather for our departure.

By this time the children had become so ensconced with their friends that they were not at all enthusiastic about leaving, and we were getting some hard lobbying to stay. This was particularly true from Heyward, but Charlotte and I were determined to move on. The weather had been good for two days and we had decided if it held we would head for Simi in the morning and begin island hopping to the Corinth Canal. But apparently two good days in a row was all we were going to get and the next day started with a lousy forecast and was followed by two days of steadily deteriorating weather. The third day was when the storm hit Mandrake.

We woke up on Feb. 15 in time for the 6:00 weather forecast—no gales but high winds—no sailing today. By about 7:00 the wind was quite strong from the east. Patrick, whose catamaran was one boat to the east of our boat, and I began to become concerned about the Danish student boat, *Columbus II,* that was moored just east of Patrick. All of us were held in place by anchors from our bows well out into the harbor and our sterns tied to the quay—this meant that the full force of the east wind was on our beams and was exerting enormous pressure on the anchors. *Columbus II* was steel, quite large, and poorly moored. We offered to help them get a line from their bow to the east quay and thereby relieve tension on their anchor. If her anchor slipped, she would push against our boats and probably start a daisy chain of uprooted anchors. Alex hopped into our dinghy and secured her line to the east quay. By this time the wind had gained considerable force, and it was obvious that we were in for trouble.

It was fascinating to watch how the sailing community reacted to the situation. Suddenly everyone was up and about offering help and advice in situations where it was needed. It was a real group effort with little or no selfish concern for one's own boat. People who had never met suddenly became friends and each person made his contribution. Patrick, with his many years of sailing experience, was quick to spot dangerous situations and ready to help fix them.

Everyone rooted deep in their boats for spare lines and a spider web of rope rapidly grew attaching the endangered boats to each other and to the east quay. Crews from the boats on the east quay, whose boats were better protected, came to the north quay to help with our preparations. Alex and Hans manned our dinghy, and in spite of winds that almost capsized them several

The Big Storm

times, managed to get extra anchors out, mooring lines across, and slipped anchors reset.

By afternoon, we had a full scale gale on our hands. Winds were varying from force 9 to force 11 with 50 knot gusts, and the situation became quite dangerous. *Alk's* anchor had dragged twice and the second time Alex and Hans along with Patrick had taken our dinghy out to reset it. It was a monster CQR weighing 80 kilos and took all of Hans' and Patrick's strength to get it up to the dinghy and hold it while Alex maneuvered them out. They placed it so far out that it would take a hurricane to make it drag again. But this didn't convince Marge that it was safe. She had been getting more and more excited as the wind had mounted and when Hans had gone to reset the anchor, something snapped. As he climbed back on the boat she began:

"Hans, we need to get out of here. It's not safe. Let's leave the harbor right now. Pleeease! Go start the motor."

We all looked at Marge wondering what was happening. Alk's motor was already started and had been running for at least an hour. In fact all of us had our motors going to keep us off the quay and to reduce tension on our anchors. Hans looked out in the harbor at the mass of lines spread everywhere. Even if he had been willing to risk trying to maneuver in the restricted harbor with winds that would almost certainly have blown him up on the rocks, the lines made it absolutely impossible. In a gentle voice Hans soothed her and persuaded her to go below and fix coffee for everyone. Periodically she would come back up on deck and start demanding that they leave, but each time he gently guided her back below.

The old salts of the harbor told us about the terrible storm when over half of the boats in the harbor had been sunk or badly damaged. It was the same storm that John had so vividly described to us. I hoped he had been right about the improvements to the jetties. The wind was so strong that we had to lean into it at a 45 degree angle. As the surf pounded on the east quay, giant clouds of spray rose into the air and drenched us.

We watched as a tanker rounded the tip of the island and headed to the southeast. The wind was pushing hard and the boat was listing heavily to starboard. Was the list preventing their rudder from controlling? We lined the quay and for a breathless few minutes it looked certain that the ship was going to be dashed onto the rocks. But by some miracle it made it past the point and then began to open with the shore.

On *Captain Spiros* we had deployed our CQR and Danforth anchors and attached two large diameter lines to the east quay. Suddenly I felt a lot better about spending all that time and money in Bodrum buying extra line, anchors, and chain, and ruining my bicycle carrying it. By night we were all exhausted, especially Alex with his work on the dinghy, but the storm was still in full force and *Searcher* had received reports that the worst was yet to come. We had no choice but to keep watching and adjusting our lines and set up a schedule with two hour rotations so we all could all get a little sleep as the storm raged on.

At about four in the morning, Charlotte and I climbed into the front end loader while Heyward and Alex took the watch. It seemed like I had just put my head on the pillow when I heard heavy footsteps overhead and talk in another language. Groggily it registered that the sounds weren't Greek, weren't Turkish, but were..."They are Arabs shouted Charlotte as she flung the covers up. What are they doing on our boat? Terrorists! Get dressed, get them off our boat!"

I pulled my pants on as I hurried through the cabin to the cockpit. No Alex. No Heyward As I emerged on deck the change was startling. It was light—we must have been asleep for hours—and there wasn't a breath of wind. There wasn't anyone on our boat either. I looked around the harbor. It looked like a giant plate of spaghetti. Lines were everywhere. Besides the lack of wind, what else was missing? People. The harbor was deserted. Everyone must be sleeping. So who had been on our boat?

Suddenly my question was answered. The Egyptian fishermen whose boats had been clustered in the northeast corner of the harbor wanted to go fishing. They had been on our boat as well as on other boats to loosen our security lines to allow them to pass. I wouldn't have believed it was possible, but they did it. By loosening the lines and pushing them down with sticks they were able to get their tall masted fishing boats clear of the mess and out of the harbor. Life had returned to normal.

A week later favorable weather conditions finally presented themselves and we were ready to leave. After the children finished their final farewells to their Danish friends and Charlotte and I had finished exchanging home addresses with other boats, we cast off our lines. Heyward's Danish beauty was in tears and all of our other friends were waving good-by as we motored away from the quay and up to the anchor.

Alex called that he was having trouble raising the anchor so I went forward to look. I sent Alex aft to steer and Heyward helped me horse in the anchor. I then saw the cause of the problem. Patrick and Hans had done too good a job with *Alk's* anchor during the storm and there it was hanging off my anchor chain. Using a boat hook and a lot of sweat, we finally got the anchor unfouled. Alex then eased the boat into forward and started his turn out of the harbor.

"Dad, the steering doesn't work"

"Sure it does Alex, you just don't have enough speed yet for the rudder to work" I replied somewhat irritated as I was quite tired from having untangled Hans' giant anchor from our chain.

"But Dad when I turn the wheel to the right the boat turns to the left!"

Instant realization—when I had reconnected the steering cables in my repair job on the steering column, I must have reversed them With a red face and quite a large audience I tried to back into our slot, but with the steering cables reversed this proved to be too complicated for my by then very frustrated mind and I simply tied onto Hans' bow. Out came the tool boxes and we proceeded to fix our steering for the third time—but Charlotte and the children helped and we finished an hour later. This time it was really good-bye and we headed off for Simi.

Chapter 7
A Winter Crossing

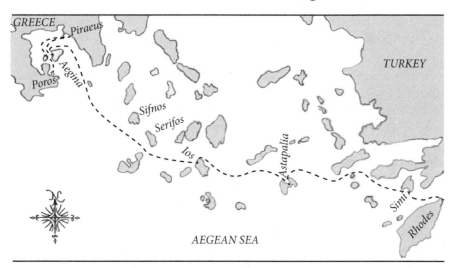

Since our aborted attempt with Demetri, I had given a great deal of thought about how we would cross the Eastern Mediterranean. There was still plenty of winter left and going directly to Malta or going via Crete didn't make sense for exactly the same reasons they had not made sense before—we could not count on decent weather for more than a day or two at a time. But a more northerly route through the Cyclades and making short dashes between islands during breaks in the weather could be done prudently.

The trick was choosing safe harbors with protection from the wind and good holding. There weren't many in the Dodecanese or in the Cyclades. But what few there were, we had carefully studied and had received good firsthand advice about them from Armand, Patrick, and Bianne. In the Dodecanese, Simi and Astipalaia had excellent holding. Then in the Cyclades, Ios was in a class by itself. After Ios, we could choose between Sifnos or Serifos, but neither was quite as good as the previous ports. From either of these islands it would then be a relatively easy day sail to Aegina. But there was a problem. There was a huge stretch between Simi and Astipalaia with no good protection. Tilos and Niseros were in the path, but offered no protection. In calm weather Niseros would probably be okay, but in bad weather it would be a disaster. There were two alternatives: a straight shot from Simi to Astipalaia which would require two days, or go out of our way on the first leg to sail from Simi to Kos then go from Kos to Astipalaia. We still weren't completely decided when we arrived in Simi.

This time our arrival into Panormittis was in daylight, and we were thrilled with the opportunity to explore the beautiful harbor. After visiting the little monastery that dominated the harbor, we visited the only other boat in the anchorage. Ian and Deborah, the English couple on *Mistress,* had been in Mandraki during the storm, and we spent the evening comparing notes for our plans to tackle crossing the Cyclades. *Mistress* was a very small sloop—only 25 feet—that they had sailed the whole way from England. They had just received the evening forecast, and the good weather was supposed to hold for the next day. I suggested leaving around four o'clock in the morning and heading straight for Astipalaia. Even with moderate speed, we should be able to make Astipalaia well before dark. Ian agreed that it made sense for us with our larger size and higher speed, but he was concerned about *Mistress'* ability to arrive before dark. Ian had another possibility, however, that wasn't open to us. Palon on Niseros did offer moderate protection, but was far too shallow for *Captain Spiros. Mistress* could stop there if she weren't able to make it to Astipalaia. But the weather was the main variable and we both decided we would wait until morning for final decisions. As *Mistres'* plans coincided closely with ours, we agreed to keep in touch by radio.

My alarm went off at 4:00 A.M. It was a beautiful night with a full moon. I woke Charlotte and by 4:30 we were underway. We were just even with Cape Knidos when we received the 6:00 A.M. forecast. Still time to divert to Kos. But no need. We couldn't have asked for a better report. Force 4 to 5 out of the east. The wind would be behind us.

As the day progressed, the wind freshened and we made very good time. If the waves hadn't started getting so big we would have hardly noticed how strong the wind was becoming as we passed Niseros. We had waited too long to reef and realized our mistake as the boat pitched wildly when we had temporarily altered course to put the third reef in the mainsail. By the time we had sighted Astipalaia the wind had reached force 6. I hoped Vathi Bay was going to be as good as it had been described.

Astipalaia is shaped like a butterfly with its right wing stretching to the east. The change was instant as we rounded the northern tip and gained protection provided by the wing. We headed down the west coast of the wing to a narrow channel that led into a harbor that was like a landlocked lake. It was the best protection we had encountered anywhere in Greece, and we were glad to have it. All the signs were pointing towards a gale, and Vathi was where we would have to weather it.

By the time we anchored, the wind was so high that no one argued with Charlotte's request for a second anchor. We tried a new technique—motoring up on the first anchor and then dropping the second from our boat rather than using the dinghy—and it almost resulted in disaster. The wind was exerting so much force that when I slowed to drop the second anchor, it almost blew us in a circle that would have wrapped the anchor chain of the first anchor around our keel. Only hard reverse and a strain on the second anchor saved us. But our two anchors were well placed and as the gale approached, I was pleased to see that we were holding nicely.

The three Egyptian fishing boats that were already moored in the harbor didn't fare as well. The crews, clad from head to foot in yellow oil skins, came out of their dwellings on shore to better secure their craft. But they had waited too long, and we watched them struggling for about two hours. They were finally successful in nesting the boats together and setting extra anchors, but only after dragging half way across the harbor and narrowly missing grounding.

As in the Rhodes storm, we set up anchor watches throughout the night. The spot I had chosen and the final direction of the wind resulted in only 10 meters between our stern and shallow water. Two anchors gave us a warm feeling of security, but the force of the wind was enormous and a sharp watch was necessary.

The fisherman combination home and restaurant off our port beam had a light we could line up with another light from a house high on the hill behind it so we had a range that would tell if we were dragging. We hoped that neither house would decide to put out its light. If that happened we would have to depend on "feel." It turned out to be a two day storm, but it stopped as suddenly as it had started and we took advantage of the break to set out for Ios.

The 65-mile trip went quickly. With Ios just in sight, we were congratulating ourselves on a smooth passage when the wind started to howl. This time we were more alert and immediately put in the third reef. We had a vigorous sail to the southern tip of the island and then enjoyed protection as we came into the lee of the shore. But the calming effect was short lived. The wind continued to pick up and we began to feel the effect of the mountains' funneling the wind and adding to its speed. On our third reef and with the high cut jib we had switched to before leaving Rhodes, the *Captain Spiros* rode nicely and we found ourselves making nine knots often surging up to ten and twelve.

As we turned into Ios bay, I began to wonder if the port really deserved the A rating for shelter that Heikell had awarded. The wind seemed to get stronger, and I became concerned that we were going to have a repeat of Mikonos. But tucked in the northeast corner was a neat rectangular harbor that was almost empty and where, magically, the effect of the wind almost disappeared. There was only one ferry along the north mole and a small sloop moored stern to from the east mole. With lots of room to spare, we moored stern to with the sloop to our starboard. But I wasn't taking any chances. I dropped our anchor almost 100 meters west of the east mole—if the wind shifted to the west our protection would be gone and I wanted to use all the chain we had to keep us off the shore.

The Frog, a restaurant just opposite our boat, showed some signs of life, and we entered. Loud music, cold Amstel, and a quick friendship with an English lady who lived there year round and taught school completed our transition from howling wind to secure warmth. Caroline told us that we had been the subject of much speculation before we had entered and that everyone was surprised to see tourists this time of year. Eyes behind the windows of what had seemed to be a deserted port had watched Charlotte steering, Margot handling bumpers, and Heyward securing lines and had drawn their conclusions concerning gender and the composition of our crew. The realization that we were a relatively normal family and not a boat full of stunning females with a hired male captain came as a surprise, and, according to Caroline, somewhat of a disappointment.

Caroline accompanied us on the bus trip up the hill to the village and introduced us to her favorite restaurant. The town was empty but the myriad of colorful pubs, discos, and hotels—all closed—told the story of what happens in this teen paradise when August arrives. Charlotte and I delighted in the history of the island and were intrigued that this was the final resting place of Homer, but the children were disappointed that the wild stories they had heard about Ios all pertained to a different season.

It was only upon arriving at the top of the hill that we were able to fully appreciate the protection of our harbor. The boiling foam far below and the bending of the trees above told the story. What we had been told had turned out to be true—Ios was the best harbor in the Cyclades. But what a strange reversal. Usually it was the town that afforded protection and a respite from the elements. But here it was only after we returned to the boat that we came out of the wind.

We awoke to a bad forecast—force 6 to 7—and wind from the north. I walked down the pier, paid the port police 450 drachmas for a two-day stay, and went back to get Charlotte for a hike. The sky was overcast and looked menacing, but we felt very little wind. As we rounded the harbor and began to climb the hill towards the western entrance of the bay, we again appreciated the extraordinary protection of our little harbor. Trees, twigs, and grass were all bent in a southerly direction and it seemed a miracle that the neat terracing and stone retaining walls could hold their own against the raging wind.

Cold, powerful, relentless—it was hard to believe the hostility of the elements, especially when they were juxtaposed in such an idyllic setting. The entire panorama was an enigma. The terracing extended out of sight in both directions, but there was no sign of cultivation. The stone walls were well constructed and were in a reasonable state of repair. But other than a few stray goats, there was no livestock to be retained. What generations had built the walls and why? Charlotte's attention was equally divided between the magic beauty of the canopy of wild flowers that stretched before us and the harsh pounding of the sea on the rocks far below.

"Oh, Heyward look at the anemones. They are so beautiful. Look at them waving and bobbing in the wind—white, pink, blue, and purple. It looks like a giant landscaped rock garden." And as we watched the flowers bobbing we could hear the report of the sea as it thrashed the rocks far below. We were both thankful we were safely ensconced in our little harbor and not fighting the elements.

After running errands in the morning and still feeling sorry for ourselves because of the force 8 and 9 winds that were reported to be everywhere in the Eastern Mediterranean, we met June. She was sitting on a bollard in front of the neighboring ketch and was carving a walking stick. Upon our arrival into Ios Peter had been very kind in helping us with our mooring lines, but this was the first time we had seen June. She invited us for tea later that afternoon. Tea turned into beer, beer into wine, and one hour stretched to two and then extended far into the night.

Although Dutch, Peter's English was quite good and June's Australian accent was charming. They had set out in early October from Rhodes to cross the Cyclades and had only made it as far as Ios. The saga started with engine problems on their first attempt to depart Ios and resulted in their enlisting Greek mechanics for the repair. This flawed decision almost cost them their motor and their boat. On their second attempt to depart the motor seized up just after they had left the protection of the harbor and entered the strong headwind of the open bay. With no sails up and no motor, only Peter's quick action and a very long anchor chain saved *Sweet Thursday* from destruction.

The next time Peter repaired the motor himself, but by the time he was finished winter had firmly set in. They were now getting ready to depart, but wanted to wait a little longer for more settled weather.

Peter and June were used to difficulties and we were mesmerized as they told us the story of their sleek ferrocement sloop and their past ten years of adventures. Choosing to build a ferrocement boat had not been the mistake. It was choosing to build it in Holland that had caused all the difficulties. In June's native Australia, this type of construction was very popular and advice could be readily obtained. But in Holland, steel and fiberglass were the media of choice for yacht builders and there was no expertise in ferrocement.

After three years of hard work—doing, undoing, and then redoing—they finally conquered their media and it was time to launch. Already they had statistically achieved the impossible—ninety percent of all do-it-yourself yacht builders abandon their project and dream well before the hull even fully takes shape. By this time in the story they had both become quite animated and Peter poured us all another round of red wine before continuing.

"The crane picked up our beautiful boat and then swung it towards the water. It was so beautiful. All the work, all the suffering, all the waiting... it was about to pay off."

"Peter, before you say it, I want to disagree. It wasn't the crane operator's fault that..."

Peter became more animated and his face turned beet red: "Ya, ya, you say it was not his fault, but our beautiful boat. Our boat. Lying on its side with a crack down the middle. Maybe it was the crane's fault, maybe the clutch slipped, I don't care. What mattered was that *Sweet Thursday* had been dropped and our dream... What about our dream!"

But Peter and June had again defied the statistics and picked up the pieces. A year later *Sweet Thursday* was launched. With the interior only partially completed and none of the rigging in place they entered the European canal systems and took a wonderful trip across the continent. From Holland to Paris and then from Paris to Southern France and finally out into the Mediterranean—and all the time continuing work on the boat. Peter stroked the beautiful interior trim as he continued his tale.

"It was very hard, but when we were finally able to leave home and come on board to live, it was all worth it. It has now been ten years and we wouldn't trade for anything."

Their trip across the Mediterranean included a long visit in Corfu and while Peter was telling us all about wintering there June interrupted. "*Captain Spiros, Captain Spiros.* Yes, I remember now. I knew when you arrived and I saw the name something was familiar. At first I thought it was just the name Spiros. In Corfu everybody is named Spiros. But now I remember. It was a Trinidad just like yours. But of course it couldn't have been the same boat."

June had our full attention. Charlotte hesitated and then asked cautiously; "Why? What happened? Was there an accident?"

"Well, yes, there was. We were not far away in the harbor when on a very windy day we saw a Trinidad full of people and using their emergency tiller. We heard later from our friend John who works on boats what had happened. It was a very large charter party and the skipper they had brought with them didn't have much experience. He jibbed the boat in a strong wind and the sheet rope caught on the steering column and tore it off."

Peter broke in: "Yes, I remember now. And the funny part was that John had said it had happened twice. Can you imagine? Two times the same accident. But the other time had been a year earlier."

Charlotte turned purple. "Everywhere we go somebody tells us about a wreck our damn boat has had. I hate Minolis, and I am beginning to hate all the Greeks. ."

Day after day, the gale continued to blow and our friendship with Peter and June deepened. During the days Charlotte and I would explore while the children tried to catch up with their work, and during the evenings we would while away the hours on one of our two boats telling stories about past experiences and sharing future plans.

June and Peter were heading for Corfu but not by the Corinth Canal. They were going to take the longer and considerably rougher trip around the Peloponnesus. It would save them some money, but rounding Cape Malea in winter was something we wouldn't have considered no matter how expensive the Corinth Canal.

I had become bogged down in reading the *Odyssey* but Peter rekindled my interest. He loaned me his copy of *The Ulysses Voyage* by Tim Severin and I promised to return it to him in Corfu. The book was fascinating. Sverin had organized and led an expedition to prove the validity of Ulysses' famous trip. He had had a replica of a sailing vessel of the age constructed and tried to recreate the trip. The book is full of exciting stories about his experiences and sets forth theories of where the locations Homer described may actually have been. After Severin, the *Odyssey* took on a new meaning for me. It seemed very appropriate that I should re-immerse myself in this classic at the final resting place of the author and in the middle of a trip where I was experiencing the ferocity of the same seas his hero had had to contend with.

After five days, the weather finally broke. The evening before we had taken hurried notes as the weather map flashed on Peter's small television. It didn't contain much useful information, but somehow it gave us confidence. The morning Greek forecast called for either force 4 to 5 or force 6—we weren't sure which—but it was so much better than anything we had seen since arriving at Ios that we decided to leave.

Sifnos was the conservative destination, but we decided that if the weather was good we would continue to Serifos, about 20 miles further along our route. The weather did hold. In fact it was one of the prettiest sailing days we had had in the Aegean. We passed Sifnos and were about to arrive at Serifos when we came up with the idea—why not continue on to Aegina? If we did, it would mean a night arrival, but we had entered so many times at night with Manfred that this didn't worry me. We took a vote, set the night watch bill, and turned away from Serifos and the warm security of Livadhi Bay.

The full moon was out and it was a beautiful night. The tanker traffic was heavy, and I was happy to have the extra light. Our night sailing was still in its infancy, and we all needed practice in reading navigation lights.

The principle is simple. If you picture a ship with a red light that shows only on the port side and a green light that shows only on the starboard side you can begin to make some guesses about the steel monster that is lurking out there in the dark. The white light that shows only from the stern further helps solve the riddle, but it can easily be confused with the masthead lights that show from all directions. If the boat is long enough it must have two of these masthead lights with the lower of the two forward—another very helpful clue. Technically, it's possible to deduct the aspect and the direction the other vessel is heading—but practically, it's very difficult and requires a great deal of practice.

But regardless of the number and color of the lights, there is another principle that we had all come to know and understand very well. A decreasing range and a zero bearing drift mean that if either our vessel or the other vessel fails to make a maneuver, we will soon become one object. And as the old naval adage goes, "A collision at sea can ruin your whole day."

Our night rule was simple. We couldn't tell whether the range was decreasing or not but we could measure the bearing drift by lining up the light on some part of our vessel and watching for a few minutes to see if it moved. If it did, we were OK. If it didn't we would change our course and hold our breath while we waited to see if the maneuver took us off the collision course.

We successfully avoided two ships that had presented us with unchanging bearings and had sighted Ay Yeoryis, a small island that sits right in the center of the entrance to the Saronic Gulf, when we began to get tired. Aegina was now only a couple of hours away and we were entering familiar waters, but we were also entering one of the busiest shipping areas in the Eastern Mediterranean. It was a time to be cautious.

The confusion set in as we sighted Aegina and began sail along its northern shore. Fishing boats don't always follow the rules of the road with their lighting and, indeed, sometimes fail to use any lighting at all. As we approached it was hard to tell if they were boats or lights on shore, but as we got closer, the random motion suggested the former. As I strained my vision through a pair of binoculars to try to make sense of the confusion on our port side, Charlotte announced a new concern to starboard.

"I have been watching and the bearing hasn't changed. It seems to be getting closer."

I switched my attention to the starboard side. This wasn't a fishing boat and it was following the rules. A high white light and to its left a low white light and right between the two there was a red one. "It's a ship, maybe large, and it's heading the same way we are," I announced and continued to watch. "The lights seem to be getting higher off the water and the bearing is not changing. It's getting close."

There were two choices. Head into shore and play dodge with the fishing boats or make a radical turn to starboard towards the ship so that we would pass astern. I chose the latter alternative but decided to alert our big friend out there so he would know what I was up to. "Ship off northeast coast of Aegina, this is the sailing yacht *Captain Spiros*. I am turning to starboard to stay clear of you. I should pass well astern of you. Over."

The radio crackled an acknowledgment and then we forgot about it in the confusion and work of tacking the boat through the wind and trimming up to our new course. But Margot thought she heard another boat calling us on the radio. "Mom, someone is trying to call us. It sounds like Deeda." By the time we settled onto our new course and had time to listen to Margot, the radio was silent. We tried but couldn't get any response so we let it drop and thought nothing more about it.

After rounding the western tip of Aegina, we lowered the sails and motored cautiously towards the harbor entrance. As familiar as we had been with Aegina, I was still uncertain and we motored past two or three times before I was ready to make the final approach. Margot spotted the critical light and we made our entrance without mishap. At 3:45 A.M. we dropped our anchor and moored stern to in front of one of the waterfront restaurants. Our crossing was over and we had arrived safely.

***

181

The next morning we woke up to warm lovely sunshine, a stunningly beautiful view of Aegina harbor, and the wonderful news that the war in the Persian Gulf was over. I didn't even fuss at Margot for having the cassette player on high as Harry Chapin boomed out:

"All my life's a circle
Sunrise to sundown
Moon rolls through the nighttime
Till the daybreak comes around

All my life's a circle
But I can't tell you why
Seasons spinning around again
The years keep rolling by

It seems like I've been here before
I can't remember when
And I've got this funny feeling
That we will all be together again"

It was the first time I had heard the song since the thousand times she had played it during our refit and the early part of our voyage. Suddenly the nostalgia of the early days, the enthusiasm, and the warmth that had greeted our arrival in Greece came back in a flood. Our life was a circle and now we were back in Aegina. And it was warm again—all was right with the world.

It made me think of another circle and wonder where it would end. Maritrans—the two-year non-compete meant that I would not be able to go back into petroleum shipping. But that didn't concern me very much. I was soured on corporate life in general, and joining any big company wasn't appealing. Subtly an idea was evolving that I wouldn't work for anybody when I got back. Whatever it was, I would do it on my own. The trip had proven we could break away—why go back to the same old thing again?

Heyward and Alex were up early to rent a scooter and explore, but Charlotte and I enjoyed having a lazy day on board and wandering up and down the waterfront. It felt great to be back in Aegina and we were even feeling a little charitable towards the Greeks. We had come to love Aegina before we had left and a now we had beautiful spring weather. We took full advantage of it and spent a day traveling over the whole island on motor scooters. Charlotte added to her wildflower collection and the cabin of

Captain Spiros began to look like a booth at the Philadelphia Flower Show.

Alex and Margot studied both before and after our outings. They had been working steadily on their Calvert lessons, even during the crossing, but they were still far behind. Heyward was taking a much more casual approach to his studies. He assured us he could finish the two courses he was taking in a week, but Charlotte and I were wondering if that week would ever come. We were also very concerned about Alex and Margot, but we stuck to our part of the bargain and left the responsibility to them.

Charlotte's Wild Flowers

After a brief side trip to Poros we headed to Piraeus. With unpleasant memories of Kalamaki still fresh, we opted for the port of Zea. But we were soon to learn again that "Greeks are Greek" and the same arrogance we had so resented in Kalamaki was also present at Zea. We weren't totally surprised when the haughty harbor-master told us there was no free space in the harbor and that we had to leave immediately—this was pretty much the normal response for a request for help. But we did become angry when, after we had pointed out that we had seen several free slots and that a storm was approaching, he kicked us out of his office.

But by this time we had a better understanding of how the game was played and we readily accepted the invitation of the Egyptian caretaker of the giant Monrovian-flagged yacht when he had signaled us to come alongside. After securely tying our vessel along the port side of *Josephena* , we climbed over the immaculate teak decks and went to the harbor-master to inform him that we were staying until the storm passed no matter what he wanted us to do. He shrugged, did a typical Greek 180 degree turn, and told us we could stay for several days if we liked, and quoted a rate that was more than twice as high as anything we had paid since leaving Kalamaki.

We marveled at our surroundings. Monrovia, Panama, Jersey, Isle of Wight—this was millionaire alley. I had never seen so much brass, teak, and fiberglass all in one place before. But even on millionaire alley and even at the exorbitant rate we were paying, the showers were still cold. The Greeks must have reasoned that any boat that merited staying in such exalted surroundings must have their own hot baths and showers aboard.

Despite the rudeness of the harbor-master, the location was ideal. Supermarkets and chandlers were a short walk away and we were close to the busses and trains that could take us to downtown Athens. I paid a visit to Minolis and picked up our mail. If he hadn't been so busy closing the final deal with an Israeli for a Jeanneau Sun Kiss, I would have characterized his reception as almost friendly.

A cultural day in Athens was a must. In exchange for enthusiasm from the children at the Acropolis, Charlotte and I agreed to spring for lunch in the Plaka. As we were walking down a narrow street we read the small sign. "Round trip to Egypt, $99.00." Everybody stopped, retraced their steps, and gathered around me and the notice. "Athens Travel Agency. Office on third floor" Charlotte read. We looked at each other. I shrugged my shoulders and said "Why not go up and see if it's real? What the heck, the war is over. It would be more fun than Yugoslavia."

It was real and Charlotte got all the details. Plenty of room—no need to make reservations until the day we were ready to travel. Suddenly we had a new focus. Warmth and Egypt—they had both been eluding us since the beginning of our trip. Now both were within reach.

One detail, however. We needed to find a place to leave our boat. Zea was out of the question. As much as we disliked Kalamaki we decided to give it a try. Bad idea. The season was about to start and the marina was in its normally grossly overfilled state. No matter that *Captain Spiros* had spent the past three years there and that we personally had paid some pretty hefty fees last fall. They were full and we weren't even Greek.

Here was where maintaining good relations with Minolis was going to pay off. He and his sister did a great deal of business with the marina and if anyone could get me in, he could. "Yes, Heywort, I can help. Meet me at the marina office at 4:00." I did and Minolis arrived half an hour late with his Israeli client in tow.

While Minolis was in the office having a combination friendly reunion, shouting match with the dock-master, the Israeli and I talked. He was a very unhappy camper. Minolis had sold him a Jeanneau sailing sloop and promised him that it would be ready upon his return from Israel. He had just returned along with a crew of his friends that were going to help him sail it back to Israel. An hour ago Minolis had broken the bad news and then the really bad news.

The bad news was that it would take two more months to get his certificate of deletion—sounded familiar. The really bad news was that it looked like a large tax that had not been disclosed to him before was going to be due. But Minolis had suggested a solution to him. Charter the boat now, sail back to Israel with his friends, and then complete the purchase and pay the taxes after the certificate of deletion had been obtained.

"Do you trust Minolis?" and "What do you think I should do?" were the inevitable questions to me.

"Have you paid him any money yet?"

A sad nod to the affirmative.

"I will give you the same advice I received from the American Embassy and several other places. Don't pay a cent more until you have the certificate. As for chartering the boat now, if you do that you have a whole lot of—how do you say in Israel?—Chutzpah!"

By this time Minolis was through with his discussions and told me that he couldn't get me into the marina. This was surprising to me because the facial expressions I had watched from the door suggested than some sort of accommodation had been reached. It then struck me what had happened. He hadn't been arguing my case at all. He had been persuading the dock-master to let the Jeanneau stay two more months so he could complete his fleecing of the hapless Israeli. "*Yassou* Minolis!"

We tried some other marinas but after two hard days of running in place it became obvious that we weren't going to find accommodations in Athens. We finally gave up and, leaving the filth of Zea in our wake, headed back to Aegina to see if we could make arrangements there.

That night in Aegina we decided to splurge and eat in the restaurant that had been Manfred's favorite. Sitting at a table next to us were two Danish families and Charlotte recognized that one of them was from the boat moored about three boats away from *Captain Spiros*. We shared our problem with them and they had a solution. Jorgen knew an Englishman in Poros who was taking care of about ten boats and he felt sure his friend could accommodate us. They had all spent the past winter in Poros and assured us that the protection was excellent. Jorgen needed to take care of some matters in Poros and offered to sail over with us early in the morning and introduce us to his friend.

It was a small miracle. The friend did have space and we trusted him. After a half hour turnover we left the boat, bags in hand, and took a ferry back to Piraeus. A train ride into Athens, a walk to our travel agency in the Plaka, and then a bus out to the airport. We boarded the plane late that afternoon and arrived in Cairo at about 10:00 that evening.

We had known that our family would be nervous about our traveling in Egypt so soon after the war. Although the war was over, peace had not yet been established. As a precaution I called the American Embassy in Athens to learn what they thought about the situation in Egypt. Not surprisingly they knew nothing, but they did give me a number to call in Cairo. I called, received a noncommittal reply, and wondered why I had bothered. We had a crew summit and the conclusion had been unanimous. No problem. We then informed our family and friends at home that we had talked with the American Embassy both in the US and in Egypt and that they had told us it was perfectly safe to travel in Egypt.

As it turned out, our biggest danger was from rip off artists in the chronically suffering tourist industry. It had been a long dry spell, and we were among the first tourists in the country since the beginning of the Gulf Crisis. They were waiting and they were hungry. Habib intercepted us as we were walking through the almost empty airport towards customs. "Hello, I am an official guide and I will check you through customs" he said with a big smile on his face as he put his hand out to receive our passports.

I was suspicious, but complied anyway. He then walked us through customs, efficiently filled out the required forms for us, and then led us into an office. "How long are you in Egypt? You come at a good time. We are glad the war is over. Saddam is a very bad man. He has hurt Egypt very bad. We have no tourists for many months." He paused for breath, motioned us to take a seat, and then got down to the real subject. "We have many travel programs. There is one with five days on the Nile and..."

It was like we had put a quarter in a jukebox and it was going to play the whole song whether we liked it or not. But it was getting close to midnight and we were all very tired. "Habib," I interrupted when he finally came up for air, "we are not really interested in an organized tour. We want to see the country ourselves and..."

"How much you want to pay? The trip on the Nile, she is only cost..." and he proceeded to quote some outlandish figure that was more than I intended to spend on our whole trip. We finally made him understand that we were serious about not wanting to buy a tour, but this only served to put him into hotel hawker mode. No, we didn't want to stay at the Nile Hilton, and no we didn't want to stay at his cousin's very fine hotel either. We were finally able to somewhat appease him by letting him call the hotel we had already picked out from our ever present *Frommer's Egypt*. He then arranged for three of his friends to take us to catch a cab.

The children and I won the wrestling match with the three men over who carried our bags and we headed off to the cab. But this did not prevent three outstretched hands as we climbed in. By this time I was getting angry. But the clincher was yet to come. It was only after the cab left that I realized the hotel we had been deposited in was not the one in Frommer I had asked Habib to call. We took the usual precaution of asking to look at the room before signing in. In this case the hotel looked so run-down that Charlotte insisted that Alex accompany me so that she would not have to rely wholly on my judgment.

It was a bad call, but Alex and I had been too tired to make a sound decision. Charlotte led the bitching as we walked up two flights of stairs past piles of garbage. The first room, the one Alex and I had passed judgment on, was only marginally uninhabitable. But the second—the children's of course—didn't even have sheets on the bed. Back down in the lobby we had a second negotiating session with Habib's cousin, but this time it was from a position of weakness because we had already paid.

He was so sorry about the sheets and immediately dispatched a servant to make up the beds. By this time it was almost one o'clock and we were bone tired. We decided to stay but Charlotte gave strict instructions for everybody to sleep on top of the sheets and not undress. When six o'clock finally came, I left the hotel with my *Frommer's Egypt* to find new lodging. When I returned, I found the four of them at a table staring at the free breakfast in front of them but afraid to try anything. Habib's cousin looked hurt and couldn't imagine why we didn't want to stay—especially since he had offered to lower the price by fifty percent.

Despite our false start, Cairo was great. At the Pyramids of Giza four of us chartered camels while Alex opted for an Arabian horse. We visited the Sphinx, Cheops Pyramid, the Pyramid of Chefren, and then several of the nobles' tombs. Alex showed off by galloping across the desert on his horse, but the rest of us were pretty conservative with our camels—particularly Heyward, who was terrified of horses and wasn't much more comfortable on his big ugly beast.

We decided to visit Aswan next. Our first class seats were terrific, but that didn't make the train run on time and it was almost midnight when we arrived. But the trip itself had been fascinating. Our route allowed us to witness the life giving qualities of the Nile—lush green vegetation along its banks and the bleak desert beyond. Most of the country is desert—it is only the thin snake of land that borders the Nile that supports life. And what vegetation! Fruit and vegetables of all sorts— bananas, rice, pineapples, and lots of plants we couldn't identify. We saw water buffalo pulling plow shares and donkeys

Margot's Camel

tied to long wooden poles that drove wells. This was the way it has been done for centuries, and probably the way it will be done for centuries to come.

The best thing about Aswan had been meeting Said. He was a displaced Nubian, one of the many casualties of the Aswan dam, and operated his lateen rigged sailboat to shuttle tourists around the many

sights in Aswan. We were so taken with him and his craft that we decided to engage him for an overnight trip up to Darwa. His eight meter felluca, *Paradise*, was typical of the traditional craft that has been used for centuries to transport goods up and down the Nile. The driving force of the vessel is a wonderful fluke of nature. For trips north, the vessel takes advantage of the current that flows from headwaters in Kenya, Uganda, and Sudan north to Alexandria where it empties into the Mediterranean Sea. For trips south, it takes full advantage of the winds that blow in the opposite direction from the current.

Cruising on the Nile

I admired the simplicity of *Paradise* with its lateen rig sail—a jib and mainsail all in one. As we worked our way north, we were constantly changing course on small tacks. But all Said had to do was swing the long tiller. The lateen sail needed no adjustment

and simply shifted from side to side each time we tacked. This was quite a contrast to all the work required on *Captain Spiros* to trim the huge jib each time we came about. Charlotte took the tiller for several hours and loved it. While she was guiding, Said told us about the Nile and about his Nubian relatives. He was a very devout Muslim and he would interrupt his stories to

Charlotte at the Helm

wash and go through his ritual during the calls to prayer.

As dusk approached, Said carefully picked a sand bar in the middle of the river for our night anchorage. He prepared an elegant dinner of onion, tomato, and potato stew and then brewed tea from Nile water. Quietly preparing all of this over his small portable kerosene stove, he explained that once you have drunk tea brewed with water from the Nile, you will always return.

Watching the sun set, hearing two cows mooing on the distant shore, and feeling the warm refreshing breeze as it blew up the Nile gave a setting to our simple but delicious meal that couldn't have been matched in any of the luxury cruisers we had watched passing us during the day. The bottle of red wine that had taken almost an hour to find in Aswan was a perfect compliment to Said's stew and we sipped it until well after dark. While the food, setting, and company were all very good, the sleeping accommodations left something to be desired. Said broke out the blankets and pillows and set up the combination tent-awning over the cockpit, but no matter how we arranged ourselves or our blankets, there was always a rib of the boat poking into one or another part of our bodies—maybe those luxury cruisers weren't so bad after all.

Said was ready to start early—which was fine with all of us as we had been up for some time. At Darwa, Said's cousin, whom he had called before leaving Aswan, was waiting with his cab to take us to the camel market. They had come from Sudan by caravan and there were hundreds of them. Babies and mothers, big ones and little ones—there were camels as far as we could see. The Bedouins stared at us like we were from Mars, but when they saw we were harmless the children came up to try to talk to us. It was a strange experience, and we never fully understood how the sales were transacted— but we had a wonderful time looking at all the nomads in their desert garb and wondering what it would be like to live their strange lives.

As Said's cousin drove through rugged and exotic countryside towards Luxor, we passed truck after truck loaded with successful purchases from Darwa and went into hysterics as the trucks in front of us would turn to the right or left. As they rounded the curves, the centrifugal force generated by the turn would force the camel's long necks and heads to sway out over the side of the truck in long graceful arcs. It

Camel Market at Darwa

was like they were scrutinizing the beauty of the landscape with the same enthusiasm as the eager tourists that trailed behind.

The temples between Darwa and Luxor and Luxor itself were interesting, but what we loved was our trek through the Valley of the Kings by donkey. Mohammet had arrived at our hotel early that morning and ushered us aboard the ferry for the trip to the west bank of the Nile. A short walk through crowded streets took to us to his stables and we each chose our mount. Small, but powerful and very frisky, our donkeys—more eager than their cautious riders—took off to see the tombs. We trotted, we cantered, we walked, and then we cantered again. All the while the five of us bobbed up and down on our little animals with arms and legs poking out in all directions and flailing about.

Heyward's donkey was the most aggressive and was determined that none of the others should steal the lead from him. Alex, who was even more aggressive than Heyward's donkey and who fancied himself an accomplished jockey of any four legged beast, tried to urge his steed to outpace Heyward's. Both my donkey and I possessed moderate amounts of aggressiveness and often found opportunities to briefly take the lead from Alex or Heyward

The Donkey Derby

The resulting mad scramble kept Margot and Charlotte laughing so hard that I was afraid they would fall from their bouncing perches. But as fun as the whole affair was becoming we all sobered as the narrow trail started to bend around sharp turns from which we could look down steep cliffs to a harsh rocky bottom many donkey lengths below. Mohammet advised that it was best not to look down.

After only a very short ride we found ourselves in completely desolate surroundings and began to understand why the Pharaohs had referred to it as the valley of the dead. It wasn't just because of the setting sun and its symbolism of the day dying. In the dessert before us everything was dead. We were beginning to feel very alone and tired when out of nowhere they appeared. There were two of them and they were selling scarabs. How could they have known we were coming? Where had they come from?

"You see, it's very nice scarab. You like? See, it is not plastic" said one of them while he held a cigarette lighter under it and almost burned his hand showing us that the treasured scarab would not ignite. The other, apparently feeling a little upstaged, began an earnest pitch to sell Margot a beaded bracelet. Margot responded by pulling a ring from her pocket and trying to sell it to her assailant.

All of this occurred as our aggressive animals continued to jockey for position. Our attention alternated from trying to brace ourselves for a sudden fall down the steep cliffs and trying to fend off our new "very nice friends" who were trying so hard to give us a special price on "beautiful Egyptian artifacts." Two scarabs and a green soap stone turtle later we sighted the Valley of The Kings below.

We marveled at the bright colors and clear paintings in the tombs of Ramses III and IV, but the main attraction, King Tutankhamon tomb, was closed for restoration so we crossed over into the Valley of the Queens. There we were able to visit the tomb and temple of Queen Hatshepsut. Margot got to see first hand the sight she had researched so meticulously the year before as part of a term paper for Springside School. What a strange feeling for her to realize that there was something actually behind those silly history books she had been forced to read and regurgitate back in her other life in Philadelphia.

**

Before the Gulf War, our goal had been to take our boat to the Red Sea and winter in Hurghada. Now we could still realize a part of this goal, but by land rather than by sea. We had to get up early to catch the first bus to Hurghada. It was crowded but comfortable and we loved threading our way up the Nile valley and then across the barren deserts that separated the Nile from the Red Sea. Pulling into village after village to pick up and discharge an endless stream of passengers, we could feel the pulse of the countryside and of the people much more than in the train,.

In Hurghada we found a quiet little hotel with a beautiful white beach that surrounded a tiny lagoon. It was blissful solitude to relax and enjoy the beach and water of our almost empty resort. But our bliss was dashed with the appearance of a speck on the horizon that gradually took on the shape of a ship and finally revealed itself as a giant aircraft carrier.

Shortly after our sighting of the speck, the USS America and her escorting cruiser arrived in Hurghada—by evening the sleepy little coastal community was transformed into a jungle of crowded hotels, crowded restaurants, and crowded streets with New Jersey, California, and Virginia accents filling the air.

In spite of the rowdiness and in spite of the naive rudeness some of the younger and less experienced sailors were displaying towards the citizens of Hurghada, the Hurghadans loved it. Tourism had been dead since the outset of the war and now their empty facilities were suddenly packed to overflowing. But more important than that, Saddam Hussein had caused incredible economic hardship in Egypt and here was a detachment of the forces that had brought victory and presumably the return of prosperity to their country.

Our children loved it also. They had been starved for companionship from back home and now they had it in spades. There were four or five groups from the ships staying at our hotel and we immediately became friends with several of them. There was something that made us all feel very proud to be Americans with the arrival of the carrier. With our proximity to the action, we felt like we had lived the war. We had watched huge US warships speeding towards the Suez Canal and we had even cheered them on through brief messages on our VHF radio. But the ships had maintained radio silence and had never acknowledged our cheering messages. This was our first encounter with the soldiers and sailors whose dangerous mission we had followed so closely and with so much enthusiasm and concern.

The USS America was the only carrier to fight in both the Persian Gulf and the Red Sea. They had flown an incredible number of successful sorties, but most incredibly they had not suffered a single casualty. It had been all success and this was their first port since entering the troubled area over six months earlier. Feelings were running high.

We became very attached to a group of six young men that formed a flight support crew on the carrier. Alex soaked up the technical accounts of their war experiences like a sponge. Heyward was delighted to be included in the orders for rounds of beer and joined them for their evening sorties into the town. Margot was old enough to attract their attention, but too young to participate. Charlotte and I watched with eagle eyes, but our new friends treated Margot more like a sister than a possible female catch.

It was a bizarre situation and setting. On the one hand we were experiencing a city full of victorious warriors just off the battle front. But on the other hand what we saw was a group of lonely boys who missed home, mother, and girl friends. And then there was us. A sole American family enjoying an impromptu vacation from a very unusual year of gypsy living. A very normal family living a very un-normal experience. The combination worked. The sailors were amazed to see a small slice of home and we loved having the opportunity to express our gratefulness for all they and their companions had done for our country. We thought about the expression we had been hearing from cab drivers and hotel clerks from Cairo to Aswan to

Luxor. "Saddam crazy. George Bush is numero uno." Here was a country who appreciated America, Americans, and our courageous President.

After three days, we decided to head back to Cairo. This time we opted for the luxury bus that left in mid afternoon. Briefcases and suitcases replaced the chickens and tied bundles we had seen on the trip from Luxor and this bus had air-conditioning. The people also seemed friendlier and we struck up several interesting conversation.

Far more interesting than the monotonous stretch of the Red Sea on our trip back to Cairo was the magical activity that began to take place about two hours before sunset. It started slowly and relatively quietly, but like a small snowball rolling down a steep hill it rapidly gained speed and momentous noise. Bags rustled as they were torn open, waxed paper crinkled as it was removed from dishes, silverware clinked, and low voices murmured as people traded condiments and instruments. Conversations became louder and more animated. Laughter broke out first in one corner and then the next.

As darkness approached the tempo increased and our neighbor across the isle explained why. We knew that the religious festival of Ramadan was in full swing and that nothing was to be taken by mouth during daylight hours. We also knew that this was an incredibly difficult time of year for the Moslems and that tempers and emotions flared. But what we had never experienced was the sense of pure joy and of camaraderie that participants in this rigorous fast share as the magic hour of sunset approaches. The atmosphere was tense, the passengers were leaning over their plates poised and ready to go, and the radio was at full blast when finally it came. The call to prayer and the official declaration of sunset. What a way to enter the bustle and confusion of Cairo.

***

Not wanting to repeat our last hotel fiasco in Cairo, I had chosen the Grand Hotel from the list in Frommer and called ahead from Hurghada. But presenting our cab driver with a definite name and address in no way diminished his determination to make his own sale. Two blocks short of the Grand Hotel he stopped in front of an establishment and then exhausted his imaginative supply of English superlatives. I was going to be polite and at least take a quick look, but the children and Charlotte took immediate and very vocal exception to this and used the opportunity of the stopped cab to climb out and walk rapidly to the Grand Hotel.

The glowing description in Frommer had been exaggerated, but probably far less so than that of our cab driver in describing his cousin's

193

hotel, and we found the accommodations quite satisfactory. As our Fezzed steward showed Charlotte and me around our room and pointed out the magnificent view from our eighth story balcony we began to get excited. But the real excitement came when we heard the shout from Heyward

"Mom, Dad, come look. There's a television in our room." Before we could get there we heard another shout, but this time full of disappointment.

"Bummer. It doesn't work."

As I entered the room and looked at the dilapidated set, I wasn't surprised. All the knobs were off and a mangy wire hung down from the back that didn't even have a plug. Turning towards the steward I asked if he could get it working. The steward gave me a quizzical, disdaining stare, threw a quick glance at the set, and then marched over and grabbed the trailing wire. He then stuffed the two bare ends into a nearby socket, turned the brass rod where a knob had once been, and proudly stepped aside as static and loud bellowing in Arabic emerged.

We had been told that it never rains in Cairo, but on our way back to the hotel from dinner on one of our last nights, it did. And with unexpected results. As the huge droplets began to fall, Charlotte noted with horror that my white shirt was becoming covered with black spots. Looking up, we quickly discovered the cause for this bizarre phenomenon. The buildings, awnings, poles, and every other structure were covered with grimy dust and dirt that had accumulated over time. Now the rain was dissolving the grime and we were experiencing black rain.

The Egyptian Museum, the souk at Khan el-Khalili, Giza at Sunset, and a day trip to the Fayyum went by quickly and suddenly it was time to leave. Completely rejuvenated and with our minds still swimming in the fascination of ancient and modern Egypt, we began our trek back to Poros and *Captain Spiros.*

Chapter 8
Corinth and the Ionian

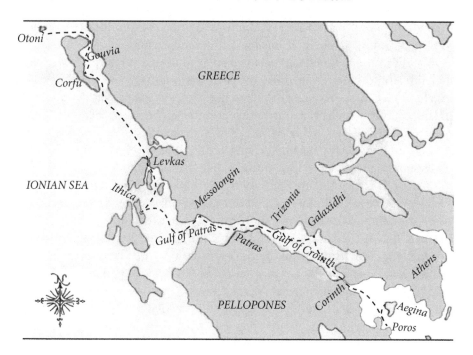

W̲e stepped off the plane into warm sunshine. Greece was sparkling. We hopped into a cab in high spirits, stopped by Minolis' office to pick up mail, and then headed on to Piraeus and bought a ticket on the *Flying Dolphin* to Poros. It felt great to be in familiar surroundings and to know our way around. After Egypt, Greece seemed like a model of efficiency. Even Kalamaki had looked good as we passed it in the cab heading to Minolis'.

Feeling the freshness of the sea breeze and watching whiter than white houses glide past as we approached Poros, we were amazed to find that many of the frustrations we had felt with Greece could have melted away so quickly, but they had. Our complex feelings towards Greece were becoming harder and harder to understand. A classic love-hate relationship. But, for the moment, it was love and we stepped off the *Flying Dolphin* in Poros fully rejuvenated and anxious to continue our exploration of these intriguing islands. The plan was to sail to Corinth, traverse the canal, visit Galaxidhi to see Delphi, rejoin the Hjorths, and then head on to Corfu, exploring along the way. Our objective was to arrive in Corfu in time for Orthodox Easter.

It was great to reclaim *Captain Spiros*. This was home and it was wonderful to be back. Despite the rigors of life on board, the familiar routines, our own beds and pillows, and our little possessions—all of this added up to a comfort that we had missed. The Englishman had done a very nice job of taking care of our boat and everything was in order. We immediately set out to restock and made preparations for getting underway.

Even the markets had changed since our departure. Warm weather had brought a better selection, and we had our bags overflowing with vegetables when we arrived at the butcher shop. Charlotte was set on a leg of lamb dinner to celebrate our return and the forthcoming visit of friends from Philadelphia so we tried our best sign language. At first we were having difficulty, but Charlotte finally coaxed the perplexed butcher into understanding with her a deep guttural "bah, bah."

Both Charlotte and I are particular about how we cook our lamb. We like it quite rare and by trial and error have developed a precise formula based on weight. We set a very short time on the timer, but when I carved the meat it wasn't red at all. In fact it was white. Strange. But I decided not to say anything—Charlotte would know I was disappointed it wasn't rare, and I didn't want to embarrass her in front of the Drakes who had just arrived.

Our celebratory dinner was not just because we were back aboard and had visitors. The Drakes had very kindly carried the cloth suitcase my mother had prepared for us that was jam-packed packed with books and was as heavy as lead. My mother had fulfilled each of the many requests that had been relayed by phone from all over the Eastern Mediterranean, and the results were now on our salon table. The children had become voracious readers and their incredible appetites for new material had now been met. I never would have believed it possible to see such excitement from them over the receipt of a stack of books.

Although we had left the states with a substantial portion of our allocated weight dedicated to books, the children had sped through most of them after the first five or six months. In theory we could have traded for new books with other boats, but each time we tried, it turned out that someone had not read one of the "to be traded" books or wanted to read it again and we couldn't consummate the transaction. In truth, what was happening was that we had become so attached to the books that we simply refused to part with them.

The reading was also very important to our social life. We all read many of the same books and at night we would have long discussions about the characters at the dinner table. Conroy's Carolina low country characters became alive, and favorites from other authors would come up time and time again. Our lives were in transition, and reading was helping us bridge the gap. We were trading in our conservative suburban life in the Northeast for what we hoped would be a more laid-back life among the salt marshes of South Carolina. Our reading provided with us with tableaus of personalities, landscapes, and styles of living that gave us a framework to compare past experiences with future expectations.

Early the next morning we left for the Corinth Canal. It was another beautiful day and we were having a great time with the Drakes. I hoped that Chris' and Carl's ears weren't getting too sore after all the talking since their arrival. Everybody felt compelled to relate all the details of our adventure to our two new passengers and often we had two or three stories going at the same time.

A swim call on our way to the Corinth Canal was a dramatic change in our routine that was brought about by the return of warm sunshine. Blue lips and sporadic shivers, but once out of the chill bath, the sun provided instant warmth and comfort—summer had returned.

As we approached the canal, I began to rethink my strategy. I had been warned many times about what lay ahead, but I had worked out my plan very carefully. The root of the problem was the tariff schedule. There were three tariffs—one for small yachts, one for medium to large size yachts, and then one for everything else. Everything else included large freighters and tankers, and by ship standards the tariff of this latter category probably wasn't exorbitant.

But the Greeks had had a little trick up their sleeves when they constructed the tariff. The tonnage ranges they used in creating their schedule were reasonable, but the method they used in their calculation of the tonnage of yachts for registration papers was not. During the endless process of obtaining the certificate of deletion, I had noted, but not been concerned about, the 23 net tons figure on the original registration of *Captain Spiros*. It had seemed like a ridiculous number as our actual displacement was less than 15 tons, but I hadn't seen where the error could cause any harm so I forgot about it.

After calling from Rhodes to find the tariff for the Canal I had realized that it was going to be a very big problem. The medium size category ended at 20 tons—we were comfortably into the large tanker category and would have to pay the same tariff as ships displacing thousands of tons.

Deeply resenting the injustice of having to pay a truly exorbitant fee for the privilege of passing through the three mile long canal, I had taken precautions. The reissue of my Transit Log upon the return from our aborted trip to Malta with Demetri had provided the opportunity. Conveniently I had "forgotten" to bring all of my papers and had to fill in the "net weight" blank from memory which I had remembered as 15 tons.

My plan was to go to the office with only my transit log and see if I could bluff my way through. The operator was immediately suspicious, but before he could sink his teeth into the problem the radio dragged him into a crisis at the other end of the canal. Wishing to get rid of me quickly, he asked how long the waterline of the boat was. In the heat of the moment I became confused and gave him the metric dimension but mistakenly called it feet.

His expression immediately changed from suspicion to relief and he quickly said: "Oh, you are very small, you pay at the middle tariff." Fortunately for me he couldn't see my boat from his seat in front of the radio. I quickly paid the yacht tariff and left praying that the radio would keep him occupied until we headed down the canal.

While we waited for the blue flag that would signal that the one way traffic had turned in our direction, I read about the history of this strategic isthmus that separates the Aegean and Ionian Seas. In ancient times warring nations would drag their ships across the land bridge. Octavian's pursuit of Antony after Actium was one of the more famous instances. Nero had tried to dig a canal but had failed. It was the French who finally succeeded and the Corinth Canal was opened in 1893.

Transiting the Corinth Canal

Our turn finally came and I took the wheel. We were third in line. There was a Greek tanker, a German yacht, and then us. The scenery was stunning but I had to focus my attention on driving. The width was less than twice the length of our boat, and one wrong turn would result in a collision with one of the limestone cliffs. Towering 80 meters overhead, the cliffs made us feel like we were rafting down the Grand Canyon. I had read about how these same cliffs could funnel wind and the devastating effects it could have on shipping, but we were fortunate to have an almost breathless afternoon.

Our overnight at the modern and uninteresting port of Corinth would have been a disappointment had it not been for our visit to ancient Corinth. Only a short bus ride away we had the pleasure of taking an evening stroll through the beautiful Temple of Apollo, and climbing up to visit the old Acropolis that towers above. Situated at the strategic crossroads between mainland Greece and the Peloponnesus and between the Aegean and Ionian Seas the ancient citizens of Corinth had thrived and had become incredibly wealthy.

The next morning when we were ready to get underway, Heyward and I cast off the lines and Alex put the boat in forward. No movement.

"Alex, are you in gear?"

"No Dad, I always try to move the boat forward leaving it in neutral."

Ignoring Alex's remark I went to the stern and looked into the water. There was plenty of wash from the screw—but still no motion. We were aground. I had been spoiled by the lack of tide in the Mediterranean and hadn't bothered to check to see if the patterns were a little different just before the choke point of the Corinth Canal. There were only a few inches of tide change, but it was enough. Our keel was firmly lodged against the rocky bottom and with all the weight of our boat pushing on the rocks we weren't going anywhere.

Standard maneuver number one—everyone on the bow—didn't work so we tried standard maneuver number two. Boom at right angles to the boat with Heyward, Alex, and Margot straddling the far end. Standard maneuver number two didn't work either so we decided to try Alex's non-standard brainstorm. He tied one end of a heavy line to the base of a statue about 30 meters off our beam and the other end to a spare halyard. He then started winching. The good news was that it worked. As the boat began its steep list towards the shore the keel came free. The bad news was that it didn't do us any good because the boat was now tightly wedged against the shore and neither hard forward nor hard reverse had the slightest effect.

We then resorted to a modification. Heyward and Alex dinghied out with the Danforth anchor and placed it about 60 meters from the middle of the boat. We then tried Alex's trick again, but this time used the anchor instead of the statue to pull our mast down. Before we achieved much of a list, a ferry passed close to us and the combination of its wake and our list did the trick. This time the strain on the halyard pulled us away from the dock and we were free.

We were now in the Gulf of Corinth, the first of two gulfs that separate the Ionian from the Aegean. Our immediate destination was Galaxidhi which was on the northeast side of the gulf. From there we would work our way through the second gulf, the Gulf of Patras, and into the Ionian. The sea was calm and there was very little wind—an ideal initiation for the Drakes. Wing and wing we glided across the glassy water and then sighted snow-peaked mountains and land.

Galaxidhi was a beautiful little port with excellent protection. We admired the pine forest along the east bank of the narrow harbor and found a spot along the quay. Although we were disappointed not to find *Et Au Alt*, we fell in love with the port. The Greeks here were noticeably friendlier and the grocery store owner even drove us back to our boat with our purchases. He also explained how to catch the bus to Itea where we could make connections to Delphi.

Spring was in full bloom during our ride to Delphi and Charlotte talked non-stop about the landscape with its wild flowers and compared it to a Monet painting. As we headed up a steep grade, both Charlotte and I spotted them at the same time. Suddenly the mystery of the not so rare lamb

back in Poros unraveled as we watched the young shepherd guide his little flock of goats and heard their little cries of "bah, bah, bah."

High up on a plateau and surrounded by the giant peaks of Mt. Parnassus sat Delphi in all its majesty. This was the center of the ancient world, the spot where the rock vomited from the stomach of Cronos had landed. Rea's deception had saved Zeus from being swallowed and had led to the stomach ache that had created a legend. Our visit to this site, often referred to by the ancients as the navel of the world,

Delphi

included a visit to the Temple of Apollo, a tour of the Museum of Delphi, and a delicious lunch in a nearby restaurant.

While we were gone, we had acquired a new neighbor in the port. Jim on *Rascal* introduced himself and then came on board for a beer. He was a wealth of information on ports to the west and I took copious notes in my log. By the time he left our boat, I had a pretty firm idea of how we would skirt the boot of Italy. In return we loaded him down with information on the Cyclades and Turkey.

Signaling that it wasn't through with us yet, the wind began to blow hard as we approached Rhion, the choke point that separates the Gulf of Corinth from the Gulf of Patras. The effect was masked because the wind was from the stern, but Charlotte's antennas were up and she persuaded me to take in a reef. Her advice was good, but I was late in following it—almost too late. The channel was too narrow to turn up into the wind and I had to either reef with full sails and the wind astern or wait until we were in wider water. As the wind was mounting rapidly, I chose the former, but the force on the mainsail was so great that we were barely able to get the reef in place and before the maneuver was completed our dinghy had flipped over twice. Fortunately our practice of removing the motor before getting underway with the dinghy in tow prevented serious damage, but the incident served as a vivid reminder of our vulnerability to the elements and the importance of paying close attention to the mechanics of sailing.

At Patros we found a comfortable mooring along one of the town quays and watched a sleek French sloop work its way into the harbor from the opposite direction. Soaking wet and in full "space suit" regalia they were exhausted. But it wasn't just from beating against the wind that they were tired. They had come the whole way from Corsica, with only two stops in between, and were headed for the Black Sea. Their goal was to be the first Western charter boat in Russia. By contrast our sail had been easy. With the wind behind us, the same force that had caused the French crew such discomfort had pushed us merrily along with the only danger being our own complacency.

Patras is the largest city in the Peloponnesus and bustles with activity. Ferries come in from Brindisi loaded with tourists and busses head out in all directions loaded with the sightseers. It was an ideal place for the Drakes to catch a bus that would take them back to Athens where they would catch a plane to Philadelphia. Their visit had provided a link to home and we were sad to see them go.

**

As we neared the Ionian we thought about the whole new spectrum of adventure that lay before us. We debated about our destinations—Chephalonia, Zante, Ithaca, and Levkas all sounded fascinating—I read one enticing description after another as we discussed the pros and cons. But Orthodox Easter was approaching, and we had decided to spend it in Corfu. We had time for some sightseeing, but it was limited.

Our relatively late departure from Patras meant one more Gulf of Patras stop before the new world of the Ionian. We decided on Mesolongion, on the mainland shore near the entrance. Heading up the narrow channel, we stared with wonder at the houses sitting on stilts in the salt marsh. It was a cross between low country South Carolina and Southeast Asia.

In the small bay at the end of the channel we circled around looking for a safe anchorage. The protection was superb, but a very strong wind was building up. We anchored carefully, went ashore for a brief visit, and then returned to the boat for a fried chicken dinner and then hours of wonderfully introspective conversation.

The trip to Egypt had been a relaxing interlude, but our life had become *Captain Spiros* and sailing. While our return had brought us back to reality, our time in Egypt had given us an opportunity to examine our new life from a distance, and we liked what we saw. Each of us had his own opinion about the benefits of the trip, but the common thread was that they were significant and we were all glad we were there.

Heyward was particularly high on the adventure and opined that he would like to do the same kind of thing with his family when the time came. This led to the inevitable discussion on responsibility, money, and how he was going to fund it. While I was glad to see Heyward wrestling with these realities, I was less enthusiastic about his proposed solution—he would simply find a wife willing to work hard enough to provide the necessary funds.

Charlotte and I were pleased with the enormous increase in family togetherness and with the opportunity to get to know our children in a new way. Although we continued to be concerned about their education, we thought that what they were missing in formal education was more than compensated by what they were learning about themselves and about the world. I still had concerns about my livelihood once we returned home but decided that it was something that would just have to wait for later.

Our entrance into the Ionian was dramatic. A deep blue, much deeper than the blue in the Aegean, greeted us, and we were poised for adventure. We had debated a great deal about our first destination, but the pull of Odysseus finally won out. We would head for his home at Ithaca. Smooth seas and a very pleasant sail led us to the spectacular approach through the narrow channel leading to Port Vathi. The lush green was in stark contrast to the ruggedness of the Aegean's rocky islands, and we approached the quaint town with excited anticipation. It was one of the prettiest views we had yet seen in Greece.

The next morning brought rain, a very stiff wind, and a healthy chill. But we wanted to spend Easter in Corfu, so we set out anyway. As the day progressed, the rain ceased and it became pleasant as we entered the second canal of our trip. Originally dug by the Corinthians around the seventh century BC, it is still an imposing sight. The five-mile-long channel separates the large island of Levkas from mainland Greece and is bordered by salt marshes that give way to green lush hills in the background. The town of Levkas, at the northern end of the canal, was charming and was home to many wintering yachts.

The harbor was crowded and the geometry of the boats surrounding my chosen berth required backing and turning at the same time, but from a direction that did not allow me to take advantage of the lateral thrust of the propeller. It's a subtle force, but an important one. When the boat moves slowly, a sudden revving of the propeller gives the stern a firm push to the side. Since my propeller rotated counterclockwise in reverse, this thrust was to port. But in this case I needed thrust to starboard to accomplish the tight turn. The maneuver was already getting away from me when Heyward missed his toss of the stern line to a yacht watcher on shore. While his second toss was successful and enabled the volunteer on shore to get it to a bollard, by this time we were almost parallel to the quay.

We had been through this before and it is never pleasant. Heyward put the stern line to a winch and we took turns slowly winching the 15 tons of *Captain Spiros* against the wind and into the quay. The knowing smiles of passing yachtsmen added to the tension as Heyward and I exchanged barbs about who was at fault for the fiasco. When we finally secured the boat we all stormed off in separate directions to cool off from the end of a strenuous day.

The distance from Levkas to Corfu was long and the day looked foreboding, but the wind was in the right direction. Apparently we had read the notices correctly about the drawbridge at the mouth of the canal, because when we approached it at 8:30 A.M. and honked, it opened and we passed through. This time the rain didn't stop, and the wind blew harder and harder. After our experience entering Patras, I didn't hesitate when Charlotte asked, and we put the second reef in the main shortly after clearing the drawbridge. I was glad we had. The wind was strong, steady, and from astern. We were speeding at eight knots towards Corfu.

Through the rain we saw it—a fort and a city high up on a hill. Corfu was huge and the surroundings were lush green. I was still trying to read the coastline as we rounded Cape Sidhero and then saw a small harbor at the base of the fort. But it wasn't until we started to skirt the northern coast of the city that we began to get a true picture of the size and magnificence of Corfu. It was crowded, and I was beginning to wonder if we should continue on to the neighboring harbor of Gouvia. We were wet, tired, and ready to get to some shelter, but something made me want to explore the old harbor before giving up. After passing through the narrow opening between the sea wall and a stone quay we found that the harbor was jammed. Not only was there no pier space, but, in true Kalamaki style, there were boats outboard of boats and then boats outboard of them. I went the whole way to the west end, turned around and was slowly heading out when Margot shouted:

"Look, it's them."

And there it was—the little white sloop with blue trim and *Et Au Alt* painted neatly on the stern. We came alongside, knocked on the hull, and four heads poked out of the companionway door. Bianne and Klaus helped with lines and two minutes later we had a new home. Bianne was outboard a large fishing boat and said the owner had been talking about getting underway, but that he thought nothing was likely to happen until after Easter.

We were all excited about the reunion and everybody was talking at once. We told them about how disappointed we had been to miss them at Galaxidhi and that we had given up on finding them. Deeda then told us about thinking she had heard us over the radio one night as they were entering the Saronic Gulf. It had been very late and she was the only one who had heard it. No one else had believed it could have been us. Nonetheless, she had persisted and had looked through binoculars as they passed the harbor of Aegina the next morning on their way to Corinth. She had seen a Trinidad and had tried to radio, but on hearing nothing she had given up and they had continued.

We checked dates on both our logbooks and there it was. The night we had sailed into Aegina and had the close scrape with the tanker it had been them that Margot had heard on the radio. The reason no one had acknowledged Deeda's call the following morning was that our radio had been off.

The next day Charlotte and I made a trip to the tourist office in the Citadel on the point we had rounded the previous afternoon and obtained information on the festivities for Easter week. We took the information back to *Et Au Alt* and went over it during lunch. Ian and Deborah of *Mistress* joined us. They had arrived in Corfu a week earlier and had become good friends of the Hjorths.

It was another reunion and this time we heard about *Mistress'* adventures. They had waited until daylight before leaving for Simi and, as the wind began to increase, they had decided to detour to Kos where they weathered the same gale we had experienced in Astipalaia. Their next destination had been Amorgos where they met the Hjorths and filled them in on our progress.

Bianne and Deeda had planned to get underway the next day to arrive in Southern France in time to meet friends and take their trip back to Denmark through the French canals. Ever since they had shared their plans with us back in Marmaris we had been intrigued with the thought. What a way to see the countryside!

We all wanted to join them, but the limitations of *Captain Spiros* made it out of the question. The same deep keel that provided us with such wonderful stability in rough seas was the stopper. The maximum for the canals was six feet and we were over this by more than a foot. Our voyage through the canals of France would have to wait for another trip and another boat.

The Hjorths were so excited to see us and so intrigued with the information we had obtained on Easter Week that they decided to remain with us for the festivities and then sail with us as far as the toe of Italy. From there they would head north and we would continue west or south.

The official activities began on Good Friday. Every high school, army, navy, church, and Greek Scout band in all of Greece must have been there. It was festive, lively, and moving, and the pouring rain and sleet did not dampen the enthusiasm in the least. We watched, followed, and joined the cheering as the bands snaked their path from one end of the ancient city to the other through the beautifully meandering streets.

We were enthralled with the city. Its rich history dates back to the Phaeacians who transported Odysseus home to Ithaca and who were rewarded by a wrathful Poseidon who turned their boat into stone. Venice's influence began in 1400 and continued until the French took over in 1797. The French laid out an organized street plan and began the arcade of buildings along the Esplanade. The result is a wonderful mixture of Venetian and French architecture. The Esplanade reminded us of buildings near Paris' Place de Vendome.

Easter Saturday brought a special treat. Just before noon, all of the city and all of the many visitors from throughout Greece gathered in downtown Corfu along streets overhung with spacious balconies. We never fully understood the spiritual significance, but it was explained to us that it had to do

Marching Band in Corfu

with driving the devil away. At any rate, at the sound of twelve, a rain of pottery thicker than the rain and hail of the previous evening came crashing down on the streets from balconies and windows. The noise, the confusion, and the debris were a magnificent display of destruction and the crowds reveled in it.

As the day progressed the notes from the continuously marching bands became increasingly lugubrious and by late afternoon had become dirges. The marching slowed and mourning crowds followed. By the time they converged at the center of the park outside the Citadel, the march had stalled to a slow walk. The sound of the clock striking midnight produced a silence that was broken several seconds later when the Archbishop shouted: "Christo Averti"—Christ has risen.

Instantly the bands switched to lively tempos, cannons boomed, and fireworks lit the skies—and the Greeks went absolutely wild. Thousands of people paraded through the streets following the bands and holding candles. Alex and Claus had somehow obtained their own stock of fireworks and did their part to add to the excitement.

Easter Saturday Pottery Smash

***

There was another aspect of Easter Week that had caught our attention. Everyone, poor and rich alike, roasted a whole lamb on Easter Sunday. There were no exceptions. Preparations for this event started well over a week ahead. As we walked along the streets we would almost trip over giant spits for sale in front of little hardware stores or be mesmerized by row after row of whole lambs suspended from hooks in butcher shops. It became too much for me, and I finally ducked into a hardware store and purchased a six-foot-long spit along with two stands to hold it.

When I showed my purchase to Charlotte, the children, and the Hjorths, the enthusiasm was instantaneous. We immediately formed a syndicate with our two boats, *Mistress*, and a Danish boat, to purchase a lamb and take it to Gouvia for a picnic. On Thursday all Hjorths and all Colemans had marched to the butcher to pick out a lamb. There were rows and rows—all hanging from their hind legs, skinless, naked, and with their teeth tightly clenched—and we made our choice. We then had our reservation pinned to it for a Saturday pickup.

Saturday morning Bianne and I took turns carrying the 33-pound beast. We needed dog-free cold storage and knew that it didn't exist on either craft. After carefully thinking the matter through, we wrapped our purchase in a plastic garbage bag, tied it lengthwise to the boom of the *Captain Spiros,* and left it there while we prepared to enjoy the Easter Saturday festivities.

***

We experienced a moving episode that Saturday in addition to the Easter happenings. Ian arrived at our boat breathless: "My friend John on *Cloud Clipper* sailed yesterday and moored in a prohibited area near the Albanian boarder. He just radioed a few minutes ago. It's blowing a gale, his motor isn't working, and he is afraid his two anchors won't hold. The wind is blowing him straight towards Albania." We then turned on my VHF and unsuccessfully tried to contact *Cloud Clipper.*

Although Ian did not immediately pose the question, I knew what he was thinking. "How big is *Cloud Clipper?*" I nervously asked, looking at the foaming surf on the other side of the breakwater and feeling the noose tightening around my neck.

Choosing Our Easter Lamb

"She's a 17-meter ketch, but with your large boat you shouldn't have any trouble towing her." I knew differently. With high winds and limited maneuverability, it would be very precarious to try to maneuver our single screw vessel into a position to extract the much larger *Cloud Clipper.* I had never even met Ian's friend John, and I was extremely worried about the prospect of taking my vessel out of its safe anchorage to conduct a mission for which it was ill equipped. But there is the code of the sea and the code of cruising families and offering help to a vessel in distress is not a matter to be taken lightly.

Locked in the horns of dilemma, I was rescued by an announcement over the VHF from *Striker* who volunteered to perform the rescue. She was larger than *Cloud Clipper,* a motor sailor, and much better equipped than *Captain Spiros* for the mission. For the next two hours we listened to the radio as the drama unfolded. With *Striker* still in route, *Cloud Clipper* managed to get her motor going long enough to get underway and get her sails up. It looked like everything was going to be okay, but suddenly the radio cracked back to life.

"*Striker* this is *Cloud Clipper*. We just lost our fore stay and have lowered all sails to avoid losing the mast. Our motor won't start and we are drifting towards Albania." The two boats then exchanged positions and I plotted them on my chart for the crowd gathering around my navigation table to study. It was going to be close.

Silence for ten more minutes then another transmission. "*Cloud Clipper* this is *Striker*. We have you in sight and will have you in tow in 20 minutes." It was a dramatic experience and one that reminded all of us of our vulnerability to the elements and our dependency on our machinery and on each other.

***

We had another surprise that day. We were sitting in the cockpit of *Captain Spiros* when we saw a familiar shape glide into the harbor. Low, sleek, green sides, a ketch—yes—it was *Sweet Thursday*. She tied up outboard our boat. By the looks we were getting from the fishing boat inboard of our by now substantial string of boats, we could tell that our welcome was wearing thin. But no matter; it was Peter and June and we were delighted to see them again.

Peter told most of the story with June occasionally adding a piece. It happened in a poorly protected anchorage near the dreaded Cape Mali. They had purposefully chosen the longer and more exposed route to avoid the expense of the Corinth Canal. It was for that reason that they had waited for more than a month after we left before abandoning the security of Ios.

It began innocently enough. The wind was beginning to pick up, and Peter had decided to set another anchor in case the wind that was then blowing from the shore should shift directions. He tied one end of the long anchor rope to *Sweet Thursday's* stern, placed the remainder of the line and a large anchor in his dinghy, and then paid out line as the wind pushed him a safe distance from the shore. It was only after he dropped the anchor over that he realized his mistake.

Peter had forgotten his oars. There he stood, 60 meters downwind from his boat with the wind pushing him steadily out to sea. He tried paddling with his hands, but against the force of the wind it was useless. He made a split second decision and it was the right one.

The cardinal rule of small boats is never to abandon the boat. No matter what. It's a rule that had been drummed into me by my father since I was barely old enough to take a boat out by myself and is a lesson taught by every mariner to every student. But Peter had found a rare exception.

June could not handle *Sweet Thursday* by herself and there were no other boats anywhere near their lonely anchorage. Face the open sea around one of the fiercest capes in the Mediterranean in a small boat in a gale, or swim for it. Peter had plunged.

By this time the wind had mounted considerably and there was a moment when June had thought he might not make it. When he finally arrived at the boat, he was so tired he could hardly climb aboard. Night was falling, a near gale was blowing, and there was no question of going after the dinghy. It had been a hard lesson.

***

Easter morning we all left in procession for Gouvia with the lamb still tied to our boom. It was Alex's fifteenth birthday, and we celebrated with a blueberry cake and special presents. As I watched him open the survival knife we had bought for him from a sporting goods store at Corfu, I couldn't help being impressed with the changes he had undergone since leaving Chestnut Hill. The youthful fat had given way to hard muscle and the boyish frame had transformed into a well-developed body. Unable to do a single chin-up and only a very few push-ups at the beginning of the trip, Alex had responded to our ribbing by adopting a rigorous exercise program. Late at night Charlotte and I would often hear him pulling himself up on ropes attached to the mast as we lay below in our front end loader reading. His program was paying off well.

In Gouvia we chose a point across the harbor from the town where there was an old abandoned church and a sandy beach. It was a perfect spot for our banquet. The Hjorths, their Danish friend Neil from *Casablanca*, a Dutch couple from *Skipjack*, Ian and Deborah, and the five of the *Captain Spiros* settled down for a hearty meal.

Neil was the only one of us who even remotely knew what he was doing and, with his guidance, we finally succeeded in running the spit in through the lamb's rear and out through the bone in its head. Sail needles and twine did the rest and we soon had the beast sizzling. Deeda showed us how to make stick bread and the children loved it. They took long snakes of dough that Deeda had kneaded a few hours before, twisted them around green sticks, and held them over the fire just like in a marshmallow roast.

We drank wine, beer, and ouzo as the lamb roasted and the conversation heated. When the lamb began to be ready on the outer edges, Ian joined the work group with a knife, fork, and plate. He sliced as the doneness penetrated deeper and deeper while the rest of us took turns at turning. At least half of what Ian sliced made its way to the serving platter and the feast began.

Lamb Roast on Gouvia Island

We were now back with the sailing community and it was great. It reminded us of the Sunday picnics at Mandraki and we felt at home. Charlotte and I found ourselves engaged in deep conversation with the Dutch couple and listened carefully to their story. They had been sailing for years. He worked on boats and she mended sails, and their little business enabled them to support themselves in their nomadic life. But what we found fascinating was the simple rule they had developed after endless controversies about prudent seamanship and sailing. They had developed one hard and fast rule and offered it to us for our consideration. He articulated it: "If von of us vants to reef, ve reef. No questions. Ve reef right then. No matter vat. Ve reef. Ja, and later if ve vant ve can argue, but the reef, she is already done."

Suddenly a light went on in my mind. I thought of Mikonos, of Cape Knidos, of Patras. He was exactly right. If someone sounds the alarm, take the prudent action right then. If it wasn't necessary, argue later. But the argument would then be from a position of security. That's far better than venturing up on the bow in high winds to try to correct a problem that could have been prevented. It was a good rule and we took it as our own from that point forward. Yes, it caused a lot of argument, but from then on they were after rather than before the fact.

Baking Stick Bread

210

∗∗∗

That afternoon Bianne lent us his "dry suit" and Heyward and I took turns scraping the bottom of *Captain Spiros*. Manfred's costly solution to anti fouling was not working and we had accumulated quite a beard. Bianne's dry suit wasn't dry and the work was very difficult. Heyward worked the hardest I had seen him work since our trip began and was a big help. I had noticed that the boat had lost a considerable amount of speed lately, and I hoped that this would help us regain it.

The next morning the Hjorths joined us and we resumed our trip westward. Our route was to be across the Ionian to the tip of the heel of Italy, across the bottom of the boot and then to the Strait of Messina where they would head north for France and we would head south for Sicily and then Malta. The first leg was out of Gouvia, through the narrow channel that separates the northern end of Island of Corfu from Albania, and then into the Ionian. We had two choices and the final decision would depend on the weather—continue across to St. Maria de Leuca or stop at the small Greek island of Othoni, about midway across.

As we departed from Gouvia we kept on the western side of the narrow body of water that separates Corfu from Albania. We had no desire to test the Albanian claims to their territorial waters. We also kept our binoculars trained in that direction to determine if we were going to have any trouble with refugee boats. But all was quiet and we rounded the northern tip of Corfu without incident and headed west.

We were blessed with strong winds from the north and clipped along at nine to ten knots, but as we neared Othoni, Charlotte began to think we were having too much of a good thing. We were not far from the choke point where the Adriatic Sea comes to an end and funnels into the Ionian. The wind had become quite strong and the sea was frothy with whitecaps—we were seeing the full force of the Adriatic concentrated in the narrow neck of the Ionian that we were crossing. In the spirit of our new reefing philosophy, I acquiesced to Charlotte's request and we radioed the *Et Au Alt*. Although they had hoped to continue, they agreed to join us.

I had not liked Othoni from the charts and I liked it even less as we entered the small man-made harbor. It was too narrow, it offered no protection from the wind, and I was nervous. As long as the wind continued from the north and we had the shelter of the island, we would be OK. But if it shifted to the south we would be exposed.

We were the only boat in the harbor, and I circled around three times, sounding as I went. I was finally able to find a spot where we would have room to swing even if the wind shifted, and we anchored. There was no margin for error—if our anchor slipped we would be in real trouble. While the stone jetties that formed the harbor walls kept the sea flat, the wind howled about us demonstrating its immense power. This would be no place to weather a gale, and I felt very vulnerable.

Shortly after we anchored, *Et Au Alt* entered the harbor. Because of her shallower draft she was able to moor along the front of the small quay at the head of the harbor. We explored the island, but, other than the friendly family that had recently come over from Albania and the tiny grocery store, there wasn't much there.

Back on board we watched a German boat seek refuge in the harbor. She anchored too close to us, and my nervousness went up a notch. All night we listened to the wind howling through the rigging and the horrendous grinding of the anchor chain as we swung back and forth on our anchor. The wind. We were always hostage to the wind. As soon as it was light, we departed Othoni and began to breathe easier.

As it turned out, both the wind and the seas were stronger than those Charlotte had wanted us to avoid the afternoon before, but now she agreed that they were better than Othoni. It's an irony in sailing that often measures designed to avoid danger result in greater danger. There is a great temptation in bad weather to seek the safety of the shore, but experience soon teaches that this is usually the most dangerous option. We waved good-bye to Greece for the last time as Othoni faded into the horizon. Italy and a whole new world lay ahead.

Chapter 9
Italy and Sicily

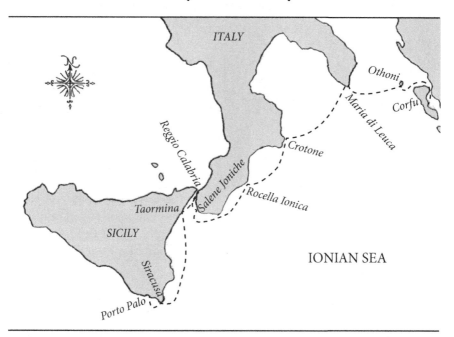

O ur crossing was rough, exhilarating, and fun—that is fun for everyone except Margot who choose to remain in the middle of the cockpit with her little yellow pail. But, in spite of her discomfort, she stood her watches and fully shared in the joy of watching the Italian shore emerge from the sea. First the huge lighthouse at Santa Maria di Leuca and then steep cliffs that came down to the sea and beautiful green fields. Lush green after the rocky dryness of Greece—what a welcome.

Sighting the light house at Santa Maria di Leuca wasn't just a change in countries, or just a milestone in passing the barrier of knock down winds from the Adriatic. It went deeper. During our winter trip across the Aegean and our subsequent trip through the Ionian, we had constantly been building up our ability to cope with our life at sea. Now, with Italy in sight, we felt that we had graduated. We had become a seasoned crew ready to face any circumstances that our new environment was likely to offer. We had met the challenge and were now ready to enjoy the adventure.

When we arrived in the little port, we already had our lines over before the local ormeggiatori had a chance to offer his services. Bianne had warned us about them, but we still didn't completely understand what role they played. Whatever it was, however, we were glad to have made it without one.

Arriving in Italy

We were now on the move and decided not to divert into the Gulf of Toronto. The cities there are mostly industrial and uninteresting, and the weather can become nasty. Early the next morning, with a brisk wind on our beam, we headed straight across to Crotone. Because of the shallowness of the gulf, the waves were tall and steep, but Margot was beginning to develop her sea stomach. Not only did she not get sick on this stretch, but she actually took one of Heyward's watches in addition to hers because he was suffering from a little fever.

Although our pilot gave Crotone low marks because of industrialization, we found it rather quaint. This time, however, we did get stung by the ormeggiatori. We needed to take on water and there was no way of doing it without dealing with the local water boss. Although the tap was right on the quay and was public, we knew that we better not turn away the man with the tool box and outstretched hand. We did, however, negotiate a semi reasonable price before we allowed him to make the connection that would have taken us less then five minutes to make ourselves.

We had not been able to obtain our Constituto—the Italian equivalent of the Greek Transit Log—in Santa Maria di Leuca so we needed to get one in Crotone. The Italians had a much more lax attitude towards customs and we completed the entire process at one location in less than an hour. I was amazed. I was also relived that we had finally officially entered Italy.

***

We would not have known about Rochella Ionica had we not been told about it by Jim on *Rascal* while we had been in Galaxidhi. It wasn't in our pilot, and the harbor was not marked on our chart. But we had been given coordinates, and the town itself merited only a tiny dot on our chart, so we didn't think we would have trouble finding it. Jim had said that it was the best, if not the only, safe harbor between Crotone and Saline Joniche on the tip of the toe.

But we had to sail across the Gulf of Squillace to get there. Squillace lived up to its ugly reputation, and we spent a miserable day beating into heavy wind. After passing Punta Stilo, I stayed glued to my binoculars trying to pick up signs of our destination. Before long I spotted it—a long gray breakwater. The wind was blowing hard and the stretch of shoreline looked totally unprotected, that is all of the shoreline except the breakwater. The presence of several cranes indicated that construction was not yet complete, but Jim had assured us that it was complete enough to afford very good protection. I was finally able to pick out the entrance and we approached slowly.

Charlotte Braves the Winds

Just as we slid into the opening between two breakwaters and I was squinting into the binoculars to figure out what we would do once inside, Alex shouted from his anchor station on the bow: "Dad, a fitting has come off the bow stay and I think the whole thing might come loose." A bow stay coming loose in heavy wind could result in a demasting and it was nothing to be taken lightly. But rocks aren't to be taken lightly either. We had them on both sides and I wasn't sure where they may be ahead. Before I could reply, Alex had begun to take exactly the appropriate action. He took a spare halyard that came from the top of the mast, attached the free end to the bow pulpit, and then winched it tight on one of the mast winches. This would do until we were safely moored.

It was a terrific man-made harbor and our only neighbors were two fishing boats. By this time the wind was blowing very hard and we took extra precautions in placing our anchors and attaching stern lines to huge rocks on shore. We then relayed information about our entry to the Hjorths to help them with their arrival. We were exhausted, and, after coffee aboard *Et Au Alt*, went to bed for an early night's sleep.

The howling wind woke Charlotte and me at around 3:00 A.M. It was blowing from the immense expanse of the Ionian Sea to the southwest and smashing onto the Italian coast. We were thankful for the wall of giant boulders that separated our little haven from the fury of the waves. By 7:00

A.M. we were too exhausted to worry anymore and after a final check of the lines retreated to the front end loader.

It was only much later the next day that we learned that Bianne had made a security check on shore shortly after we had gone back to bed and found that one of our lines had worked loose. How many times would we have to learn the same lesson? He had re-secured the line for us and all was well. But what would have happened if he hadn't caught it?

Although we had hoped to continue the following day, the weather put it out of the question. The town was two miles away, and I decided to walk in to explore. Before I got more than a short distance down the dirt road a car pulled up and offered me a ride. When I was about to get in, another car came up and they argued over who would get to take me. What a greeting to Italy. We were well off of the beaten tourist path, and the Italian hospitality was overwhelming. My host drove me around the town showing me all the places of interest, took me by his shop, and then dropped me off at the only bank in town and made introductions for me.

While I was changing money, Bianne walked in. Apparently the second driver had found him and treated him to the same attentions. We went from store to store, intoxicated by the wide variety and excellent quality of the salami, cheeses, vegetables, and pastas. But buying was very time consuming. It was the same in every shop. They wanted to know where we came from, what we were doing, how we liked Italy, and, of course, there was the inevitable story about their cousin or brother or sister in New York, Chicago, or Los Angeles. Charlotte, Deeda, and the children joined us, and, after about three hours of solid shopping, we walked back to our boats with all the wine, cheese, beer, and produce we could carry.

But the best was yet to come. The night before Bianne had given a cassette with Danish-American music to one of the fisherman on the boat next to his. That evening the fisherman had reciprocated by giving Bianne a huge slice of swordfish, and Deeda had us over for a delicious seafood meal.

**

The abandoned oil port in the town of Saline Joniche was a scene from a post World War III movie. Tall concrete breakwaters led the way into a huge basin with piers that could accommodate giant oil tankers, and it was completely deserted. Deserted that is except for tiny *Et Au Alt* and a small fishing boat tucked away in a corner of the facility. Huge oil tanks, a high storm fence, and a network of newly paved roads completed the scene. I had read in one of our guides that the facility had been built several years earlier but had never used. Some poor Italians had lost a lot of lira on this one.

We had learned enough about the system to surmise that the gruff looking man standing beside Bianne was an ormeggiatori. The scowl on his face told us that Bianne had probably been successful in not using him. Heyward's toss was perfect and the line landed in Bianne's extended right arm before the ormeggiatori could push him out of the way. Bianne smiled politely and pretended to interpret the loud tirade from his neighbor as friendly chat. In a very gentle and soothing voice he started to speak in Danish. We were able to recognize two words that Claus had taught Alex, and this tipped us off as to the probable content of the rest of the dialogue. I fought hard to keep from laughing and avoided any eye contact with the frustrated ormeggiatori.

After we finished mooring the ormeggiatori stormed off. We had heard that handling them was not always easy. On the one hand, no one wanted to pay for services they didn't need. But on the other hand no one wanted their boat cut loose at midnight. Heikell had used the term "little Mafioso" to describe this peculiar Italian phenomenon. We were all a little concerned that we might have made an enemy—and one that had teeth.

Heikell's pilot described a well-equipped supermarket not far from the harbor, and in Italy, unlike in the Greek Isles, supermarkets were real supermarkets. This was incentive enough. With baskets in hand we set off for the hike. The road through the harbor was long and deserted. Finding a cab was out of the question. We walked, but not for long. Honk honk. He came up from behind just as we were leaving the entrance of the port. "Bon journo. You need I give you a lift?"

This was our first introduction to Luigi, the captain of the lone fishing boat moored in our same corner of the harbor. His smile was sincere and we immediately knew we had made a friend. Not only did Luigi take us to the giant supermarket, he accompanied us through the isles showing us the best deals and then, as we left with three shopping carts full of items we had dreamed of for the past three months, he wrangled a deal with the cashier so that we were immediately able to get our free set of plastic plates. We then crowded into his car, filling his trunk and our laps with our purchases, and headed back to the boat where he helped us unload the groceries and then came on board for a visit.

Luigi was delightful. His wife was from southern France and his French was quite good. He told us all about fishing along the Italian coast and even offered to take us out with him on one of his trips. After helping us sample some of the wine we had purchased and sharing many stories with us, he said good-bye and left.

Two minutes later he returned, and quite upset: "My car, it is gone!" We all had the same thought at the same time—the ormeggiatori! We told Luigi about our arrival and he turned pale and left again. While he was gone, we became quite worried and speculated about what had happened. Luigi's friendly help had probably turned insult into injury for the ormeggiatori. Free rides to the supermarket for HIS customers was definitely not good for business. A half hour later a very subdued Luigi returned. Yes, he had found his car—the ormeggiatori had taken it, but only as a joke.

Some joke. This was a clear warning that we would have to be more careful about ormeggiatoris in the future.

The next day we decided to have a picnic. We scoured the deserted port for wood, set up the spit I had bought in Corfu for the lamb, and roasted two whole chickens. Luigi joined us for an aperitif but would not stay for lunch. The ormeggiatori glowered at us from a distance but never came over. It was our farewell feast with the Hjorths. Our next stop would be Reggio Calabria, a little to the north and right across the Straight of Messina from Sicily. From there the Hjorths would continue north and we would head west to Sicily.

***

Reggio Calabria was our first real city in Italy. The principal harbor was large and well protected, and there was also a yacht harbor. We made the mistake of choosing the latter. Once comfortably moored we got the bad news. The little attendant explained. This was not simply a yacht harbor. It was a marina. And the fees were exorbitant. It didn't look like a marina, but our attendant pointed out that the amenities included a cold water shower at the end of the quay and, for an extra charge, electricity. Bianne and I weren't at all sure he was legitimate, but he led us to a little shack and produced a receipt pad with the name of the harbor printed on it. We were tired and had no desire to move our boats, so we decided to pay the ransom wondering all the time if our attendant was just another ormeggiatori.

We broke out the bike and all headed into town for some shopping. After finding a huge supermarket, I took the bike to find a bank while everyone else shopped. My banking complete, I then rejoined the group in the grocery store so we could load everything on the bike before returning.

When I arrived, Charlotte, Heyward, and Margot had filled one cart and were working on a second. Alex had gone in search of a particular fishing lure. About five minutes after I had joined the group, Alex returned. "Dad, I didn't know you were here. Where's the bike?"

"Very funny Alex. You know it's right where I left it—right in front of the store" I said with a sinking feeling that he wasn't joking. We had been warned many times about theft in Italy. Alex had even rigged a lock for the dinghy. Heikell had a special section in his pilot on it. I had locked the bike everywhere I had taken it, but this time I had been careless. I knew I would be in the store only a short time, it was daylight, and the street was crowded. Besides, the bike was rusty, the wheels were bent, and it was in such deplorable shape, I couldn't imagine that anyone would take the trouble to steal it.

I was wrong. I ran out of the store with Alex and the bike was gone. We searched for several blocks in all directions, but it was useless. We decided that my leaving the bike unlocked and unattended was an insult to the character of the Italians and that an offended street thief had probably stolen it on principle.

***

Our travel plans were still uncertain. West to the Balearics or South to Africa? With some bite still left in the Mediterranean winter, we wanted to head south. Malta and then Tunisia—that was my vote. But did we really want to return to an Islamic country so soon after the war? Our neighbors to starboard gave us the encouragement we required. The French crew of *Kanumera* were on their way from the Red Sea to La Camargue in Southern France. They couldn't speak too highly about Tunisia. For two hours they told us tales of Bizerte, Sidi Bou Said, Tunis, Kelibia, and Monastir. But it was mainly of Sidi Bou Said that they talked. No matter that it was a hot bed of PLO leadership. Located on the site of ancient Carthage and only a short commuter train ride from Tunis, it was the gem of the Mediterranean. And the Gulf War? "No problem. The Tunisians are super—you will like them very much."

While this report didn't exactly give us a green light for Tunisia, it certainly served to whet our appetites. We decided that we would definitely go to Malta and from there decide whether to go west to the Balearics, or to continue south to Tunisia.

Farewell to the Hjorths

Early the next morning we said good-bye to the Hjorths and left Reggio Calabria. The Hjorths had a less favorable weather forecast than we had, and it looked like they would be heading into a storm system that was developing along the southern part of the Tyrrhenian Sea. We were concerned for them and kept in touch on the VHF until we finally lost contact late that morning. The Hjorths had become very close friends, and we were going to miss them terribly.

Our trip would take us across the Strait of Messina, and we were delighted to have a calm forecast for our crossing. Our pilot had warned of strong tides, whirlpools, and treacherous squalls blowing off the highlands that dominate both shores of the narrow body of water that separates Sicily from Italy. This was a place to be respected.

Circe had warned Odysseus about Scilla and Charybdis. On Scilla, the Italian side, there was the six-headed, long-necked monster that would pluck sailors from their craft. Next to Charybdis, on the Sicilian side, there was a giant whirlpool that would suck ships to their doom.

I remembered a more practical reference point. Twenty years earlier I had been an officer aboard a nuclear submarine cruising below the surface of the Mediterranean. While our depth gave us protection from the capricious weather of the Mediterranean, our unexpected rerouting through the Strait of Messina gave our navigator and many of the officers much cause for concern. Pouring over charts, studying bottom contours, and plotting the currents of this unique body of water was one of the most vivid memories I had retained from my brief naval career.

Light winds pushed us over flat seas. Our trip was calm and, with one exception, uneventful. Half way across and before we could tell if the drizzling rain was going to stop or turn into a squall, a small sparrow chose *Captain Spiros* for refuge. Its choice of a landing spot was unfortunate. The tiny claw gently alighting on Charlotte's knee couldn't possibly have caused

Charlotte's Friend

any harm, but judging from the loud scream she must have thought that one of the horrible heads of Scilla had found its prey. After the initial shock, the sparrow was great company and he stayed with us the whole way to Sicily.

We stopped for the night in Naxos which is just south of Messina, enjoyed a brief visit to the medieval city of Taormina that dominates the heights above the harbor, and left the next morning for Syracuse. Shortly after our departure our attention was riveted ashore—2,800 meters high, snow peaked, and magnificent, Mount Etna dominated the western horizon as we headed south. As we passed, Charlotte read to us about how an eruption in 1669 had destroyed the city of Catania, and we all watched the mountain looking for activity.

But the real attraction for me that day was the Cicople. We sailed up close to the huge black rocks that were marked as basalt pillars in my pilot. I pulled out my well-worn copy of the *Odyssey* and read to everyone about Odysseus' encounter with the Cyclopes Polyphemus. After narrowly escaping being eaten by blinding his captor, Odysseus had taunted the enraged Polyphemus by yelling at him as he headed seaward. Polyphemus had responded by hurling giant boulders in the direction of the shouts and had very nearly done our hero in. The Cicople were the rocks that Polyphemus had hurled.

As we rounded Maniace Castle in our approach to Syracuse, we began to appreciate the beauty of this ancient capital. The old town of Ortiga had been founded by Corinth in 735 BC. This had been the scene of much history and much power. At one time it was wealthier and more powerful than any city in Europe. Brutality and despotism were hallmarks of its past. It had rivaled Athens for power, defeated its fleet in 415 BC, and had forced the defeated army to die a slow death in a huge stone quarry. But in 212 BC the city was sacked by the Romans who robbed it of its art and riches and put to death its favorite son Archimedes. Ortiga also had its role in mythology. This was the island where the sea nymph Calypso had detained Odysseus for seven years.

Charlotte was still reading to us as I was scanning the western shoreline to decide on a spot to anchor. Syracuse Bay stretched to the west and didn't give much protection, but the long finger of Syracuse and Ortiga gave excellent protection from the north and east. At the southern end of

Winding Streets of Ortiga

the ferry quay and under the ramparts of the city we saw a lone English motor yacht at anchor and decided to join it.

John and Pat of *Princess Christina* and their mate Dave welcomed us and gave us practical information on Syracuse. I was a little nervous about our anchorage, but they assured me that it was OK. Alex and Heyward fixed pizzas—homemade dough and all—and we had a quiet evening on board.

By the time I was up the next morning the wind had changed direction and was now coming from the west. My first glance outside convinced me of the folly of my choice of anchorages. By the time I had the children up and the motor running, it was too late. The wind was now blowing quite hard, and loosening our stern lines would have resulted in our being blown into *Princess Christina*. We were stuck.

But there was no way I was going to rely on just one anchor—especially with the wind partially on our beam. Alex and Heyward groaned, but set out in the dinghy with the heavy Danforth, its chain, and the end of a second anchor line. I watched with admiration as they drove the dinghy into the strong wind, found the perfect placement off our starboard bow, and then dropped the anchor. I still felt vulnerable, but at least we now had holding power.

Dave and John were much less concerned than I was about the weather. Perhaps it was their much smaller size and their powerful motors that gave them confidence—If the conditions got worse they would have a much easier time of getting underway than we would. They had both watched our maneuvers of the morning and complimented Heyward and Alex on their skill in anchoring.

Our enjoyment of Syracuse was marred by our precarious anchorage. Under the conditions, I could not leave the boat unattended, so we had to take shifts going ashore. The streets were so inviting that we all wanted to take an outing—I was determined to change our anchorage as soon as the weather permitted.

More or less captive on board, Charlotte decided to use the opportunity to pursue the special French lesson module she had purchased from the Calvert School to enhance the children's' French. Alex was so hopelessly behind with his normal courses that he was successful in avoiding the session. Heyward wasn't subject to any formal educational requirements. This left Margot as the sole pupil.

It started badly. Sitting at my navigation table studying the charts that would take us to Malta I was only half tuned in to the drama that was taking place at the dinette table.

"Ça va, Margot?" from an exuberant Charlotte who was finally getting a chance to impart her love for the language to her daughter.

Silence from Margot.

"Ça va, Margot?" A long pause and then with more force and less exuberance: "J'ai dit Ça va, Margot?"

From a very exasperated Margot: "Mom that's beginning French. I learned that at Springside. This is a real dorkey course."

Refusing to give up Charlotte continued: "Ça va ou ça ne va pas, Margot?"

Alex lowered the Calvert book he had been taking refuge behind and interjected: "Margot's right, it's a dorkey course."

Charlotte exploded. "Alex, you be quiet. Nobody asked you. I went to a lot of trouble to buy this course and I want to teach you and Margot to speak French."

Margot reluctantly: "OK Momma, ça ne vas pas."

Charlotte with enthusiasm returning: "Dis quelque chose, Margot."

Alex from behind his book: "Merde. Dis merde, Margot."

It went straight downhill from there. I was happy that I had had the foresight to turn on my tape recorder at the outset and sat patiently waiting for the shouting match to end.

The replay was even more entertaining than I had expected. After the lessons had been put neatly back in their box, I fixed popcorn and played the tape. We all laughed until we cried. Margot's impatient disgust for the whole exercise was occasionally interrupted by Alex's displays of gutter French, and Charlotte had responded with a richness of vocabulary that impressed us all.

The next morning it was calm when we woke so I decided to walk over to the canal that separated Ortiga from the mainland. It was crowded but offered protection. We also walked over to investigate the private yacht harbor, but they were so snooty that I decided I would rather face the weather.

The canal was the obvious choice, but by the time we had returned to *Captain Spiros* it was almost too windy. I decided to try anyway.

The canal was deep, narrow, and extended for about 200 meters before it was crossed by a bridge. My initial thought was to moor on the left side just forward of the 50 foot ketch we had seen two days earlier. She had executed a perfect Mediterranean mooring about 50 meters to the north of us—and all with only one person. We had been impressed.

But there wasn't room and I had to shift my attention to the tangle of fishing boats to my right. Now halfway down the channel, I was running out of room. I had already begun to execute my 180 degree turn to abort our mission when I saw the fisherman waving to us from the stern of a boat immediately to our starboard. He looked sincere so I put the boat in reverse, shifted the rudder, and had Heyward toss the fisherman a line. Alex passed a line from our bow to another fisherman and they began to pull us in. It hadn't looked like there was a place, but they had had sympathy for our plight and helped us moor. Once the hospitality had been extended we knew we could have complete confidence in our new neighbors. In the space of a few minutes we had gone from a very precarious situation to a secure berth with new friends.

Now Syracuse became alive for us. Victor, the owner of the ketch on the other side of the canal, came over for a beer and told us about the city. He was a native Syracusan and told us about the places we should visit. That night we all left the boat, explored the city, and had dinner ashore.

Our decision to change anchorages had been a good one. Dave called us on the VHF shortly after we had moored and filled us in on the forecast he had received on his single side band radio. Force 7 from the southwest. They had decided to shift berths and were headed to the far side of Syracuse Bay. With the strong blow the next day, there was no question of leaving. Instead we took advantage of the fantastic vegetable market in Ortiga and also made several trips to the supermarket. We were becoming very fond of the city.

The next morning it was calm. I was ready to leave, but Charlotte was a little nervous. To allay all fears, I grabbed the binoculars and invited Charlotte to join me for a walk to the Maniace Castle where we could get a good view of the weather outside the harbor. It was a pleasant walk and calm seas greeted us from the castle. It was going to be a go. On the way back to the boat we passed the spot where we had previously been moored and a totally unexpected sight greeted us. *Princess Christina* had returned and they were enjoying the sight also.

There must have been over twenty of them—radio controlled model speed boats—all making loud whirring noises and throwing up sheets of spray over their sterns. Their crews were more fun to watch than the boats themselves. Gaudy lettering on fancy sweat shirts and jackets gave identities and winning records for their craft. We couldn't tell if they were arguing, cheering, or simply having a good time. Probably it was a combination of all. The boats were traveling at thirty miles an hour and were executing tight turns that I thought would have been impossible. I was worried that one of the little missiles could put a hole right through the hull of *Princess Christina,* but Dave and John seemed unconcerned. We were sorry that our children weren't with us to enjoy this little Sicilian redneck delight.

An hour later we were on our way to Porto Palo. Tucked in a small harbor just around the southeastern tip of Sicily, Porto Palo was an ideal striking out point for Malta. The harbor was jammed full of fishing boats so we circled three times before deciding on a spot that didn't seem too hemmed in. By dark we were finally settled. If the weather held, tomorrow would be the big day.

Chapter 10
Malta to the Balearic Islands

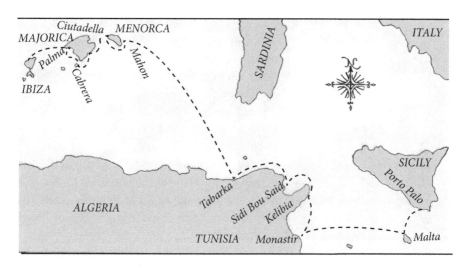

I had carefully plotted our course on the large-scale British Admiralty chart I had purchased at Corfu. I also had plotted our course on the more detailed charts of Malta that I had Xeroxed from the copies other boats had lent me. But the problem with Xeroxed charts was that it was often difficult to distinguish land from sea. 70 miles of open sea stood between us and Malta and I was taking all precautions The wind was a little higher than Charlotte would have liked, but the weather forecast had been good so she agreed, and early on the morning of April 22 we left Porto Palo and headed for Malta.

Charlotte had articulated her concerns to me the night before: "I need to conquer or allay my fear of the Mediterranean which is becoming stronger every day. It's a stupid fear—out of ignorance—it's smart to be conservative and careful—reef the sails—don't sail in bad weather and all of those kind of things. But when I look at a chart or think about leaving, I'm scared. And it's mostly the wind that scares me. I'm afraid of a giant wind building up out of control and then we can't do anything."

We had the wind behind us, the swells were only moderately high, and we were booming along. But both Charlotte and I knew what a powerful wind from astern could do and we were exercising every precaution. Before our departure we had put in a second reef and rigged the preventer, but I couldn't resist the temptation of pushing things a little. Alex had been pestering me to use the spinnaker pole since Demetri had drilled us on its

225

use outside of Simi. This was the time. Wing on wing—the huge pole kept the jib out even if our course wasn't exact, and having it out significantly increased our speed.

Alex Rigging the Whisker Pole

But as the wind picked up, the power became scary. The Charlotte-anemometer was spinning high and a serious argument was developing between her and Alex. I couldn't quite picture what effect a jibe would have on the stout aluminum pole and our low-cut jib, but visions of shredded sails and broken rigging was enough to convince me that Charlotte probably had a point. Besides, I wanted to slow down a little so I would have plenty of time to figure out how to get into Malta. We unrigged the pole and reefed the jib. But even then we were still speeding along at almost 10 knots.

The wind was from the northeast and the sea was churning. As we approached the coast I had difficulty reading the shoreline. Where was the entrance into Marsamaxett Creek? With sails up, the wind pushing us straight for the rocky coast, and waves tossing us about, I had an uneasy feeling as I scanned the coast looking for the entrance that I thought should be close. Sure, it was there—but the fact remained that we were in a small boat bobbing around and had no place to go except into Malta. Going 70 miles back to Sicily with the wind on our nose or skirting Malta to sail another 180 miles to the North African coast were both equally unpalatable.

I temporarily put out of my mind the statement in our Malta pilot that it can be unsafe to enter the harbor in very strong winds from the northeast and continued to strain my eyes through a tightly clenched pair of binoculars to find the clues that I was searching for. And suddenly—there it was. There is no feeling quite like finally sighting the anticipated buoy or seeing the unmistakable landmark that provides a sure path to protection from the uncertainties of the sea. Watching Grand Harbor and Marsamaxett Creek take shape was warm security. And then there was the thrill of entering one of the world's greatest harbors.

We followed Marsamaxett Creek to Manoel Island and then turned right into Lazzaretto Creek. Although British rule had long since ceased to exist, British efficiency was a legacy that was still very much present. Customs, papers, and a berth were taken care of in less than half an hour. The price was right—the equivalent of $30 US per week. And, had we understood correctly? Were warm showers really part of the bargain?

No one could believe it when I returned to the boat less than an hour after departing. When they heard the news, they grabbed towels and made a beeline to the showers. After a month of wash bowl baths, this was pure luxury. It was a worthy cause to which the major focus of our first night ashore was directed.

Entering Malta

The next morning was even more amazing. They actually honored my request for a transfer to the more protected and more convenient berths at Msida Creek. At 7:30 A.M. the attendant came with instructions and we made the move. We were now comfortably installed and ready to explore the many wonders of Malta, many of which we had read about in Bradford's *Great Siege of Malta* and Monsarrat's World War II novel, *The Kappillan of Malta*.

Visiting the harbor, the forts, and the countryside we relived the Knights of St. Johns' victory over Suleiman the Magnificent's 40,000 troops with only 600 knights. By this time we felt quite close to the Knights having wintered in their old capital in Rhodes and having moored in the shadows of their magnificent castle in Bodrum. Reading about the steel will of la Valette, about how he ensured the incredible defeat of the Turks, and seeing the city and fortifications he created made our visit come alive.

Our social life at Msida Creek marina was active. The big event of the season was coffee, beer, and cake aboard *Impossible* to welcome Belgian Jean-Marie and his Filipino wife's five-day-old baby boy. They had a Moses basket and it reminded Charlotte and me of the similar basket we had used to transport Heyward when we had first been introduced into the joys of parenthood. While we remembered the happiness and sense of fulfillment in new parenthood, we couldn't quite relate to how they could hope to cope with a newborn baby on board a sailing vessel.

Daniel and Sibyl of *Foxquitrot* also became good friends. Daniel had built his 45 foot steel ketch and left a successful accounting practice in Belgium to see the world. He and his wife had no children and at age 35 decided there was more to life than being successful business persons.

Daniel had never sailed before he built his boat. But they had both taken the plunge and were now thriving on the experience.

They had spent the winter in Monastir, Tunisia and told us what it had been like during the Gulf War. Before meeting Daniel, Charlotte and I had been worried about the prudence of visiting Tunisia, but he assured us that even during the war the Tunisians couldn't have been nicer. During their stay, both he and Sibyl had grown to love the country. They had lots of names for us so that even before arriving in Tunisia, we had lists of friends.

Daniel was a wheeler-dealer. During the winter he had gotten to know many of the officials in the major Tunisian yacht ports. In order to make our arrival easy, he had suggested that we carry two boxes of shot gun shells with us, hide them in our boat when we cleared customs, and then give them to the Monastir chief of police. Shamir was an avid hunter and Daniel was sure he would not only be delighted to receive our gift, but would also be sure to express the "proper appreciation."

While we were a little hesitant to act on this bit of advice, Daniel's tip on Taoufik was to prove to be pivotal in our plans. Daniel was an avid scuba diver and had taken advanced lessons from Taoufik in Tabarka where Taoufik was chief instructor for Tunisia's largest diving school. Daniel said we should be sure to look him up and enroll in the scuba school. Suddenly the children became completely dedicated to Tunisia as our next destination.

Daniel was a good example of how the intelligence net operates in the sailing community. After several late nights of cocktails and lively discussions aboard *Captain Spiros* and *Foxquitrot* we had gained Daniel's accumulated experience of a winter of sailing in Tunisia. He, in turn, profited from the detailed information we provided on Greece and Turkey and the best routes and ports to get there. We lent each other guides, maps, and even charts so that we could make copies of what we needed.

We also took extensive notes. The reverse side of pages in my ship's log were full of notes that recommended one port highly and warned about hazards in another. By the time we were ready to leave we had very good information that would have been almost impossible to obtain in any other way. Putting all the information we had together confirmed our already heavy leaning towards Tunisia. If we had been wavering before, Daniel's account of Taoufik and the scuba school had made the decision.

***

Its hard to say at what point in a trip, an experience, or an adventure that it starts to be ending rather than beginning. But that point clearly started for us in Malta. I became concerned about selling the boat, my future livelihood upon return, and about the children's return to schools. Charlotte and I attacked all three fronts with vigor.

My little Toshiba laptop was busy and I produced letter after letter to brokers all over the Mediterranean and in the states. I wrote Minolis in Athens, Camper Nicholson in both Rhodes and Palma, Henri Wauquiez in France, and Peter Dodds in Charleston and enclosed an impressive listing of the marvelous capabilities and equipment of *Captain Spiros*. My goal was to determine the best place to dispose of our floating home once the trip was over.

While I had talked about the market for boats like ours in every place we had been, up until then the conversations had been only theoretical. Putting the specifications on paper made it real. Although the letters were a good start, I decided to test the local market as well.

Christian had been politely enthusiastic as he read the description of *Captain Spiros*. But his real interest lay in what we were doing and where we were going next. We enjoyed trading sailing stories. Charlotte was in a super listening mode as Christian gave us a blow-by-blow description of his experience in sailing a 60-foot boat over Skerki Bank in the middle of a gale. Shallow water and heavy seas resulted in enormous waves that broke suddenly and with tremendous force. Christian's boat had suffered enormous damage and had almost pitchpoled. He felt lucky to have lived through the experience.

Christian then introduced us to his father, Captain Paul, who also politely looked at the information and photos I had brought with me. "Its a very pretty boat Mr. Coleman. But tell me, how did you and your family decide to live on a boat in the middle of the Mediterranean?"

From there we went into his sailing experiences. If Christian had given Charlotte food for thought, Captain Paul's, advice almost unraveled her. "So you are going to Tunisia. It is a very pretty place. But be careful of the Gregale. It comes from the north and can blow for days. If it's bad, it can push you right onto Libya, and I don't think you would like to meet Mr. Kadaffi. Then you wouldn't have to worry about selling your boat. No, you should be very careful. Now is the time for the Gregale."

As we left the offices of the broker and wandered down Ta' Xbiex Sea Front I tried to soothe Charlotte. "But Charlotte, Skerki bank is between the western end of Sicily and Tunisia. We won't even come close. And Libya— that's two hundred miles south of Malta. We are sailing to the west. And, besides, you know I won't leave unless the weather conditions are right." But Charlotte wasn't convinced, and I knew what was next. Until our boat was safely moored in a Tunisian port with lines fast, the Gregale and Skerki bank would become subjects of daily conversation and would be used as yardsticks of prudence on any sail plan that I was to develop.

We were beginning to formulate a final plan of action for the remainder of our trip. After Tunisia, we would go to the Balearic Islands where we would make an all out effort to sell the boat. If unsuccessful, we would leave the Mediterranean and sail to the Canaries where we would leave our boat and catch a plane back home. Charlotte and I would then return in the late fall or early winter to sail the boat to the Caribbean and from there eventually back to the US. The final decision would hinge on the relative strength of the markets for sailing yachts in the Balearics and in the US.

In April the winds blow hard in Malta and we were stuck on the island. Shortly after our meeting with Christian and Captain Paul, a Gregale had developed and seemed to go on forever. Each day we would declare "We will leave tomorrow if the weather is good"... but when morning came, both the weather forecast and what we saw outside said no.

Finally the break in the weather we had been looking for seemed to have come and we went over to *Foxquitrot* for final good-bye cocktails. Pouring over *Foxquitrot's* charts, Daniel and I had a long discussion about Tunisia. Monastir would be our destination and Daniel gave me the details on some of the logistics. It sounded like a wonderful place, and we looking forward to it. Daniel wrote Francois' name on a piece of paper for me and told me I should look him us as soon as we arrived. He was living with his wife and daughter on a steel ketch, and they had all become good friends during the winter.

We were up at 5:15 the next morning and ready to leave. The children were grumbling about the early hour and I was pretty tired myself. But Charlotte was the unhappiest of all. "Its a Gregale. Are you crazy. What about Libya?" While I wasn't particularly worried about Libya, Charlotte had a point. The wind was howling and our experience had been that what we saw in the morning we could count on doubling by noon.

That evening Doug from the English boat *Elamylan* came on board with a weather fax that indicated we should have good weather the next day. He also gave us the name of a broker in Palma and encouraging news on the sale of our boat. Doug then proceeded to almost hypnotize Alex with a description of a special metallic tape he had somehow managed to "acquire" from the British Navy. Placing the tape on strategic locations on his mast and spreaders made his boat look the size of an aircraft carrier to radar. The tale went on. Coming out of Sicily, he had been stopped by a mystified Italian Naval vessel that searched his boat from stem to stern to find out what he could be carrying that could make his boat look so large. Our biggest problem became how to pry him and Alex apart so that we could get some sleep before setting out early in the morning.

While we have never been able to determine if Doug's story about the metal tape was true or not, his weather forecast turned out to be accurate and we departed from Malta at daybreak the next morning with moderate seas and light wind.

***

Leaving Malta the unfamiliar had now become familiar, and unlike our arrival we enjoyed the comfort of recognizable landmarks. We now had beautiful sea views of the walks and bays we had enjoyed by land. Rounding the northwest tip of the island we passed the familiar ferry docks where we had departed for Gozo a week earlier and passed close to the small island of Comino that sits right in the middle of the channel between Gozo and Malta. The light on the south west tip of Comino would serve as my last landmark.

I set our course for the tiny island of Lampedusa, about midway in our 180-mile trip to Monastir. This was by far the longest trip in our voyage and I had done some careful planning. Lampedusa is one of three islands in the Pelagie Island chain that sit isolated between the coasts of African and Malta. While Lampedusa was the best of the three, its protection was marginal. The harbor was shallow and the approach tricky—I had no desire to enter at night. My plan was to use it as a reference point. The lights would make it easy to spot and I would keep it well to port. My calculations indicated that we should pass it around midnight.

It was nice to be at sea again and we settled in for the two-day trip. The wind was gentle and we had a very pleasant day. At sunset I used my sextant to check our compass heading and was pleased to find it was very accurate. As darkness approached we set the night watch.

After much discussion we had decided on two-hour shifts. I wanted two people on each watch and either Charlotte or I had to be one of the two. This worked out to Margot and me for the 9-11, Charlotte and Alex for the 11-1, Heyward and me for the 1-3, and then Charlotte and Margot for the 3-5. Since daylight would come a little before 6:00, I decided to trust Heyward and Alex with the 5-7. After that we would go back to our normal one-hour rotations.

Staying up at night staring at a compass rose and looking out for shipping can get old very quickly. It defies the laws of nature how quickly two hours of sleep can go, and how long two hours of watch can drag on. But our by now seasoned crew responded well to the challenge. Margot had become a pro on the wheel and had the best eyes in the family. She would always be the first one to spot a light on the horizon and was a great help in determining what it was and whether or not it was a problem for us. The fact that I would let Heyward and Alex take a night watch by themselves was the ultimate measure of how far I felt they had come along.

In spite of her ultra cautious nature, Charlotte had become quite an accomplished sailor. She loved to take the wheel and had become very good at keeping track of tankers or any other lurking hazards. Again, my willingness to let her take a night watch showed my confidence in her seamanship.

Sighting the exotic African coast as the sun rose was exhilarating, but it brought with it a new danger—Tunny nets. Daniel had warned us about them. They are giant fishing nets with steel cables that often extend over several miles and are generally very poorly marked. There was one that was very large near the small island of Kuriat just offshore Monastir. It didn't take much imagination to visualize the problems running into one could cause and I approved of the wide berth that Charlotte gave the island.

***

Monastir was quite a change, a very modern marina surrounded by expensive shops and restaurants and even a Club Mediterranean. The marina officials were polite and efficient and, amazingly, the price was very reasonable. It was a mark of how accustomed we had become to life on a sailboat that everyone didn't immediately rush to the showers or rush off the boat to explore the city. Glad to be in port and tired from our two days at sea we were perfectly content to remain on board and relax.

Upon our arrival in port we had received a very warm welcome from the yachts that had wintered there. Simon and Linda of *Zaylan* took our lines and persuaded us to moor on the quay next to them. Simon was Lebanese from Beirut and Linda was from New England. Wolfgang and Doris of *Susie Q* and a German couple on a Hallburg Rassey were there also.

Simon was very bright and articulate, but when he broached the subject of Zionism some of his logic and most of his objectivity seemed to evaporate. It was his thesis that all problems in the Middle East stem from Zionism. When he began to explain that Arabs never used to fight with each other before Israel came into being, I knew that his opinions had to be taken with a large grain of salt. One thing that Simon told us was certain—feelings run very high in this part of the world and you have to be careful when expressing political opinions. Simon helped provide a key for us in understanding the incredible attitude the Tunisians had towards Saddam Hussein and the Gulf War.

Simon explained to me that the Tunisians believed in Hussein because they did not want to believe in Westerners. They had seen too many victories for the West and too many defeats for the Arabs. They wanted to believe in Hussein so much that they were blinde to facts and guided only by emotion. I saw this first hand during a visit to a photocopy shop in town. Wolfgang of *Susie Q* had lent me his copy of a pilot on the Canaries and I wanted to Xerox sections of it. The owner of the shop was well dressed, intelligent, and very well educated. I made the mistake of striking up a conversation with him about the war.

He was polite, but firm. Hussein had had a right to march into Kuwait because it had formerly been owned by Iraq, and, besides, the Iraqis had not done anything to harm the Kuwaitis. It was only after the US came into the picture that anything was done to the Kuwaitis. It was clearly all George Bush's fault. He then went on the offensive. The killing of civilians in the bomb shelter had been outrageous. In response to my suggestion that the US had had data indicating that it was a military target he angrily stated that that was no excuse and then pointed out that the US should have been much more careful before bombing. As for the atrocities at the end of the war—again this was all Bush's fault. But most incredibly he felt that Hussein had won the war—Hussein had stood up to the US and the Allies and he was still in power and still controlled a substantial army.

I was to learn that this view of the war was widely shared by educated as well as uneducated Tunisians. At first I thought this was perhaps due to slanted newspapers and strict censorship, but as Simon had pointed out this could not be the cause—good French newspapers and magazines had been widely available all during the war, and both BBC and Radio France were quite easy to receive and carried excellent news coverage.

Simon had been right. The Tunisians believed in Hussein because at all cost they wanted to believe in an Arab victory over the western world. They were quite capable of accomplishing this by simply twisting their logic around. Ironically, as Simon tried to explain the reasons behind the distorted views of the Tunisians, I could see the same distortions and twisted logic in his explanations of the situation in Lebanon.

***

Shortly after mooring, we met Daniel's friends Francois, Francoise, and their twelve-year-old daughter Clemence who all lived aboard *Jonathan*. Francois was a sculptor and they had been cruising for three years. They had just returned from a land trip in Southern Algeria and were full of stories. A car and camping equipment gave them enormous flexibility to visit places by land as well as by sea. When they moved to a new port, Francoise would drive the car and Francois and Clemence would sail the boat.

Clemence did not speak English, and it was interesting to watch how Margot and Alex communicated with her. They spoke in English (and a little French) and she replied in French (and a little English). These communications worked, and they became quite good friends as their linguistic aptitudes continued to increase. The family included Margot and Alex in their activities and took them to Sousse for a day trip. Alex told us that the lamb chop he had for lunch was the best he had ever tasted. The fact that Clemence was quite good looking did not escape Alex's notice, but, unfortunately, the lamb chop was as far as he got.

Most things in Monastir were easy to find. But finding a Tunisian flag was not. I had felt vulnerable entering port without a courtesy flag and was determined to obtain one before we left. I thought it would be simple enough. But after trying every store, stall, and stand in town I discovered that Tunisian flags simply weren't commodity items. I asked Linda and Simon where they had obtained theirs. They laughed and then Linda explained that after looking for two weeks, she had finally decided to make her own.

I didn't give up that easily. No luck at the Syndicat D'Initiative de Tourism Tunisienne and so I decided to try their city hall. After being shuttled through five offices, I finally met an official who promised to help. I was to return to the same office the next day at the same hour and he would have my flag. I was skeptical, but made the trip anyway. I couldn't believe it. Right when I got there—not half an hour later, and not in another location—there was my friend. And he was holding a genuine Tunisian flag. He absolutely refused to take any money for the flag and he and his companions wished me "bonne chance et bonne voyage."

One night our dinner was interrupted to say good-by to Fritz. Fritz was German and lived aboard a 50 foot Morgan along with his two huge motorcycles. He had bought the Morgan in the United States and had sailed it over a few years earlier. His girlfriend had just arrived that day—he had been waiting for weeks—and he was determined to set out for Malta right away.

"But Fritz, there are 40 knot winds blowing and the forecast says it will get worse—do you think tonight is the best time to go?" With a big grin on his face and his admiring girl friend watching he gave us his macho answer "This is the kind of weather I like—my boat is built for it—it should be a great trip!"

After saying good-by we went back to our dinner scratching our heads. "Perhaps I am too cautious" I suggested—which brought forth a five minute dissertation from Charlotte on how dangerous the weather can become and Fritz must be completely out of his mind.

The next morning Simon told us about the drama that had unfolded over the VHF radio that night. Fritz had found Charlotte's Tunny net about an hour after leaving Monastir. His keel became caught fast in the steel wires. With 40 knots of wind and a very rough sea pitching his boat around, Fritz donned his scuba gear and went overboard to untangle the net while his girlfriend rolled around the cockpit violently ill. A few hours later he somehow managed to get out of the net and then limped on to Lampedusa where he spent what was left of the night. We have often wondered whether or not the romance survived this episode.

A couple of days later we woke up to see a mast gliding by our cabin porthole. Up on deck in a second we talked to Wolfgang and Alice—they had sifted through two or three equally unreliable weather forecasts and had decided it was time to end their winter hibernation. They were off to Kelibia. Charlotte and I conferred hurriedly and made a decision—"Monitor channel 22—we will be right behind you."

Half an hour later we had said good-by to Linda and Simon and our other friends and were on our way. The seas were flat and there was no wind, but Charlotte had her eyes peeled for the "coup de vent". In her opinion there was no way that all of that wind could have disappeared so quickly.

We caught up with Wolfgang and Alice, but they developed engine problems, and *Susie Q* had to turn back. We had grown quite fond of them and were disappointed to lose their company. Wolfgang's description of how he had bought his boat in the Canary Islands and his detailed description of the many fascinating ports had whetted our appetite to go there. He told us about his camel ride to an active volcano just a few miles from emerald green water and described the many beautiful warm beaches. His glowing accounts had started us thinking very seriously about altering our itinerary to take in this intriguing group of islands.

As we drew close to Kelibia, it began to look like Charlotte's "coup de vent" was finally coming. A light wind turned into 10 then 20 and then 30 knots with gusts up to 40 knots. Our Tunisian courtesy flag looked like it was about to tear into ribbons. The wind was off the land, however, so the sea was flat, and we had a very invigorating sail. Everybody seemed to be enjoying themselves when Margot spotted the Tunisian gun boat.

In spite of Charlotte's well-executed ship collision avoidance maneuvers the boat continued to close. It finally became obvious she wanted us. Us! Pandemonium broke out. I was dispatched to the VHF to see what she wanted. "Tunisian vessel this is *Captain Spiros*—what do you want?"

No reply.

By this time the boat was getting very close, and we could see two soldiers on the bow signaling to us to come on the radio. I went back below and finally establish contact.

"What's the name of your boat?"

Captain Spiros.

"What is your nationality?"

"United States" I replied, noting that our large US flag was waving in the breeze 30 feet from their bow.

"Where are you going?"

"We are headed for Kelibia. We departed from Monastir this morning. What do you want?"

Silence on the radio, then some motion on the bow of the vessel. We became concerned that they were going to try to board us—a move that unquestionably would have caused damage in the strong wind. Finally a reply: "When you are in Tunisian waters you must fly a Tunisian courtesy flag."

I thought angrily to myself about the three days in Monastir it had taken me to find a Tunisian courtesy flag and directed their attention to our starboard yard-arm where our gift from city hall was proudly fluttering.

"Oh, it's OK then. You may proceed to Kelibia" And off they zoomed leaving behind a large tail of spray.

That evening, quietly moored along the long quay in the fishing port of Kelibia, we were still wondering what the afternoon episode was all about when they came aboard. Two uniformed soldiers and an inspector. They brought the startling news that we were being investigated by Interpol in connection with a stolen yacht. They then very politely asked if we would mind not leaving port until the investigation was complete.

I was then asked to accompany the inspector to his office and was questioned for about an hour. He was kind enough to relieve me of the burden of having to keep track of my ships papers and passports, and put them under lock in his office. In the meantime a guard had been posted on the quay to make sure we didn't misunderstand their request not to leave port.

Midway through the interrogation, Charlotte came into the office to "help me" answer their questions. Not being a business person and not having had the opportunity to work with lawyers Charlotte was willing to offer more information than I was willing to volunteer and refused to heed my glaring looks begging her to be quiet.

They were looking for a Gulf Star 50-foot ketch that had been stolen in July. My explanations that my boat was a French Jeanneau and not an American Gulf Star , that it was a sloop with only one mast and not a ketch that had two masts, and that the length was 48 feet and not 50 feet were getting me nowhere.

My ships papers made it worse. The fact that my boat claimed to have a corporate owner (Seabiscuit Corporation) and that I was only skipper seemed to lend even more to the suspiciousness of my situation. I had a sinking feeling that my legal advice to limit my liability by forming a corporation was just about to backfire on me in a big way. I was muddling my way along when Charlotte had appeared.

"Oh, that must be the *Sun Queen*, the sailboat we looked at in July" she offered as I cringed and fired off a quick phrase in English that I knew he wouldn't understand: "Don't volunteer information, only answer questions he asks!" Oblivious to my comments and painfully clear body language Charlotte proceeded to tell the inspector of how we had sent our broker Minolis to look at the boat and we had even put in a bid—and later how we had heard that it had been stolen.

When the inspector told us that the boat had been spotted going through the Suez Canal, that the crew was English speaking, that children were on board, and that she had been flying an American flag, I felt the noose tightening. I had barely finished explaining that my boat had never been anywhere near Egypt when Charlotte added, before I could kick her under the table, that although we had been in Egypt our boat had remained in Greece during our trip.

That night there was utter pandemonium aboard *Captain Spiros.* First there was the postmortem. "Charlotte, you told him too damn much— this thing is getting so complicated we are going to be kept here for months."

"Nonsense—he obviously knew about our role in looking at the Gulf Star and Egypt is stamped in all of our passports—which he now has."

The children were about equally divided between Charlotte and me—they thought it would make sense to tell them as little as possible, but on the other hand they didn't want us to look like we were hiding anything.

Heyward and Alex offered the cheerful observation that they thought we were probably in one of those countries where you are presumed guilty until proven innocent. It was Margot, however, who was able to properly sum the situation up. "Gee Dad, no matter what happens we never seem to get bored." As I caught glimpses through the porthole of the uniformed figure shuffling around on the dock, I thought about what Margot had said.

She was right. With all of our papers seized and a guard posted to watch our boat we certainly weren't bored.

Realization dawned slowly. As we discussed the events of the day after dinner, the pieces suddenly seemed to come together. Mrs. Weber's strange call to my mother from Switzerland asking how our trip was going had puzzled me when my mother had told me about it right after we had returned from Egypt. When I had been pursuing the *Sun Queen* I had only corresponded with her husband and had never talked with her at all. Why would she call asking about us?

It was now obvious. Mrs. Weber, or someone impersonating her, had been playing detective and had tried to pry information out of my mother on false pretenses. Her call had been successful. My mother told her that we were doing great and had just gotten back from a wonderful trip to Egypt.

While I had still been in the states, Minolis had looked at *Sun Queen* on my behalf. He had climbed all over the boat, inspected it from stem to stern, and then reported to me that it was in lousy shape and that he could find a much better boat for me. The day after Minolis' inspection, the boat had been stolen.

I had only learned about the theft when I was outfitting *Captain Spiros*. Minolis told me that he needed the photos of *Sun Queen* he had taken for me. When I asked why, he had hesitated at first and then finally confided that the boat had been stolen and that he had been asked to help find it. He thought the pictures might help. I remembered this clearly because I had a very hard time locating the pictures. I also remembered the impression I had after looking at them again. After all my difficulties with *Captain Spiros* the photos of *Sun Queen* had looked almost pristine.

Charlotte and I compared our versions of what we thought the inspector had been driving at during his interrogation. It had been in French and we had understood the basics, but some of the nuances could have gone over our heads. Did he think Minolis had stolen the boat and then sold it to us? Or, did he think we had stolen it? How far had the investigation already gone? Who exactly was conducting the investigation? He had mentioned Interpol several times—who exactly was Interpol?

We had tried to call the American Embassy. But by the time we had finally obtained the number and persuaded the inspector to let us use his phone for a long distance call, it was past working hours on a Friday night. Not surprisingly, there had been no response.

Our interview with the inspector had ended with lots of questions in our minds and few answers. He politely informed us a special team of inspectors from Sousse had been summoned and were due to arrive in the morning. They would then conduct a very thorough investigation of the whole affair. We were up late that night trying to figure it out. But clear answers wouldn't come. We would just have to wait for the arrival of the inspection team in the morning.

At 8:00 Saturday morning they arrived—four of them. Mr. Hamadi was their chief and, with a great deal of self-importance, identified himself as a member of Socotu (whatever that was). He was impeccably polite, but very cagey.

"How did you get my name and why are we being investigated?"

"We know a lot about you, Mr. Coleman. Our investigation has been very thorough. You are from Florida, aren't you?"

"No, I'm from South Carolina." It only occurred to me later that I had forgotten about my brief residence in Florida as I was selling my interest in Maritrans. "How did you get my name and what do you want?"

"Please, Mr. Coleman, let us ask the questions."

He then produced a picture of *Sun Queen* that resembled our boat about as much as a Volkswagen Beetle resembles a fire truck. He also had a huge folder with a mass of data giving all of the specifications. "Our job," he stated, "is to determine whether or not your boat is the stolen boat."

He and his cronies then proceeded to crawl all over the boat measuring everything and taking lots of photographs. They meticulously recorded serial numbers, brand names of equipment, and asked detailed questions about our itinerary.

At the end of about two hours of this Mr. Hamadi finally concluded that our boat was definitely not the stolen boat and apologized for any inconvenience he may have caused. He then invited us to Sousse where he promised us a couscous dinner. He also gave us a number we could call to get a final report on their investigation.

"Oh, and Mr. Coleman, I am glad it turned out that the stolen boat wasn't your boat—it would have been very bad for you if it was. Also you should be glad that the investigation was conducted in Tunisia—in another country like Italy or Greece it would have been real trouble for you."

Charlotte and I waved good-by. We were glad to see them go and glad to be off the hook. But somehow we thought that it had been a great deal of trouble, even though we had been so fortunate that it had occurred to us in Tunisia.

The only other yacht in the harbor was a French ketch that arrived after us. Ever since their arrival the French couple had been eyeing us suspiciously. Watching the continuous flow of inspectors and soldiers on our boat asking questions, taking measurements, and snapping photos, they probably thought we were drug runners. After the police retreated, Charlotte tried to strike up a conversation with them.

"Hello. My name is Charlotte. We are from the United States. This has been crazy. They thought we stole a boat from Greece. But we didn't even sail to Egypt. And the boat they thought we stole had two masts. And..."

Charlotte then noticed that the husband, whom Alex had tagged "the man with no belly button" was staring at her with suspicious and judging eyes. She also noted that Alex had been right. He didn't have a belly button. She gave up the effort and politely said good-bye. This was simply going to be one set of friends we were not going to make.

**

After the police had finished making us wait, the weather took over, and we were locked into Kelibia for another two days. Charlotte and I took advantage of this by visiting some of the historic sites, and the children took advantage of the time to accelerate their academic efforts.

Margot was making the most progress of all and now had a target completion date of June 5. Even though Alex had accelerated up to three lessons a day, his target completion date was June 20. Heyward used his own brand of logic that none of the rest of us was able to understand to set his completion date at anywhere between June 5 and June 20.

Kelibia was a good hub for exploration. In ancient times it was known as Apsis and had been founded by Agathocles the Greek. In Roman times it had allied itself with Carthage and consequently had been destroyed by Skipio Africanus. The principal site of the city itself was Bordj, an impressive Byzantine Castle. Perched high on a hill overlooking the harbor and city, it dominated the countryside.

We took a cab ride to El Haouaria that is at the northeastern tip of the country. Unfortunately we were two weeks too late for the main event of the year. The Hawk festival had taken place in the beginning of May. Half removed posters told us of the hunts, dances, and festivities that had marked this important festival. But that wasn't the reason we came.

El Haouaria was within walking distance of Cape Bon, the rugged cape that faces the juncture of two huge expanses of the Mediterranean. From the south giant waves travel over three hundred miles from Libya to crash into seas that have the thousand-mile stretch from Gibraltar to gain strength. And to add interest, the ominous Skerki Bank lurks less than fifty miles to the north. This was an area that Charlotte wanted to see so that we would have some idea of what lay in store on the next leg of our trip. Fortunately for our forward progress, it was a beautiful day and relatively calm. We explored the caves and grottoes that honeycombed the hills of the cape and then returned to Kelibia.

The morning of May 20 was beautiful. After an early morning reconnaissance of the fishing market and obtaining weather advice from a number of the old salts, we decided to chance the Cape. It turned out to be a beautiful day with moderate wind and smooth seas—a perfect day to round Cape Bon.

Cape Bon

Sidi Bou Said was our destination. Located near the site of ancient Carthage, Sidi Bou Said was the crown jewel of Tunisia. We pulled into the crowded harbor and nearly rammed a fishing boat while we were trying to get into a narrow berth. Instead of responding with anger, the fisherman on the endangered boat took a line from us and spent half an hour helping pull us into our small berth. Later Arbi paid a visit and brought us a kilo of the best shrimp I have ever tasted. He was about Heyward's age and became a great friend of the family.

In spite of the fact that Sidi Bou Said was the site of the Palestinian Headquarters for Tunisia, it was a fantastic place. It's the playground for Tunis and the setting was beautiful. The path from the port to the city goes up a steep hill that is blazing with exotic wild flowers. Looking up, there is a beautiful city of white-washed buildings, and looking down, there is a magnificent view of the sparkling blue Mediterranean.

Each time we made the climb up to the city, Charlotte would detour to the little stand that produced the Arabic equivalent of a doughnut. As we watched the owner go through his ritual in creating the little pastries, he would see the longing look in Charlotte's eyes and give her a free one. After that, there was no choice—we would leave his stand with two each.

Sidi Bou Said was an ideal jumping off spot for visiting Tunis and Carthage. We took advantage of both. In Tunis, we spent a morning weaving our way around the Casaba, visiting museums, and enjoying the exotic sites. After paying off the bribe—lunch in a nice restaurant—we released the children to wander around on their own and then make their way back to Sidi Bou Said. By this time they were thoroughly sick of sight-seeing, and to get them out on any kind of outing was a major undertaking that required a special incentive.

Charlotte and I then made our way to the American Embassy. In between phone calls to decide on the menu for dinner that night and who should bring what, Greta gave us her undivided attention as we spun our tale of woe. "How far had the investigation on us gone? Was it possible other countries could be on the lookout for us? What steps should we take? Could she please have the Embassy call the number that Mr. Hamadi had given us to try to get more information than we were able to obtain?"

A week later we got our reply—the investigation was only carried out by the insurance company and Interpol had never been involved. And, oh yes, the report of sighting the vessel in Egypt had been incorrect—it hadn't been the stolen vessel.

We chose to believe the embassy and put the matter out of our minds—except that one day I will probably write Mrs. Weber a nasty letter for playing detective and causing us all the trouble. Minolis' role? Who knows—we were sick of him and didn't really want to find out. We had recently learned from a fax from our US broker, Castlemain, that Minolis had cheated them out of their share of the commission on our boat.

As we were purchasing our tickets at the Carthage Museum, a great surprise. Francois, Francoise, and Clemence of *Jonathan* arrived in their little car to visit Carthage. We all spent a delightful morning admiring a mixture of remnants of Greek, Roman, and Carthaginian cultures and then went back to the *Captain Spiros* where we had a final farewell lunch. We purchased two kilos of shrimp from Arbi and invited him to join us. During lunch Francois announced their decision. Just the day before they had decided to return to France and resume their old life. Their sailing days were finally coming to an end.

***

The children were very anxious to start their scuba lessons. We had met Daniel's friend, Taoufik, when he had been visiting marina officials in Monastir and we had made preliminary arrangements with him to take his course. The weather was finally becoming warmer, the winds were abating, our great adventure with Interpol was over—Tabarka and scuba lessons awaited—it was time to move on.

In order to be sure of arriving at Tabarka in daylight, we needed to leave Sidi Bou Said in the afternoon. After lunch and after Francois, Francoise, and Clemence had left, we made a quick decision. Thirty minutes later we began our final stretch in Tunisia. Our trip would take us along the northern Tunisian coastline almost to the Algerian boarder.

The trip was smooth except for Margot and Charlotte's 3:00 A.M. watch. They had the stretch offshore Bizerte where the density of fishing boats was incredible. By this time in the trip we had become fairly competent in interpreting navigation lights. But the Bizerte fishermen had apparently developed their own unique code for lights at night, and if there was a system, we never succeeded in unraveling it. At one point they came upon an anchored open cockpit fishing boat with its skipper asleep in the bilge and almost had a collision. They were so busy that Charlotte didn't even read to Margot about how they were passing the most northern point in Africa as they glided past Ras Enghela.

Although I had tried to joke about the laxness of the fishing boats during the times they had rousted me from bed to help them avert disaster, Charlotte didn't think it was funny at all. She had collapsed into an exhausted sleep when their watch was over and I had taken over. My watch was uneventful and then I turned it over to Heyward and Alex for their 5:00 to 7:00 watch. They had the exhilarating experience of seeing the rocky African coast line turn into flat desert sand and then into giant sand dunes. Later that morning we spotted the beautiful Genoan fortress that clearly marked the entrance of Tabarka.

Taoufik was waiting for us on the dock. We were surprised to see the modern marina facilities that included water, electricity and showers—our pilot had indicated that it was only a fishing harbor. After I had negotiated a price with Taoufik, we headed for our assigned berth.

Alex could hardly finish helping tie up the boat he was so anxious to get to the diving school to sign up. He was very nervous that a 15 year old might not be eligible and wanted to resolve the issue as quickly as possible. We somehow managed to keep everyone on board long enough to secure the boat before heading for the school where we were told to come back in the morning for our first lesson. Alex interpreted this as full acceptance and decided not to broach the delicate matter of age.

The next morning we headed for the diving school to have our first dive. Heyward and Alex were about to go berserk they were so excited. Charlotte categorically refused to even consider scuba diving, but Margot appeared willing to be coaxed into it. All five of us went out on the little diving boat. Heyward, Alex, and I had our "baptism dives" that officially enrolled us in the course. Charlotte had been careful not to bring a bathing suit to further emphasize her views about diving, but Margot had speculated that on a later trip she might give it a try.

For the second in our series of twelve dives, a Tunisian television crew accompanied us to do a documentary on Tabarka for the Tunisian national television. An incredible amount of equipment was loaded onto our small boat and we met the director, his girl friend, and the TV crew. The director, a Tunisian Walter Cronkite, explained the thoroughness with which they do these documentaries in all parts of Tunisia and always with a well-known historian and well-known geologists to give the cultural view of the territory as well as the tourist view.

"Where are the geologist and historians for this segment?" I inquired.

The director quickly changed the subject and finished the greasy sandwich he had brought aboard. A half hour later the fun began.

We reached our diving site and dropped the anchor. While the divers were getting dressed to dive, the TV crew stumbled around the wildly pitching deck trying to assemble their complicated equipment. As we grouped in the water to get ready to go under for our dive we could tell that all was not going so well with our media friends. The equipment was becoming a tangled mess, the TV crew was obviously slowing down, and "Walter" looked like he wished he had not eaten the greasy sandwich.

Our dive was great. Down to 15 meters. Alex and Heyward, enjoying the new-found freedom of swimming under water without worrying about air, were turning somersaults, swimming upside down, and generally having a grand time. When we returned to the surface half an hour later, all hell had

Scuba Diving in Tabarka

broken out on the diving boat. Last night's couscous was dripping down the side of the boat and six green heads were drooping over the gunnels. The TV gear, now a hopeless tangle, was sliding up and down the deck as the boat bobbed like a cork on its anchor.

One of the TV crewmen was so sick he had to be emergency evacuated back to port in a special Zodiac tender that had accompanied us. For some reason they decided to also take the divers back in the tender—perhaps they were worried we would get tangled in the TV cables.

We really enjoyed the diving course. Tabarka is one of the few places in the Mediterranean where coral grows and the coral reefs are one of the main attractions. Our instructors took us to several different places. At a cliff where huge fish would come right up beside us, Alex was examining a shellfish when a large Merlot approached and took it out it out of his hand. Heyward showed his first interest in navigation when he wanted me to teach him how to fix the position of this cliff with ranges so we could come back to the cliff later and fish.

There was another place where underwater mountains were riddled with caves that were encrusted with coral and teaming with sea life. Although we found the cave diving fascinating, it was nerve racking and claustrophobic to be in the middle of one with a diver in front and another behind. The problem was exacerbated by our fellow diver from Gabes—a six foot klutz whose deportment was even more ungainly underwater than on land. He might have been tolerable if it hadn't been for his gigantic flippers. Each time we came to a cave he would push and pull his way to the front of the group and then all we would see was the wash from his frantically gyrating body. One time Flippers almost knocked Alex's mask off and I felt obligated to talk to the instructor about it. But in the end, I wasn't too worried. It just served to make Alex and the rest of us better divers.

Our Diving Instructor

Margot joined us during one of our early dives to take her "baptism dive." She loved it and decided that she would like to take the full course. But this time the instructors did raise the question of age and she had to be content with only two dives.

On most days we made two dives—one in the morning and one in the evening. But on some days it was too windy in the afternoon to go out, and the instructors used this time to teach us the theoretical part of the course. After ten days and twelve dives, we obtained our certificates. It was amusing watching Alex and Heyward take their oral exams in French and calculate pressures and volumes in bars and liters. Alex dazzled them by calculating the result of a complicated formula in his head (I think he guessed) and Heyward's diagram of the human ear was so original and amusing that they decided to give him a passing grade.

***

Back on the *Captain Spiros* other adventures were taking place. For some reason the Tunisians found our boat fascinating. Most of the time we were the only sailboat in the harbor, and they took delight in climbing aboard to take pictures of themselves. We reluctantly tolerated this with soldiers, but generally chased children and teenagers off. One day, Madam Slim, President Director General of Societe Financiere de Gestin, arrived on the quay beside our boat in a big car and announced that she would like to come aboard. She was accompanied by her mother and her friend who was a director of the diving school and manager of the grand Mimossa Hotel.

Charlotte had accepted their kind offer to come, and when I returned from our diving, the conversation was in full swing. They told us about plans to develop Tabarka that involved a great deal of money from the Kuwaitis, the Saudis, and the Italians and promised to drive us around the area. The conversation became even more interesting when a French couple from the French embassy in Tunisia, whom I had met diving, joined us. They started to fill us in on a recent coup attempt in Tunis that had apparently taken place while we had been in Monastir. Madam Slim and her entourage did not seem to be comfortable with the topic nor with Veronique's graphic description of the gory details, but before she could find a way to change the subject, a sudden diversion spared her the trouble.

It started with footsteps on deck, laughing, and then a rainstorm in the main cabin. In one swift motion Charlotte was on her feet, out the hatch and screaming at the young boys who had thought it would be a cute trick to turn on the hose that extended into our water tanks. Turning on the water would not have been bad if the boys had not tripped over the hose during their unauthorized caper and thereby diverted the live nozzle through a hatch and into our living room.

***

Not many sailboats came to Tabarka while we were there, so that those that did were very special and, in all cases but one, led to great friendships. The French boat we had seen in Kelibia arrived two days after us. Eyeing us like we were escaped convicts, the man with no belly button and his wife kept their distance and departed the day after they arrived. We were delighted when the small French sloop *Thalmege II* sailed into port, and we met Henry and Sophie Ledeun. They were the best friends we made in Tabarka. Henry was an ex-business entrepreneur turned painter and writer.

Sophie was also a painter and they did many paintings together. They were both from Brittany and gave us a beautiful watercolor of a small Brittany fishing boat that now hangs in the living room of our home. They left before us, but we made plans to meet at a small fishing village near Malaga, Spain if our travels took us that far. They told us a lot about Caleta de Velez and we hoped that we would see them there.

＊

Nadher was an enigma that we were never able to quite figure out. We first saw him on a walk up to the old Genoan Fort on the point. We were a little suspicious of the rather tattered looking man on the lonely road and kept our distance when he tried to talk to us. Later we saw him again, but this time aboard a fishing vessel, the *Ayoub El Bahr*. Then, able to put him in the context of a lonely fisherman, we felt comfortable striking up a conversation. Nadher proceeded to explain the intricate technology of the many different kinds and colors of nets he carried aboard his vessel. He was an encyclopedia of knowledge about fishing and sea life in the Mediterranean, and we were mesmerized. We invited him to our boat, where, after downing a good portion of our final wine reserves, he proceeded to make us a fishing lure out of the top of a tuna fish can. This, he explained, would enable us to catch sword fish as we sailed past the shallows around Isle de Galite just offshore Tabarka.

Nadher had consumed so much wine that, as he was putting the finishing touches on his masterpiece, I was afraid he would cut a finger off on the sharp edges of the tuna fish can. In the interest of keeping his limbs in tact and in keeping a little of *Captain Spiros'* rapidly declining supply of spirits in reserve, I announced that we were completely out of wine. A half hour later and with a little help from Heyward and me, Nadher left.

After that night, he came over to our boat daily, inviting us to dinner on his boat (which we refused) and offering to take the children fishing (which they accepted). We thought he was genuine, but there was something about him that made us suspicious. Heyward in particular was nervous around him. One morning he brought us some fish as a gift, and they were excellent. Charlotte and I were so touched that we took the last bottle of wine out of our larder, fixed a bowl of popcorn, and joined him on the beach as he told us his life's story under a full moon. His mother and twin brother had died during birth, and he had been brought up by his uncle. He claimed to be 22—he looked more like 30—and was searching for the perfect wife. He loved families—he had never had one—and really liked being around ours.

In spite of all of the many things we liked about Tunisia, some of the social and cultural aspects were fatiguing and we were ready to leave when the diving course came to an end. Even though Tunisia was probably one of the most enlightened of the Arab countries, the way men treated women was disturbing. Charlotte and Margot felt very uncomfortable going into town by themselves, not from a safety point of view, but rather because of the general low esteem that the Tunisians seemed to show to western women.

When we were ready to check out of Tabarka Charlotte went to the customs officer to pick up our papers. But instead of giving them to her, he asked her a bunch of fresh questions and held on to them. Finally she left in frustration without the papers. A few minutes later she returned with Alex and the officer immediately handed over the papers and seemed to pretend nothing had happened before.

It was this attitude that was beginning to grate on us. It reminded me of the arrogance of Mr. Hamadi presenting himself as a representative of Interpol instead of admitting he was just an insurance company employee. It was the same attitude that induced people to freely come on board our boat, or to approach us with an over familiarity that often seems suspicious. After awhile these things became quite annoying. It was easy to see why Westerners who live in Arab countries often become so frustrated.

It was also interesting for us to note the enormous contrast between Turkey and Tunisia. Although Turkey was Islamic, it was not Arab and this made an enormous difference. The Turks were very friendly to us without being overly familiar. We were also impressed with their extreme industriousness. This was very different from the Arab attitude of *en shallah* or "god willing"—or the even more literal translation of "maybe I'll do it or maybe not with emphasis on the maybe not." But the biggest difference was that the Turks didn't seem to have the chip on their shoulders that was so apparent with many of the Tunisians.

* * *

Before leaving Tabarka, we received a couple of faxes via my mother regarding the sale of our boat. Henry Wauquiez had answered my letter from Malta and advised that the market for boats had collapsed in the Mediterranean as a result of the Gulf War and the recessions in Europe. Another fax from our broker in Charleston informed us that the US market was still bad, but may be improving. This news affected our thinking about our itinerary. Instead of leaving the boat in the Balearics, we began to think more seriously about the Canaries.

The other decision we needed to make was whether to head straight north for Sardinia and then sail to the Balearics or whether to head to the northwest and make it in a straight shot. Carloforte in Sardinia was 120 miles north and it would entail only one night underway. Port Mahon in the Balearics was 300 miles northwest and would have meant three days at sea. I had researched Sardinia and we were not opposed to the idea of spending a couple of days there. But the weather and sea were the most important considerations. The water between Sardinia and North Africa is relatively shallow and in a big blow it can become quite rough. While the dreaded Skerki Bank would have been well to the east of this route, it was near enough to still give Charlotte some concern. By going directly to Port Mahon, we avoided the shallow water, but also increased our time at sea and hence our vulnerability to a bad storm.

The overriding concern originates in the Alps, flows down the Rhone Valley, and then deposits its enormous force into the Gulf of Lyon. From there it sweeps across the open stretch of the Mediterranean and blows powerfully onto the shores of North Africa. It is called the Mistral and is the mother of all winds in the Mediterranean. We had been hearing tales of the Mistral ever since we had begun our sailing adventures in the Mediterranean. It was the end of May and fierce storms were still real threats. We needed to be sure that no Mistral would blow during our trip. Each day we would eagerly devour the weather forecast Taoufik would bring to us from the marina office. In the end, the forecast made the decision for us. After waiting several days, we received a forecast that almost guaranteed no Mistral for the next three to four days, and the wind was coming out of the north. I gathered up all our Sardinia tourist information, put it into deep storage, and, 1:00 P.M. on June 1, we set our course for Port Mahon.

***

We were blessed with fantastic weather. The wind was east enough from north to allow us to carry full sail. It was fun to be at sea again and we settled down to the routine. At sunset I carried out a compass check and then we made preparations for the evening. Although the wind was moderate, we put a second reef in the main—this was becoming standard for night sailing—I had absolutely no interest in going up to the bow in the middle of a night storm to reef.

During twilight we had an early dinner with only one person on watch. But when darkness set in, we went to our two person two-hour rotation. This meant port and starboard for Charlotte and me, but only until the 5:00 watch when Heyward and Alex could take their watch alone. We were becoming increasingly confident in our abilities and, although this was our longest trip so far, we were ready for it and were relatively relaxed.

Immediately upon leaving Tabarka, we had deployed Nadir's tuna can lure in hopes of catching the guaranteed sword fish. It was fun hoping, but we crossed the shallows with not even a bite. While our fishing results did not surprise us very much, the complete lack of shipping did. From two hours out of Tabarka until three hours before we entered Port Mahon we didn't see a single ship. I couldn't believe it. We were crossing the principal shipping lanes connecting the Western Mediterranean with the Eastern Mediterranean and I had been prepared to play tanker dodge for three days. What a break.

The children did very well on the trip. They had all continued in their development as competent seamen, but more importantly were beginning to take an even greater interest in the mechanics of what we were doing. Margot read one of my technical books titled *Storm Sailing* and started asking me a bunch of questions I couldn't possibly answer. I was used to this with Alex, however, so I didn't have too much trouble in giving the appearance that I was thoroughly familiar with all the topics. Even Heyward had started asking technical questions that broached critical topics such as "can a strong sea really rip one of our winches off the boat."

I used the trip to improve my navigation skills. I had gathered all the proper almanacs and mastered the calculations for sun lines with my sextant, but our three-day trip gave me the opportunity to gain practical experience. I was very pleased with my noon fixes and happy to know that if our Satnav were to fail, I could still figure out where we were. If we did decide to sail to the Canaries, being able to rely on our sextant as a back-up would be essential.

It was a real feeling of accomplishment to watch Port Mahon rise over the horizon and confirm that my calculations had been correct. We arrived and moored a little before noon. After three days and two nights at sea, it felt great to sail into the wonderfully protected harbor and find an anchorage.

Perched on the eastern end of the Isla de Menorca, Port Mahon is one of the truly great harbors of the Mediterranean. The island and the port have both seen much history, but the part of Charlotte's readings that caught our attention most was when the French had invaded the island in 1756. Their leader, the Duc de Richelieu, had a special sauce served at his victory banquet in Paris and named it after the harbor—sauce mahonesa.

Menorca was as big a change for us as Monastir had been from Malta and Italy. We had become so accustomed to the backwardness of the

Tunisians that to find ourselves in sophisticated European surroundings was another culture shock. Charlotte, Margot, and I took a cab to the supermarket and we could hardly believe our eyes. The giant store was a Spanish version of the US institution and even offered purchase by Visa! We went wild. Six shopping carts filled to the brim, an unhappy cab driver, a dangerously overloaded dinghy, and then we were back on board *Captain Spiros* for a feast of spare ribs, Doritos, and good Spanish beer. It looked like we were going to enjoy the Balearics.

Cala Cova

The weather was sunny, the water warm, and the beaches sparkled with emerald green water. Menorca is surrounded by little coves that give excellent protection and are great anchorages. On our way to Ciutadella on the western end of the island we stopped at several of these coves where we thoroughly enjoyed the warm beauty of the sandy beaches surrounded by low mountains. Swimming for the adults and serious study for the children as they entered the final stretch in their Calvert lessons made our days go quickly and pleasantly.

Ciutadella is Menorca's second largest port and has a very protected harbor. It was the ideal jumping off point for the next leg of our trip to Majorca. Manuel was waiting on the Club Nautico dock to take our lines and our money. We had been warned that Club Nautico was a snobbish Spanish club whose members rarely ventured closer to the sea than the glass-enclosed balcony from where they could sip their sangria and watch visiting yachtsmen being ripped off.

We were forced to land at Club Nautico because a boat show was in progress in the port and all of the public docks were being used. Grudgingly we handed over the ransom that Manuel demanded and then settled down to endure the loud music. Blaring from speakers across the channel where they were exhibiting various models of jet skis, the music was almost as obnoxious as the exhibits.

Our neighbor was a ketch from Scotland, and cocktail hour had been in progress during our delicate job of mooring next to them. As soon as our lines had been secured and we had settled with Manuel, they had invited us on board. I was happy to accept the invitation because Murray had given me a nine out of ten on my stern to mooring. This was in sharp contrast to the normal grumbling and criticism I had grown to expect from "Lord of the Lines" Heyward, "Anchorman Alex", and "Bumper Queen" Margot. "Gee Dad, why did we have to use so many lines—especially the big heavy one that's so hard to coil" from Heyward Or "Let's not anchor, I think we should go alongside instead" from Alex, who would like to shift the work over to his brother. Or from Margot, just at the critical moment when I would be trying to judge when I need heavy reverse to keep from ramming the neighboring boat, "You said we were coming in on the starboard side and now I have to change all the bumpers to the other side—why can't you make up your mind." But the unkindest comment of all, that could come from any of my crew at any time, was: "Why can't we do it smoothly like all of the other boats instead of making it so difficult?"

At any rate, Murray obviously had a good eye for fine seamanship and it was with pleasure that we boarded his vessel to have the first gin and tonics of our trip. There was no ice, of course, but it tasted great anyway. Murray then gave us a fascinating account of his smoked salmon exporting business that he runs during the portion of the year he isn't sailing.

***

After beating into the wind the whole way to Majorca, we explored several coves along its southern coast and then headed for a small island that is owned by the Spanish Army. Our visit provided some excitement.

Puerto de Cabrera, with its isolated beaches and surrounding cliffs, was spectacular. We read in our pilot how 7,000 of Napoleon's soldiers were taken prisoner, transported to the island, and then left to die because of a lack of food and water, but we failed to read the part in our pilot that warned against going ashore because of current military security. Unfortunately for Alex, he opted to take his customary afternoon wander on shore and dinghied over. We heard his shouts and saw his arms wave as the two men dressed in fatigues wrestled the dinghy out of his hands.

In addition to being anchorman, Alex acted as "mother of the dinghy" and anyone who tried to do damage to our Zodiac or Yamaha motor had to contend with him. We could see enough from the boat to be worried, but there was nothing we could do. There was a fierce interchange that lasted for five or ten minutes during which we had added to the confusion by shouting from the boat at the men not to steal our dinghy. Alex had then returned to the boat and told us his sad story. The men were soldiers and had explained to him by punching a hole in his prized dinghy that no one was allowed to come ashore.

***

Palma and the reality of trying to sell our boat were next on the agenda. We carefully avoided going anywhere near the swish Club Nautico as we entered the harbor and moored next to an English boat at the public quay beside Paseo Martimo. Our first order of business was to find the American Express office so we could pick up mail that had been forwarded by my mother. While it was great getting news from back home, news of the huge legal fees I had incurred on the fallen-through sale of our house in Philadelphia was not. It was another reminder of how difficult the entire process surrounding taking our trip had been. We were about to encounter another reminder. Selling our boat was going to be very difficult. I visited every broker in Palma and the story from each of them was the same—the market in the Mediterranean was dead. But if we were willing to leave our boat in their custody, they would try hard to sell it, an effort that would include a very significant weekly storage charge.

Charlotte and I knew how to translate this message. After we left our boat with the friendly broker, we would get a series of letters informing us that we needed to decrease the price lower and lower. And meanwhile, the expense of taking care of it would go up and up. On top of this, the harbor of Palma was very exposed, and I was not at all comfortable with the safety of leaving my boat there.

The decision not to leave our boat in the Balearics was easy, and we were almost on our way to the Canaries. But I had one last broker to see before we gave up completely. I took the long walk down the Paseo Martimo, past all the luxury yachts, past the swish Club Nautico, and then across the street to the De Valk office where I met Adrian.

De Valk was headquartered in Holland, and Adrian thought that might be the best place to sell our boat. It had easy access to French, German, and British buyers and the market there hadn't been nearly as bad as in the Mediterranean. In addition, De Valk had its own boat yard and would take care of our boat at no additional expense. It sounded tempting to me because it could solve the boat sale problem. But I was a definite minority.

Alex was still set on crossing the Atlantic, and the Canaries represented the first step. But the main objection from everybody was the thought of heading north. We had been cold for so long and finally we had found warmth. Why give it up? And there was the matter of beating against the Portuguese trade winds. A trip to Holland would entail over 800 miles along the entire Atlantic coast of the Iberian Peninsula straight into the prevailing Portuguese trade winds and then a trip across the dreaded Bay of Biscay. Heading to Holland was not a popular concept.

I found myself in a difficult position. I weighed the possibility of a family mutiny against the financial consequences of taking the boat back to the US to face a dead market. Adrian smelled my hesitation and immediately pulled out his mobile phone.

From the bow of *Captain Spiros* he made a call to his associate in Holland. Menno assured me that our boat would do well in Holland and urged me to give him a call when we got to Gibraltar. I agreed with Menno that if we were still interested when we arrived in Gibraltar, I would fly to Holland and talk with him. This compromise left everyone only moderately unhappy.

Palma itself was a beautiful city. From our quay on the Paseo Martimo, we were an easy walk away from one of the prettiest central squares we had ever seen. We explored the town and ate delicious tapas at a restaurant a neighboring yachtsman had recommended. We also noted the yachtsman's advice for our next anchorage and I plotted a course for Cala Portals.

Late the afternoon before leaving, we received more hope on selling our boat. Alex was the first to spot it, but both Margot and Heyward quickly confirmed his observation. I came on deck and confirmed their conclusions. It definitely was a Jeanneau Trinidad that was heading for the slot just to our starboard. Jean Luc was French and both he and his wife ran a charter business on their Trinidad. They thought it was a lovely boat and had friends in Marseilles who were looking for a Trinidad to start their own charter business. Although I knew it was a long shot, it boosted our spirits at a time when they needed boosting, and we traded addresses. Jean-Luc would contact his friend and if he were interested, they would leave a message for us at the principal marina in Gibraltar.

But the Trinidad wasn't the main event of that afternoon. After Jean-Luc had finished his third aperitif and left, Margot emerged from her cabin with a big smile on her face. She had just finished her last exam, and it was ready for mailing. That night we had an appropriate celebration.

Leaving Palma was more than just leaving another port. It was the end of the idea of a quick sale in the Balearics and the beginning of another phase of our adventure. We weren't sure if it would end in a long trip south to the Canaries or a hard cold sail to Holland. But we did know it would be exciting.

***

Smooth water, light winds, and a warm sun have their price, and we began to understand the currency better as we circled Cala Portals looking for a spot where we could anchor and not be on top of another yacht. We had finally caught the tourist season and were about to have our first encounter with the third estate of the sailing community—the charterer.

Eric couldn't have been nicer and showed a surprisingly small amount of embarrassment as he climbed aboard our boat carrying a large battery. "Oh, I just left the refrigerator running last night" he explained as casually as if he had accidentally dropped a jar of mayonnaise overboard "and she's pretty dead now. Would you mind awfully giving me a charge?"

Fortunately I had jumper cables and didn't have to go through the tortuous process of removing one of my batteries to find a place for his. As I cranked up the engine to give him an hour charge, I began to think about how different our two worlds were. I had three batteries on board and would go into a panic if even one of them became low. The nightmare of all cruisers is to find a dead engine at the moment of need. Visions of *Captain Spiros* splintering on harsh rocks would follow such a thought, and the whole affair would leave me in a sweat.

But Eric wasn't in the least bit concerned and returned to his chartered Beneteau carrying his battery as if it were a cup of sugar he had just borrowed from a neighbor. We had enjoyed chatting with him and his young son during the charging and were surprised and greatly pleased when they returned an hour later with ice cream cones for everyone. As we were finishing our cones, we heard the crash on our stern.

The young Spanish boy who had been annoying everyone by speeding around the small cove on a jet ski finally cut it too close. His wild maneuvering through the maze of vessels ended with a crunch as his jet ski and the stern of *Captain Spiros* became one. Charlotte exploded like a coiled spring and was sure our anchor had slipped and we were up on the rocks. We rushed to the stern and watched as the young boy and his de-manned jet ski both bobbed up and down in the water. Our relief in not being damaged and not having to fish an injured Spaniard out of the water turned into anger.

We scolded him that a small cove was not a good place to race around on his jet ski. We also told him that he was lucky he hadn't killed himself, that we were lucky that he had not holed our boat, and that jet skis were not at all fun for people who were not riding them. An apologetic "Si Senior" and then he was gone. Ten minutes later his friend was driving the same jet ski around in an even more reckless manner.

Our last island in the Balearics was Isla Espalmador, a small island just south of Isla de Ibiza. It was both South Carolina Low Country and the Caribbean merged into one with green sparkling water setting off the large white sand dunes. There were other sights besides sun and sand on Espalmador. Margot had noticed it first. The man in a neighboring boat had apparently forgotten to put on his bathing suit. We had seen a lot of topless bathing in the Mediterranean but this was taking it one step further. Alex pointed out that a girl in another neighboring boat had also forgotten her bathing suit—and then we realized that this was the norm for Espalmador. And so went another chapter in the continuing education of our children.

Chapter 11
Around the Iberian Peninsula

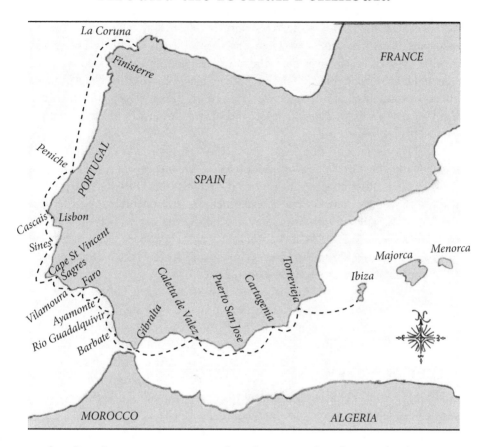

After dinner on our second night at Espalmador we made a snap decision. It was 105 miles to mainland Spain and we wanted to arrive in daylight. I went to the navigation table and made the calculation. Five minutes later we had the anchor up and were on our way. By this time night sailing had become routine, and we made the trip easily. Alicante light was visible far offshore, and we had the comfort of being sure of our position as we neared shore. At about 6:00 the following afternoon, we pulled into the small fishing village of Torrevieja, but not before catching our first blue fish of the trip. Our five-pounder made a superb dinner as we celebrated our first day in Spain.

Torrevieja put us half way down the Costa Blanca. This was where we would begin our long haul around Southern Spain to Gibraltar. Our choice had been excellent. Not only did Torrevieja provide excellent protection, it had a huge supermarket and a great vegetable market. We availed ourselves of both and set out the next morning for the South.

We missed the opportunity to visit the giant inland sea, Mar Menor, because it was too rough to make the narrow channel safely, so we pushed on to Cape Tinoso, just outside of Cartagena. Colonized in 223 BC by Hannibal's brother Hasdrubal, this was the point at which Hannibal launched his march into Italy. From our quiet anchorage at the base of a high hill that housed an enormous ancient fortress, we enjoyed thinking about the historical significance of this strategic location and of its relationship to Carthage that we had visited so recently.

The peace and quiet was marred by the approach of a high speed vessel with the Guardia Civil on board. Our pulses raced—could this possibly be another chapter in the episode of the stolen Gulf Star? Happily, it was only a routine passport check and quiet was restored after they filled out their mass of papers. But in this case they did the writing, a pleasant contrast with Greece and Turkey. With its proximity to Africa there was a great deal of drug smuggling along the Spanish coast, and these visits by the Guardia Civil in quiet anchorages were to become the norm.

We had warned Alex that we would not leave Gibraltar for the Canaries or anywhere else unless he was finished with his Calvert Course. And, as an additional incentive, we told him that he would not be able to leave the boat in Gibraltar until he was done. As Margot lounged around and basked in the glory of being finished, Alex labored away. It was an interesting sight to see him at our portable cockpit table as the boat glided along the coast of Spain, working on geography, history, and math while the rest of us sunned ourselves on deck and watched the porpoises.

Our anchorage near Puerto de San Jose marked the end of the Costa Blanca and the beginning of the coast of Almeria. The following morning we rounded the formidable Cabo de Gata, but the June weather was beautiful and being terrified of capes had become a thing of the past. We had become so relaxed that we didn't even mind when we were unable to receive weather forecasts. Down came our heavy duty Yankee jib and up went our very much larger Genoa. The increase in performance of *Captain Spiros* was significant.

Schools of thousands of dolphins surrounded us on the trip to Caleta de Velez as we basked in the sun and watched the Spanish coastline glide by. In the port of Caleta de Velez there was an unusual laxness. We had to walk all over the long docks and shore to finally find someone who had the authority to assign us a berth. With polite indifference they told us to stay where we liked and didn't bother to assign a price. But as we looked around the reason became obvious. This was a fishing port that had not yet been discovered by the yachting community and a Club Nautico was not to be found. Henry's recommendation had been excellent.

We hoped to find Henry and Sophie. When we had said good-by in Tabarka they had given us an address and dates when they would be there. Our rushed trip around the Spanish coast had been partly to have our arrival meet these dates, and partly to arrive in time to attend the Sunday bullfight in nearby Malaga. But our thorough search of the port confirmed what our cursory survey upon arrival had suggested. *Thalmege II* was not there. With difficulty we tracked down the address they had given us, but were disappointed that their friend was nowhere to be found either.

While the bull fight we saw in Malaga was fascinating, the real highlight of our visit to Caleta de Velez came with the Feast of San Juan in the neighboring town of Torre del Mar. That night the beach was full of huge wooden structures, a band was playing, and the whole town, toddlers included, were out walking along the boulevard. At midnight all the wooden structures were set on fire and there was a brilliant display of fireworks. While the significance of this display was obscure to us, we were drawn in by the warmth of the people and their joie de vivre. It was a wonderful evening.

Early the morning of June 25 we left Caleta de Velez and began our last stretch along the Costa del Sol. We had seen many dolphins on our trip, but never so many and never so large as those we saw as we neared Gibraltar. Was it the nearness of the Atlantic? Excitement was in the air as we approached.

I had read a great deal about the strait and the strange phenomenon that occurs there. It dates back to the Ice Age when the Mediterranean was still a separate body with no connection to the ocean. But as the ice began to thaw and the water level rose, the narrow isthmus that connected Europe with Africa was overrun and the Strait of Gibraltar was born. But even with the strait, the Mediterranean is essentially a land-locked sea and this is what makes it different. The only way water can leave the Mediterranean is through evaporation and this is made up by a constant flow from the Atlantic in through the strait. This explains the lack of both tides and current everywhere in the Mediterranean. But this is not the case at all in the narrow strait. Through this three mile channel flows all the water that must make up for evaporation for the entire Mediterranean and the currents can be awesome.

Mountains on both coasts of the narrow channel give the strait another special feature—strong wind. From the west, the powerful Poniente can come howling through the strait often bringing heavy clouds and rain with it. And from the east the formidable Levanter can suddenly arise and quickly build up to gale force. East to west or west to east, transiting through the strait can be very tricky for a sailing craft. But this was something we would have to contend with later. Gibraltar was our destination and it is situated on the eastern approach to the strait.

At Gibraltar

We had all been craning our eyes to see the "Gib," and when it finally appeared we were struck with its size and majesty. It was a clear day and as we got closer we could also see Sidi Musa, the huge peak on the African shore that formed the other Pillar of Hercules. Charlotte read to us about Tarik-ibn-Zeyeb and how in 711 AD he invaded Spain from Morocco and began an occupancy that was to last until the fifteenth century. They had named the peak after him. Tarik's Mountain or Jebel-Tarik—and thus the name Gibraltar was born.

The port of Gibraltar was gigantic and crowded. We passed harbor after harbor, and each was full of war ships, tankers, and freighters of all descriptions and sizes. Alex counted the guns along the ridge as we passed the commercial harbor on our way to the northern end of the harbor, and we noted the huge amount of traffic from US war ships and supply vessels en route to or from the Persian Gulf.

Our destination, Marina Bay, was sandwiched in a little cove that had the airport runway as its northern sea wall. Like Malta we saw British efficiency, but this time it wasn't once removed. A quick stop at the port office just opposite the marina and we were through customs and ready to proceed to a berth that had already been assigned to us. The customs officer had described to me the incredible activity Gibraltar saw during the Gulf War and explained that there was still a lot of activity in the port engaged in demobilizing the Allied Forces.

Gibraltar brought not only the end of our trek across the Mediterranean—it brought to a head the dilemma of what to do with the boat. The fork in the road had finally come, and now we had to make a choice. Contemplating a five-day trip in the Portuguese trades with the wind on our stern and constantly warmer weather with the intriguing Canary Islands at the end had fortified us during our forced march around the Spanish Coast. But there was also the reality of the situation to consider.

Our trip was coming to an end, and we all had new chapters in our lives to face. Selling the boat in the Canaries was out of the question, and keeping it there over a long period was impractical. Leaving it there would necessitate coming back in the late fall or early winter and sailing it across the Atlantic. While Charlotte and I would have loved to do this, we knew that it could have a very disruptive effect on whatever new life we were creating. My plan was to buy or start a business, and leaving my new enterprise for a three to four week Atlantic cruise didn't strike either of us as very realistic.

The pressure of the decision was on, and after the initial exhilaration of our arrival in Gibraltar, depression set in. At first I thought we were just tired from the long trip, and we went to bed early to try to catch up on our sleep. But after a night of tossing and turning, I knew it was the decision that was bothering us. As far as the children were concerned, our destination was definitely the Canaries. And for Charlotte and me, it was certainly what we wanted to do. We decided to wait one more day before tackling the decision.

We spent that day getting ready for a long trip south. We refueled, restocked, and fixed various broken items. Just outside the marina there was a great chart store and I was able to purchase the two charts I would need to get to the Madeira Islands and then the Canaries. And I was able to obtain a pilot for the Canaries. But I hedged my bets. For both purchases I negotiated the right to return them for charts and a pilot for the Bay of Biscay and the English Channel.

After a long talk with Charlotte well into that evening and a good night's sleep to collect our thoughts, the situation became clear. If the De Valk alternative was real and not just another broker's sales pitch, we would pursue it. It would be my job to determine the viability of selling our boat in Holland. Early the following morning I took a flight to Amsterdam and met with Menno and his associate Peter at Bruinisse, the site where I would leave the boat if we took it north to Holland.

Bruinisse was not only a charming little Dutch community nestled just south of Rotterdam, it was by far the cleanest and best run marina I had seen since leaving the states. I began to develop confidence in Menno, Peter, and their firm, De Valk. De Valk is the largest yacht broker in Holland and I was impressed with their operations. We discussed the problem of my getting the boat the 1,500 miles from Gibraltar to Bruinisse and Menno said they could help.

Willem, a skipper De Valk often used, was going to go to the Balearics to make a short delivery for them and was then going to Peniche, a small fishing port just north of Lisbon, Portugal, where he owned some land. After a few phone calls and some negotiations Willem agreed to meet me in Peniche on July 12 and then sail with me back to Holland. He would also bring a friend who would be helping him with the Balearics delivery.

This idea was appealing. It would mean that even if we encountered delays, I could get Charlotte and the children back home by the beginning of August and in time for school. Willem and I could get the boat back by ourselves. If we adopted this plan, I would be able to make firm plane reservations for them and then drop them off somewhere along the route in time for them to catch a flight in late July. Without making a firm commitment, I told Menno and Willem that I would discuss the whole matter with my family and give them an answer as soon as I got back to Gibraltar.

An hour out of Gibraltar I had an impulsive thought and acted on it right away. The stewardess was very cooperative and agreed to pass my request on to the pilot. Five minutes later she was back at my seat and motioned to me to follow her forward. She told me to take the vacant jump seat just behind the pilot and then left.

They were so busy with the approach that I wasn't sure if they had even noticed my arrival, but after a short time the copilot broke the silence: "So you are living on a sailboat and want to see the Strait of Gibraltar from the air. Well, you will get a great view. What kind of boat do you have?"

What luck. George was a sailor and he understood perfectly my request to do a little reconnaissance before our transit. Not only did I get an excellent look at the channel and the state of the seas, I also learned from George how I could get an official air control weather forecast before setting out. After our landing, I invited George to come join us for afternoon cocktails and then walked across the runway to the marina and our boat.

On the way back to our boat I thought about the coming discussion and knew it would be heated. This was the moment of truth. For almost a year we had been living a maverick life. It had had its rewards, and it had had its shortcomings. Would we continue it? We all had been responding to this question in different ways, but with results that were amazingly similar. Heyward and Alex often talked of crossing the Atlantic, but their concerns about school and friends at home led them in a different direction. Margot's endless conversations with Charlotte about the garden she would plant when we returned to Wadmalaw, Heyward's concerns about room arrangements in our small house, my gnawing concerns about my next livelihood, Charlotte's efforts to sort through and understand the school structure in Charleston—

these were all indicators of the overwhelming pull back to tradition. Even before our discussion began, I knew where it would end—we were ready for re-entry. But I also knew it would be a different kind of re-entry. While we would go back to our old world, I felt that we would all play by a different set of rules. What would this new set of rules be? How would it affect our daily lives? I wasn't ready to answer this yet, but I did know things would not be the same.

When I was back on board, we held our family summit. Alex was particularly disappointed at the prospect of missing the sail to the Canaries and made strong passionate arguments for his case. We were all getting tired and no one was very enamored with a hard sail to Holland which would be against the wind most of the way. But there was agreement on one point. The trip was coming to an end and it would be best to put the *Captain Spiros* to bed so we wouldn't have the burden of moving her again once we got back home.

We finally reached a compromise and it contained two key provisions for the children. One was a firm departure date before the end of July and the other was the promise of a nice visit to Philadelphia before returning to South Carolina. There were also other concessions. We would confine our travels to short relaxing day hops from Gibraltar to Peniche so everyone could enjoy the Atlantic coasts of Spain and Portugal. After that we would pick up Willem in Peniche. From there on, while we would sail hard, Willem and the helper he planned to bring would take the brunt of the workload and the children would be able to "enjoy the cruise." No night watches and only light cleaning duties.

At about three that afternoon George came and brought his girlfriend with him. He was full of advice, tips on ports to visit, and sailing anecdotes. Charlotte was having a great time until we got into the weather discussion. During our flight I had seen that the waves were only moderately high. I had also noted that the wind was in the right direction for our passage—east to west—a good strong Levanter. George had pointed out that the Levanter was only in its first day and would probably continue a day or two. When both George and I agreed that tomorrow would be an excellent day for our departure, Charlotte couldn't remain quiet any longer.

"The weather report says it's blowing force 9 at Tarifa. I'm not going to sail in a force 9."

"But Charlotte, Tarifa is a choke point and it always blows hard there. Besides, I saw it from the air this morning and it didn't look even close to a force 9. And we have to have the Levanter to get through the strait. What happens if the wind shifts and comes out of the east? We could be stuck here for a week."

George nodded his agreement with my logic, but Charlotte would have none of it. She had been particularly quiet when George had quoted "when barometer is high, let sails fly." As far as she was concerned, no sails were going to fly either that day or the next. The scales tipped in favor of family harmony and we decided to stay in Gibraltar one more day.

Our extra day in Gibraltar was July 1 and it turned out to be a very special day. Alex finished and mailed in his Calvert Course. His confinement on board finally over, he and I walked into Gibraltar. It was the first time he had been permitted to leave the boat since arrival. I was glad that he was finally getting the opportunity to see the port. After visiting the town, we walked over to the chart shop and I exchanged the Canaries charts and pilots that I had previously purchased there for those to the north.

A few days earlier Heyward had completed his courses. Now they were all done. Charlotte and I breathed a huge sigh of relief. Maybe we hadn't ruined their educations after all. There was still the task of finding schools for the three of them back in South Carolina, but at least it would be with a successful academic year behind them instead of incomplete correspondence courses. We were very proud of them.

It had been a strenuous day, but now that the decision had been made, some of the pressure was off. We had chosen the fork to the north. Weather permitting, we would depart in the morning. I stayed up late that night planning for our trip to Portugal.

***

Charlotte and I were up early and we were both nervous. The day before, winds of force 8 had been reported around Tarifa and the forecast that morning called for more of the same. But I was worried that the Levanter we had had for three days now would soon be over. The previous day I had extracted a promise from Charlotte that if it were no worse the next day, she would be willing to leave. Reluctantly she agreed to her promise. My interpretation of the ambiguous current charts in our pilot and the advice from the marina office put 11:00 A.M. as the ideal departure time to catch the most favorable currents.

At 10:45 we left the marina, put a third reef in the main, and with only a handkerchief of a jib set out across the Bay of Gibraltar. The bay was flat and there was practically no wind, but I had made a bargain with Charlotte and knew better than to try to make any modifications to her precautions. We had company. Two elderly Norwegians Alex and I had met in the chart shop the day before zipped past us under full sail. They waved gaily and I felt a little foolish, but bit my tongue and said nothing.

As always in tight situations such as this, Charlotte was at the wheel. Adrenaline was flowing, and we were taking no chances. As we approached a giant tanker, Charlotte started veering to the right.

"Head a little more to your left and pass just behind his stern" I suggested.

The compass continued to swing.

"He's so big, I don't want to come anywhere near him" Charlotte exclaimed as she continued to veer her home, children, and household effects to the right.

"But Charlotte, he's anchored."

"No he isn't. Look how much closer he has gotten."

I decided that it was not the time for a lecture on the physics of relative motion so I was ready to let the matter drop. The children, however, always quick to seize the opportunity to enter a good argument, picked up the ball. Alex grabbed the binoculars and announced that he saw the anchor chain. Heyward, who had yet to be nervous about anything on the trip, made fun of Charlotte's concern, and said we could go close whether it was anchored or not.

Margot, presented with the happy prospect of disagreeing with her brothers and at the same time taking up for her mother, explained to Alex in her new sailor vocabulary that he was crazy and that there obviously was no anchor chain. The adjectives that Margot used in her attack on Alex were sufficiently vicious to change the whole course of the argument and, after Charlotte's wide arc to the right, we forgot about the tanker.

Soon after crossing the bay, we came out of the lee that the gigantic Rock of Gibraltar provided and began to feel the power of our Levanter. Bianne and Deeda had called them White Horses and Margot's eagle eyes picked them out on the horizon. Our roller coaster ride was about to begin. The white caps became bigger and bigger and the increasing agitation of the water gave us early warning of what was to come. Just off Tarifa it finally hit us. It was sudden and it was strong. Force 7 with gusts to force 8.

Thanks to Charlotte, however, we were ready as the strong wind on our stern gave us a sudden burst of speed. As I watched our Norwegian friends fight to reef their sails in the powerful wind, I felt less embarrassed about our early precautions and was glad we had followed Charlotte's cautious advice. Properly reefed, *Captain Spiros* could take almost any sea and watching her plow smoothly through the troubled waters around Tarifa gave me a warm feeling of security as we headed for the open Atlantic. It had taken us a long time, but we were finally beginning to learn the importance of being ready. It only takes a small mistake or oversight to turn an exciting sail into a tense situation. The Dutch couple in Corfu had been right, and I silently thanked them again for their sage advice.

****

Carefully avoiding the gigantic tunny net that extended over three miles offshore, we entered our first Atlantic port. After passing rows and rows of moored fishing boats, we pulled up to a dock, and then went onshore. Barbate de Franco was a quaint little fishing village with a beautifully protected harbor and was very different from the Spanish Mediterranean. There was less pollution, fewer tourists, and beautiful sandy beaches. Even the people at Club Nautico were friendly—and the mooring was only moderately overpriced.

Early the next morning we set out and I began the day with the first of two serious mistakes. Rather than trust the marked channel between the north jetty and the landward end of the tunny net, I decided to round it to seaward. It turned out to be a long wet trip into a steadily increasing wind and it seemed that we would never reach the boats that were moored at the end. Perhaps it was my impatience and desire to get on with our trip after this unnecessary two-hour delay that had led to the second mistake.

I still wasn't completely comfortable with the RCC Pilot Foundation's writing style and was having trouble understanding how to use their pilot, *Atlantic Spain and Portugal*. It was about two hours after rounding the tunny net that I finally figured out that in reading about east to west routes only half of the hazards are cited. The other half are cited in sections on west to east routes. As I began reading about approaching Barbate de Franco from the west I turned white. "Passing Trafalgar light beware of the Placer de Meca reef and the dangerous ridge, Bajo Aceitera, that extends two miles from the reef." It went on to talk about agitated seas and shallow water. The pilot gave two alternatives to give the reefs a wide berth. Pass close to shore or stay at least three and a quarter miles offshore. The transition from absolute calm and relaxation to sheer panic can take place very quickly. I couldn't believe I could have made such a mistake. I hurried below and checked my chart. We were right on top of Placer de Meca Reef. Which way should we go? Further out to sea, or closer to shore? I posted Margot on the bow to spot for banks and asked Alex to call out every change in depth from our fathometer at the navigation station.

I hoped that my interpretation of the tide tables posted at the Club Nautico in Barbate de Franco had been correct. By sheer luck we were on a high tide and this gave us an extra three feet. As Alex called out 16 feet, 15 feet, 14 feet, 16 feet, I could visualize the narrow space between the bottom of our keel—seven feet below us—and the rocky bottom. What would happen if we grounded? What would happen if the wind picked up? How would we get off a reef that extended three miles?

"Dad, the water gets dark ahead. Does that mean it's shallow?" Margot shouted. We were about equally split on our opinions, and I was still vacillating when Alex shouted "11 feet."

My decision was made. I swung us hard to port and gritted my teeth as we headed away from land. Then from Alex "12 feet ,14 feet, 14 feet." It was the longest half hour I have ever spent, but luck was on our side and 11 feet was the lowest number I heard from Alex.

Once off the reef and after our rattled nerves had a chance to settle back down, we began to relax and enjoy the day. I studied the entrance to Cadiz through binoculars and decided to forego the confusion and bustle. Instead we headed for the Rio Guadalquivir, the giant river that snakes the whole way up to Seville. After our trek across Bajo Aceitera I was a little nervous about our long approach into the Rio Guadalquivir. I was also very confused by the buoys marking the entrance of the channel. Different colors on the four quadrants and strange stripes. This was something new.

Out came The Macmillan & Silk Cut Nautical Almanac and my pilot for the Eastern Atlantic. But none of the pictures quite lined up with the buoy that prominently stood at the southern side of the channel entrance. But there was one that was close and it read "Port Closed."

Port closed? How could the entrance to Seville be closed? It didn't make sense, but the marks were there for a reason, and, after having been burned at Bajo Aceitera, I wasn't going to take any chances. I waited until I saw a large vessel heading out of the channel, and then entered the long approach. We anchored a short way up the river just off Coto de Donana where there was a huge national park that was famous for the abundant wild-life that can easily be seen grazing from the river. We didn't have time to make the 55-mile trip up to Sevilla, but decided to go ashore to explore. While we were a little disappointed not to see any wild animals, we thoroughly enjoyed our short hike across the island and an evening swim. The highlight of the evening was fixing the two blue fish that Heyward and Alex had caught that afternoon. Alex turned his into deliciously fresh sashimi and Heyward pan fried his in olive oil and garlic.

***

Early the next morning we were underway again. We had noticed that after Gibraltar the sailing was quite different. While the winds were stronger than the June and July winds in the Mediterranean, they were predictable, and we were no longer at the mercy of abrupt and radical changes. The waves were higher, but more spread out so that there was little if any pounding when we headed into them.

Although the open water was less daunting than in the Mediterranean, entering ports presented a new set of challenges. Along the Atlantic coasts of Spain and Portugal the gradually sloping shoreline often results in shallow bars forming at the entrance of harbors. The other challenge was that now that we were comfortably away from the quirks of Gibraltar, we were experiencing tidal ranges over six feet and they would increase as we headed north.

With our seven-foot draft and the large tides, there were many harbors that were simply too shallow for us. In addition, rip tides can be very strong and would often exceed the speed of our boat. The bottom line of all this was that we had to choose our ports very carefully and enter only under ideal circumstances.

We carefully orchestrated a high tide arrival at the bar of the entrance of the Rio Guadiana, the river that separates Spain from Portugal. This was the trickiest entrance we had made so far, and I was cautious. The chart in my pilot said nine feet and the tidal range should have given us another six so I thought we should be OK. But to make sure, I cheated and followed a large fishing boat as he wove his way around the bar. Once in the river we opted for Ayamonte on the Spanish side and anchored next to a large Canadian ketch.

Alex and I rowed over to shore to explore and buy groceries. On our way back we were amazed by the strength of the current and could hardly make way against it. We decided to stop by the Canadian boat and see what we could find out from them about our surroundings. Tim immediately invited us on board and introduced us to his crew. They were simply taking the boat out of Portuguese waters for a day for the owner in order to comply with certain Portuguese regulations and were happy to give us a tour.

Tim explained the bizarre story behind the 52-foot ketch. It was a Robertson design and had a center cockpit. The owner was a cabinet maker and had built the boat himself. Once the hull and basic rigging had been completed, he had launched. His plan was to finish the details as he sailed his dream craft around the world. His first voyage was from Canada to the Azores. It was also his last. Sea sick, scared, and discouraged he had abandoned his dream. He had had the boat sailed on to Portugal and there it waited under Tim's care until a buyer could be found.

Alex and I laughed as we saw the huge four-poster bed in the gigantic aft cabin—but my laugh was a little hollow. For many years before our trip, I had dreamed of constructing a yacht that we would one day sail around the world. I had devoured the Roberts catalogues in my landlocked workshop in Chestnut Hill and mentally built each of the beautiful boats in his catalogue of plans. Had I pursued this dream, I probably would have chosen a boat similar to this ketch and would have felt I was still making a compromise by not building larger.

After Tim's story, I found myself wondering why I had wanted to see the boat so much. But I knew the answer. And I suspect it is the same with all boat lovers. I was subconsciously deciding on what my next boat would be like. When I would buy another and where I would sail it were other questions—but that I would buy another was certain. After living on our 48-foot boat for a year I had come to realize that even it was too big. Looking again at the mammoth after cabin confirmed the soundness of the 40-foot maximum Charlotte and I had set for our future craft.

Tim gave us a lot of helpful information on Portugal and told us about the beauty of the southern coast that we were about to traverse. It's called the Algarve and, according to Tim, is one of the most beautiful stretches of coastline in the world. Tim highly recommended Vilamoura and told us to look him up on his boat, *Just Passing Through*. We decided to make it our next stop.

On our way to Vilamoura, we kept looking at the pretty pictures of Faro and Cabo de Santa Maria, and it reminded us of Bulls Bay in South Carolina. We were concerned about the currents and tricky entrance and convinced ourselves that we should pass it by. Two miles from the bar, however, we saw a medium-size ship coming out, so we decided to give it a try. The current swept by the buoys that marked the channel with so much force that they lay almost flat. Just to the right of the channel was a long jetty, and I knew that a loss of power would have us up against it in minutes. But we were going against the current and this gave me considerably more control as I worked my way up the channel. Once in, we turned to the left and began the long approach to Faro.

But as I examined the charts in our pilot, I didn't like what I saw. I also knew that there was a reason that the pilot had stamped prominent in places throughout: "charts not to be used for navigational purposes." It wasn't just for liability. The channels were constantly shifting and what might have been accurate when the pilot had been published may be totally unreliable as little as a year later.

As we passed a particularly attractive sandbar I decided to forgo a visit to Faro and instead opted for the isolated beauty of the little sandbar island. It took a long time to get situated in a spot where our anchors would hold us off the sandbar and at the same time keep us safely out of the channel. But we finally succeeded and were rewarded by a magnificent view of salt marshes and the Atlantic. It was one of the prettiest spots we saw in Portugal and we spent the remainder of the day wandering around our island and clamming.

The next day we arrived in Vilamoura and were back in civilization. It was also our first official entry into Portugal and the first place we were able to obtain Portuguese money. The marina there was by far the nicest and most expensive we had seen on our trip. In less than an hour we were able to check into both the country and the marina. I was delighted to see that they used floating docks as the tidal range was now up to nine feet, and mooring to a stationary dock would have posed a full-time job in adjusting lines. Just as we finished mooring at our assigned berth, we looked up to see the carpenter's ketch coming into the harbor.

We went over to the neighboring pontoon and helped them with their lines. Tim and his very haggard crew then told us their story. They had run out of fuel shortly after leaving Ayamonte and had been forced to negotiate the bar under sail. The boat handled so poorly that it had taken them almost two days to get back to Vilamoura. They greeted us like long lost friends and we agreed to meet them at their favorite watering hole, Hellie's, after dinner.

Hellie's was booming when we got there. Tim, Phil, and Mario were feeling no pain and had apparently forgotten all about their recent trials and tribulations. Phil bought a round of beer for all of us and Margot had downed almost half her glass before I realized she had been included in the circle. Over the noise and confusion I was having a hard time understanding what Tim was trying to tell us. But after getting him to repeat it a third time, I realized that I hadn't been hearing him incorrectly after all. Druids. He was telling us all about Druids. He had apparently converted Phil and Mario and was now working on us. I could tell Charlotte was only listening with half an ear, but when she heard Druid repeated for the third time, she went into a long spiel about how much she had enjoyed reading *Sarum*, but wasn't it awful with all those human sacrifices.

I asked Tim if they still followed the practice, but he ignored my jibe and continued with his sermon. It was a back-to-nature movement and he was extolling its advantages over formalized religions such as Christianity. I had been trying to find a way to change the subject when Heyward rescued me. He and Phil were in a deep discussion about the relative merits of the bagpipe and the guitar when they pulled Tim into their conversation.

"You have never heard a bagpipe until you have heard Phil" Tim slurred. He then urged Phil to return to *Just Passing Through* to fetch his pipes. The noise in Hellie's didn't hold a candle to Phil and his regal entrance. The

Phil's Bagpipes

loud wailing of pipes followed him up the stairs, and he stole the show. Tune after tune with Tim and Mario leading dances continued until after 3:00 A.M. Finally the neighbors complained and we were all very politely asked to leave—por favor.

***

Vilamoura was a resting point, a time to take stock of our situation again. Since we had finally made our decision to head north, life had become a great deal more relaxed. True we had chosen the more difficult course, but we had not yet reached the difficult parts, and the decision was no longer a worry. It was great to have a definite destination, even if it wasn't the one everybody had wanted. And July 25 had become a date we could plan around. Charlotte and the children had already contacted friends in Chestnut Hill to arrange their visit. The end was becoming real.

But having time to stop and think brought up a topic that had largely been swept under the rug during our decision making process. Biscay. Everyone we met who had sailed their yachts down from Northern Europe had their own story, and they were all hair raising. Trips were always planned around crossing the Bay of Biscay at the proper time of year, but even then the might of that giant body of water gave each traveler his own special demonstration of what could happen.

Although the French can visualize their country as a straight-sided hexagon with one side bordering the Atlantic, other people cannot. In fact, from the northwestern tip of Brittany to the southern boundary with Spain, there is a substantial bow inland. Drawing the line from Brittany to the tip of

271

the Iberian Peninsula that juts far out into the Atlantic accentuates this bow. It's the body of water contained in this giant bow that makes up the dreaded Bay of Biscay. Biscay is the end of the road for waves that have their origins on the other side of the ocean, and when storms come out of the west they deposit their full fury on the exposed French coast. It is a body of water to be respected.

The *Amoco Cadiz* wasn't the first nor was it the last to learn what happens when there is no more sea to leeward and the rocky coast of France is all that is left. While each story I heard was different, and each mariner's advice had its own unique message, there was one common thread. Give the French coast a wide berth. A hard blow from the west can last for days, and safety lies in being far from land.

Charlotte had listened to all of the stories we had heard about Biscay with rapt interest. Bianne's had struck a particular chord with her. *Et Au Alt* had made it over half way across and they were beginning to ease their guard. August had been the right choice and they had not encountered any winds over force 6. They were about to put behind them the major hurdle between Denmark and their Mediterranean destination. Bianne had said that these were the thoughts that were flowing through his mind as he stood his early morning watch. He wasn't sure what made him look behind just when he did, but it had made all the difference. Like a mountain appearing off their stern was the bow of a huge tanker. *Et Au Alt* was about to become kindling and her crew fish bait. More by reflex than by reason, Bianne violently pushed the tiller away from himself. The tiny craft responded immediately and Bianne sat there shaking as he watched the high sides of the tanker speed by with only a few meters separating steel from fiberglass.

Charlotte was not keen about sailing across Biscay, but up until Vilamoura she hadn't had a chance to get her worries together and it was a subject we hadn't yet discussed. The topic came up obliquely. Even before our late night at Hellie's we had decided to take a day off for rest at Vilamoura. While the children slept late, Charlotte and I walked among the fishing boats. As we passed poster after poster with pictures of gigantic sharks hanging by their tails and their proud captors standing by, we met Pattie Leary.

A young man with blond hair and a weathered face, Pattie was sitting on a stool in front of one of the shark photographs splicing a line. When we explained that we were on our way to Holland, Pattie looked up from what he was doing and gave us his full attention. "Don't fool around with Cape Finisterre" he stated with a trance-like stare focused on Charlotte. "I almost lost my life there. It's where the Devil lives. Have you looked at your Admiralty Chart and found Finisterre light? Do you know the number?"

He then glared at us in silence. But before we could even think of giving a response to his bizarre question he proclaimed in a sinister voice: "Its number 6666. Yes, 6666! And that's the sign of the Devil."

While we were digesting this bit of information he gave the end of his line to Charlotte to hold, whipped out a huge knife, and quickly hacked off the loose ends of his splice. In the process he almost hacked his thumb off also. Charlotte watched, horrified, as the blood ran down his arm. He licked the blood off with a silly grin as if it were nothing and continued his monologue. "If I were you, I would go well out to sea before rounding Finisterre. It's the home of the Devil. Stay away and then go straight on to France or England. Don't go near Cape Finisterre!"

Charlotte was having a difficult time deciding whether to concentrate her concerns on his injury or on his warning. She offered to return to the boat to get him a bandage, but he shrugged off her offer for help as he wiped his bloody hand all over his shirt and his ragged jeans. Pattie cut quite a figure as we left him standing there. Blood was on his hands, shirt, trousers, and all around his mouth. He had a silly grin on his face that seemed to emphasize his warning: Don't go near to Cape Finisterre.

When I started quoting to Charlotte: "Water water everywhere and all the boards did shrink..." she didn't think it was very funny. The first thing she did when we were back on the boat was look up Cape Finisterre on our charts. It did look formidable—right at the northwest corner of the Iberian Peninsula We had learned enough about the geometry of capes to realize that this would be a tough one.

Worries about Finisterre brought up worries about Biscay and that afternoon we had a long discussion about the remainder of our trip. I explained that Willem had agreed to bring all the necessary charts and that he had crossed Biscay many times. While this made me feel better, it didn't completely ease my concerns. I didn't need to learn again about the importance of self-sufficiency and I wasn't about to put all my eggs in the Willem basket. The charts I had bought in Gibraltar would get me safely as far as Brittany, and I had already done a fair amount of research on the trip. But my initial idea of stopping in Brest was undergoing a radical change as I studied my charts and pilots in detail.

There were two big problems with stopping in Brest. First, it would mean hugging the French coast of Biscay for at least a portion of the trip, and everyone I had talked to had advised against this. Second, once we left Brest we would face one of two bad alternatives. One would be to sail between Isle d'Ouessant and the coast in what looked to me like one of the most treacherous channels in the world. With tidal ranges that could exceed 20 feet and currents that in some cases could exceed the speed of our boat, there was no way I was going to try this without local knowledge. The other alternative was to sail back to the west and round Isle d'Ouessant to seaward. This would involve retracing a great deal of ground.

I had concluded that the only option was to bypass the west coast of France entirely and make land-fall in England. As this plan did not please Charlotte in the least, I decided not to confide with her about my principal worry. My charts ended at Isle d'Ouessant. If we were to continue to the southern coast of England, it would have to be done relying entirely on my pilot with its greatly abbreviated charts for the final stretch. Hoping that the arrival of William would eliminate this last wrinkle or that I might be able to purchase the last chart in Lisbon, I tried to put the worry out of my mind. At any rate, for Charlotte Cape Finisterre had replaced Biscay as the principal concern. From that point on, the first question she would ask anyone we met who looked even remotely nautical was what they thought of Cape Finisterre.

That night we made preparations to leave Vilamoura and I opted to move the boat to the fuel dock so that I could complete my check out with customs that night and get an early start in the morning. There was a strong breeze blowing across the pontoon to which we were moored, but I ignored the warnings from Charlotte and the children. "If you guys had it your way we would never leave port" I chided and put the boat in reverse. As I saw our bow crash into the stern of our neighbor and heard the crunch, I realized I should have heeded the sound advice from my crew.

Fortunately the damage was limited to our boat and was relatively minor. It was, however, minor damage to a major item. Our starboard running light had been mangled and we no longer had the ability to safely sail at night. Instead of getting underway at daylight as I had planned, we sat and waited until the marina chandler opened so I could purchase a replacement running light.

During our wait we struck up a conversation with the English couple on the very beautiful and very old wooden yawl that had tied up outboard us the night before. The story of how they had purchased their ancient craft in a bone yard near Dover and then spent two years fixing it up was intriguing, but it was the account of their sail across Biscay from England that interested us most.

Their advice to us was consistent with what we had been told before. Give the coast of France a very wide berth. They also agreed with my assessment that Brest wasn't a good idea. They said that Southern England should be our destination after leaving the Iberian Peninsula, and that Portsmouth would be an excellent choice of places to stop. I took copious notes in my pilot and on my log as we poured over their well-worn charts of the English Channel.

By some incredible stroke of good luck, the chandler had a running light that I thought could be mounted and was reasonably similar to my other light. On our way out of the breakwater, I finished the installation and we were back in business.

Our destination was Sagres, a small open bay that is located on the eastern edge of the south western tip of the Iberian Peninsula. It's the southern-and western-most point of West Europe and was called O Fim do Mundo by the ancient Portuguese navigators. It's the spot that Prince Henry had chosen to locate his think tank where he had trained the series of famous Portuguese explorers who had opened up the Atlantic coast of Africa.

The End of the World was a pretty apt description for Sagres. It's the first point at which the full force of the Atlantic falls upon the Portuguese coast and we were awed by the barren harshness of the rocky cliffs that surround the bay. The wind picked up considerably as we approached the bay, but it was coming overland from the north and the sea was flat. Because of the funneling effect of the cliffs, the wind became stronger as we approached shore and the rigging was moaning with its force as we dropped our anchor about a hundred meters off shore. I paid out plenty of chain for good holding, and then, surveying the wide exposed openness of the bay to the south, prayed that the prevailing northerly would not change during the night.

I would not have felt comfortable leaving the boat alone with the strong wind, but the children volunteered to stay so Charlotte and I dinghied ashore to explore. A walk through the little town and then a long walk down a narrow road led us to the Sacred Promontory or "sleeping place of the Gods." This was where Prince Henry had built and we walked around the walls that enclosed the huge courtyard with its mosaic compass rose in the center.

Always eager for reconnaissance, we walked to the Atlantic side of the courtyard and looked at the huge waves below as they deposited their force on the rocky coastline. Through the mist we could also see Cape St. Vincent. Large and foreboding, it was the first hurdle we would have to clear on what we knew was going to be an arduous trip north. This was the point at which we could expect to feel the combined forces of both the Algarve and the Atlantic weather patterns. But for the moment we were lost in thoughts about the past. It had been interesting to read about the feats of such figures as Vasco Da Gamma and Dias in history courses, but it was not until I looked down from the ramparts of Prince Henry's old fort and saw the violence and loneliness of the sea below that I could begin to understand what kind of men they must have been.

During our visit to the fort we met Trench, his wife, and his two daughters. They were from South Africa and lived aboard *Stardust*, the little sloop that was anchored next to us. They told us that they were going to round Cape St. Vincent in the morning, so we agreed to keep in touch via VHF. They also informed us that we could pick up the BBC 4 Atlantic shipping forecast at 12:30 P.M. and that they planned to be guided by that in making their final decision whether or not to depart. After seeing the power of St. Vincent we were delighted to have someone to consult with concerning our next leg.

We had just gone back into a deep sleep after waking up to record the BBC 4 midnight weather forecast when we heard a loud voice: "*Captain Spiros, Captain Spiros!*" Charlotte shot out of bed like a rocket. Who was calling? What had happened? Could the anchor be slipping? In her mad rush to the cockpit she tripped over the two buckets of recycled dish water she had placed in front of the sink for morning dishes.

It was Trench shouting to us as *Stardust* circled our boat. "The weather forecast is great" he shouted above the wind. "We are leaving now. Do you want to join us?"

Charlotte and I had a quick conference. She let me know in no uncertain terms that she didn't consider a force 6 to be a perfect weather forecast and in addition there was no way she was going to try Cape St. Vincent in the dark. "We want to get a little more sleep before we leave" I shouted to the oilskin clad figures huddled in the stern of *Stardust*. "We will meet you in Sines tonight. Please come over for cocktails when we arrive."

"Delightful! We will monitor channel 6. Stay in touch" Trench shouted and then they were off.

Five-thirty came early, but the wind had abated a little so we pulled up the anchor and headed for the cape. The wind and the seas steadily increased as we neared Cape St. Vincent and I could tell it wasn't going to be an easy passage. Before any of us had a chance to really get worried about the wind, however, a worse problem presented itself. Fog. This was something we had not yet encountered, and it was terrifying. As the jagged silhouette of Cape St. Vincent receded into the mist, realization set in. We were blind.

A few moments after we were completely engulfed, Charlotte shouted: "What's that noise? It sounds like a siren." I rechecked the chart to make sure what I was telling her was correct, but she wouldn't be convinced that it was only an audio navigational aid on the Cape St. Vincent light house. She was so nervous that she could hardly get into her safety harness.

I stayed below at the navigation station glued to the radar screen, and Charlotte clutched the wheel. "Contact about two miles off the starboard bow, drawing nicely to the right" I shouted. "Yes, I hear his siren and he sounds close" Charlotte replied.

"No, the siren is Cape St. Vincent Light and it's about five miles off our starboard beam... Don't worry, this contact won't be a problem."

We went through the same drill several times, but after about an hour the fog lifted and we were around the cape. We were so relieved to have our vision back that we didn't even think about the force 6 wind and huge swells.

In spite of her nervousness, Charlotte had become a very good boat handler. Once we were in the middle of a difficult situation she would never panic. She had done an excellent job during the fog, and I thought again how important teamwork was in handling our craft. Below, staring at the radar, I had been the eyes, while she had remained riveted to the helm and provided the control.

While all of the commotion was taking place, Heyward had quietly gotten up, put on his foul weather gear, and helped by spelling Charlotte and relaying information back and forth. Later that day Charlotte and I had a long talk about how much Heyward had matured since we had left Philadelphia, and how important it was to us to see him perform so well under difficult circumstances.

Sines is a small fishing port about half way up the coast to Lisbon. In spite of weariness from the day's activities, we were glad to welcome Trench, Marylin, and their two daughters Laura and Susan, when their dinghy came alongside. Age and experience differences were put aside as we sat around our dining table late into the evening sharing stories. I enjoyed watching how animated Margot, Alex, and Heyward became as they told stories about our trip. It was moments like this that made all the trouble we had gone through seem worthwhile.

We all laughed as Trench told about his attempt the previous summer to sail directly to England from Sagres. Following the advice of his pilot and of other boats who had made the trip, he sailed straight west in order to get past the Portuguese northerlies. His plan was to continue west until the northerly wind clocked around to the west, then he could change course and proceed to England on a broad reach. After several days of hard sailing that took them 400 miles west of Portugal, they still had not picked up favorable winds. During breakfast on the fifth day they had decided to sail the 400 miles back to Portugal. They each had their own version of the discomforts of their aborted trip and now planned to try again, along the coast instead of out to sea.

After the glow of cocktails wore off, we decided that maybe their story wasn't so funny. After all, we were headed in the same direction, and turning back after 400 miles definitely wasn't part of our game plan.

As we departed for Cascais the following morning, we noted that the trips were becoming progressively more difficult. We were now bucking the Portuguese trade winds and were virtually guaranteed to have the wind on our nose as we worked our way north. The best we could hope for was relatively light wind and moderate seas. That day we were lucky and made good time against a light breeze. As we passed the very formidable looking Cabo Espichel, just south of the approach to Lisbon, I was glad we had been so fortunate with the weather.

Cascais is right at the mouth of Rio Tejo which continues on to Lisbon. It is a lovely community that has a well-protected harbor surrounded by a sandy beach. We agreed with the advice in our pilot and decided to use it as a base for the break we had decided to take to visit Lisbon. Apparently a lot of other people had the same idea, and the bay was full of boats at anchor. We chose a place not far from the beach and spent a quiet night aboard resting for our outing.

Before boarding the train for Lisbon, we found a large bookstore and obtained a copy of *Frommer's Portugal On 5 Dollars A Day*. During the short ride I turned to the section on Cascais and read: "A small resort town outside of Lisbon. Besides being a great place to shop, it is the jumping off place to make the short bus ride to Boca do Inferno where you can watch giant waves pound down on the rocky coastline." I quickly flipped the page hoping that Charlotte had not been reading over my shoulder and turned to the restaurant section for Lisbon.

We had a wonderful day in Lisbon. First, a memorable lunch featuring that special combination of sea food and pork that makes Algarve cooking so delicious, and then a search for nautical charts. After getting lost twice, I finally found the chandler that handled admiralty charts. The good news was that they had a current version of the nautical almanac so I wouldn't have to make the adjustment from my 1989 version when using our sextant. The bad news was that they were missing the chart I needed to navigate across the channel to make the southern coast of England. We still had the blind spot.

Charlotte and I were up at six o'clock the following morning. The BBC 4 midnight forecast had been a "go" and the wind had abated a great deal. Force 5 to 6 from the northwest wasn't ideal, but it was acceptable.

Charlotte took the wheel, I raised the anchor, and we let the children get more sleep.

"How far to the cape?" Charlotte inquired.

"There are two capes" I replied. "Cabo Raso and Cabo de Roca. The first one is about three miles away."

"Which one is Boca do Inferno" she asked, trying to keep the concern out of her voice. Apparently she had read the section in Frommer after all.

"Cabo Raso, is the first one" I replied. "I can see it through the binoculars, and it doesn't look too bad." But Charlotte could see the wall of whitecaps we were approaching even without the benefit of binoculars and was not convinced.

"I don't want to go around the Mouth of Hell in the middle of a gale" she opined as the whitecaps drew closer.

"First of all it's not a gale. It's probably blowing a force 5 at the most. And besides, we should be out of it right after we round the cape." I had tried to keep my voice as matter of fact as possible and took out our anemometer to give her more assurance.

At about that time the wall of waves and a heavy wind hit us simultaneously. Charlotte was about to go into overdrive. My readings on the anemometer didn't help the situation. Even fudging the numbers, I was forced to admit to a steady force 6 with gusts up to force 7. "It's an interesting coastline" I stated trying to switch the subject. "I bet we will really like Peniche."

"I want to turn back NOW. I thought we agreed to never sail in a gale!"

I knew it was useless to argue that because the wind wasn't force 8 or higher it wasn't a gale so I tried another tact. "This is always a difficult cape and we have to round it to get to Peniche to meet Willem. It's better to go now while we have a decent forecast. If we wait we risk being obligated to sail in much worse weather. We both know the boat can easily handle it. If we can stick it out just a little while longer, we will be past the cape."

"Heyward, if you don't turn this boat around now, I promise I will never sail with you again."

By this time, all the noise on deck had woken the children, and they were watching the scene unfold as they peered out of the cabin. "Dad, I think she means it" Margot stated. Looking first at Charlotte and then at me Alex chimed in: "Yea, Dad. She really doesn't want to go." Then they all stared at me waiting for a decision.

This was serious. Charlotte had not merely threatened to divorce me or to push me overboard. She had threatened to never sail with me again!

Reluctantly I acquiesced and Charlotte turned the boat back towards Cascais. With the wind on our stern we flew over what then seemed like calm water. The tension eased and everybody's spirits lifted as we sped back to port.

I looked longingly as I saw a sailboat rounding the cape and heading towards us, but Charlotte started shaking her head and exclaimed before I could say anything: "Don't even think about it! We are going back. NOW!"

Back in Cascais I succeeded in putting a call through to Menno in Holland and told him that we would not make our July 12 deadline in Peniche. I explained that we were in Cascais and would set out as soon as the weather permitted. Menno told me he had just talked to Willem and reported that he was already in Peniche. The plan was that Willem would check the harbor for our boat each day. Menno expected another call from Willem shortly and would pass on to him that we were on our way.

In spite of Menno's assurance, I was getting nervous about missing Willem, and the July 25 flight date for Charlotte and the children was rapidly approaching. Charlotte did her best to placate me and even fixed a curry dinner with all the condiments for us that night. We agreed to get a good rest and set out on the third reef in the morning, even if it was blowing a force 6.

At 12:30 A.M. we woke up to my alarm radio blaring out the end of "Sailing By" on BBC 4. It always struck us as an odd contrast when the soothing music ended and the forecast began. It started with the Irish Sea and then worked its way south. A soft voice proclaimed the weather conditions in a matter of fact fashion that completely belied the content of the message. As we lay in our bed listening, we could picture what it must have been like in the cold wet surroundings of the areas the soft voice was describing. Inevitably the Irish Sea and most of the North Sea was being bashed by fierce gales. As the forecast moved south, it became better, but force 7 and 8 seemed like the norm for Biscay and Finisterre. When the voice neared our region, we strained our attention and turned on the recorder. "North, North-West force 7" We both cursed and went back to sleep.

In the morning we woke up to very light wind, but there was the matter of the lousy forecast. I wasn't going to suggest setting out in a force 7, but Charlotte, being a very good sport, suggested we go ashore to see what the Portuguese Port Police said about the weather. Their guess, or at least our best guess at a translation of their best guess, was for a force 4 to 5. This was all the assurance we needed so we dinghied back to *Captain Spiros* and set out for Peniche for the second time.

This time we were well rested and had a third reef in the main. Charlotte was very calm and I was quite proud of her as she steered us towards the wall of white caps again. Margot summed it up nicely: "Mom, you need to figure out what you are worried about. Sure, we will all be uncomfortable, but as long as we are careful there is no danger."

I began to measure the wind again but when it started gusting up to force 8, I put the anemometer away in order to keep from hurting morale. Both the *Captain Spiros* and her crew performed admirably. After a vigorous trip around the cape, the wind calmed down, and the trip to Peniche went smoothly. When we entered the harbor I scanned the shoreline for two able body seamen, but nothing I saw suggested a Dutch delivery skipper and his mate. We were anchored near the shore with our large American flag waving when the self-proclaimed social director of the port motored up in his small dinghy.

As I took the line Travis handed to me he boomed out: "I say old bean, is there anything I can do to help you get familiar with Peniche?"

"Yes, we would love some information. Won't you come aboard for a drink?"

"A marvelous invitation, old bean. Don't mind if I do". Two hours and several beers later Travis zoomed off to visit an English boat that had just arrived and was circling around looking for a good spot to anchor, but not before he had given us the complete infrastructure of Peniche, and filled us in on the gossip concerning most of the dozen or so yachts in the harbor. Travis' boat, *Rhiannon* had been in Peniche almost two weeks and this made him the resident expert. No, he had not seen two Dutchmen hanging about, but he would keep his eyes out for us.

The afternoon turned into evening, and still no Willem. It was July 12, we had pushed very hard to get to Peniche, and I was very concerned that he had not yet appeared. Sensing my frustration, the children started their ribbing. It began with Heyward's "Hey dad, did Menno really tell you Willam was here?" Then from Alex "Menno—sounds like M E N N O...L I S". After this there was a good laugh at my expense as we all conjured up images of our shifty friend and of all his maneuvering to sell us *Captain Spiros*. Heyward then added: "Hey Dad, did Menno promise to take you out fishing?" I managed to silence this round of laughter by pointing out that If Willem didn't show we would cross the Bay of Biscay by ourselves flight or no flight.

By 10:00 the next morning there still were no signs of Willem, so I decided to go into town to see what we could do for entertainment while we waited. On my way in Travis hailed me over to his boat. *Rhiannon* shared a mooring with another British boat, and before I could even get my line over Bill and Eddy of *Beatnick* handed down a giant jelly jar glass full of Portuguese red wine and insisted I come on board for a pop. I'm not sure what time happy hour started at the British mooring, but it was certainly well in progress by 10:30 A.M. They suggested a restaurant in town, and I invited the whole group over to our boat for cocktails that night.

We explored the little town and had an excellent lunch at Travis' recommendation, the Maritmo restaurant. I had pork and clams Algarve—a delicious dish that is somewhere between roast pork and Manhattan clam chowder, and made a mental note to myself to try to fix it with Wadmalaw clams when I got back to Charleston. After lunch I went to the post office to phone Menno in Holland again. He assured me that Willem was there and had probably just missed me the previous night. "Don't worry, he will show up!" I brought this reassuring news back to the boat, but somehow didn't feel very reassured as I scanned the shoreline searching for our crew.

Travis, his wife Frieda, Bill, and Eddy dinghied over to *Captain Spiros* punctually for cocktails, and we had a great time. Travis was a Scot who had served during World War II with the Highland Regiment. He kept us all in hysterics as he described dining in with the regiment and explained an elaborate system of marching over mirrors to ensure that none of the troops wore anything under their kilts. Alex wanted more specific information on whether or not certain parts of the anatomy become cold during winter marches over the Scottish moors, and the conversation went downhill from there.

Bill and Eddy were professional delivery skippers taking a busman's holiday in sailing Bill's boat back to England. They all assured me that Willem should have no trouble finding our boat, and, besides, the weather wasn't good for setting out so I should relax.

The next day came and still no Willem. I began to panic. It was then July 15 and I needed to get the troops to London by the 25th. I began to consider modifying our route to head for Brest instead of Portsmouth. This would give them more time to get to London in time for their flight. But for them to leave, I needed to have Willem—otherwise there was no way I could get the boat to Holland. I made another call to Holland, but they hadn't heard from Willem since his call to Menno just before I had left Cascais.

I dinghied over to the British mooring and, after the mandatory jelly jar full of wine, conferred with Bill, Eddy, and Travis. Travis had received a weather fax and the wind was supposed to drop that night. Bill and Eddy planned to leave around midnight or as soon as the wind had died down. Travis theorized that Willem really hadn't made it to Peniche yet and was probably hitch hiking from Spain.

Charlotte and I conferred and decided that we should leave with Bill and Eddy and take advantage of the weather to get past the difficult stretch of Portugal and Spain we had remaining. We both wanted calm weather for passing this rugged coastline and the whole thing with Willem was beginning to smell very fishy. Menno had said Willem was in Peniche, but he obviously wasn't. We were beginning to wonder if he were going to show up at all. I called Menno that night. Having no further word from Willem, he agreed we should take advantage of the weather and continue north. I told Menno I would call him from my next port, which I thought would probably be La Coruna. We would then try to hook up with Willem at that time.

I checked with the Brits again that night. Travis had scouted around the harbor checking with other boats and had confirmed his earlier forecast for good weather. Eddy had modified his plan for an early morning departure because he thought Bill was too drunk and needed some sleep before getting underway. I looked over at Bill and agreed with Eddie's assessment. A jelly jar later I was back on board *Captain Spiros* for an early evening.

I dreamed about Willem not showing up at La Coruna while Charlotte had visions of Pattie and Cape Finisterre dancing through her head. Our deep sleep was briefly interrupted by the end of "Sailing By" and BBC 4's confirmation of Travis' good weather report—"Finisterre: variable, force 3 or 4." We woke up refreshed and ready to strike out on our three day sail to La Coruna. As we motored out of the harbor I made one last scan of the quays for Willem. There were no likely candidates, so at 6:30 we departed.

The trip north was rather pleasant—at least for the first two days. We made good progress motor sailing, and, after our force 8 experience around Cabo Roca, fears about the strong winds seemed to have disappeared. By noon on the second day, we thought we had broken the back of the trip. Charlotte fixed an excellent lunch and we were all relaxed.

Midnight and our encounter with Cape Finisterre changed everything. My plan was to go halfway between the cape and the busy shipping lanes as we rounded the northwestern tip of the Iberian Peninsula. I thought that late at night was a good time for the passage because normally the wind dies down in the evenings. Charlotte had been reluctant to make the passage in the dark, but there had been no practical alternative, so we had plowed on. As we neared Finisterre my plan seemed to be working. The wind was very light, and there was practically no swell. There was a moderate amount of shipping, but we were not having any trouble reading the lights and staying clear. It would have been an easy passage except for one small detail. Fog.

At 1:00 A.M. Charlotte and Margot came off watch and I went on. I was just getting settled and Charlotte was about to go to bed when we saw it come rolling in. Suddenly fog as thick as pea soup surrounded, us and we could barely see our own running lights on the bow. Charlotte stayed on the wheel and took the boat off of auto pilot while I stayed glued to the radar.

We were all familiar with the relative bearing drill. As long as the relative bearing to other vessels is changing everything is OK. If it isn't changing, you change it by changing the course of your own vessel. Our normal practice was to monitor the relative motion of other vessels by lining them up with some spot on our vessel and watching to see if the spot changed. But in the thick fog we could barely see the lights on our own boat much less those of other boats.

The small radar screen at my navigation station was our only eye. Other vessels showed up as small blips and we were always at the center of the screen. The drill was to watch the blips and keep track of what they were doing. If the relative bearing wasn't changing, the blip would move across the screen towards the center. That's when we needed to do something to make the bearing start to change. This something was generally a radical turn in a direction that I hoped, but couldn't be sure, would take us away from the approaching vessel.

For the next four hours I stayed glued to the radar set while Charlotte steered.

"Contact three miles away—40 degrees off the starboard bow— drifting nicely to the right, won't be a problem" I shouted so Charlotte could hear me from her position at the wheel and then went on to examine the other three or four blips on my radar screen.

"Is he big? What's he going to do next? Why did we get right in the shipping lanes?"

I ignored the questions that Charlotte knew I couldn't answer and went on with my reports. "Another contact two miles off our Port beam— drifting left—he's already passed us. Here's one that will come a little close— now 10 degrees off the starboard bow and drifting slowly to the right—now a little less than two miles away—he should pass about one half to one mile off our starboard—see if you can see him as he goes by."

Charlotte gave me the answer I expected, "No, I can't see anything." We had just proved empirically that our visibility was less than a mile.

As long as we could pick up the contacts on radar, and as long as their bearing drifted, we were okay But there were a couple of problems. We couldn't pick up some small fishing boats on our radar, and some contacts didn't drift.

"Contact 10 degrees off the starboard bow—about three miles away—I'm not getting any drift yet." I shouted as I waited to see if I could detect any bearing movement at all to determine which would be the easiest side to pass him. His range decreased to two and a half miles and still nothing. We were going to have to take action to avoid him. "Come 30 degrees to your left."

Charlotte complied, but still no bearing drift. He must have had a slight left bearing drift that I had failed to detect before our turn, and I had chosen wrong. The range was now slightly less than two miles.

"Change course 60 degrees to your right—quickly please!" This would put us back 30 degrees to the right of our original course and, hopefully, result in bearing drift to our left. "It looks like we are getting a little drift to the left, but I'm not sure yet. He's about a mile away." We waited. "Yes, he's definitely drifting to the left, but not by much. He's going to come close. By now he is less than a mile away."

As the contact disappeared into the "noise" at the center of the radar screen I had a sinking feeling that maybe I had miscalculated his drift. "He should pass down our port side in just a few moments. Look hard for him—he should be close."

My warning was unnecessary. Charlotte already had the fog horn in one hand and a flashlight in the other that she was shining on our sails. "Honk, honk" and then we heard a reply. It sounded like it was coming from our port side. Good, I had guessed correctly. We then saw the lights towering above us and watched as a huge ship appeared out of the fog about 200 yards off our port beam.

We continued in this manner and it seemed like the night would never end. During all of the commotion Alex woke up and quietly put on his foul weather gear. He was a big help and relayed information between Charlotte and me. When I couldn't provide answers for some of Charlotte's more elaborate questions, he improvised and gave answers on his own.

At about 2:00 A.M. Charlotte inquired: "Have we passed the Cape yet?"

"Actually there are three capes. We have already passed Finisterre and are now just off the second, Cabo Torinana. We will be past the third cape in about an hour or so" I replied, purposefully not mentioning that the name of the third was Cabo Villano.

By 4:00 A.M. we had passed Cabo Villano. This put us along the north coast of Spain and the worst part of the fog was over. Heyward and Margot had also gotten up and they spelled Charlotte so she could get some sleep.

For the remainder of the trip to La Coruna we had intermittent fog, and when we approached the harbor, the visibility was very poor. The charts of the entrance in my pilot were confusing, so I waited until I saw a small ship entering, and, hoping he knew what he was doing, followed him in. At 4:00 in the afternoon, bone tired, and utterly drained from our long night, we dropped our anchor in La Coruna harbor just off the yacht club.

It had been a very difficult evening and day and I was really proud of Charlotte and the children. No one had complained and they had all worked very hard to get us past the fog safely. As with most of our tense situations at sea, the greatest danger had been that someone would panic and do the wrong thing. The cumulative experience all of us had gained, however, made this quite unlikely and we all knew we could rely on each other.

In spite of her apparent nervousness, Charlotte had become quite a seaman. It was interesting to watch her reaction to danger. When we were in situations that demanded cool judgment, she would calm down and focus all of her attention on the problem. It was only when things were really OK that she would rattle off her concerns and seem to be near panic. Her nervous factor was at its worse when we were deciding whether or not to go. Once past that hurdle, she did great. That night her performance had been superb.

After going below to get cleaned up in preparation for going ashore, I was greeted by a stony silence from the crew. They were waiting for me on deck and Charlotte was the spokesman. "We aren't going across the Bay

Discussing Our Trip Around Finisterre

of Biscay! I really didn't like last night! Why did we have to pass the cape at night and why did you take us in the middle of the shipping lanes?" At this point the conversation began to get teary.

In a calm voice I tried: "We were never in the shipping lanes—all we were seeing was coastal shipping close to shore and…" Tears gave way to anger as she cut me off: "I never want to go in a sailboat again—I won't even go with you to the fuel dock to take on fuel!"

Detecting that she might be a little upset, I suggested that she come ashore to the yacht club with me while I called Menno. As we pulled away in the dinghy the children called: "Don't let him change your mind Mom—we don't want to go across Biscay"

The yacht club at La Coruna was very nice. On the third floor there was a huge bar overlooking the harbor and, much to my surprise, a telephone

286

capable of making international calls. While I was waiting for my turn on the phone we met Reg Brown of the Guernsey yacht *Whitefly* and his two crewmen Neil and Andy.

Finally my turn with the phone came, and I was able to reach Menno. Willem had shown up in Peniche two hours after we had left and had just missed us. He was calling in every two hours to find out where to meet us next. This was great news, and I told Menno to get in touch with him and tell him to meet us in La Coruna right away. Menno agreed to do this and estimated that Willem would be in La Coruna late that evening or early the following morning.

Meanwhile Charlotte was deeply engrossed in a conversation with Reg and his crew, and they had just bought us a round. They were planning on leaving the next day to cross the Bay of Biscay on their way back home to Guernsey. They could receive weather faxes on board and the outlook for Biscay was excellent. Although we were really tired, Charlotte invited the Guernsey group for cocktails at 6:00, and we were in high spirits as we dinghied back to the boat. Somehow the children weren't surprised or disappointed when Charlotte announced to them that Willem was on the way and that we were heading for Brest in the morning.

The next morning I dinghied in again—but still no Willem so I Called Menno again. "Don't worry, Heyward, I Talked with Willem last night. There is a train strike in Portugal and he will drive his car. It's only 600 km so he should be there by mid afternoon." I made some quick calculations—we could still make it. The crossing to Brest would take three days and the troops could take a ferry from neighboring Roscoff to England. There was still time—but barely.

Back on *Captain Spiros* my announcement of my conversation with Menno and of Willem's latest delay were greeted with skepticism. Alex quibbled: "Are you sure Menno has really talked with Willem?" Heyward joined in: "Why don't you ask Mennolis to come with us instead—then he could show us his fishing tricks."

I ignored their jibes and put them to work to take advantage of the time we had until Willem's arrival in the afternoon. I put Heyward on the laundry detail. Margot came with me for last minute provisioning, while Charlotte and Alex stayed on board to begin packing to be ready for a quick departure at Brest.

Four, five, six, and then seven o'clock and still no Willem. Plans for Brest began to fade—we were running out of time. We went to bed late that night—but still no Willem. Brest was out.

In the morning we were sitting in the cockpit finishing our breakfast and trying to decide what to do next when we saw the row boat with two men weaving its way towards us. "It must be them" I exclaimed optimistically. The children looked at me like I was crazy, but the boat continued to approach. In a soft voice I called: "Willem?" There was no reply. But the boat kept getting nearer. This time more confidently and louder I shouted: "Is that you Willem?"

A small affirmative nod from the blond head in the stern and a few minutes later they came on board. They were both dead tired from an odyssey that still has me confused. There had been a general strike in Portugal and not only could Willem not get a train, he could hardly drive his car. Protesting farmers had cut down trees and blocked all the major highways. Willem had only been able to make it by driving east to Spain and then north and he had been on the road over 24 hours. He and his companion, Dick, were exhausted and obviously needed rest before setting out.

We talked over our time schedule and decided that the best thing to do was to get Charlotte and the children transportation to London from Portugal and then Willem, Dick, and I could set out the following day for Holland. I was successful in obtaining tickets on a charter flight that departed the next day from Santiago, which was only 60 kilometers away.

The Maria

That night we had our last dinner on board together and were treated to a spectacular sight in La Coruna Harbor. Exact replicas of the *Nina*, the *Pinta*, and the *Santa Maria* sailed past our anchorage to enter the harbor to a 21 gun salute. They were en-route to the beginning of the voyage that would commemorate the 500th anniversary of Columbus' discovery of America. Later that evening the sky exploded with fireworks. We had had no idea it was coming, but what a way to celebrate the end of our one year adventure on the *Captain Spiros*!

The next morning Willem drove us all to the airport. He sped down the highway in his old Chevrolet at almost 90 miles an hour, narrowly missed hitting a bus, and managed to get lost three times before we got to the airport. "I hope he drives boats better than cars" was Charlotte's parting comment to me as I waved goodbye to them at the airport.

She and the children were going to London where they would have a three-day adventure before taking their flight to New York. They would then have the promised visit to Philadelphia before returning to Charleston. I would meet them back in Charleston. As I watched the plane take off, I could hardly believe they were gone. After all we had gone through together it would be hard to adjust to being on *Captain Spiros* without them.

My Crew Heads Home

On the way back to La Coruna Willem explained to me: "I missed that bus by two inches. But that's all it takes. And that's all it takes with boats too." The trip to Holland was going to be interesting.

Chapter 12
The Final Stretch

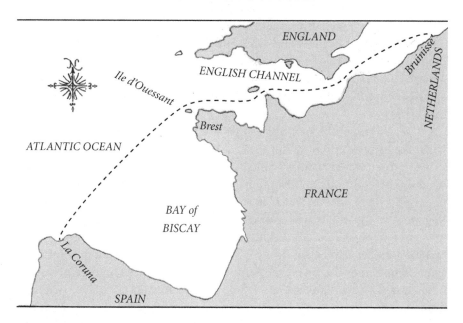

Willem doesn't like to depart in a hurry. He believes it causes accidents. When we arrived back at La Coruna Yacht Club from taking Charlotte and the children to the airport, I was anxious to leave and begin the trip. After all, I had been waiting for almost a week to start. But to accommodate Willem I suggested a beer at the Yacht Club before returning to the boat. Willem accepted with pleasure and half way through was gracious enough to order a refill for both of us. This continued until I succeeded in breaking the chain by putting down all my Spanish money on the bar and informing Willem and the bartender that after that I was out of pesetas.

Back on board *Captain Spiros* Dick had been contemplating replacing our Genoa with the smaller Yankee as he had promised to do before we left. But he had decided to wait for our return before undertaking any serious work. The three of us then changed the sail, deflated and stored the dinghy, and tied everything down very securely.

By this time it was getting late in the afternoon and Willem suggested dinner before getting underway. I thought this was taking the "not being in a hurry" concept a little too far and volunteered to fix dinner if we could get underway right away. When I brought three cold beers on deck to celebrate our departure, this clenched the deal, and at about 6:00 P.M. on Sunday, July 21, I pulled up the anchor of the *Captain Spiros* for the last time.

After finishing a third helping of the Nazi Goering I had prepared, Willem helped himself to a generous glass of red wine and explained to Dick and me how he normally worked shipboard routine. Basically he would be on watch the whole time, and Dick and I would rotate four hours on and four hours off. No two of us should ever talk about the third when he wasn't present. Normally Willem cooked, but my Nazi Goering was sufficiently palatable that I would share cooking duties with him, and Dick would do the dishes.

I had no problem in agreeing not to talk about either Willem or Dick when they weren't present, but I asked Willem why he didn't prefer to have a one in three watch rotation which would have given each of us four hours on and then eight off. Willem quickly explained that it would not be safe to have only one person on watch at a time and that it was much better his way. Reluctantly I agreed to wait and see how it worked out.

Two weeks before picking up Willem my Satnav had developed a serious gremlin. After turning it off, it was very coquettish about coming on again. Sometimes the on switch responded with Chinese hieroglyphics and other times with a blank screen. While my sextant was a reliable back up, I didn't want to count on this in the fog prone area of Biscay. My solution had been to tape the Satnav switch in the "on" position and warn my crew on pain of keel hauling to leave it there.

As part of my due diligence process with Willem I alerted him to the fact that our Satnav could die at any moment. Willem was not in the least concerned. "You von't believe my navigation system" he boasted. "Vone fix a day is all I need. And I have a very simple system with the sextant I vill show you later. Ve vill go north for vone hour out of La Coruna and then put the boat on a compass course of 030 degrees. This is the course that goes straight to Isle d'Ouessant. Currents vill set us to the vest for the first half of the trip and to the east for the second half, so ve don't have to vorry about them."

Willem was right—I didn't believe his navigation system. But it worked! We followed his plan and after turning on to 030 degrees we didn't change course for three days. I was amazed to see how close we came to Isle d'Ouessant.

Our first night, Sunday, was very calm and during my 8:00 P.M. to midnight and 4:00 A.M. to 8:00 A.M. watches I began to understand how Willem's watch system worked. I stayed in the cockpit watching for tankers while he slept soundly in the dining area. While his snores kept me company and I was confident that I could arouse him from his slumbers with a two by four if I should need help, somehow I felt I was standing the watch alone.

In the morning at 6:00 A.M. I managed to wake Willem from his comatose sleep. Thrusting a cup of hot coffee into his hands I explained to him that I would be more comfortable with our watches together if during daylight hours he watched for tankers while I pursued other interests. He quietly accepted his coffee and acquiesced.

The wind shifted to the east and blew a steady five to six. With our Yankee out we made six knots and had a very pleasant day. William's navigation plan kept us right in the middle of the shipping lanes, and we had ships in sight almost constantly.

Shortly after his arrival Willem had spotted our portable generator that had been submerged in salt water during our fiasco off Cape Knidos. It was still on board only because I had been too lazy to dig it out from under a pile in the bow compartment and throw it away. He announced that he was going to repair it.

While I skeptically watched, he proceeded to disassemble the unhappy piece of equipment, and the rolling deck quickly became a mass of screws, parts, and dirty rags. Dick acted as a workbench, vise, and consultant, and the show went on for about four hours. As hopelessly frozen parts emerged from the carburetor, I kept thinking the exercise was over and that Willem would give up—but Willem's ingenuity was limitless. A ball point pen and our air horn turned into a high pressure air cleaner, oil was sprayed everywhere, a scrap of sandpaper became a precision file and miraculously—"cough cough cough"—it was working!

On Tuesday the wind shifted to the west and picked up considerably. We were beginning to see a little of the strength of the Bay of Biscay that I had heard so much about from other yachtsmen. During the elegant lunch Willem had put together, a powerful gust hit us and we heeled heavily to starboard. As my mind was racing with thoughts about finally finding Charlotte's coup de vent, I was greatly reassured to see Willem leap up from his seat next to the companionway. With the graceful movements of an experienced seaman, Willem saved our half full-bottle of wine from spilling a drop with one hand and with his other hand swiftly closed the companionway hatch.

"Ve don't vant all of that noise and confusion outside to ruin our lunch" he explained as he proceeded to tie a string from the mouth of the wine bottle to a fitting just above the center of our dining table so that our wine would be safe no matter what the wind did. This "relaxed attitude towards sailing" was new to *Captain Spiros* and I felt I was learning a lot watching how

Willem's Wine Pendulum

Willem approached shipboard routine. While I had always insisted on having someone on deck at all times, this wasn't completely necessary as long as someone periodically went on deck to make a check. The trick was to go frequently and to make a thorough check while on deck. Our auto pilot was very reliable, and with the boat properly trimmed, even strong gusts of wind or radical shifts in wind direction did not need instant attention.

From his perch at the dining table, Willem could monitor our radar screen and he claimed to have been able to tune it to pick up even small fishing boats. As the boat continued to lurch heavily back and forth in the strong gusts of wind, I felt our greatest danger was that one of us would be hit in the head by the bottle of wine as it swung off the table on its string during big rolls.

During a particularly violent gust, Willem deftly caught the swinging bottle of wine, poured himself a glass, and proceeded to tell us about some of his previous deliveries. "Ve vere taking a 50-foot sloop past the Southern coast of Inkland in heavy fog ven ve vent under the anchor chain of a huge tanker."

"Wait Willem—I must have misunderstood you. You must have gone BY the anchor chain, not UNDER it!"

"No—ve vent unter the chain!"

"How could you have gone under the chain?"

"It vas by accident."

"I realize it must have been by accident. Couldn't you see the tanker once it was very close?"

"Ve never saw the tanker. Suddenly it became very dark on our port side and on our starboard side ve saw the chain going straight up in the air. Ve passed right between the tanker and chain and never touched anything!"

I didn't think Willem could possibly top this story—but he did. "VE vere delivering a boat from Brest to Holland during the vinter. A nut case had stolen the boat from Holland and had abandoned it in Brest with no engine. He had even taken all the batteries so Ve didn't even have navigation lights. All ve had vere flashlights."

"During a bad gale in the Inklish Channel at night a ship vas on a collision course with us and couldn't see our boat. The batteries in our flashlights vere all dead by this time. Ve vere in real trouble!"

"What did you do?"

"Ve tried to get out of his way, but ve couldn't, so ve lit our jib on fire. That got his attention and he changed his course."

I shuddered when I heard these stories and was glad my navigation lights were working.

That night, just before dark, Willem and I put the third reef in the main as the wind was continuing to gain strength. Near midnight we sighted the powerful light on Isle d'Ouessant and entered the western approach to the English Channel. With a continuous stream of tankers about one or two miles to our port and a very hostile shoreline to our starboard I began to appreciate how formidable this area can become.

On Wednesday we sailed off the coast of Brittany and began to encounter patches of heavy fog. I hoped Willem was right about his claim to have tuned our radar to be able to pick up all fishing boats and also said a silent prayer that we wouldn't come close to any anchored tankers.

While Willem was cleaning out our vegetable bins and throwing out items that were growing hair or becoming too juicy, I noticed that we didn't seem to be accumulating much trash. Before leaving us in La Coruna Charlotte had grilled Willem on his attitude towards pollution.

"Should we take rocks along to sink our trash at sea?" Charlotte had inquired.

"No it's not necessary. I light the bags on fire and what doesn't burn sinks to the bottom" Willem explained. He then made a show of breaking a beer bottle in mid air with a winch handle so that the pieces settled into the sea off our stern. This seemed to satisfy Charlotte and she let the matter drop.

As I watched Willem cleaning I began to realize that I hadn't seen any burning bags of garbage floating away from our boat. At about that time Willem switched his efforts to the refrigerator and half full cans and bottles began to fly up out of the companionway and over the side.

In response to my horrified stare Willem stated "In France they recycle this stuff. They have hundreds of people picking it up off the beaches." The stream of refuse continued. At about this time Dick jumped into the conversation. As he watched Willem toss an empty reinforced box that had housed some of the less expensive wine we had consumed he opined "I would love to have a box like that if I were shipwrecked on a desert island."

In his search through our supplies, Willem came across two giant cans of okra that I had purchased in Turkey. "Vat is this" he asked, truly mystified as he stared at the strange shape pictured on the can.

As the children had scorned my purchase and threatened to throw it overboard, I was delighted that finally someone had expressed an interest and offered to fix a Charleston Gumbo for him and Dick. They cautiously accepted my offer and that night they had their first introduction to the slippery vegetable.

As I was cooking our gumbo, I was disappointed to discover that this Turkish version of okra was not only bigger, tougher, and slimier than any okra I had ever seen, it was canned together with awful looking tomatoes. My concerns were unnecessary—after the first few cautious bites, their wrinkled noses became smooth and they began to shovel it down at an ever-increasing pace. I had to think hard before answering Willem's question about which family of vegetables okra belonged to—but finally stated "the bean family" with strong conviction in my voice.

***

It was much colder in the channel and the swells were reaching four to five meters. We had originally planned to stop in Guernsey to pick up fuel, but the wind had been with us for most of the trip and our fuel consumption had been low. Our dwindling supply of red wine was almost the deciding factor, but Willem finally conceded that he could manage to consume white wine if our red ran out and it became absolutely necessary.

As we sailed past Guernsey, Willem shared the story of his life with me. His wife had died of cancer some years ago and left him with a young daughter that he had educated by taking her around the world with him on sailboats. I was amused by his description of how he would march his daughter into museums and shove her in front of paintings to force feed her culture. His second love, who had accompanied them on these trips, had also died of cancer a few years later. The most recent woman in his life was Winnie, and we toasted her birthday while we watched the shoreline of Guernsey glide past.

Willem then told me the incredible story of how he and Dick had missed me in Peniche. The trouble had started in Malaga, Spain.

They had driven his vintage Chevrolet from Holland to Malaga where he was to pick up a boat to deliver to Antibes, France. There the brokerage firm had refused to release the boat to them because mooring fees were still due. After a series of calls to Holland, Willem finally managed to get the boat released and then sailed it to France. His troubles had just begun.

In Antibes he discovered that it was impossible to take a train along the coast to Malaga where he wanted to pick up his car. He had neglected to take into account one small obstacle—the Pyrennes mountains. The brokerage firm manager in Antibes had offered to lend him a car, but when he went to pick it up the police thought he was trying to steal it. Rather than embarrass the manager with the police, Willem and Dick made a quiet exit to the train station where they boarded a train to Bordeaux.

They arrived in Bordeaux low on funds and exhausted. After spending the night in the woods, they took a train to Madrid and from there another train to Malaga. Already way behind schedule, they called Holland to let them know they were on their way. This was then relayed to me in Cascais as "they are in Peniche and waiting for you there."

The trek from Malaga to Peniche was not easy. In normal circumstances it's a hard two-day drive, but nothing that happens to Willem is normal. A general strike in Portugal made the roads almost impassable and Willem finally arrived in Peniche one hour after we had declared an end to our three-day wait and had left. Travis had intercepted Willem and told him, incorrectly, that we had set out for Figueira de Foz, a small port about 80 miles north of Peniche. Willem and Dick immediately re-boarded their Chevy and headed for Figueira de Foz in hot pursuit.

That afternoon Willem searched in vain all over Figueira de Foz . He even persuaded a fishing boat to lend him their VHF and tried to reach us by radio. At about that time we had been 40 miles off the coast of Portugal and well on our way to Cape Finisterre—which was far out of radio range. When darkness set in, it became apparent that the *Captain Spiros* was not going to stop in Figueira and two frustrated and very tired Dutchmen drove slowly back to Peniche to wait for news from us.

Our phone call from La Coruna set the next chapter of Willem's odyssey into motion. He persuaded a Portuguese friend to come with them to Lisbon so that the friend could drive his car back to Peniche after he and Dick had boarded the train to La Coruna. But in Lisbon there was a general strike in progress and the trains were not running. And that had not been the worst of it.

The general strike was getting worse, and farmers were felling trees across the highway in an effort to bring the country to a standstill. Undaunted, Willem led his trio east until they crossed the Spanish border. There he planned to board a Spanish train and send his Portuguese friend back with his car.

Portuguese bureaucracy took over where the strike left off. At the boarder the Portuguese police refused to allow Willem's Portuguese friend to drive a car registered in Holland in Portugal. Willem had argued, but to no avail—it was the law!

The problem had now shifted over to how to get the Portuguese friend back home. After unsuccessfully trying to flag down the third bus, Willem realized that stronger measures would be necessary. When the fourth bus came he was ready. He sped by it and forced it off the road by pulling in front of it at an intersection. The astonished bus driver was no match for Willem's quick wit, and a few minutes later his friend was comfortably speeding back home in the bus while Willem and Dick began to wind their way up the Spanish highways on the long trip to La Coruna.

After hearing this astonishing story, I felt foolish for ever having doubted that Willem would arrive in Peniche and find us. Travis, Bill, and Eddy had been right when they had urged me to relax in Peniche and to take life easy until Willem arrived. Although I had suspected that their advice had been good, relaxing was something that I had still not learned to do, and after three days of waiting, I simply had not been able to sit still any longer.

Before retiring that night, Willem told me about his military career. Twenty two months in the army—two of them in the brig. His lax attitude towards government property finally got him into big trouble when he absconded with a large truck to make a visit to his girlfriend in a nearby village. He hadn't noticed that the truck was full of tank batteries and his little caper had prevented an entire tank convoy from getting under way for two days.

With Willem finally asleep, I enjoyed a few hours of solitude as we rounded Alderney and continued up the English Channel towards Cherbourg. The continuous stream of tankers to our port kept me company, and in a strange way I felt very relaxed.

Later that morning Dick and I were treated to an unexpected surprise. Willem announced that he had fixed us an English breakfast. He had combined a can of baked beans with their cousin, the remaining can of Turkish okra, and topped the whole affair with several fried eggs. Glad that there was no more okra left, I promised Willem that I would give him full credit if I ever fixed "Okra Willem" back in South Carolina.

Although the sky was overcast, the sea was calm, the wind was on our stern, and it was a relatively nice day for the English Channel. We all relaxed as we sailed past Le Havre on our way to the heavy shipping lanes near Calais and Dover. Before I had a chance to worry about staying out of the way of tankers in the choke point of the Channel, Willem raised another area of concern. He had forgotten to bring charts for the approach to Antwerp.

Being cautious by nature, I had not wholly relied on Willem's fulfillment of my request to bring all necessary charts from the Western Approach of the English Channel to Bruinisse, Holland. As a hedge I had bought a very extensive pilot that included most of the ports from the North Sea to Spain and a few extra charts, but nowhere did I have any charts of the narrow, constantly shifting channel that winds its way through the shallow water leading inland towards Antwerp. We would have to find our way to Vlissingen and the southern entrance to the canals of Holland based on the knowledge in Willem's head.

We breezed past Calais late that day with excellent visibility, but a very dark evening greeted us as we approached the chartless stretch of our journey. For the first time during our trip Willem showed a slight degree of uneasiness. A buoy with a reflector clearly stood out on our radar screen and, based on our most recent Satnav position—Willem finally acknowledged the value of this frivolous electronic toy—it probably marked the entrance to our channel. But on which side should we pass? Close scrutiny with the aid of our searchlight still did not provide a clear answer to the riddle. Without an up to date chart the buoy number, shape, and coloring scheme was insufficient to give us a definitive answer to this crucial question.

With over seven feet of keel beneath us and a falling tide, we had no choice but to wait until a passing tanker could give us the empirical data we needed. We didn't have to wait long, but once past this buoy our guiding tanker was too far ahead of us to help with the next buoy. We followed ship after ship in this manner for the next several hours until finally one of our guiding ships turned out to be a dredge with a long dredge line deployed. Frantic and unorthodox search light signals from the dredge to us and back combined with a lot of Dutch cursing over the VHF nudged us in the right direction to escape the horseshoe of dredge pipe we had inadvertently entered. Relieved and very tired we entered the lock at Vlissingen at 3:00 A.M. Saturday morning and moored in the entrance of the Kanaal Door Walcheren. Sleep came instantly.

***

Much to my surprise Willem had us all up at the break of day and we promptly got the vessel underway. I could tell that Willem's first explanation that he didn't want me to have the hassle of dealing with customs was only a partial truth so I continued to probe. Well... he and Dick had forgotten to bring their passports, and besides there had been that trouble he had been having with various Dutch tax collectors and... I immediately recognized the soundness of the logic that had resulted in Willem's prompt daylight departure and dropped my line of questioning.

A warm sun shone down through clear blue skies, and almost all of Holland must have been out either bicycling along the canal or engaging in water activities in it. We watched the flat Dutch countryside flow past us as we motored up the canal and then watched hikers, bikers, trains and cars stream over the bridges as we patiently waited for them to open. At locks, boats would mass like a swarm of bees until the entrance of the lock opened. The swarm would then make a cautious, controlled rush into the lock. The first boats in would secure lines to the sides of the lock and then take lines from their neighbors and secure them along side. This continued until there wasn't enough room for even a small boat to enter, and the lock doors would close.

Suddenly we found ourselves eyeball to eyeball with a mass of humanity and frozen into position while the lock slowly filled to its new level. Unlike elevator etiquette that demands one look at a blank spot on the wall and try to ignore the presence of the other fifteen passengers, the lock crowd reacted with pleasant nods and small talk in numerous languages.

The family in the ketch tied along our starboard side was finishing a huge fried chicken lunch while the elderly Dutchman in the small sloop to our port was teaching his grandson how to bait a hook. A French couple in a nearby power boat were having a domestic squabble which didn't seem to bother the five bathing beauties in another boat as they drew admiring stares from the entire community. At the next lock we saw the same people, but all at different stages of their ongoing dramas. This was people watching at its best.

At about noon we entered Ooster Schelde, a very large lake that was full of craft of all descriptions. Traditional Dutch design sailboats with their giant leeboards and gaff-rigged sails mixed among modern sailing boats and motor cruisers that ranged from modest to obscenely extravagant. Oddly the vessels for which the canals were originally built looked out of place against the background of their flashy companions. Husband and wife teams, often assisted by their young children, meticulously primped and painted their already immaculate long narrow commercial barges. As these barges passed us with their potted plants in all windows and bicycles on deck, I felt envy for the simplicity and mobility of their lives.

The lock between Zijpe and Grevelingenmeer was the last leg of our trip through the canals and lakes of Western Holland. Once through, we entered the immaculate and fully equipped marina at Bruinisse. Five minutes after the lines had been secured, three salt-encrusted sailors with fresh shaves and clean shirts were off to explore the surroundings.

A cursory check of the closed De Valk office failed to produce Menno or Peter so we headed over to the Sailor's Inn. Willem's orders for a continuous stream of Heineken began to concern me because I didn't have any Dutch money, and the restaurant had already made it clear that they would not accept my US dollar traveler's checks. Within minutes of Willem's suggestion to the worried waitress that we would simply charge the tab to De Valk, Peter magically appeared.

Peter was Dutch efficiency personified. Of course the tab would be on De Valk—and not only for our refreshments but for dinner as well. Did I need any Dutch money? Peter would be glad to lend me enough for the weekend. He arranged for us to have the choice table in the corner overlooking the harbor, told me to meet him on Monday morning to begin the process of making the boat ready for sale, and then was off—leaving me his car telephone number if I should need to reach him. What a change from the Mediterranean!

It was a memorable evening. Willem took a brief break from cocktails to give Winnie a call in Muiden, a small town near Amsterdam, and she joined the three of us a couple of hours later. Beer, wine, hors d'oeuvres, and Irish coffee came in a continuous stream, and Winnie arrived in the middle of the feast. Winnie was everything Willem was not. She had driven a solid two hours from Muiden, but didn't show any signs of impatience when Willem insisted she have a full-three course dinner and kept the wine flowing. She had recently taken a job in the harbor master's office in Northern Holland and Willem chided her for this because it kept her from coming with him on his trips. She answered his chiding with a sweet smile.

We rehashed the story of Willem's wanderings from Antibes to La Coruna, and she filled in the missing pieces of the puzzle by describing all the communications she had relayed back and forth. Willem, Dick, and Winnie then spun tales of past trips and of good times together. I was fascinated with their stories and felt compelled to accept their invitation to come to Muiden and spend the weekend on Willem's barge.

Well past midnight, when the restaurant management was getting uneasy about the duration of our continuing party, the practical side of Winnie finally took over. She mobilized her two Dutch mariners and their American friend and began to herd us all towards her Deaux Cheveaux. Two hours later we were in Muiden.

***

301

Captain Spiros had been moved while I had been in Muiden. It was now closer to De Valk's office and in the middle of the other boats they had for sale. At first I was a little angry, but then realized that this was the first step in transferring control. In a funny way, it was the first step in our parting. I inspected the mooring lines with suspicion and checked around the boat to make sure nothing was damaged. But I was dealing with Dutch efficiency and everything was in order.

Peter was waiting for me in the office. We had a lot of work to do and both of us were ready to get started. "How was your weekend with Willem?" he asked. Before I could reply, he pulled a slip of paper out of a folder in front of him and asked: "How many people were at your party at the Sailor's Inn on Saturday night?"

Sensing that Peter's inquiry had gone beyond polite conversation and wondering what he had fished out of the file on his desk I cautiously replied, "there were the three of us until Winnie joined us later on in the evening."

With an incredulous look on his face Peter began reading: "twenty five beers, three bottles of wine, and nine Irish coffees... and there were only three of you?"

"Well, as I said Winnie joined us and..." I could tell by the penetrating stare Peter was giving me that my reply wasn't very convincing, but I plowed on anyway "and we were all pretty hungry after our long trip."

I thought about questioning the validity of the bill—after all twenty five beers did sound like a lot—but upon reflection the numbers Peter had so sanctimoniously cited weren't at complete variance with my recollection of our festive evening. I said nothing and waited for his scolding.

"Do you know how much the bill was for your little party?"

I didn't, but knowing that Peter was about to tell me, I remained silent.

"Two hundred and ninety eight guilders!"

By now I was able to put my finger on the cause of Peter's discomfort. He probably thought we had taken advantage of his generous offer to buy dinner for the three of us—and perhaps he even considered our consumption of alcohol to be excessive. I was about to offer to pay for the bill when he interrupted my thoughts.

"We have paid the bill but will include it with other expenses incurred by the boat and deduct it from the proceeds of the sale."

I now began to understand the real meaning of the term "Dutch treat." Glad to be off the hook, I readily agreed to this treatment of the bill.

Suddenly Peter was all smiles again, and we settled down to the work of preparing *Captain Spiros* for sale.

***

Remove all of our personal belongings, clean the boat from stem to stern, arrange shipment of our belongings back to Charleston, pull the boat out of water, and then negotiate necessary repairs and a reasonable price with De Valk. It sounded pretty straightforward, but it wasn't. Having lived on the boat for almost a year and having accumulated countless items for entertainment, comfort, and survival I knew it was going to be difficult. Charlotte knew it also and for that reason had tried to do some of it before leaving me in La Coruna.

Charlotte's efforts had been doomed to failure from the start. To thoroughly clean the boat it was necessary to remove belongings. To remove belongings it was necessary to put them somewhere. Therein lies the problem that plagues anyone foolish enough to try to make a home on a sailboat. It's hard enough with a couple—but try adding two teenage boys and a twelve-year-old girl to the stew and the pot boils over.

Guitars, drums, walkmen, bead collections, a wind surfer, and a very comprehensive library competed for space with the tools, navigation books, travel books, supplies, foul weather gear, clothing, medicines (a year's supply of drugs for any and every emergency), and the pottery and baskets Charlotte had so lovingly collected. And all of this was superimposed over the large quantity of supplies necessary for the running of the boat—spare sails (they are huge), mooring lines, extra anchors and chain, spare parts, two dinghies, an outboard motor, two sets of oars (difficult items to store), snorkel gear for five, and the list goes on. If something had been broken and replaced, I kept the old one as a spare. NOTHING was thrown away. The resulting accumulation was overwhelming. Charlotte's futile attempt at serious cleaning in La Coruna was typical of earlier efforts. In cleaning one space the mess she was forced to make in other spaces to accommodate the proliferation of items was worse than the original mess.

After thoroughly cleaning our room, replacing displaced items, remaking the bed, and rearranging the other rooms she had disturbed with the displaced items, she noticed the huge box full of pottery and books that normally lived in the huge bin directly below the cushions of the bed she had just made. We all suppressed smiles as we heard some words that we previously had not realized were part of Charlotte's vocabulary. This had marked the end of her final attempt at cleaning *Captain Spiros*.

Even if Charlotte had been successful in her cleaning efforts, the trip from Spain to Holland would have undone anything she could have accomplished. With the boat sealed tight during the voyage, the damp air saturated all the sheets, pillows, and blankets on board. A large part of the trip had been very cold, and, despite double layers of clothing, we had wrapped ourselves in all the bedding material we had to ward off the chill caused by the moisture laden air.

Wet foul weather gear, saturated clothing, and three human moisture generators put so much water into the air that when we arrived in Holland all the beds were wet to the touch, and the walls and ceilings in all the state rooms were coated with mist. There was nothing else to do for it. Everything had to come up on deck to dry out before I could even think about packing. And I had to pack before I could even think about cleaning.

With its 48-foot length and 15-foot beam, the *Captain Spiros* was a large boat, and its boom, lifelines, and the two layers of clothes lines I had rigged around the perimeter of the vessel provided an enormous area to hang clothing. But it was barely adequate for the task. It was a sunny warm day which meant, by Holland statistics, that the next day would probably be rainy and cold. I acted quickly and before noon all sheets, blankets, pillows, towels, foul weather gear, clothes, duffel bags, and anything else on board capable of picking up moisture were hanging.

The marina at Bruinisse was very swish and I was acutely conscious of the image we must have cut. Peering out between wet blankets and sheets I would watch immaculately dressed Dutch and German yachties strolling down the pier admiring sleek Swans, Hallburg Rassys, and Moodys. When their discerning seaman eyes would finally focus in my direction I could see the look of horrified shock and could only imagine what they thought lay buried behind the giant tent of tattered blankets and underwear. Fearing that the marina would come aboard and insist that I immediately clean up this spectacle, I left the boat and didn't come back until dark, at which time I had to take everything back below deck to avoid the dew.

That night I could hardly sleep thinking about how I was going to dispose of the incredible array of junk that we had accumulated. Just leaving it there wouldn't work—after all I had to sell the boat. Throwing it overboard would probably have resulted in my arrest. The nearest Salvation Army was over four thousand miles away so that was out. Besides, these were our family possessions and if I unilaterally disposed of them I would probably be subjecting myself to criticism from other family members when I returned home. Clearly I had to make a shipment back home—but how?

The next morning I found the answer. A container. At first the idea had seemed ridiculous—a whole container for our possessions? But after talking with Datama of Rotterdam I found that a short container (20 ft.) to Charleston was more economical than boxing and shipping what I had. Besides, the logistics, for once, would be simple. They would truck the container to Bruinisse and all I had to do was load it. One month later I could claim my possessions in Charleston. Simple. I couldn't quite picture how big or how small 30 cubic meters was, but it sounded more than adequate and there would even be room for the wind surfer.

I began to pack in earnest. Huge dinghy boxes I had obtained from the marina chandler began to fill up with fishing rods, snorkel gear, clothing, bedding, books, and endless assorted items. I tried to remember Charlotte's parting instructions. "The bag under our bed in the forward right compartment is old clothes we don't need anymore. Try to give it to a boat with children. Take the spices we bought in Tunisia, but throw away the ones we had in Turkey—you know, the baggies held together with green rubber bands in the middle drawer forward of the sink. Be sure to bring all the children's books, but you can get rid of the box of books in the top shelf behind Alex's toilet."

It was hot and stuffy in the boat and the confusion was overwhelming. My initial attempts at an orderly organized approach quickly degenerated into chaos. Half-full boxes covered all the free surface areas that weren't already covered by articles waiting to be packed. Do we really need to keep these five storm kerosene lanterns or would the three brass lanterns I had already packed be enough? As I stood there with the lanterns in my hand vacillating, it suddenly came to me. It was so simple. Everything goes!

Having made that decision, the rest was easy. Lanterns, dried beans, lines, and baskets, went in a steady stream into the waiting boxes. By this time I had abandoned any semblance of an attempt to select or sort as I packed. My efforts were focused on getting everything into the boxes and getting all of the boxes off of the boat. I took grim satisfaction as I thrust the bag of old clothes into a half full box. If Charlotte wanted to get rid of them or the baggies of Turkish spices with their green rubber bands, SHE could do so at her leisure in Charleston. I was packing EVERYTHING.

Boxes filled the cockpit, covered the bow, and were jammed everywhere in the cabin when I began to shuttle them ashore into De Valk's store room where they would await the container. Filling, sealing, and then stacking, I created a mountain of boxes that completely hid the small cart that De Valk had loaned me. Slowly, very carefully, I inched the mountain down the dock towards the store room. It would have gone smoothly if I hadn't tripped and pushed a large and untied box into the water. My retrieval efforts were rewarded with a wet empty box. Its entire contents had disappeared into the murky marina water.

What had been in the box? I recalled throwing most of the snorkel gear into the box when a frightening thought came to mind. My sextant. With relief I remembered that I had put it in a smaller box surrounded with bedding. But the only way I was going to find out what had gone over was through retrieval.

I approached the group of young boys who had been swimming around a neighboring boat and asked them if they wanted to earn some guilders. Cans of tuna fish, soggy boxes of dehydrated soup, and not so dried garbanzo beans found their way onto the dock from outstretched hands. By this time cocktail hour was approaching, and couples in neat casual attire were slowly working their way down the dock towards the Sailors Inn. The unsightly mess that was collecting at my feet was becoming embarrassing, and I decided that if asked directly I would explain that I had been on the way to the garbage bins when the accident had occurred. When flippers, masks, snorkels, and storm lanterns began to appear I realized that this tack wasn't going to work so I asked the boys to put everything they found on deck to dry, left them some guilders, and set out for the Sailors Inn myself.

After relaxing over a couple of beers I decided to call home and let Charlotte know how the packing was progressing. Her raised voice carried clearly above the heavy static: "We must have a bad connection—it sounded like you said you had decided to pack EVERYTHING." Trying to change the subject I explained that it was much easier that way and besides, we could probably use most of the items. But Charlotte continued persistently "Please, not those awful blankets -not even Minolis would..."

Before she could finish I interrupted with: "Look, they will make great padding for packing" and jokingly added that they were a lot better than the dried Turkish soup.

"Soup? You packed soup?"

"Calm down, the soup is gone, it fell overboard with the snorkel gear and..." Fending off Charlotte's disappointment over the loss of our snorkel equipment wasn't easy, but I finally got the conversation over to the more stable topic of the excitement she and the children had had in their visit to London and our conversation ended on a happy note.

The next morning I took a break from heavy cleaning to meet with Peter to negotiate a price for the boat. Knowing that a suggestion to reduce price was inevitable, I decided to use the meeting to tie down exact costs for all the services that De Valk would perform and save our pricing arguments for later. While the Dutch were efficient and honest, I had learned many lessons from my dealing with the Greeks. I knew that any "undefined expenses" would turn into unpleasant surprises for me when they found their way into the inevitable invoice. And besides, my recent encounter with Peter had demonstrated that in Holland not only was there no such thing as a free lunch, but that the rule applied to dinners as well.

***

August 1 was a big day -*Captain Spiros* was to come out of water. At 8:00 A.M. Peter's helpers, Hans and Jonn, were buzzing around the boat coiling lines, touching up paint, and arranging deck equipment so the boat would look ship shape. On the way to the crane, they were going to take photos for the marketing brochure and they wanted the boat as presentable as possible. To my question about whether or not we should clean the ugly black smoke ring off the side of the boat around the diesel exhaust they replied: "don't worry, it won't show up on the photo—we will take the picture into the sun. But we need a BIG flag—buyers like to see big pretty flags."

The large American flag that Atilla had given to us in Turkey fit the "big" part of the bill but Mediterranean winds had shredded the last inch and the overall appearance could hardly be described as pretty. Out came Peter's razor sharp pocket knife and a couple of minutes later *Captain Spiros* was flying a beautiful non regulation American flag.

With Peter in a dinghy full of photographic equipment and Hans and Jonn on deck, we were ready to get underway. From Hans: "Would you like to take us out?" A little irritated at the question I nodded yes. Of course I would get us underway—why would anyone even ask! I gently nudged the throttle forward. Nothing. A little more, but still nothing. From Peter in the dinghy "You need to give it a lot of throttle, it's sitting in the mud."

"You mean we are aground!" My critical inspection of the boat upon return from Muiden had obviously not been critical enough. It had never occurred to me that they would have driven *Captain Spiros* onto the mud.

"Don't worry. It's soft mud. You just need to push the throttle the whole way forward to break out." I looked at the bow of the elegant motor sailor moored at the pier opposite my slip just two boat lengths away and then back at Peter. "Oh yes, when you break free of the mud pull back on the throttle right away so you don't hit your neighbor."

Full throttle and still no motion—and then a little bit of movement. Half way out of our slip and suddenly the movement began to accelerate rapidly. Full reverse and a hard turn to the right! I think I ruined the Dutch couple's breakfast on the motor sailor, but as Willem had explained to me back in La Coruna, missing by a few inches is all that is really necessary.

Captain Spiros Comes out of the Water

As Peter circled us in his dinghy taking pictures and ordering various course changes I was keenly aware of losing control of my boat. When we approached the pier with the huge crane I didn't even object when Hans offered to take the wheel. Suddenly I was an observer and the intimate relationship I had developed over the past year with *Captain Spiros* was coming to an end. My mind was still occupied with the thrust astern and to port the screw was now giving the boat as Hans eased her into reverse, and I mentally added this vector to the vector of our slow forward motion to determine if the maneuver would have the desired effect of gently nudging us against the pier—but it was only an academic exercise. I no longer had control.

The boat inched its way out of the water and I was able to clearly see the cause of the two knots we had lost over the past few months. In spite of the many underwater brushings Heyward, Alex, and I had given to her bottom in the frigid Mediterranean waters, an enormous beard had developed. For the fiftieth time I cursed Manfred and the extravagantly expensive and extremely difficult to apply Teflon anti fouling paint he had persuaded us to use. But I chalked it up to experience. Next time we would use traditional self polishing anti fouling in spite of its effectiveness, low cost and ease of application.

Peter gave *Captain Spiros* a prominent position along the long raised platform De Valk had constructed to show its vessels. We occupied a corner so that passersby could see the boat along its starboard side and along its stern. The boat had already attracted a great deal of attention, and Peter told me that the entire marina community had been talking about the large French built sloop and its "very busy" American owner.

That night it felt strange as German and Dutch couples would stop their strolls down the platform to critique my vessel and would stare at me through the port holes as they examined the interior. My feelings were largely spared because I couldn't understand most of their comments, but the expressions on their faces and the tone of their guttural comments was enough to arouse my sensitivity, and I began to look forward to my final departure. After more hard cleaning I went to bed and ended a very strenuous and emotional day.

Peter was coming at 11:00 and I still hadn't cleaned the refrigerator. The bilges were only half done and I still had the heads, engine room, and bow compartment to clean. With only two hours to go, I made a quick decision. Cosmetic cleaning! When they stepped aboard, I had just finished mopping the floorboards and cleaning the counters and table top. Skin deep it looked great. I was ready to discuss price.

Parked at Observation Walkway

But first we had a few more details to settle. We agreed upon a price for anti fouling paint and a new waterline. Reluctantly I agreed to new upholstery and then the discussions turned to cleaning. Peter started to explain how De Valk's comprehensive cleaning service worked: "Polish, teak waxing, bilges—a thorough cleaning inside and out…"

"How much?" I interrupted.

He quoted a figure. For the first time it seemed low—especially compared with what I had been subjecting myself to. I gave an unenthusiastic, negotiating "okay" while inwardly I rejoiced at the sudden realization that my duties aboard *Captain Spiros* had abruptly come to an end. We listed all of the costs incurred to date including the bill for Willem's party and then itemized all future costs. I began to see that selling the boat wasn't going to be cheap. We then had a long discussion about what the boat would be worth in its new pristine condition and finally arrived at a selling price. No sooner had we agreed upon this price than he talked me into a 15 percent reduction. Then he was off.

With nothing left to do but pack my clothes and arrange ground transportation to Amsterdam for my flight back to the US, I had a strange feeling of freedom. Since my arrival in Athens a year earlier there had always been more to do than I could possibly accomplish. Stepping off the boat to wander around and do nothing was pure joy. Another example of Dutch efficiency as I left—Peter had already posted a for sale sign with the new lowered cost.

At 6:00 A.M. the next morning my bus to metro to train journey to Amsterdam was about to begin. I had allowed myself an extra hour to have a leisurely breakfast on board and then walk around the boat before leaving. With bags in hand I stared at the stout keel and sleek lines of the hull.

Thoughts of Cape Knidos, our near tragedy coming into Mandraki, fog off Cape Finisterre, and the many other times we had relied on the integrity of *Captain Spiros* to keep us out of danger flooded into my mind. As I walked away from the platform I recalled the wonderful evenings when our priceless discussions around the dinner table extended well into the nights. The duties we shared, the cultures we came to know, the friends we made all flashed past and before leaving the marina I turned to look at our boat one last time.

"Good-bye *Captain Spiros*. You have served us well, and I will always remember life on board. It has been a fascinating experience."

Epilogue

Life returned to normal but with important changes. We bought a house in downtown Charleston—a place where we had always wanted to live but thought we could not because of a lack of business opportunities in my profession. Charlotte succeeded in getting our children enrolled in schools and they resumed their formal education, but this time, as much better students with a lifetime of topics for school essays. The only rough spot in their reentry was in again becoming "viewed as children." Their hard won equality in the sailing world was now gone, but not their determination to be taken seriously, and the experiences they accumulated gave them the tools they needed.

Following the new rule I had set for myself in never again working for someone else and honoring the non-compete with my former business, Maritrans, I started a business in an entirely different industry, and became completely absorbed in making it successful. But the travel bug had bitten, and nine years later Charlotte and I were back on the high seas—this time it was just the two of us on what was to become a six-year sailing trip around the world. It's all there in my first book, *The Next Port*.

Request for Review

Thank you for reading my book. This was my second book and it was inspired by the success of my first book, *The Next Port*. The purpose of my writing is to share our adventures with others and explain how we were motivated and able to put our normal lives on hold and set out to explore the unknown.

If you have enjoyed the reading, I would be grateful if you would write a review so that others might be encouraged to also share our experiences. I love getting reviews and read all of them.

To submit review use the link below.
http://www.amazon.com/review/create-review?&asin= B00BLLT85A

About the Author

Heyward Coleman served as a submarine officer in the US Nuclear Navy before entering a business career. His education includes an MA in nuclear physics from Duke University and an MBA from the Harvard Business School. Initially in the oil and gas industry, he became a senior officer and part owner of a large oil shipping company. After selling his interest in the company, he founded an environmental laboratory that specialized in radiochemistry analysis. During his career he cultivated a love for travel and adventure. Now retired, he and his wife divide their time between their home in Charleston, SC and cruising the canals and rivers of Europe on thier powerboat, *Magnolia*.

Coleman is the author of two books. *Where the Wind Blows* is his second book and covers his adventures after leaving the shipping company in 1989. His first book, *The Next Port* tells about his 1999-2004 trip around the world in a 42-foot sailboat.